The Orwell Mystique

A Study in Male Ideology

Daphne Patai

The University of Massachusetts Press

Amherst, 1984

Publication of this book was assisted by the American Council of
Learned Societies under a grant from the Andrew W. Mellon Foundation.

Printed in the United States of America

LC 84–8488

ISBN 0–87023–446–3 (cloth); 0–87023–447–1 (paper)

Library of Congress Cataloging in Publication Data

Patai, Daphne, 1943–

The Orwell mystique.

Includes index.

1. Orwell, George, 1903–1950—Political and social views.

2. Masculinity (Psychology) in literature. 3. Women in literature.

4. Sex role in literature. 5. Feminism and literature. I. Title.

PR6029.R8Z753 1984   828'.91209   84–8488

ISBN 0–87023–446–3

ISBN 0–87023–447–1 (pbk.)

For Gerald

———————

*People can foresee the future only
when it coincides with their own wishes,
and the most grossly obvious facts can
be ignored when they are unwelcome.*

GEORGE ORWELL

Contents

Acknowledgments

At various times in my research for this book I have been aided by the staffs of the Lilly Library at Indiana University; the Berg Collection at the New York Public Library; and, above all, the George Orwell Archive, at the library of University College London, and I would like to thank them all for their help. In addition, I found the readers' reports on an earlier draft of this book helpful and stimulating and want to express my gratitude to those readers who took considerable time and trouble to set down lengthy comments and lively objections.

Finally, a number of friends-and-relations read parts or all of the manuscript at one or another stage in its composition and gave valuable criticism and support. To all of them go my deepest thanks and the promise that next time we meet I will not talk about Orwell.

Parts of chapter 8 originally appeared, in slightly different form, in *PMLA*, October 1982 and March 1983, and *Women's Studies International Forum* 7, no. 2 (1984).

Published works by Orwell quoted in *The Orwell Mystique*

The Collected Essays, Journalism and Letters of George Orwell. Edited by Sonia Orwell and Ian Angus. 4 vols. New York: Harcourt Brace Jovanovich, 1968. (Cited in the text as CEJL.)

Down and Out in Paris and London. Harmondsworth: Penguin, 1975.

Burmese Days. Harmondsworth: Penguin, 1967.

A Clergyman's Daughter. Harmondsworth: Penguin, 1964.

Keep the Aspidistra Flying. Harmondsworth: Penguin, 1963.

The Road to Wigan Pier. Harmondsworth: Penguin, 1962.

Homage to Catalonia. Harmondsworth: Penguin, 1962.

Coming Up for Air. Harmondsworth: Penguin, 1962.

Animal Farm. Harmondsworth: Penguin, 1951.

Nineteen Eighty-Four. Harmondsworth: Penguin, 1954.

Other material by and about Orwell, utilized in this study, is held at the George Orwell Archive, University College London Library (hereafter: Orwell Archive); the Berg Collection of the New York Public Library (hereafter: Berg Collection); and the Lilly Library at Indiana University, Bloomington (hereafter: LL).

Preface

One day in the early stages of working on this book I was asked by a friend what it was that drew me to Orwell. I remember answering: "His passion and his honesty." Given the enormous changes in my understanding of Orwell over the past several years, I have often recollected this scene and wondered how it was that, at one time in any case, I was in such agreement with majority opinion about Orwell. I have a few ideas about this now, and possibly they will help explain certain aspects of the Orwell mystique.

First of all, I think my answer reflected a general assent to received opinion about Orwell. The extent to which our presumably personal, subjective, "authentic" responses to a given writer are shaped by prevailing ideas seems to me to be a largely unexplored and undiscussed issue. As readers, we tend not only to repeat what others have said, but also to have our own vision fundamentally altered, deflected, or constricted by a chorus of consensus. I have reread earlier drafts of this book and note that I was often, at that point, still writing in what I now call the "honorific," carefully couching criticism in words of praise and general agreement with the gist of the Orwell myth. As a result of continued rereadings of Orwell's work, however, I came to see that a passion for appearing honest and actually being honest are very different things, and that saying what one thinks can be as much an act of aggression as a display of lofty principles. Something else struck me as well: that the critic who praises Orwell for his "honesty" is saying not only, "Orwell is honest," but also, "I am honest too; I too care passionately about these issues." By praising Orwell, one thus affirms one's own moral condition.

I initially set out to explain Orwell's pessimism and eventual despair in terms that were compatible with his general reputation and the honor that is routinely done him. As I became more and more aware of the profound misogyny and preoccupation with manhood in his works, I still tried to hang on to an interpretation that would not so much challenge earlier views as complement them or register a small disclaimer. Once I had thought further, however, about what I was actually encountering in Orwell, it became impossible to reconcile my own observations with received opinion. And I also began to suspect that much of this opinion was simply mistaken—the result perhaps of the very ideological cluster my work was attempting to unravel. As a result, while my main theme is now Orwell's androcentrism— which in my view explains his despair—a secondary focus of the book is the Orwell cult itself. Although I have not made an exhaustive study of it, I believe my characterization of this cult, as the year 1984 seems to be proving conclusively, is accurate.

It seems to me that Orwell's real importance will ultimately reside not in his critique of totalitarianism or in his much proclaimed but, as I shall show, rather limited "honesty" and "decency," and not even in his occasionally valuable essays on language. Instead, both Orwell and the cult that arose around him in the mid-twentieth century will eventually be viewed as a problem in intellectual history and ideological consumption. In the future, I think, interest in Orwell will focus not on his work but on the phenomenon of his fame and what it reveals about our own civilization.

March 1984

One

Introduction:

The Orwell Myth

"A writer's political and religious beliefs are not excrescences to be laughed away, but something that will leave their mark even on the smallest detail of his work." So wrote George Orwell in 1943 (CEJL, 2:276). This is a moderate version of another statement of Orwell's: "All art is to some extent propaganda" (2:239–40), which in turn is a variation on yet an earlier and more extreme dictum: "Few people have the guts to say outright that art and propaganda are the same thing" (1:257). Orwell prided himself on having "the guts," and several generations of critics have joined in the celebration. He was above all a man of strong opinions, on everything from Communists to cups of tea, and he expressed these opinions in a characteristically vehement form in essays, letters, journalism, and books of fiction and reportage. But it is not only overtly expressed opinions or political and religious "beliefs," as Orwell says, that define a writer's ideology, although these have provided the core of most Orwell criticism. It is the totality of a writer's ideology—which must not be narrowed to his "politics" in the usual restricted sense of that term—that leaves its mark, and frequently this is even more effectively revealed through the indirections of fiction than in intentionally polemical writing. The premise of this book is that the essential ideology at the heart of Orwell's work as a writer and a thinker can be understood only by exploring his ideas about masculinity and femininity. For to focus on Orwell's depiction of masculinity and femininity is not merely to add women to a picture from which critical discussion has largely excluded them (though this in its own right would correct the myopic view of most criticism); it is also to examine in the most fundamental way how Orwell construes the social reality of which he is a part.

ORWELL'S REPUTATION

Orwell is a writer whom people like to take in parts, accepting some of his words, ignoring or suppressing others. Since well before his death in 1950, this habit has characterized critical reaction to him.[1] But Orwell has also inspired an altogether different order of commentary, directed not at the writer but above all at the man. In this vein, V. S. Pritchett, in his obituary of Orwell, referred to him as "the wintry conscience of a generation" and "a kind of saint" who "prided himself on seeing through the rackets, and on conveying the impression of living without the solace or even the need of a single illusion." [2] This assent to Orwell's own judgment of himself is typical of the dominant trend in critical response to Orwell, but it can be sustained only by disregarding those recurring aspects of Orwell's writing that point to a very different image of the man and the writer. Earlier (1946), Pritchett had called Orwell "the most honest writer of our time." [3] With statements such as these, Pritchett has come to be one of the main sources of the Orwell myth. Yet calling Orwell's outspokenness "honesty," as so many subsequent critics have also done, often means merely that his "truth" resembles the critic's own. Since Orwell also wrote many objectionable untruths, involving slurs on individuals and groups—national, racial, religious, sexual, and political slurs—critics have faced a dilemma in making claims for his "honesty" and "decency." These two words, so frequently applied to Orwell, were among his own favorites, and critics who project them onto Orwell seem to mistake the act of referring to a quality with the demonstration of that quality in his own behavior. The major strategy that has evolved over the past few decades for dealing with the problem of Orwell's frequent less-than-decent verbal assaults is to briefly acknowledge, only to brush aside, this aspect of his writing, as if it were a minor and perhaps regrettable lapse but no serious reflection on the man.[4]

As critical opinion has filtered through the public realm, however, a mystique has come to surround Orwell that frequently prevents even the simple recognition of those important strains in his work that contradict his public posture. "Outspoken" would hardly inspire the myth-making process, which depends upon the language of moral absolutes, as Pritchett so clearly discerned. By now, Orwell's name has become a kind of talisman, linked to a moral stature that is assumed to be unassailable. To cite Orwell in support of one's position *is*, therefore, to assert the self-evident rightness of that position. What is of interest is that Orwell can be used with such ease to defend opposing claims, yet this state of affairs never calls into question his moral stature and role as a touchstone of right thinking—whatever one thinks that is. Critics who have studied Orwell frequently praise him for different reasons, some for his alleged political acumen, some for his "prose like a windowpane" (another instance of projecting onto Orwell himself something for which he expressed concern), some for his journalism or his essays, some for his fiction. And more often than not each critic rejects Orwell's claim to greatness on grounds other than the ones the particular critic subscribes to. Thus, many of his greatest supporters view him as *not* an important political thinker, or *not* a gifted novelist, or *not* a major stylist, or *not* an insightful literary critic and essayist—without, however, challenging his basic stature.

What have we here, then? A writer almost universally acclaimed but one who arouses broad disagreement about what it is we are to admire in him. These disagreements have accompanied Orwell from early in his career to this day.

In 1946 Orwell proclaimed: "Every line of serious work that I have written since 1936 has been written, directly or indirectly, *against* totalitarianism and *for* democratic Socialism, as I understand it" (CEJL, 1:5; Orwell's emphasis). Still, the fact remains that none of Orwell's books is *for* socialism as much as it is *against* something else. This is why Orwell can be omitted from studies of British socialist novels in the twentieth century.[5] Though Orwell identified himself as a "democratic Socialist," he produced no socialist novel, and his writings were useful to the antisocialist cause as early as *The Road to Wigan Pier* (1937), with its violent attack on socialist cranks. This attack is still functional today, as can be seen from the fact that William Buckley chose to reprint one of Orwell's nastiest passages about socialists as a "Guest Editorial" in a 1982 issue of the *National Review*.[6] Orwell's anti-Communism became a prominent feature of his work after his months in Spain in 1937, as recounted in *Homage to Catalonia* (1938), but it was only with the publication of *Animal Farm* (1945) that he emerged as a potential cold warrior of unusual force, a position confirmed and further intensified by the publication in 1949 of Orwell's last and most famous book, *Nineteen Eighty-Four*.

By 1955, the *Spectator's* political commentator, Henry Fairlie, could name Orwell as the teacher of the "new Conservative protestors," whom Fairlie describes, in what could well be a capsulized portrait of Orwell's public persona, as "the rebels against authority, the eccentrics who wish to challenge order, the opponents of the prevailing climate of opinion, the odd few who wish to keep ideas moving. These are the people who would have been on the Left in 1906, and who were on the Left in 1939." [7] Nearly thirty years later, Orwell's name and reputation are evoked to similar effect by American neoconservatives. Thus, Rael Jean Isaac and Erich Isaac dredge up Orwell's attack on pacifists (during World War II Orwell accused pacifists of being secretly attracted to Hitler and of being "objectively pro-Fascist") in order to bolster their own attack on the nuclear freeze movement. [8] In this way, Orwell is taken out of his time and, in disregard of his few but strong warnings about atomic weapons—for example, "Either we renounce it [the bomb] or it destroys us" (CEJL, 4:19)—is used to endorse the nuclear arsenal.

A more interesting example of Orwell's appropriation by neoconservatives is provided by Norman Podhoretz's recent article "If Orwell Were Alive Today"—whose very title is a telling indication of the power of the Orwell myth. Podhoretz's argument, and the subsequent rejoinder by Christopher Hitchens, claiming Orwell for the socialist camp, especially illuminate the techniques of the Orwell sweepstakes. Podhoretz begins by establishing Orwell's authority through some judicious quotations. Irving Howe, he recalls, considered Orwell "the greatest moral force in English letters during the last several decades," and Bernard Crick numbered Orwell, with Hobbes and Swift, among the three greatest political writers in the English language. Since Orwell (Podhoretz states) is "the greatest political writer of the age," it is important to have him "on one's side." [9] But there is a problem: Orwell did call himself a socialist. Podhoretz's way of dealing with this inconvenience is interesting. He could have argued that Orwell was mistaken in his self-appraisal (as some Marxist critics have asserted while analyzing Orwell's deeply conservative strains), but to do this would be to deprive Orwell of precisely that on which his moral stature rests: his alleged concern for justice, decency, equality. Instead, Podhoretz argues that were Orwell alive today he would have become a neoconservative because he would see that capitalism has realized most of what he wished to accomplish via socialism. By this ploy (especially intriguing given the difficult economic times so conveniently ignored by Podhoretz), Orwell's moral stature remains intact, while the glow of his unquestioned moral authority is appropriated for Podhoretz's purpose.

Christopher Hitchens replied to this provocation with a long and irate comment, in which, unfortunately, he revealed that he knows less about Orwell than does Podhoretz. Hitchens believes that his hero could not possibly have said some of the things Podhoretz attributes to him. Regarding the statement that British rule in India was as bad as Hitler's in Europe, Hitchens declares that "Orwell never wrote or thought [sic] anything of the kind." And he labels as "wholly false" Podhoretz's assertion that Orwell became "a wholehearted patriot." Like Podhoretz, Hitchens buttresses his case with well-chosen quotations that support his image of Orwell. Podhoretz, however, can cite chapter and verse in a rejoinder: Yes, in 1937 Orwell did write that British rule in India was just as bad as German fascism.[10] But another citation is needed to complete the reference. If, in correcting Hitchens, Podhoretz had cited the whole of Orwell's comment, it would have directly undermined his own position: "I do not see," Orwell wrote, "how one can oppose Fascism except by working for the overthrow of capitalism, starting, of course, in one's own country. If one collaborates with a capitalist-imperialist government in a struggle 'against Fascism,' i.e. against a rival imperialism, one is simply letting Fascism in by the back door" (CEJL, 1:284). Nor does Podhoretz point out that this passage provides a typical example of Orwell's habitual tendency toward extreme generalizations that are suddenly reversed, for by January 1940 Orwell would be writing to Victor Gollancz: "What worries me at present is whether the ordinary people in countries like England grasp the difference between democracy and despotism well enough to want to defend their liberties. . . . The intellectuals who are at present pointing out that democracy and fascism are the same thing etc depress me horribly" (1:409). And later that same year, having forgotten his earlier allegiance to the idea that war would make England go fascist, Orwell sneers: "Already it is customary among the more soft-boiled intellectuals of the Left to declare that if we fight against the Nazis we shall 'go Nazi' ourselves. They might almost equally well say that if we fight against Negroes we shall turn black" (2:102). And yes, as these passages and many others from Orwell's wartime writings reveal, he had indeed become an ardent patriot, writing of "the spiritual need for patriotism and the military virtues, for which, however little the boiled rabbits of the Left may like them, no substitute has yet been found" (1:540). Christopher Hitchens's assumptions about what Orwell could not possibly have said, thought, or felt reveal a key phenomenon in the Orwell myth: the compulsion to overlook or ignore those writings of Orwell's that tend to undermine the purpose one is trying to make him serve.

A similar instance of selective reading appears in the Podhoretz/Hitchens exchange on Orwell's anti-Semitism and anti-Zionism. Podhoretz ponders Orwell's lack of awareness of the evils of nazism and links this to Orwell's "curious hostility" to Zionism.[11] Yet he does not explain why Orwell's anti-Zionism is a "curious hostility" while his anti-Communism is an important truth. When Orwell's views do not match his own, Podhoretz seems content to treat them as inexplicable, or as curious lapses; when they do coincide, he holds them up as semisacred writ. Hitchens, on the other hand, considers Orwell's anti-Zionism a sign of his unusual perspicacity, which tells us more about Hitchens than about Orwell.

Such talking at cross-purposes has plagued commentaries on Orwell for decades. But in the Podhoretz/Hitchens exchange, the full force of the Orwell myth, now at its height, is apparent. No longer is it a matter of Communist attacks on Orwell versus capitalist or socialist defenses of him. His status—not primarily as a writer but as a moral exemplar, a symbol of ethical and political rectitude—is now virtually beyond question. To Hitchens and Podhoretz this status is a foregone conclusion, and their disagreement is only about who can rightfully claim him as his patron saint. But it is vital to note that this is not merely intentional distortion of Orwell on the part of his readers. There is, indeed, enough contradictory material in Orwell's writings to warrant many positions, many extrapolations. At the same time, Orwell's characteristically assertive manner of writing invites readers to accept as conclusive whatever opinion he is expressing at any given moment. This can be explained partly by his extensive journalism throughout the late thirties and forties, much of it ephemeral but responsive to changing political realities. I believe, however, that a better explanation of the ease with which Orwell can be appropriated for divergent political ends lies in his approach to writing and his rhetoric.

First of all, as a writer Orwell was primarily stimulated by negative impulses: He needed to write *against* something. If one takes at face value, for example, his attacks on socialists in *The Road to Wigan Pier* and his designating the totalitarian society of *Nineteen Eighty-Four* as "English Socialism" or "Ingsoc," then it makes sense to regard him as something other than a socialist. If, however, one chooses to believe his statements identifying himself as an internal critic of socialism, then one can go on claiming him and his reputation for the socialist camp. Clearly, every attack on something contains at least the seed of a positive idea in the name of which the attack is pursued. The reader is free to concentrate on one or the other aspect of such a text.

Second, as many commentators have noted, Orwell is a conservative by temperament—a longing for the past being one of the constants of his work—but he was also a revolutionary at various moments in his life. This combination helps explain the contradictory impressions of the man and his thought one can draw from his writings, contradictions that cannot be accounted for by arguing that he holds complex and hence multifaceted views. Orwell is equally simplistic and extreme at each end of the spectrum: as sarcastically opposed to militarism in 1938–39 as to pacifism thereafter. In 1938 Orwell blamed the "pansy left" and "hack-journalists" for trying to stir up war fever, while "ordinary decent people" opposed war with Germany (cejl, 1:332), but by 1940 Orwell is charging the "pansy left" with revealing its cowardice by *opposing* the war while "pro-Fascist" pacifists ("Fascifists") try to hush up "the fact" that the working class is (so Orwell asserts) almost always antifascist (2:226–28).

But there is a logic running through these mutually contradictory attacks. Not only his continuing anger at the Left but also the values implicit in his assaults remain the same. Even during his brief antimilitarist phase in 1938 and 1939, Orwell in effect accuses those men who were promoting war of not being real men; they take this position, he argues, because of the softness and security of their life in England. They hunger for blood out of lack of experience of it. A few years later, on the other hand, in arguing that the "real working class" is "never really pacifist," Orwell maintains that this is so *because* of their experience of violence. "To abjure violence it is necessary to have no experience of it," he now says—once again accusing his opponents of lacking these true badges of manhood (2:167). Orwell's values and orientation have not changed: The charges of cowardice, lack of firsthand knowledge of war and violence (which, by this contrast, emerge as things to be valued in themselves), continue to provide the core of his critique, whether he happens to be scourging the Left for promoting war or for opposing it.

Certainly Orwell's extravagant and loose accusations are not surprising in a polemical writer, but Orwell is hardly the "magnificent" polemicist John Wain considers him.[12] There is marked crudeness and oversimplification in his writing as he typically indulges in ad hominem attacks rather than offering explanation and analysis. E. P. Thompson notes that this is a characteristic device in Orwell's polemical style: "He continually replaced the examination of objective situations by the imputation of motive."[13] Orwell was always ready to toss labels at people of whom he disapproved. In his "London Letter" to the *Partisan Review* in early 1942, for instance, he asserted that Julian Symons "writes in a vaguely Fascist strain" (CEJL, 2:181). Subsequently, Orwell became friends with Symons and publicly retracted his comment.[14] Yet this did not keep him from continuing to attach labels to individuals on the basis of mere gossip or his own careless judgments—as in a 1946 "London Letter," in which he writes: "Wyndham Lewis, I am credibly informed, has become a Communist or at least a strong sympathiser" (CEJL, 4:188).[15]

Orwell enjoyed making lists; he kept track of his reading, his income from writing, foreign expressions that he thought should be replaced by English ones, popular songs at different stages of recent history, clichés, and many other things. He also kept, toward the end of his life, a notebook on over eighty people he considered politically unreliable. In three neat columns headed "name," "job," "remarks," Orwell set down his judgments. We do not know what purpose this notebook (primarily in Orwell's own handwriting with occasional notations in another hand) was meant to serve, but it provides a perfect example of the claustrophobic cold war mentality soon to become embodied in Sen. Joseph McCarthy, in which individuals are scrutinized to determine their possible Communist connections and political "reliability." Orwell notes religious affiliations and physical ailments, and attaches labels to identify character, sexual preference (when it deviates from the norm), and politics. Thus we find: "Zionist"; "Political climber"; "Outright F-T [fellow traveler]"; "Sympathiser only"; "Probably venal"; "Dishonest demagogic type"; "Previously C.P."; "Tendency towards homosexuality"; "Strong sympathiser only. Could change." [16] But it is not merely the notebook's demonstration of Orwell's descent into a vigilante mentality that is disturbing; it is also the smug tone of one totally confident in his judgments of people and ready to label them according to narrow criteria, an attitude visibly at odds with Orwell's popular reputation as an opponent of all forms of totalitarianism. But the seeds of such a catalogue were already in Orwell's mind well before the late forties. In a 1942 "London Letter," he comments on the phenomenon of "quisling intellectuals" on the Continent and says: "If the Germans got to England, similar things would happen, and I think I could make out at least a preliminary list of the people who would go over" (CEJL, 2:183). And yet, only a few years earlier, in his 1939 essay "Inside the Whale," Orwell had written that what most frightened him about the war in Spain was the "immediate reappearance in left-wing circles of the mental atmosphere of the Great War." People "rushed straight back into the mental slum of 1915. All the familiar war-time idiocies, spy-hunting, orthodoxy-sniffing (Sniff, sniff. Are you a good anti-Fascist?)" (CEJL, 1:517–18).

One of Orwell's favorite rhetorical strategems is the blanket generalization, often blatantly biased. I offer a few examples only: "No real revolutionary has ever been an internationalist" (CEJL, 2:103); "All left-wing parties in the highly industrialized countries are at bottom a sham. . . . A humanitarian is always a hypocrite" (2:187); "I have never met a genuine working man who accepted Marxism" (1:532). His writings are littered with such sweeping assertions, a rhetorical technique that brushes aside reservations and challenges by the sheer force and confidence with which these declarations are made.[17]

A further aspect of Orwell's habit of generalization is apparent in his preferred narrative postures. The first of these may be called the voice-of-the-people stance, in which Orwell invariably identifies his position with that of "everyone." But in fact he places some limitations on who this "everyone" is—restrictions that cannot help but have a coercive effect on the reader. "Everyone" turns out to be all thinking people, all decent people, all sensitive people, all honest people—so the reader who dares to disagree with Orwell's dicta must accept the ostracism implicit in these formulations. A few examples of this rhetorical strategy will make the point: In *The Road to Wigan Pier* Orwell tries to explain why "so many normal decent people are repelled by the only remedy, namely by Socialism" (191); by contrast, "Everyone who has given the movement so much as a glance knows that the rank-and-file Fascist is often quite a well-meaning person—quite genuinely anxious, for instance, to better the lot of the unemployed" (187). "People know that in some way or another 'progress' is a swindle" (168), Orwell asserts earlier in the same book, and, in the same vein, "A generation ago every intelligent person was in some sense a revolutionary; nowadays it would be nearer the mark to say that every intelligent person is a reactionary" (177). Such statements recur throughout all of Orwell's writings and are also embedded in his fiction. More than ten years after *Wigan Pier*, Orwell still strikes this posture. In his 1948 essay "Writers and Leviathan," he writes: "Take for instance the fact that all sensitive people are revolted by industrialism and its products" (CEJL, 4:411). This particular sentence is overdetermined, for Orwell's opinion is here further called a "fact"—another favorite tactic of his. To the end of his life Orwell utilized this constraining rhetoric. In a notebook (now held at the Orwell Archive) that he kept shortly before his death, one striking passage reveals both his typical rhetorical claim (that he merely expresses what everyone thinks) and his often bizarre views: "Who has not felt when talking to a Czech, a Pole—to any central European, but above all to a German or a German Jew—'How superior their minds are to ours, after all!' And who has not followed this up a few minutes later with the complementary thought: 'But unfortunately they are all mad'?"

Orwell's other main narrative tactic, the voice-in-the-wilderness, though it seems to contradict his voice-of-the-people stance, in fact complements it. In its dramatic form it becomes a David-versus-Goliath scenario, with Orwell casting himself in the role of David, single-handedly engaging in verbal duels. It is this rhetorical device that Orwell deploys in the 1936 declaration cited at the beginning of this chapter: "Few people have the guts to say outright that art and propaganda are the same thing." This is another example of Orwell's recourse to overdetermination; not only the statement's simple declarative form but also the intimidating tone with which Orwell leads into it. Evident well before Orwell's experiences of newspaper censorship and distortion of events in Catalonia in 1937, this belligerent stance comes to characterize his polemic against the Left.

Between them, these two rhetorical strategies seem designed to appeal to virtually everyone. The voice-in-the-wilderness has an obvious attraction to those who see their place in the world as constantly under attack by restive masses and an uncontrollable and hostile radical opposition. Orwell acts as a whistle blower for this group, telling the awful truth about the Left. The voice-of-the-people posture, on the other hand, is obviously populist, suggesting that Orwell is indeed everyman, in touch with what the masses (at least those among them who are honest, decent, etc.) really want. Those who disagree are cast into the role of elitist opponents or obscurantists unwilling to admit obvious truths. It is easy to see how these contrasting appeals make Orwell attractive to two quite different groups, as the Podhoretz/Hitchens exchange demonstrates.

Seeing himself as the sole bearer of truth in a world peopled largely by cowardly and dishonest leftists (he had much less to say about the Right), Orwell set himself up as a judge over others, determining according to his own lights the "tests" that alone would redeem them. In August 1944 he wrote to John Middleton Murry (whose pacifism Orwell had attacked), "I consider that willingness to criticise Russia and Stalin is *the* test of intellectual honesty" (CEJL, 3:203; Orwell's emphasis), apparently confident that he himself has passed this test many times over. Orwell's respect for "anyone who is willing to face unpopularity" (3:191), a further aspect of his voice-in-the-wilderness stance, requires him to overestimate the strength and extent of his opponents.

Thus, as late as the winter of 1947/48, we find Orwell still claiming that it takes courage to criticize the Soviet Union and that newspapers such as the socialist *Tribune* simply kowtow to what is fashionable (4:395–400).[18] Commenting on this strain in Orwell's writing, Mary McCarthy refers to his "habit of making avowals to his readers, often in a truculent manner. For instance he admits suddenly that he has never been able to dislike Hitler. Such a confession 'expects' that the reader feels the same but has not had the bravado to declare it." Repeating Nigel Dennis's statement that Orwell's appeal was "to what everyone knows in his heart," McCarthy then points out that "this is less a soft appeal than a challenge, sometimes a species of blackmail or bullying: if you think you dislike Hitler, you are a hypocrite or a toady of fashion and you had better think again."[19] Orwell prided himself on this posture, as he makes clear in a 1946 essay entitled "Why I Write," in which he remembers himself as a child: "I knew that I had a facility with words and a power of facing unpleasant facts" (CEJL, 1:1). Actually, his writings reveal that he frequently needed to distort or magnify the "facts" in order to create opportunities for "facing" up to them.

The role of this coercive tone in sustaining Orwell's claim to moral rectitude has been, in my view, generally overlooked. His reputation for self-imposed austerity also contributed to the moral authority granted to him by members of his own class (less readily given, presumably, to a genuine working-class critic). Orwell's censoriousness is an important element in the creation of the mystique surrounding him. A good illustration of this process at work is provided by Anthony Powell, who recollects that he was apprehensive about his first meeting with Orwell because a mutual friend, Cyril Connolly, had pictured Orwell as a "severe unapproachable infinitely disapproving personage."[20] Orwell's adventures and reputation, as well as his earlier writings, had preceded him, and Powell was anxious to make the right sort of impression. When, by chance, he was introduced to Orwell in a restaurant (in 1941), Powell imagined that Orwell would not approve of his patrol uniform: "It was no doubt bad enough in his eyes to be an officer at all; to be rigged out in these pretentious regimentals, at once militaristic and relatively ornate, would aggravate the offence of belonging to a stupid and brutal caste." Instead, Orwell showed interest in Powell's uniform and expressed nostalgia for the days in Burma when he himself used to wear trousers strapped under the foot, saying: "Those straps under the foot give you a feeling like nothing else in life." [21] Powell goes on to describe his friendship with Orwell in highly ambiguous terms, overtly praising Orwell while conveying the impression that, with his self-imposed Spartan ways, his ill-concealed dandyism, and his "consciously battered old tweed coat," [22] Orwell was acting out a role.

Other friends of Orwell's display similarly ambiguous feelings toward him. Malcolm Muggeridge, who refers to Orwell's attire as "a sort of proletarian fancy dress," also praises Orwell while conveying a general impression of a lack of sincerity in him—duly laughed away as Muggeridge refers to him as "a card, a dear fellow." [23] In fact, something of the laundering process that accompanies such memories of a famous friend surfaces if one compares Muggeridge's later comments with his diaries. After an initial meeting in Paris, he and Orwell met again in London in 1945. Muggeridge describes Orwell in his diary at that time as "exactly like Don Quixote, very lean and egotistic and honest and foolish; . . . a kind of dry egotism has burned him out." [24] Although consistently expressing his affection for Orwell, Muggeridge also writes, on January 26, 1950 (five days after Orwell's death): "Read through various obituary articles on George by Koestler, Pritchett, Julian Symons, etc., and saw in them how the legend of a human being is created, because although they were ostensibly correct and I might have written the same sort of stuff myself, they were yet inherently false—e.g. everyone saying George was not given to self-pity, whereas it was of course his dominant emotion." [25] Yet in writing of Orwell some twenty years later, Muggeridge makes no mention of this self-pity, treats Orwell's extravagant statements with good-natured indulgence, and praises him for his "true humility . . . and inflexible honesty." [26]

These contrasts between contemporaneous and subsequent reactions to Orwell are of importance because they indicate that the farther we get away from his own lifetime, the stronger is the hold of the Orwell myth. Of the dozens of articles that have appeared on Orwell in newspapers and popular magazines in the last few years, almost none deviates from the honorific tone. And this despite the fact that not only details of Orwell's life but extremely astute analyses and commentaries on his writings are readily available. Perhaps the best, in the sense of most accurate and insightful, of these critiques are those by E. P. Thompson and Raymond Williams, though other critics (such as Mary McCarthy, Terry Eagleton, and Frank Gloversmith) have also made clearheaded observations about Orwell.[27] Disregarding the Orwell myth as much as possible, these writers have read his words without the obfuscatory veil generally cast over them. But what is most interesting is to observe that the facts that these critics point to, instead of merely repeating received opinion about Orwell, have apparently made no dent in the Orwell mystique, which has continued to flourish, ever more so as the year 1984 approached.

Whether contributing to the Orwell mystique or challenging it, commentators on Orwell have remained largely insensitive, however, to certain aspects of his work. In a writer so notably torn by contradictions, even the antagonisms and the terms in which he expresses them provide a startling unifying thread. It is my contention in the following chapters that there is an identifiable "ideological cluster" at the heart of this angry and contradictory writer. The concept of an ideological cluster helps us to see what it is that unifies Orwell's diverse pet peeves, his fear of socialism and the machine, his nostalgia for the past, his misogyny, his attraction to the experience of war, and the conservatism apparent in his carefully circumscribed challenge to hierarchy and inequality. The ideological cluster that, as we shall see, clearly emerges from Orwell's work can be expressed in one word: androcentrism.

ORWELL AS A WRITER

The point of the preceding pages, emphasizing the coercive and generally problematic sides of Orwell, is not to condemn him but to show the immense discrepancy between what he actually wrote and how he has come to be viewed. Although Orwell's reputation has by now metamorphosed into an independent entity, not strictly linked to what he wrote, he is, nonetheless, primarily a writer and not the cultic hero into which he has been transformed. In the chapters that follow I therefore return to his books, both fiction and nonfiction, and secondarily draw upon his extensive shorter and in many cases more ephemeral writings.

Orwell's posture as truth teller and challenger of conventions, gadfly of the intellectuals and implacable critic of the consummately smug, does not seem to be one that would earn him much popularity among those same intellectuals. How, then, can his fame be explained? Many of his greatest admirers, after all, believe that his importance is not primarily the result of literary merits. One easy answer suggests itself: To be a "leftist" anti-Communist was an increasingly respectable position as the 1940s wore on. It protected one from the charge of simpleminded anti-Communism motivated by mercenary considerations and allowed one to be high-minded, a defender of justice and fairness for all—this from the point of view of left-leaning intellectuals. To pro-capitalist anti-Communists the matter would, of course, appear in a much simpler light. *Animal Farm* and *Nineteen Eighty-Four* without a doubt made Orwell the most popular anti-Communist writer of his time (and ours). But is this all? How does such a writer signal to his readers that he is indeed "safe," that he does not mean to deprive them of cherished ideas, habits, and beliefs? One suitable technique would seem to be to show in some way that there is agreement between himself and his readership about fundamentals, so that his harangues and challenges would not be viewed as an unbridgeable gulf separating him from his readers. I believe that Orwell does this through his cultivation of a traditional notion of masculinity, complemented by a generalized misogyny. Quite apart, then, from the problem of how such attitudes influence a writer's own thought, they play a role in Orwell's fame and popularity. While Orwell's attacks on the "pansy left," pacifists, and other numerically small groups are an essential part of the ideological cluster that pervades his work, they could too easily be dismissed as amusing or ornery, misguided or intentionally provocative, but at bottom a passing diversion. The substantial stuff, the meat of the issue (an appropriate image given Orwell's hostility to vegetarians), lies in the insistent adherence to a gender polarization that assumes male centrality and superiority. This feature of Orwell's work has never been addressed, though critics of all persuasions have now and then noted his toughness, his "Kiplingesque" strain. At a time of rapid social and technological change disruptive of the traditional family, Orwell reassured his readers that even a man who depicted himself as a great challenger of the powers-that-be could be counted on not to rock the boat.

Orwell was born in 1903. He was growing up while women in England were fighting for the vote, but not a word about this is recorded in his writings, whereas his prejudices and preconceptions, often in the form of an apparently innocent (i.e., unquestioning and unquestionable) "natural" tendency to insult and denigrate women, appear frequently in his work. I suggest that an unacknowledged communication was occurring here between Orwell and his typical readers, a quite successful communication in view of the fact that it has never cast his reputation into any doubt. At the base of his apparent challenges lay the reassurances of perceived similarity. His disdain for deviations from traditional masculinity (epitomized for Orwell by vegetarians, sandal wearers, homosexuals, pacifists, and the rest of his menagerie of bêtes noires) [28] must have soothed and calmed many of his readers, who sorely needed this reassurance as they read through his angry and pessimistic texts. In *Keep the Aspidistra Flying*, for example, Gordon Comstock rants and raves about the money world and women's commitment to it, but the text does not go beyond this flood of words to induce the reader actually to think about the relationship between these two, money and women, or, rather, lack of money and women. Still, these themes lurk in the text, and, were it not for the complicity of critics and readers, they would surely have been noted long since.

Orwell's reputation today depends upon a peculiarly passive readership, passive in its acceptance of claims about Orwell's decency, honesty, and integrity. Where are the women readers of his works who heard and took seriously the misogyny of his texts,[29] who felt excluded from the concerns for "mankind" he professed? Perhaps they did not have access to the press, as did his male readers; or perhaps their own perceptions tended to be diminished, even stilled, by the roar of respect he seemed to generate.[30] There is a disruption of meaning,[31] a dissonance, once the reader of Orwell's work assumes a gender different from that which Orwell explicitly addresses. And when Orwell does not do so explicitly, what kind of reader does he implicitly invoke? A male in most instances, and a British male of his own class specifically, sharing his prejudices and perhaps enjoying hearing them voiced. But it is important to note how narrative not only addresses a certain kind of reader but in effect creates that reader. One instance of this has already been noted: Orwell appeals to common sense, to what everybody knows, and to what every intelligent person is bound to think, in such a way that different perceptions are obscured, inhibited. When the reader is a woman, imagining as a woman (rather than identifying with a male, as is in fact often the case), she becomes aware of being excluded by the narrative; of being outside the intimate narrative framework of author-text-reader; alone, even put in the wrong for having other than the assumed reactions. Orwell appeals to the reader's snobbery and encourages the reader not to challenge the prevailing definition of reality that the text creates. Women readers thus find themselves as effectively excluded from the magic narrative circle, as say, the Burmese in *Burmese Days* are from the European Club. So the reader who has broken through the habitual identification with men (which, under the circumstances, involves a violation of her own identity and experience) finds herself alone in unexplored territory, somehow excluded from the intimacy and complicity of the male text that addresses itself to other males.[32]

Apart from this problem, Orwell's work, as a whole, reveals a curious ambivalence about the possibilities for positive human change and growth. From mere ambivalence and then pessimism, however, Orwell moves to a position of despair, most forcefully expressed in his last novel, *Nineteen Eighty-Four*. This progression is in my view a logical consequence of Orwell's commitment to a not clearly articulated paradigm that polarizes human beings according to sex roles and gender identity and legitimizes male displays of dominance and aggression. Women figure in this paradigm primarily as a category of human beings in contrast to which men can experience a sense of centrality and superiority. Orwell's unquestioning adherence to this concept of manhood—and to the narrow world view that follows from it—exacts a considerable price; it is what eventually leads to his despair.

Orwell may not have been aware of the extent of his preoccupation with manhood and masculinity, but he was certainly conscious of his own misogyny and antifeminism. In a letter to his friend Brenda Salkeld in 1934, he comments on a talk with a man who "is a bit of a feminist and thinks that if a woman was brought up exactly like a man she would be able to throw a stone, construct a syllogism, keep a secret etc. He tells me that my anti-feminist views are probably due to Sadism!" (CEJL, 1:136). In his journalism, Orwell found it appropriate to display his misogyny repeatedly. In a review of a novel by Joseph Conrad, for example, he comments: "One of the surest signs of his genius is that women dislike his books" (1:227). The force of Orwell's androcentrism is apparent not only in his work itself but also in the critical response to it: Most critics have simply affirmed this view of the world and have resolutely ignored the contradictions that recur between Orwell's stated principles and the underlying implications of his texts. Such contradictions, evident in various guises throughout Orwell's works, appear above all in the novels, because the very act of creating characters and setting them in motion implies a certain loss of control on the part of the writer. If the contradiction is a deep and important one (such as that manifest in the critique of imperialism made by Flory in *Burmese Days* and the reality of his exploitative relationship with his native mistress), traces of the problem the author is trying to ignore or suppress will seep into the work, often at every level. Orwell himself was aware of this potential, as a number of his comments reveal, but he apparently believed himself to be a fully conscious human being, one who did not need the advice he gave to others. He therefore felt free to indulge rather than question his own ideology.

The relationship between manhood and misogyny, though not a simple one, is surprisingly well delineated by Orwell in one of his earliest writings, a short story he published in the Eton school newspaper, the *Election Times*, in 1918. This story, entitled "The Slack-bob," is, in Bernard Crick's description, "about a boy who pretends to be in the Rowing Eight to impress some sisters and, when they invite themselves down on Open Day, has to pretend to be injured—it ends, 'Moral: honesty is the best policy.' " [33] But the story is in fact about the pressures of gender role training. The seven sisters, "all big fat noisy girls with red hair," Orwell writes, both encourage and taunt the unathletic protagonist and in effect require an athletic performance of him; so "By the end of the day He [sic] had told them that He was going to win junior sculling, & probably be in the Eight next year. But this made them so fond of him that he wished he had told them the truth." [34] The boy wants nothing to do with these girls, does not want them to be fond of him, but is unable to avoid conforming to the masculine behavior they seem to expect of him and from which they derive vicarious satisfaction. As a result, the sisters announce, a few weeks later, that they are coming to watch him win junior sculling. He pretends to have injured his arm and gets both attentions and criticisms that he does not want, both kisses and charges of "Coward!" from the different girls, who then have tea in his room and announce that they will appear the next year to watch him in the Procession of Boats. Hence the story's moral. In its way, this is an illuminating parable on the pressures boys feel to acquire and act out a masculine identity. The emphasis on athletics, the fear and anxieties about succeeding, the antagonism and disdain toward girls who, nonetheless, have a peculiar power to ridicule the boy—these tensions appear in the story and will reappear in almost all Orwell's subsequent fiction.

Orwell's commitment to androcentrism, as the following chapters demonstrate, has everything to do with his achievements and his failures as a writer, as well as with his political vision. His adherence to a traditional and damaging notion of manhood, which I call hypertrophied masculinity, illuminates problems relating to both the technical and the ideological aspects of his work.

In using current terminology such as "androcentrism" and "gender ideology," I am perhaps inviting the objection that I am applying anachronistic standards to Orwell. I think this is a spurious objection, which can be answered in two parts. First, feminist writing and agitation have gone on throughout this century (as well as, of course, the nineteenth century), as Dale Spender reminds us in a recent book bearing the title *There's Always Been a Women's Movement This Century*.[35] In fact, in the chapters that follow I repeatedly cite sources from Orwell's own time reflecting on women's position in England in the early twentieth century. These materials were certainly accessible to Orwell, had he been receptive to them. Second, although he rarely wrote on works by women, in 1945 Orwell did review one of the most important feminist works of the century: Virginia Woolf's *Room of One's Own*. His comments on this book (to which he devotes one-fourth the space allotted in the same article to Viscount Samuel's

Memoirs) are remarkable for his uncharacteristically circumspect and wary tone; he neither engages the book nor strongly contradicts its premises. He is clearly on his guard.[36] But there is a more important point to be made regarding the standards to which I am holding Orwell. They are those he himself proclaimed: honesty, decency, egalitarianism, justice. And it is by these very standards that, as I shall show, he must be found wanting. Orwell identifies himself as a political writer, and it is because of his purported concern for justice and equality that he has developed a reputation as a moral exemplar. The work of such a figure should be able to withstand scrutiny in terms of the values he professed. But Orwell's works reveal his failure to adhere to his own standards, and any celebration of him not modulated by appropriate criticism will simply repeat that failure. Orwell is not a good man gone wrong who, as some would like to claim, simply could not take on everything and just happened to omit consideration of the gender hierarchy from his repertoire of highly publicized concerns. As we shall see, Orwell in fact supports the gender hierarchy in every possible way, by acts of both commission and omission in his writing, and this is what gives many of his moral claims a peculiarly hollow sound.

In a 1946 essay (CEJL, 4:65), Orwell wrote: "Even a single taboo can have an all-round crippling effect upon the mind, because there is always the danger that any thought which is freely followed up may lead to the forbidden thought." He was right.

Two

Roles of Empire

There is a scene early in *Burmese Days*, Orwell's first novel, in which five Englishmen have their prebreakfast drinks at the European Club, their sole bastion against the four thousand Burmese among whom they live. The Englishmen fall into argument over the order they have received to accept an Oriental as a member of the club. Degrees of racism divide these men. At one extreme is the rabidly racist and vulgar Ellis, a company manager; at the other is the novel's protagonist, the "Bolshie" Flory, who has spent fifteen years working for a timber firm in Burma and is notorious for his friendship with an Indian physician, Dr. Veraswami. Although the issue of race divides these Englishmen, they are united by their privileged status not only as white Britishers but, especially, as white males.
Orwell writes:

"Did you hear that one about 'There was a young lady of Woking'?" Maxwell said. . . . He completed the biography of the young lady of Woking and there was a laugh. Westfield replied with the young lady of Ealing who had a peculiar feeling, and Flory came in with the young curate of Horsham who always took every precaution. There was more laughter. Even Ellis thawed and produced several rhymes; Ellis's jokes were always genuinely witty, and yet filthy beyond measure. Everyone cheered up and felt more friendly in spite of the heat. [26]

Male sexual humor thus establishes a bond, however ephemeral, among these men. But discussions of *Burmese Days* typically focus on the issue of imperialism, while ignoring the appearance within the novel of quite another major theme: that of sexual and social identity and the linkage between them.

Burmese Days (1934) is not only Orwell's first published novel; it is also his first book that explicitly deals with the issue of domination. Much has been made of the impact on Orwell of his five years (1922–27) in Burma as a policeman in the service of the British Empire and the feeling of guilt with which this personal participation in power and domination left him. Orwell was to describe his reaction in the autobiographical section of his later book, *The Road to Wigan Pier:*

> I was conscious of an immense weight of guilt that I had got to expiate. . . . I felt that I had got to escape not merely from imperialism but from every form of man's dominion over man. I wanted to submerge myself, to get right down among the oppressed, to be one of them and on their side against their tyrants. And, chiefly because I had had to think everything out in solitude, I had carried my hatred of oppression to extraordinary lengths. At that time failure seemed to me to be the only virtue. [129–30]

Orwell is here talking about the desire for "social" failure that moved him to seek the experiences described in his first book, *Down and Out in Paris and London* (1933). He wanted to opt out of the class he had been born into; however "shabby genteel" his family (and Orwell made it out to be a good deal shabbier than in fact it was), nonetheless it was part of the privileged class. As we shall see in the next chapter, he thought he could escape from this class by how he chose to live and relate to other people. But when, a few years later, Orwell came to write about his five years in Burma, he did not see that man's dominion over man, in general, is also quite specifically the male's dominion over the female. *Burmese Days* is the only work of Orwell's in which the issues of class, race, and sex all appear, and it thus provides us with a unique opportunity to examine more closely the precise contours of Orwell's critique of domination.

IMPERIAL MANHOOD

The structure of *Burmese Days* can best be understood by reading it as a drama. The time is 1926; the scene is the lush landscape of Upper Burma. Orwell said later that in every novel about the East the real subject is the scenery (*Wigan Pier*, 97); but this is hyperbole, for the scenery is not nearly as important to his novel as the human conflicts developed within it. The central stage set is the European Club in the town of Kyauktada, in which the English hold forth. Two main dramatic threads are interwoven. The first is the ambition of a villainous Burmese official, U Po Kyin, to acquire prestige and power among the English. Rather than deal with the actual problems of rising Burmese nationalism in the post–World War I period, Orwell focuses on this more limited drama, as U Po Kyin schemes to improve his standing by attacking and discrediting various other people—beginning with Flory's Indian friend, Dr. Veraswami, and ending with Flory himself. Orwell's state of mind at the time he wrote this novel becomes clear when we consider that there is hardly a single positive character in the entire novel. Both Burmese and English are depicted in extraordinarily negative terms, all pursuing their egocentric ends.

The second main thread of the novel has to do with Flory's desperate efforts to resolve the issue of his isolation and loneliness, for his hatred of imperialism has set him apart from the five other Englishmen in Kyauktada. Flory's status as an outsider is symbolized by the disfiguring blue birthmark on his cheek. But he is by no means an unambiguous hero; Orwell carefully presents him as a man constantly compromised by the imperialism of which he has been a part for fifteen years in Burma.

In keeping with its rather primitive dramatic structure, the novel's action often progresses by startling entrances and exits and perfectly timed chance events. Two new characters appear in the course of the novel. One is a young British woman, Elizabeth Lackersteen, on whom Flory pins his hopes of salvation, which in turn cause him to dismiss his Burmese mistress, Ma Hla May. Just when Elizabeth, desperate for a husband, is ready to accept Flory, a young British aristocrat named Verrall appears, clearly a better catch for Elizabeth but ultimately an elusive one. This triangle is worked out against the background of the political machinations of U Po Kyin, whose success finally depends upon Flory's failure and humiliation. While possessing many farcical elements, Flory's drama, as it turns out, is a tragedy, and Flory, the novel's sole critic of British imperialism, is driven to suicide at the end. But the political impact of the drama is blunted by the fact that Flory's suicide is not due merely to cumulative revulsion at his part in an oppressive system. Rather, it is instigated by his petty humiliation at the hands of his cast-off Burmese mistress. Instructed by U Po Kyin, she makes an ugly scene in front of the entire European community, and this in turn leads to Elizabeth's final rejection of Flory.

Orwell's "Kiplingesque" side, as Malcolm Muggeridge has called it,[1] is manifest in *Burmese Days* most clearly in the grudging admiration conveyed by the text for Verrall, who despises soft living and who looks, elegantly astride his horse, like a centaur: "Horsemanship and physical fitness were the only gods he knew" (193). Verrall (a pun on virile and feral) abhors women. Though he succumbs now and again, he is always able to escape their clutches in time. The portrayal is in many respects satirical, yet Flory admires and envies this man and agrees that he is a better mate for Elizabeth and, indeed, a "better man" (215) altogether. This is, of course, the same Flory whose judgments about imperialism the reader is meant to take seriously and honor. Thus Orwell simultaneously supports and undermines his protagonist, adding to the difficulties of interpreting his novel. In all Orwell's novels, the central moral and ideological problems faced by his chief characters are clearly spelled out; at the same time, as invariably happens in fiction, Orwell creates in Flory a figure whose traits reveal more than his creator is able to control. Thus the novel presents no irony in its treatment of Flory's conventional notions of masculine identity and reflects instead a lingering commitment on Orwell's part to that late-nineteenth-century public school ideal known as "muscular Christianity."[2] We shall see, in a later chapter, how Orwell's writings on war reveal his own adherence to this background, but what is important for present purposes is to understand the ideal of manliness against which the Englishmen in *Burmese Days*, including the "Bolshie" Flory, measure themselves and what this has to do with imperialism.

In a study of the image of India in British literature, Allen J. Greenberger explores how the Victorian concept of "manliness" was enacted in India. Since manliness was seen as the opposite of both childishness and femininity,[3] it is not surprising that the empire should appear to its defenders as a paternalistic enterprise: the British "father" caring for and disciplining the Indian "child." A whole series of characteristics were thus attributed to the Indians, all of which stress their similarity to children and women as traditionally perceived: lacking in self-discipline, governed by emotion rather than reason, untrustworthy, senselessly cruel, tending toward hysteria. A few of the positive traits associated with women and children also appear in this portrait: The Indians have innate simplicity, energy, intuitive awareness of people, and they are happy even though their lives appear harsh to Europeans.[4] These ideas reveal the extent to which an androcentric view of the world, which places men (especially husbands and fathers) at the center of reality, can be adapted to imperial purposes. British servants of the empire did not need to acquire a new ethical code in order to step into the role of domination; such an ethic was already available to them in their ideas about masculinity. They merely extended it to a different object, a new kind of "woman."

How well this ideology worked in Burma is apparent in a passage from Orwell's *Road to Wigan Pier*, in which he ingenuously describes his attitude toward the Burmese:

But one did not feel towards the "natives" as one felt towards the "lower classes" at home. The essential point was that the "natives," at any rate the Burmese, were not felt to be physically repulsive. One looked down on them as "natives," but one was quite ready to be physically intimate with them; and this, I noticed, was the case even with white men who had the most vicious colour prejudice. When you have a lot of servants you soon get into lazy habits, and I habitually allowed myself, for instance, to be dressed and undressed by my Burmese boy. This was because he was a Burman and undisgusting; I could not have endured to let an English manservant handle me in that intimate manner. I felt towards a Burman almost as I felt towards a woman. [124]

Orwell defends this attitude by reference to the "fact" that "most Mongolians have much nicer bodies than most white men" (124). They have firm-knit skin and relatively little body hair, and they are beardless and seldom go bald (124–25). Interestingly, Orwell nowhere expresses such admiration for these qualities in women, which suggests that their real significance is to aid in the ideological transformation of Burmese males into social "females." Other details appearing in *Burmese Days* reveal the implications of this racial and "sexual" domination. When Flory receives an "anonymous" letter from U Po Kyin containing a covert threat, he does not consider it important: "no Englishman ever feels himself in real danger from an Oriental" (75). The point is reiterated much later in the novel when the European Club is surrounded by Burmese angry over Ellis's attack on a Burmese boy. Flory's attitude is described: "He had been watching the scene almost with detachment—dazed by the noise, indeed, but not much frightened. He always found it difficult to believe that Orientals could be really dangerous" (236).[5]

If the native men are viewed as women, the corollary attitude among the British men is a preoccupation with their own status as males, and this is precisely what we find in the chummy masculinity of the European Club, as satirized by Orwell. One expression of this attitude is the eagerness of some of the Englishmen for that archetypal rite of manhood: war. Westfield, the district superintendent of police, laments the "paper-chewing" he is reduced to and says, "God, how I wish the war was on again!" (25). He complains about the position of the British in Burma, where "beggars of natives know the law better than we do. Insult you to your face and then run you in the moment you hit 'em. Can't do anything unless you put your foot down firmly. And how can you, if they haven't the guts to show fight?" (30). Orwell himself used nearly identical language in his short piece "Shooting an Elephant," written a few years after *Burmese Days*: "in an aimless, petty kind of way anti-European feeling was very bitter. No one had the guts to raise a riot," but harassment was common (CEJL, 1:235).[6] This is a typical example of the close correspondence that exists between Orwell's own views, as expressed in his extensive nonfiction, and the views he attributes to his characters.

In the novel, Westfield hopes for a native rebellion. "God, if they'd only break out and rebel properly for once! . . . But it'll be a bloody washout as usual. Always the same story with these rebellions—peter out almost before they've begun. Would you believe it, I've never fired my gun at a fellow yet, not even a dacoit. Eleven years of it, not counting the War, and never killed a man. Depressing" (106–7). He is eager for the Burmese to "have the guts to show a bit of fight for once. Then we'll call out the Military Police, rifles and all. Plug a few dozen of 'em—that'll clear the air" (107). Westfield is upset when the longed-for rebellion falls apart at once: "They caved in like the funks they are. The whole district's as quiet as a bloody girls' school. Most disappointing" (219). Later, he learns that he has missed a "veritable riot": "It seemed fated that he should never kill a man. Depressing, depressing" (242). Orwell is clearly ridiculing this eagerness for violent confrontation. Yet, as we shall see in chapter 5, only a few years after writing these scenes Orwell himself was anxiously wondering how long it would take him to shoot "my first Fascist."

When Maxwell, one of the Englishmen, is murdered, Ellis can hardly contain his eagerness for a battle. In this state of mind he attacks a group of high school boys, both verbally ("Do you call yourselves men? You sneaking, mangy little rats!") and physically, by hitting a boy across the face with his cane (230), an episode that resembles an actual event in Orwell's life in Burma.[7] The boy ends up blinded, and the makings of a rebellion seem at last present as the Europeans find the club surrounded by angry Burmese. Ellis is beside himself because the Europeans have no rifles: "My God, we won't get another chance like this in a hundred years! If we'd only ten rifles here, how we could slosh these b——s!" (235). It is in this situation that Flory gets the opportunity to play the hero, by swimming to the police lines to take command. Unlike his countrymen, however, Flory is not interested in doing battle with the Burmese, and he tells the police to fire above the crowd, to disperse it. But in other respects he shares in their preoccupation with manhood, as we shall see.

Flory was twenty-four in 1914 when the war broke out. Although he was due for home leave, he "dodged military service, which was easy to do and seemed natural at the time" (64). As in many other parts of the novel, the narrative now abandons any pretense of neutrality and tells the reader how to understand this action: "In reality, Flory had dodged the War because the East had already corrupted him, and he did not want to exchange his whisky, his servants and his Burmese girls for the boredom of the parade ground and the strain of cruel marches" (64). Flory's failure as a man is reiterated throughout the novel. He gives vent to both his loneliness and his hatred of imperialism, only to turn these into an attack on himself: "Did all his trouble, then, simply boil down to that? Just complicated, unmanly whinings; poor-little-rich-girl stuff? Was he no more than a loafer using his idleness to invent imaginary woes?" (69). Orwell repeatedly presents Flory's self-hatred as a deeper truth than his attacks on imperialism. In one scene he does not have the "nerve" to fire at a dog baying outside his house and then goes into a diatribe against himself, "without heat, however, for he was too accustomed to the thought. 'Sneaking, idling, boozing, fornicating, soul-examining, self-pitying cur. All those fools at the Club, those dull louts to whom you are so pleased to think yourself superior—they are all better than you, every man of them. At least they are men in their oafish way. Not cowards, not liars. Not half-dead and rotting' " (59). This particular outburst has been brought on by Flory's behavior that evening at the club. He had signed his name to a letter informing the deputy commissioner of the club members' disinclination to allow a "nigger" into the club and thus had publicly betrayed and insulted his Indian friend, Dr. Veraswami. This leads to several more pages of self-directed insults. Flory acts as if calling himself a coward and recognizing his fear of going against the views of his peers are sufficient expiation. Guilt thus becomes a substitute for action. The explanation given by the narrative of Flory's capitulation is as follows: "He had done it for the same reason as he had done a thousand such things in his life; because he lacked the small spark of courage that was needed to refuse" (61). This would have led to a row, to nagging and jeers: "At the very thought of it he flinched; he could feel his birthmark palpable on his cheek, and something happening in his throat that made his voice go flat and guilty. Not that! It was easier to insult his friend, knowing that his friend must hear of it" (61). Orwell here ironically repeats the words "his friend," as he calls our attention to this betrayal of friendship.

Terry Eagleton has pointed out that Orwell uses the birthmark to exculpate Flory from responsibility for his failure to act according to the moral principles he professes.[8] Orwell tells us that Flory's trouble can be traced further back than his fifteen years in Burma and the lesson he had learned there not to go against the opinion of the other Englishmen. The trouble "had begun in his mother's womb, when chance put the blue birthmark on his cheek" (61). Eagleton argues that "the birthmark is a telling detail which the novel can mobilise in support of its thesis that moral stances are impracticable." In this way the novel "suggests that Flory's weakness is in the 'nature of things' rather than in his response to a particular moral situation." Eagleton concludes: "The two elements (the birthmark and ideological conflict) are, of course, closely interrelated in Flory's history; but the fact that the genetic issue finally predominates over the social question seems to throw the burden of Flory's tragedy, not on to his moral and political conflicts with his fellow-countrymen, but on to what he physically and unchangeably is." [9]

Eagleton focuses, correctly, on Orwell's ambivalent characterization of Flory, who is unable to break with the class he attacks. But Eagleton's analysis does not show what Orwell's protagonists obtain from their identification with their class. More is at work in the novel, and Orwell's own text reveals what it is that binds his protagonists to their class: If they were to follow through with the rejection of their privileged status, they would eventually be led to a rejection of the even more fundamental privilege they enjoy by virtue of being males. Flory rejects imperialism, but he cannot bear to be thought of as less than a man.

Orwell's tendency to valorize roles according to their congruence with a masculine identity is apparent also in *The Road to Wigan Pier* in the chapter depicting his changing attitude toward imperialism. His work in the Indian Imperial Police as "part of the actual machinery of despotism" (127) was looked down upon even by the other Europeans in Burma. He refers to an occasion (described in *Burmese Days*) in which a Burmese suspect was made to bare his buttocks to ascertain, by the presence or absence of scars from earlier bamboo floggings, if he had ever been imprisoned before. An American missionary witnessed this scene one day and said to Orwell: "I wouldn't care to have your job" (128). Orwell's anger and shame are violent here: "So *that* was the kind of job I had! Even an ass of an American missionary, a teetotal cock-virgin from the Middle West, had the right to look down on me and pity me!" (128). Commenting on this passage in an essay on Orwell's imperial attitudes, John Gross notes its clear implication that Orwell "felt himself trapped in a role which, contrary to its conventional rating, was essentially unmanly." [10] Deviation from a masculine appearance also arouses Orwell's anger, as we shall see throughout his works. In *Burmese Days* this is evident in Flory's reaction: "Nasty old bladder of lard! he thought, watching Mr Macgregor up the road. How his bottom did stick out in those tight khaki shorts. Like one of those beastly middle-aged scoutmasters, homosexuals almost to a man, that you see photographs of in the illustrated papers. Dressing himself up in those ridiculous clothes and exposing his pudgy, dimpled knees, because it is the pukka sahib thing to take exercise before breakfast—disgusting!" (73–74).

Flory's anxiety about his own masculinity takes the further form of a fear of attractive women, especially when they appear as confident adults rather than as uncertain children. When Elizabeth, having snubbed Flory, arrives at the club elegantly dressed (because she is hoping to meet Verrall) Flory's reaction is extreme: "She looked so modish, so adult, that he feared her more than he had ever done" (182). It is the possibility of rejection, with its implied specter of female dominance, that is so threatening to Flory, as he makes clear later in the novel: "Is there anything in the world more graceless, more dishonouring, than to desire a woman whom you will never have?" (214).[11] While Elizabeth is hoping for a marriage proposal from the more eligible Verrall, Flory brings her the improperly cured leopard skin, symbol of the failure of their hunting episode to unite them permanently. He feels at a miserable disadvantage: "She was wearing a silk shirt and jodhpurs, and she was a little sunburned. Even in his memory she had never been so beautiful. He quailed; on the instant he was lost— every scrap of his screwed-up courage had fled. Instead of stepping forward to meet her he actually backed away" (206–7). And the narrative reiterates: "So great was his fear of her that he stepped hurriedly away" (207). This fear is rapidly translated into fantasies of violence, which would presumably redress the balance of power. When Flory cannot get past Elizabeth's "dreadful tee-heeing brightness," he thinks: "Go on, say what you came to say! Seize her in your arms; make her listen, kick her, beat her—anything sooner than let her choke you with this drivel!" (208). Defeated, he goes home and has "obscene" hallucinations of Elizabeth and Verrall and finally weeps in the arms of a fat prostitute thoughtfully provided by his servant (211). Thereafter, the narrative authoritatively declares, Flory comes close to seeing Elizabeth "almost as she was—silly, snobbish, heartless—and it made no difference to his longing for her." He now berates himself for his base envy of "the better man who had beaten him" (215), a definition of the situation remarkably at odds with Elizabeth's true position and intentions. When Elizabeth is "yielding" or when she clings to him like a child, he is reassured. When she appears to Flory as an adult, he is afraid of her. The status of their relationship can be established at all times by the degree of his fear or confidence. What is at stake here is control: When he is in control, the narrative reveals, all is well between them. To the extent that he loses control and it passes to her, the relationship is problematic.

Something of the sexual and racial hierarchy at work in the novel is indicated in a chapter in which most of the major plot lines are brought together within the space of eight pages. First, Flory is berated at the club for his friendship with Dr. Veraswami, called "Very-slimy" by the racist Ellis. Ellis also labels Flory a "nigger's Nancy Boy," thus indicating that Flory has placed himself outside the white man's definition of manliness (white, heterosexual, racist) by his friendship with an Indian. Westfield then reminds Flory of the five beatitudes of the pukka sahib, and Flory is so disgusted that he announces his intention to propose Dr. Veraswami's name for club membership at the next general meeting. Throughout this scene Flory is preoccupied with Elizabeth, wondering why she had snubbed him that morning. He does not know that Verrall has been spotted as a better "catch" and Elizabeth is therefore redirecting her energies. Later Flory blocks her path and insists that she explain her behavior toward him; it is apparent in this scene that the sole authority she possesses is the power to reject him. The narrative states: "She was not going to explain. She was going to leave him in the dark—snub him and then pretend that nothing had happened; the natural feminine move" (184). When he forces the issue, Elizabeth clings to the pretext that she has discovered he was keeping a Burmese woman. And now, though Flory thinks the accusation isn't "even true" (since he had recently thrown out Ma Hla May), he recognizes his guilt:

He had not even the heart to be angry any longer. For he had perceived, with the deadly self-knowledge and self-loathing that come to one at such a time, that what had happened served him perfectly right. For a moment it seemed to him that an endless procession of Burmese women, a regiment of ghosts, were marching past him in the moonlight. Heavens, what numbers of them! A thousand—no, but a full hundred at the least.... Their heads turned towards him, but they had no faces, only featureless discs.... The gods are just and of our pleasant vices (pleasant, indeed!) make instruments to plague us. He had dirtied himself beyond redemption, and this was his just punishment. [186] [12]

But Flory's awareness, as this passage shows, is deeply flawed. He, in effect, feels guilty about the wrong thing: He has "dirtied himself beyond redemption"—the very words suggest the sahib's view of a dangerous social descent and the possibility of contamination whenever he engages in sexual relations with native women. Flory's failure to accept responsibility for his action is evident when Ma Hla May suddenly appears and corners him, just as he had cornered Elizabeth. She demands money and threatens to make a scene, and Flory's guilt at once changes into anger and the desire to humiliate her (though Orwell does not label this "the natural masculine move"). Flory deliberately throws on the ground the money and the cigarette case she has extracted from him. In this scene Ma Hla May is described as a wretched woman following him "like a disobedient dog" (188). There is an inevitability about Flory's interactions with her that is in sharp contrast to Orwell's critique of imperialism. Despite his tendency to exculpate the British now and again, Orwell does depict their behavior as resulting from a particular social and political institution that could be changed. The personal relations between men and women, on the other hand, appear to be beyond human control, even when those relations clearly suffer from many of the same problems of domination and inequality. Flory casts stones at the men who dishonestly benefit from the empire and asserts that lying corrupts.[18] He even includes himself among these men to some extent, but his guilt seems to be intended as a sign of his moral superiority, as if he alone were able to face the truth, even the truth of his own complicity. Yet he has lived a lie of the most intimate sort, not in the abstraction of imperialism and his economic exploitation of Burmese lumber, but in the personal use he has made of Ma Hla May (and her many predecessors) while treating her, both before and after her dismissal, as beneath contempt. Rejected by the other men at the club for his friendship with an Indian, by Elizabeth supposedly for his affair with a Burmese woman, Flory suffers a loss of masculine status. But there is someone even lower than he, someone he can still humiliate—Ma Hla May, who is both female and oriental—and, in the scene discussed above, he does not hesitate to do so.

Ultimately, Elizabeth judges Flory in terms much like his own. After the "shameful, squalid" scene in the church, she is prepared to face even spinsterhood and drudgery: "Never, never would she yield to a man who had been so disgraced; Death sooner, far sooner. If there had been mercenary thoughts in her mind an hour ago, she had forgotten them. She did not even remember that Verrall had jilted her and that to have married Flory would have saved her face. She knew only that he was dishonoured and less than a man, and that she hated him as she would have hated a leper or a lunatic. The instinct was deeper than reason or even self-interest, . . ." (264). It is the ugly scene, the public disgrace, that Elizabeth finds insupportable, not Flory's sexual relations with a Burmese woman. Not what a man *is* but what he appears to be is what counts; and Flory, in this scene, has totally relinquished his position of male dominance by his inability to control the behavior of the outraged Ma Hla May. This, of course, is precisely what U Po Kyin intended: Such an attack on his manhood was bound to permanently discredit Flory.

The most important truth we can know about Flory is not that he hates imperialism and is disgusted by the racist remarks of his countrymen but that his separateness is seen, both by himself and by others, as a failure to be a man. By his appreciation of Burmese culture and by his occasional defense of the natives, he has broken with the posture of the dominant sahib and thus muddied the clear distinction between Englishmen and inferiorized, feminized Burmese. This is why Ellis refers to Flory as a "nigger's Nancy Boy." [14] The breakdown of racial and cultural segregation implies the breakdown of that more fundamental identity established by gender. Flory has become less than a man, and this is a judgment he makes of himself as well—though from an opposite position: In Flory's eyes, his lack of ability to act on his beliefs (as the racist Ellis, for example, acts on his) makes him, indeed, less than a man. But manhood is the basic issue, and the sense of self-worth of these men is articulated in terms of manhood and masculinity. Thus, while attempting to combat his colleagues' ideas, Flory is unable to defy the conventional polarization into valued male and devalued female, though only such a challenge would solve his dilemma by enabling him to transcend his guilt at being "unmanly" and evolve into a human being.

But Flory, of course, also profits from his occasional status as a hero in Elizabeth's eyes. His generally recognized "heroism" when the Burmese surround the club, in conjunction with Verrall's subsequent getaway, ensures that Elizabeth will finally "yield" and agree to marry him. Although aware of the irony of this situation, Flory is willing to enjoy the benefits it brings to him, while treating Ma Hla May in much the same manner as Verrall treats Elizabeth—as someone to be quickly disposed of once his purposes have been served. Flory thus fully utilizes the privileges of his masculine role. That this role overlaps the imperial role is no accident: Both are based on the same premises of presumed centrality, and domination and inferiorization of an "other."

INFERIORIZED PEOPLE

To judge individuals or groups as "other" is to assign them an identity essentially unlike one's own. The ideological function of this classification is easy to understand: " 'Domination,' " writes Barry Adam in his study of inferiorization and everyday life, "exists in the social structuring of life limitations, by which one group (the dominators) successfully maximizes its life chances by minimizing those of another (the dominated)." [15] But in order to ensure the acquiescence of the dominated, an ideology develops that explains their restricted options and devalued social identity in terms not of what *we* (at the center of reality) do to *them* but simply of what *they* are.

In the case of "natives" and women, domination can be made to seem justified by seeing both as some sort of slightly subhuman (because non-Anglo-white-male) group. To the material injury of domination is thus added the psychological and spiritual injury of inferiorization. At the same time, within the colonized societies, where male domination also occurs, the women are further viewed as a subgroup by their own men, which in turn justifies their continued subservient status. What this scheme of things shows is that both the Anglo women and the native men are in an ambiguous situation: the Anglo women for belonging to the ruling race but the wrong sex; the native men for belonging to the ruling sex but the wrong race. Only the native women and the Anglo men, in their respective positions at the bottom and top of the scale, provide clear examples of the hierarchies of race and sex working together.

Whenever people organize and explain their world according to set categories and divisions, we can expect those elements that refuse to fit neatly into their assigned places to arouse anxiety and hostility. From this point of view, it is the memsahib's status as an anomaly that explains the antagonism directed at her. In British literature relating to the empire she is a staple caricature, resented by British and Indian alike, and from Kipling to Orwell there is little change in the stereotype.[16] The memsahib's anomalous status is due to her "right" race but "wrong" sex. The Burmese despise the white women in a way they do not despise their white male masters. Behind this hatred one can read the anger at a deviation from the sex rule that demands male supremacy. Do the Burmese women hate the white mistresses for the same reason, because they transgress, in everyday life, this rule of male dominance? Yet they transgress it only in part, and on sufferance, with the authority of their own men behind them, for even while exercising their authority over their servants they are still "only women" and bound by "kinship"—by gender identity—to all other women, to the class of the powerless. In his negative characterizations of Mrs. Lackersteen and Elizabeth, Orwell relies extensively on the memsahib stereotype. Mrs. Lackersteen is lazy and domineering, concerned only with social status and keeping her husband in line. And Elizabeth, in her dislike and disdain of the Burmese and their culture, has the makings of the perfect memsahib, a potentiality that is later realized, as the novel's closing paragraph sarcastically informs us.

The legendary antagonism of native servants toward their white master's wife is a minor theme developed in *Burmese Days*. In one particularly interesting scene, Flory's servants bemoan the changes that the household will undergo if Flory marries Elizabeth. More is involved here than the possible resentment servants may feel at seeing their authority dwindle. As Flory's male servant expresses his intense dislike of Englishwomen, the narrative informs us: "Neither [of the Burmese women present] took Ko S'la's remarks as a stricture upon her own sex, Englishwomen being considered a race apart, possibly not even human, and so dreadful that an Englishman's marriage is usually the signal for the flight of every servant in his house, even those who have been with him for years" (110). In the many scenes at the club during which the Englishmen make humiliating comments about the Burmese men, Orwell never felt the need to provide such an explanation for the men's lack of sensitivity to criticism of other men. Apparently it never occurred to him to expect men to assume that any criticism of a man, or of a group of men, was a criticism of all men. But women are, from the point of view of this narrative, beings apart.

A complementary example of the kind of unity attributed to women occurs in another scene of anomaly in the sexual and racial hierarchy. Orwell writes: "The Burmese women repelled Elizabeth more than the men; she felt her kinship with them, and the hatefulness of being kin to creatures with black faces" (113). This is an intriguing passage. No such "kinship" is mentioned among the men, and thus it is not explained why the Englishmen should not feel a similar hatred based on presumed kinship. What Orwell really defines here is the inescapable "difference" of women. All women are different from men, and in this "difference from" there is also a "sameness," which Orwell calls a "kinship" with all other women. The passage invites a meditation on the concepts of sameness and difference as they apply to men and women, but the terms of the meditation are set by men, at the center of reality according to their own definitions. It is in their views and values that we find the "otherness" that makes all women kin, regardless of racial, cultural, or class differences. What Orwell could have said here, but missed saying because he missed seeing it, is that Elizabeth hates her own status as a powerless woman, which she sees reflected back at her in the even more powerless and despised dark-skinned woman who is, like herself, not a man. Beyond racial and cultural antagonism, deeper than that, lies the androcentric division of the world into a male center and a female periphery.

Elizabeth's "kinship" to Ma Hla May is again underscored by her relationship with Verrall: "U Po Kyin's version (he had a way of being essentially right even when he was wrong in detail) was that Elizabeth had been Flory's concubine and had deserted him for Verrall because Verrall paid her more" (215). What is of interest is the degree of editorializing Orwell has allowed himself in this passage, clearly meant as a criticism of Elizabeth, not of the social situation that gives her these particular options and not others. Orwell uses the fact of female prostitution in one or another guise as an occasion to further discredit women.[17]

Once we have become attuned to this aspect of the text we experience throughout the novel the tension of Orwell's refusal

to address this problem. An odd sort of hypocrisy creeps into
the text as a result. We watch and wait, listen to Flory's self-
accusations, to his attacks on his colleagues, on the institution
of empire (understood in simplistic terms as mere "theft"—which
disregards the many other aspects and motives of imperial expansion), and we see, ironically, how quite another meaning, beyond
Orwell's projected one, pervades the work: Flory is destroyed by
his own dishonesty, his inability to recognize and come to terms
with his personal exploitation of others—not as a mere agent of
the empire and member of the European Club but as a man personally benefiting from male domination of women, from their
continued inferiorization and economic dependency. These are
the hidden issues in Orwell's novel. That they are issues at all is
acknowledged only to the extent that the victims are blamed for
their situation; for their prostitution and for clinging to such
status (always derivative) as they can obtain. But Orwell is not
able to contain his meaning as he tries to do, and his very characterizations of women allow the larger problem, of male domination and female subservience, to seep into the work. Orwell's
inability to confront this problem is especially clear in the novel's
last line, when Elizabeth Lackersteen is described in purely negative terms as the perfect memsahib, which is blamed on Nature.
Orwell's narrative, however, has shown us that what is involved
is the scramble for security and status of a person with highly
restricted options: marry in Burma or end up poverty-stricken
back in England. The authorial voice one hears throughout the
third-person narrative thus comes to judgments at odds with the
information made available by the text.

In contrast to the feeling of degradation that, we are told,
Elizabeth experiences at being of the same sex as a "black"
woman, one unusual incident reveals the type of bonding that
Orwell envisions between white and "black" men. Elizabeth's
best moments with Flory occur during her first experience of
hunting, the occasion for a long set piece that stresses her intense,
clearly sexual reaction. She is described as helpless and paralyzed
with excitement as she handles a gun and contemplates killing
an animal. She succeeds in hitting a bird, which one of the native
beaters places "limp and warm" in her hand: "She could hardly
give it up, the feel of it so ravished her. She could have kissed it,
hugged it to her breast. All the men, Flory and Ko S'la and the

beaters, smiled at one another to see her fondling the dead bird"
(158). What is going on in this scene? A sexual innuendo merely?
Bonding in presumed male superiority over a female who, temporarily, is encroaching on a male preserve—hunting? But this
scene is of special interest also because the description of Elizabeth's reaction, her excitement at the hunt, her "natural" feeling
for a weapon, is clearly intended to convey to the reader her pred-
atory qualities: Killing arouses her sexually. A woman who hunts
is depicted as unnaturally bloodthirsty; a man who hunts is simply a hunter.[18] This is a fascinating illustration of the symbolic
significance of crossing gender boundaries. The complicitous
smiles exchanged among the men perhaps help set things right
and compensate for the shock the beaters feel at seeing a woman
handle a gun.

In general, however, the anomalous status of Burmese
males ceases to be a problem once they are turned by the white
men into social females, that is, into powerless inferiors. White
men, at the top of the hierarchy, can do this. White women cannot do this to Burmese men without bringing to mind their own
social inferiority; hence the ambiguity of the women's relationship to their male servants and their awareness of vulnerability.
This is why, although an Englishman is not afraid of the Burmese
(as Orwell explains), his novel reveals that an Englishwoman *is.*
Yet Orwell's narrative ridicules Mrs. Lackersteen's fear of rape
and her political ignorance: "To her mind the words 'sedition,'
'Nationalism,' 'rebellion,' 'Home Rule,' conveyed one thing and
one thing only, and that was a picture of herself being raped by a
procession of jet-black coolies with rolling white eyeballs" (131).

SEXUALITY AND SOCIAL STATUS

Ma Hla May, described in the novel as Flory's "mistress,"
is in fact a sexual servant, as we learn the first time she appears:
"Ma Hla May came in, kicking off red-lacquered sandals in the
doorway. She was allowed to come to tea, as a special privilege,
but not to other meals, nor to wear her sandals in her master's
presence" (49–50). She is "an outlandish doll, and yet a grotesquely
beautiful one," and she is regularly compared either positively to
a kitten or negatively to a dog. Flory speaks to her in terms that

leave no doubt about their master/servant relationship: " 'Go away,' he said, pushing her back. 'I don't want you at this time of day' " (50). Yet, petulantly, he complains to her: "You only like me because I am a white man and have money" (51). In fact, Flory had bought her from her parents two years earlier, for three hundred rupees. Orwell's descriptions of sex—and not just in this novel, as we shall see—tend toward the model of a male-using-an-object, but such use extracts a price in guilt: "When Flory had done with her he turned away, jaded and ashamed," and she now becomes "nauseating and dreadful to him" (52). He gives her money and says: "Get out of this room! I told you to go. I don't want you in here after I've done with you," and when she protests that he treats her like a prostitute, he says: "So you are. Out you go" (53). Ma Hla May accepts these humiliations because she loves "the idle concubine's life," as well as "the visits to her village dressed in all her finery, when she could boast of her position as a 'bo-kadaw'—a white man's wife; for she had persuaded everyone, herself included, that she was Flory's legal wife" (51). What the narrative does not tell us, however, is that open cohabitation counted as de facto marriage in Burmese customary law. A Burmese woman with a foreign mate was viewed by neighbors and friends as a lawfully wedded wife, but problems arose in cases of separation or inheritance, for the foreign man's law considered these women as mistresses and their offspring as bastards. "Many a case has come to light," one scholar has written, "in which foreigners have lured young and ignorant Burmese women into what seemed to be a marriage and later, when it suited them to do so, repudiated the union on the strength of their own personal law." This situation, which clearly functioned to the detriment of Burmese Buddhist women, continued to prevail after Burma passed into British rule, and only after World War II did a law go into effect protecting the rights of Burmese Buddhist women living with non-Buddhist men as wife and husband. Formalizing the marriage was not required, since it was governed by Burmese customary law.[19]

Orwell's novel may inadvertently represent a case of cross-cultural misunderstanding, with Flory and Ma Hla May operating from different paradigms. But although Orwell depicts Flory as having genuine interest in Burmese culture, Flory is given no awareness of this problem. Instead, we see the situation only from his point of view, which includes the usual wretched admission of guilt, after he casts her out. Since Flory's viewpoint predominates, the reader is invited to consider Ma Hla May as, in fact, a money-grubbing prostitute from beginning to end. Orwell even redeems Flory by providing details of the disasters that befell his Burmese dependents after his death: "Ma Hla May is in a brothel in Mandalay. Her good looks are all but gone, and her clients pay her only four annas and sometimes kick her and beat her. Perhaps more bitterly than any of the others, she regrets the good time when Flory was alive, and when she had not the wisdom to put aside any of the money she extracted from him" (270). These are odd lines for Orwell to have written, for they recall the much-despised Mrs. Lackersteen's they'll-be-sorry-after-we're-gone attitude, but they are consistent with his overall ambivalence toward domination.

An interesting detail appears in Orwell's depiction of Ma Hla May. "She believed that lechery was a form of witchcraft, giving a woman magical powers over a man, until in the end she could weaken him to a half-idiotic slave. Each successive embrace sapped Flory's will and made the spell stronger—this was her belief" (52). In the scene in which she begs Flory to take her back, to let her live in his house even if he marries Elizabeth, this motive again appears: "Perhaps even now she thought that with her arms around him and her body against his she could renew her power over him" (148). A similar view of female sexuality appears fifteen years later, in Orwell's last notebook, which contains, among other things, brief passages that are perhaps sketches for future fiction. One such passage, written in early 1949, reads:

There were two great facts abt women which it seemed to him that you could only learn by getting married, & which flatly contradicted the picture of themselves that women had managed to impose upon the world. One was their incorrigible dirtiness and untidiness. The other was their terrible, devouring sexuality. . . . In the long run even the motive behind their sexuality became uncertain. Perhaps it was sheer sensuality, but perhaps again they simply felt that sexual intercourse was a way of keeping the man under control. At any rate, in any marriage of more than a year or two's standing, intercourse was thought of as a duty, a service owed by the man to the woman. And he suspected that in every marriage the struggle was always the same—the man trying to escape from sexual intercourse, to do it only when he felt like it (or with other women), the woman demanding it more and more, and more and more consciously despising her husband for his lack of virility. (Different in the working class?) [20]

This passage also provides a good example of Orwell's tendency to break through his narrative frame and impose generalizations that seem to express the author's, rather than the character's views. Throughout *Burmese Days* this occurs, frequently marked by a shift to the present tense and an editorializing tone. The perspective on sexuality presented in the notebook is oddly consistent with the beliefs attributed in the novel to Ma Hla May. And, indeed, it is because of Flory's sexual relationship with her that she has grounds for recrimination and can justly berate him at the end of the novel. Were she not known to be his mistress, the European community would simply sneer at the scene she makes in public. Their sexual relationship has, in this sense, given her some power over him. Immediately after this scene, as Flory begs Elizabeth to marry him anyway, he offers the promise never to approach her sexually. Theirs would be a purely companionate marriage. Is it female sexual "power" that he is afraid of, or is this merely a fitting sacrifice to atone for past sexual misdeeds and to reassure Elizabeth that she need have no contact, however indirect, with the despised Burmese woman—as if by renouncing carnal relations with Elizabeth he would protect her from his own contaminated body? But Elizabeth, by now, seems to have learned that prestige is the breath of life (as Flory thinks early in the novel [76]), and she will not sacrifice her own "prestige" for the sake of redeeming Flory's.

Ironically, Flory now confronts the backfiring of the system he has embraced. Desperate for a listener, he did not care about Elizabeth's personal feelings but sought to profit from her economic need to make a marriage. But since he accepts this state of affairs, he should in no way be shocked when by the very same code she rejects him once his social value as a husband has declined. Flory knows he can "get" Elizabeth after Verrall rejects her. But by the same rules that allow Verrall to find her an unworthy mate, she can reject Flory, and she does so. Thus, inhumane and impersonal social rules end by undermining the very characters who have supported them, as if proving that complicity with the wrong values is likely to lead to one's undoing.

The failure of imperial ideology to continue to beguile Flory with its image of the superior white male may explain his need to cling even more tightly to the remaining part of his masculine social identity. He can see through the sahib role, but he cannot go so far as to question how this role functions in the creation of a male identity. He feels lonely and isolated (not to mention hypocritical) as a nonbelieving imperialist surrounded by true believers. Acting the role of superior and benefactor to a woman in the role of dependent and inferior—that is, becoming a husband who has a wife—is one way of salvaging his social identity. What he lacks is not human companionship. He could have that; he could, for example, take a native wife or choose a lover he likes instead of one he merely uses. But this would not do; he needs the public acknowledgment of his "normalcy," his successful demonstration of manliness, and this can come about only through the conventional sort of marriage to an English-woman.

Flory's desire for an Englishwoman in his life is also a desire for order. He cuts down on his drinking when Elizabeth appears; he dresses better and shaves twice a day. She is not a force of darkness or disorder as is Ma Hla May with her uncontrolled behavior and money-grubbing ways. Unlike the Englishmen who defend their imperial presence as a civilizing, controlling force, Flory sees the empire as an unethical exploitation that corrupts the British. At the same time (although Orwell never connects the two themes), Flory is caught in a relationship of exploitation and abuse with Ma Hla May, which "lowers" him, drags him away from the purported standards of culture of his own group. Through Elizabeth he seeks to set things right, fantasizing about the life they will have together, with Elizabeth as genteel culture bearer, homemaker, civilizing agent. They will be so civilized together that they will break through the material barrier of imperialism's ugliness. In his fantasy, they will both be the appreciators of Burmese culture; they will transcend their status as outsiders and exploiters, at the same time as their conjugal bliss will re-create a peculiarly English style of life.

When the path of marriage and normalcy is closed to him, self-destruction appears as the only remaining gesture he can perform. Thus the heroic demand that one be prepared to die for one's country is transformed into the demand that one die, period.

Ironically, Flory may be redeeming himself by this gesture—showing himself capable of action after all; at the same time, his suicide recalls his earlier moment of intimacy with Elizabeth, which also involved shooting. If Elizabeth agreed to marry him despite everything, he could go on. Without her, there is no redemption. Not only has the imperial role failed him, but also the personal illusion of manhood according to the definition he has uncritically accepted and acted on. Flory's defeat is implicit in his temporary success at the club—both are based on erroneous public notions about what qualities are to be valued in a man. When he acts as a dominant male, "saving" the English (though he is aware that this was no great feat), he is rewarded by the club members and by Elizabeth. But similar social judgments eventually are his undoing. In failing to live up to the demands of the masculine role, an essential part of which is personal control of females, Flory is ultimately damned.

WOMEN AS A MUTED GROUP

While Orwell himself is vocal on the subject of women, his women characters are themselves muted. What does Elizabeth, for example, want apart from marriage and "prestige"? We know far too little about her, for we see her either through Flory's eyes or through the third-person narrative informing us of her past life and present feelings—but this narrative, which contrasts ironically with Flory's romanticized view of Elizabeth, is only a transparent screen for Orwell, whose sarcastic narrative voice is heard with special clarity in his depictions of women.

Elizabeth provides a good example of what it means to be a member of a muted group. However much she is admired (that is, desired) by the men at the club, her life is largely defined by their perceptions: She is husband hunting; she is part of what one survivor of the British Empire in India has called the "fishing fleet," and if she fails to catch a husband, she will go back to England a "Returned Empty."[21] What can she say to lend dignity to this position? She may inspire fear in Flory, but he is perfectly aware of her real status in the community. Ellis articulates her position for the edification of the men at the club:

"She's come out to lay her claws into a husband, of course. As if it wasn't well known! When a girl's failed everywhere else she tries India, where every man's pining for the sight of a white woman. The Indian marriage-market, they call it. Meat market it ought to be. Shiploads of 'em coming out every year like carcasses of frozen mutton, to be pawed over by nasty old bachelors like you." ... He went through a pantomime of examining a joint of meat, with goatish sniffs. This joke was likely to last Ellis a long time; his jokes usually did; and there was nothing that gave him quite so keen a pleasure as dragging a woman's name through mud. [104–5]

And, we are told, "there was much smutty talk about Elizabeth" at the club (105). The men joke among themselves about her presence—they are not muted on this subject, but she is; even with her aunt it is a hardly mentionable topic. But her muting goes far beyond this level, for she does not, cannot, question the social reality that places her in this position.

A muted group, according to the anthropologist Edwin Ardener, is a group that is rendered "inarticulate" by the dominant structure. A group is muted "simply because it does not form part of the dominant communicative system of the society—expressed as it must be through the dominant ideology." [22] Cheris Kramarae explains how this theory applies to women:

The language of a particular culture does not serve all its speakers equally, for not all speakers contribute in an equal fashion to its formulation. Women (and members of other subordinate groups) are not as free or as able to say what they wish, when and where they wish, because the words and the norms for their use have been formulated by the dominant group, men. So women cannot as easily or as directly articulate their experiences as men can. Women's perceptions differ from those of men because women's subordination means they experience life differently. However, the words and norms for speaking are not generated from or fitted to women's experiences. Women are thus "muted." Their talk is often not considered of much value by men—who are, or appear to be, deaf and blind to much of women's experiences. Words constantly ignored may eventually come to be unspoken and perhaps even unthought.[23]

Orwell was especially alert to the ways in which language can be used as an instrument of domination, as indicated by his comments about British class distinctions in *The Road to Wigan Pier*, his essay "Politics and the English Language," and his creation of Newspeak in *Nineteen Eighty-Four*. Even in *Burmese Days* he shows a fine sensitivity to the role of language as an important index of social status and potential power. This is why Ellis is infuriated, early in the novel, by the servant at the club who speaks good English. The servant says, "I find it very difficult to keep ice cool now," and Ellis replies: "Don't talk like that, damn you—'I find it very difficult!' Have you swallowed a dictionary? 'Please, master, can't keeping ice cool'—that's how you ought to talk. We shall have to sack this fellow if he gets to talk English too well. I can't stick servants who talk English" (25). Not speaking the language well is an important part of an inferiorized social identity. It helps justify the bad treatment of the servant, the brutalizing, and the racist remarks.

The two Eurasian men in *Burmese Days* (with whom Flory sympathizes) are also exposed to some ridicule, often merely by their not-quite-correct English, presented by Orwell in a manner reminiscent of Thomas Anstey Guthrie's Victorian satires of Anglicized Indians. Even Dr. Veraswami appears in a slightly comical light by the narrative's focus on his language. And Elizabeth's language is also disparaged; it is a kind of sublanguage, full of dramatic gasps and emphases but devoid of substance. She expresses herself in a caricature of "female" speech patterns, which are commonly thought to rely more heavily on adverbs than does the speech of men.[24] "Oh, I simply adore gardening"; "What a perfectly divine view you have from here"; "But of course I simply adore reading" (80, 81), Elizabeth says, making it clear to the reader that we are to view with ironic distance Flory's enchantment at having come upon this young Englishwoman in Burma. Beyond this stereotyped gushing, Elizabeth is unable to articulate her thoughts: "I think reading is so wonderful. I mean, what would life be without it? It's such a—such a—" (81), and Flory is happy to finish her sentences for her.

Eurasians, natives, women—all are in one way or another muted, put at a disadvantage by their illegitimate or imperfect command of the model language, which is that of the white male masters. It is this that lends special irony to Elizabeth's later refusal to explain herself to Flory; she uses her silence as a weapon against him, rejecting communication. And Ma Hla May, who says so little throughout the novel, ironically defeats Flory at the end by means of a verbal attack. Elizabeth, in fact, is muted in much the same way as Ma Hla May, though she seems to have more power by virtue of her status as a white woman. Flory shuts her up by dictating her responses. Hoping to make her share his views, he tells her what will "interest" and "amuse" her—which usually involves contact with the "natives," the very thing she fears and wants to avoid. Rather than make any effort to understand her feelings, he seeks only to deny them. When he wants to take her to the native market, she thinks that "it was all wrong, somehow. However, she followed, not feeling able to explain her reluctance" (120). Flory wants her to enter his world; he seeks to divide his loneliness by half. While his sentiments, whether of love, guilt, or self-hatred, are presented as deep and sincere, Elizabeth's unworthiness is a foregone conclusion, and the narrative brings no insight or sympathy to bear on her particular situation. Elizabeth not only finds it difficult to speak her truth, she finds it difficult even to locate that truth, since the terms available to her are largely those created by the male-dominated society in which she must function. Hence she is unable to challenge the conventional definition of her situation.

We see the same constraints at work again in relation to Ma Hla May, who is defined by men's truth as a prostitute. Her final appearance as an abject, filthy creature is a fitting retribution: She acts out the role she has been cast into, and Flory finds that the disgrace is now his. But she is still limited in her alternatives, and in order to retaliate against Flory effectively she must choose from among the roles ordained for women by the dominant structure. The fact that she is acting as a tool of U Po Kyin, and has presumably sold her services to him, merely reinforces her status as a muted being, unable to escape from the paths men make available to her.

Even Elizabeth's aunt, the lazy, nagging Mrs. Lackersteen, is seen to be muted, for nowhere in the novel is there a word about her perception of her status as the sole Englishwoman in town until Elizabeth's arrival. She is merely one of Orwell's many stereotyped females. This is all the more striking since the one fact intended to explain Flory's reactions (his pathetic attachment to the unsuitable Elizabeth, his cowardice at the club) is his loneliness, his isolation among a group of Englishmen who do not share his values or ideas. Yet, concerning Mrs. Lackersteen, Orwell thought it unnecessary to tell us even how long she had been in Burma without the company of a single other Englishwoman. While depicting Mr. Lackersteen with restrained sympathy—as a genial alcoholic womanizer whose sexual harassment and attempted rape of Elizabeth are viewed within the narrative as lighthearted lapses or high-spirited good tries—Orwell portrays Mrs. Lackersteen as a one-dimensional memsahib.

But Orwell's female characters are not merely muted. To the extent that they are given voices they are also derided; first, by the actual description of female voices as unpleasant, a recurring feature in Orwell's fiction; second, by the scorn typically permeating portrayals of women throughout the novel. This is especially clear in such characters as Elizabeth Lackersteen's mother. Elizabeth's father was an alcoholic,

by nature too optimistic to put money aside in prosperous phases. Elizabeth's mother had been an incapable, half-baked, vapouring, self-pitying woman who shirked all the normal duties of life on the strength of sensibilities which she did not possess. After messing about for years with such things as Women's Suffrage and Higher Thought, and making many abortive attempts at literature, she had finally taken up with painting. Painting is the only art that can be practised without either talent or hard work. [85–86]

Orwell's sneering comments about this character make all the more revealing his equally negative portrayal of Elizabeth, for if she rebels against such a mother she must in some sense be right to do so. But Orwell makes her out to be as reprehensible in her own way as was her mother.

In the various scenes in which Flory tries to introduce Elizabeth to Burmese culture, Orwell's point is not only to reveal Flory's loneliness and need for companionship but also to contrast their reactions. To do this he makes Elizabeth reject almost everything she encounters—except, that is, her passions for shooting and riding. She is uncomfortable among the Burmese, finds them smelly, is offended by the provocative dancing she sees, and is horrified at the bound feet of two women in a Chinese merchant's shop. She has never heard of foot-binding and considers it barbaric. Flory explains to her that beauty is just a "matter of taste" and "hence such practices are no queerer than bustles or crinolines" (123). No connection is drawn between Flory's protests against British power over the Burmese and this example of male power over females, which results in a painful and permanent crippling. And Elizabeth, the female character, has no words with which to explain why she is repelled at the sight of the bound feet.[25] By embedding this detail within the general demonstration of Elizabeth's supercilious reactions (immediately afterward she is truly horrified at seeing a child urinate on the floor), Orwell reveals his own blindness. And Elizabeth, unable to articulate her objections in language Flory might respect (the language of power and justice), is effectively muted.

At the end of the novel, Orwell could not resist taking a final swipe at Elizabeth, thus sacrificing the symmetrical structure he could otherwise have given his novel. We need to recall that the novel opens with U Po Kyin and his intrigues. After recounting Flory's suicide, Orwell adds a final chapter summing up the fate of the other characters. As he wrote in a letter to his agent, Leonard Moore, in February 1934, resisting the suggestion that this tidying up be omitted: "I hate a novel in which the principal characters are not disposed of at the end" (CEJL, 1:134). The most important result of Flory's suicide was that Dr. Veraswami was ruined, "even as he had foreseen. The glory of being a white man's friend—the one thing that had saved him before—had vanished" (268). After depicting Dr. Veraswami's fate, Orwell focuses briefly on Flory's servant Ko S'la and his two wives, not without including a few misogynistic comments;[26] and then, even more briefly, on Ma Hla May. Orwell depicts the rise of U Po Kyin in the English community, his extraordinary success in winning honors and decorations from the British he has so perfectly manipulated, and—with typical irony—his death before he has been able to ensure equal success in the next world through the good works of building pagodas. This would have provided a perfect closure, paralleling the novel's opening scene. However, Orwell goes on to the pièce de résistance: the bitter description of Elizabeth Lackersteen's marriage and subsequent life as a memsahib. Defined as someone who is hard, terrorizes her servants, never learns Burmese,[27] gives charming dinner parties at which she puts subordinate officials' wives in their places, and has an "exhaustive knowledge of the Civil List," she fills, the novel concludes, "with complete success the position for which Nature had designed her from the first, that of a burra memsahib" (272).

This final stress on Elizabeth's unalterable nature deflects the reader's attention from the overt theme of the evils of imperialism, for though she is indeed a member of an oppressor class and nation, as a woman in a patriarchal society she is certainly not its typical representative. In fact, she enjoys the fruits of colonialism only through kinship and association with the dominant group—males. Yet, as we shall see in Orwell's subsequent novels, misogyny is often used to refocus our attention away from the dilemmas and contradictions of his heroes, as if to excuse their personal defects by casting a bright light on some still greater flaws in women as a group. This is the logic of the novel's last chapter: Flory, as irresolute and corrupt as he was, nonetheless is remembered with longing by the people whose downfall followed his death. Even given the pervasive misanthropy evident in *Burmese Days*, Orwell's depiction of Elizabeth has an unusual severity, a hard edge absent from his handling of the far more dangerous (because more powerful) male characters. In addition, Orwell's negative portrayal of women seems to have its source in some not fully articulated belief about femaleness itself.

The clarity of Orwell's drawing of the character of Elizabeth contrasts sharply with his ambiguity in the treatment of Flory which, as many commentators have noted, makes it difficult to situate Orwell's own attitude toward his protagonist with any certainty. Furthermore, revelations of male character in Orwell's writings are generally softened by a feeling for context, an appreciation of men's social situations shaping their actions. So typical a distinction is this with Orwell that he at times makes man simply a victim of his environment, thus exonerating him. Orwell's short sketch "Shooting an Elephant," also set in Burma, provides an interesting example of this, as it pursues the theme of the futility of imperialism. But quite other forces are also at work in this text. Most important of these is the complete reversal of the roles of victim and victimizer. The narrator alone cares about the loss of the elephant's life, while the natives who "force" him to kill it are merely "a sea of yellow faces . . . all happy and excited over this bit of fun" (CEJL, 1:239). The description of the Burmese evokes an image of children on an outing, a quite traditional expression of imperialist ideology, as we have seen. Orwell writes that the incident reveals "the real motives for which despotic governments act" (1:236).

Here was I, the white man with his gun, standing in front of the unarmed native crowd—seemingly the leading actor of the piece; but in reality I was only an absurd puppet pushed to and fro by the will of those yellow faces behind. I perceived in this moment that when the white man turns tyrant it is his own freedom that he destroys. He becomes a sort of hollow, posing dummy, the conventionalised figure of a sahib. [1:239]

Regardless of the better feelings or more sensitive perceptions of the oppressors, they are compelled to behave in a despotic manner because, Orwell says, "every white man's life in the East, was one long struggle not to be laughed at." The white man must forever try to impress the "natives" and must therefore do what the "natives" expect of him. "He wears a mask, and his face grows to fit it. . . . A sahib has got to act like a sahib; he has got to appear resolute, to know his own mind and do definite things" (1:239).

Orwell here attempts to appeal to the enlightened self-interest of the dominant, rather than make any moral claim. But in setting up this reversal, the deeper meaning of the episode is concealed. In "Shooting an Elephant," the narrator acts not merely as an agent of the empire but also as an individual man. It is not, after all, the empire or its dignity that is at stake. Even if the Burmese found him an unworthy individual, his authority would continue to come from the institution he represents, regardless of his personal deficiencies. It is easy enough to imagine a man reacting differently to this situation. If he did not fear looking like a fool, he would be free of his need for affirmation from the people around him and would not need to kill the elephant. The narrator's conventional sense of what defines a man constrains him as much as the despised Burmese anxiously awaiting the elephant's execution.

In fact, "Shooting an Elephant" is about the interaction between dominated and dominator, not about imperialism specifically. Orwell here approaches a recognition of the congruence between the demands of a "normal" masculine gender identity and the imperial role—both based on notions of superiority, centrality, and domination. But he does not follow through with a critique of domination in itself. Instead, he confines his comments to imperialism and even contrives to blame the victims while depicting the imperialist as the sole person possessing genuine awareness of the scene's significance. This is a characteristic stance with Orwell: It is difficult for him to attribute full consciousness, as we shall see, to whoever fills the role of Other in his particular scheme of things, whether the Other consists of "natives," women, or—as in Nineteen Eighty-Four—proles.

In Burmese Days, Orwell expresses, at times violently, his revulsion at the institution of imperialism, at the practice, that is, of regarding an entire nation or ethnic group as means to the "center's" ends. Orwell's own critique of imperial domination is conveyed by many subtle details within the novel: the servants' zealous regard for their masters' status as typical Englishmen; the self-alienating effort to identify oneself with the oppressor (evident in nearly all the native characters); the painful interiorization of the label of inferior (the rejection of Indian culture on the part of Dr. Veraswami, for example, so that he takes on the role of defender of the empire in the face of Flory's assaults on it). There is an incipient morality here of true egalitarianism. But it cannot develop, for Orwell never allows this incipient morality to mature into a rejection of all forms of domination, all instances of using others as means to one's own ends.

Two interrelated aspects of *Burmese Days* account for this failure. One is Orwell's inability to confront the issue of manhood as an accolade that must forever be defended and won anew. The second is the novel's disregard for the problem of personal exploitation—beginning with Flory's relations with his Burmese mistress. These failings undermine the moral position that the novel, on the most generous interpretation, attempts to set forth. As a result, Flory is indeed a blemished character. He is marked not merely by his frequent failures to stand by his Indian friend or to speak up for his beliefs—these, after all, are part of Orwell's critique and explained by his theory that imperialism corrupts the imperialist. More importantly, the novel reveals but never addresses Flory's inability to have a humane relationship with a woman. Orwell does not allow him to recognize that he lives in a society in which women are seen as means to ends pursued by men— whether as sexual or household servants or as "holy vessels" destined to reproduce the race. At heart Flory accepts the imperial posture of domination as the only possible model of relations between the sexes, a view that is not a subject of Orwell's critique and that has been equally disregarded by commentators on the novel. Flory's ambivalent protests against the hypocrisy of the British, against the ugliness of imperialism, appear in the last analysis as signs of his desperate effort to contain the contradictions within his own life. He has no ethic or positive code of behavior that goes beyond an occasional argument over the blatherings of his fellow club members.

Above all, *Burmese Days* articulates a male reality, and it is Flory's inability to recognize this reality, to come to terms with his own role as an agent of domination, that explains his failure. He finds himself split. He wants to forgo the privileges of whiteness while retaining whole those of maleness. Were he to address this division in himself, he could conceivably transcend its limiting effects and embark on a genuine human relationship not based on domination and privilege. To begin to notice the importance of the human relations portrayed within the novel is to see the continuity between official and personal roles, the public and the private realms. It is not general despair over imperialism, after all, that drives Flory to suicide but, more immediately, his loss of manly prestige. Ironically, this loss comes about through two women, Ma Hla May and Elizabeth, neither of whom possesses the personal autonomy enjoyed by Flory. They are colonized people, and the colony they belong to is the female.

Three

Vagabondage and Labor:
The Masculine Mystique

Orwell returned to England from Burma in late August 1927 and resigned from the Indian Imperial Police within a few months. Then began his social descent. After five years as a policeman, Orwell wanted to break with the class of the oppressors to which he belonged by birth and by profession, and so for periods of varying length, between 1928 and 1931, he lived out his new role, first in London and then in Paris.[1] Later on he investigated the lives of the unemployed and of coal miners in the north of England, and there his descent took an obvious and physical form: into the mines, again for purposes of reporting. His final descent was geographical—south to Spain, to write on and participate in the Republican struggle against Franco. From each of these descents came a volume of reportage: *Down and Out in Paris and London* (1933), *The Road to Wigan Pier* (1937), and *Homage to Catalonia* (1938). In addition, two novels, *A Clergyman's Daughter* (1935), and *Keep the Aspidistra Flying* (1936), utilized material from his experiences of poverty and reworked the theme of descent in fictional form. Orwell's social descent was accompanied by his literary rise, for throughout the thirties his activities and visibility as a writer increased. This ascent, too, was something for which he labored hard. Through the public account he gave of it, the embrace of failure became a source of success.

Down and Out in Paris and London and *The Road to Wigan Pier* have generally been seen in terms of Orwell's desire to break with his own social class and as examples of progressive and polemical reporting. But they are also something more: narratives of a process of masculine self-affirmation.

DOWN AND OUT IN PARIS AND LONDON

Orwell's attraction to departures from his own social class long antedates his first published book, *Down and Out in Paris and London*. The first of his letters in the four volumes of his *Collected Essays, Journalism and Letters*, written in the summer of 1920 when he was seventeen and still a student at Eton, begins: "I have a little spare time, & feel I *must* tell you about my first adventure as an amateur tramp. Like most tramps, I was driven to it." He proceeds to recount how, while returning to his family's summer home, he missed a train and had to spend the night in a farmer's field. The letter ends: "I am very proud of this adventure, but I would not repeat it" (CEJL, 1:11–12). Pride and the sense of adventure are still evident when Orwell composed *Down and Out* in 1930 and 1931, but he was later to provide a quite different explanation of his activities. As he wrote in *The Road to Wigan Pier*: "I wanted to submerge myself, to get right down among the oppressed, to be one of them and on their side against their tyrants.... At that time failure seemed to me to be the only virtue" (130), Orwell states, unaware that failure pursued vigorously becomes another object of ambition. Having served the masters in Burma, he now wanted to be on the side, so he thought, that by its very circumstances could never play the oppressor role. The contrast—as well as the linkage between the two roles—is perfectly expressed in the words of Lord Rosebery who, in 1893, declared: "An Empire such as ours requires as its first condition an imperial race—a race vigorous and industrious and intrepid. In the rookeries and slums which still survive, an imperial race cannot be reared." [2]

Although Orwell was in fact working within an established tradition—one that Peter Keating, in his book *Into Unknown England*, has called "social exploration"—his later cultivation of class guilt, combined with his readers' lack of awareness of this tradition, seems to set him apart from other writers in this genre. What would appear to be the continuation of his boyhood impulse toward "adventure," therefore, stimulated in addition by the need for suitable material for a book (he was trying to become a writer and was in search of a subject), takes on existential and psychological dimensions in the minds of those who approach *Down and Out* through the prism of Orwell's later statements and reputation.

Social Exploration. Keating relates the literature of social exploration to the need of the British reform movement in the early nineteenth century to gain knowledge of the new urban-industrial conditions of life. "Out of this concern," he writes, "there develops a distinctive branch of modern literature in which a representative of one class consciously sets out to explore, analyse, and report upon the life of another class lower on the social scale than his own; the reverse procedure being, of course, not really possible, except in satire." A modern variant of the journey motif, this literature is distinguished from the earlier type by its narrower social focus and its reformist aim. In its purest form, Keating states, the literature of social exploration "tells the story of one person's journey into an alien culture and offers the detailed results of his findings"; it is thus related to Royal Commission reports and to subsequent sociological studies, as well as to the novels of writers such as Dickens and Mrs. Gaskell.[3] Temporarily becoming one of the poor, as Orwell did, is, in Keating's words the "most spectacular aspect of the explorer's role." Keating traces the vogue for disguise back to James Greenwood, author of *A Night in the Workhouse,* published in 1866, and comments, "The use of disguise did not bring with it a corresponding change in personality, the transformation was largely external; but it added a dash of flair to the explorer's journey, and the felt need to put on, as it were, a uniform in order to enter the life of the poor, carried in itself lessons about class distinctions which the explorers understood and used." [4] Orwell himself, as many critics have observed, relied on Jack London's *People of the Abyss* (1903) [5] for his description of the effects of putting on old clothes, and with substantially the same aim: "Attempted disguise," writes Keating, "is as much an attempt to break from one form of status as it is to adopt the trappings of another." [6]

Around the turn of the century, the literature of social exploration popularized the idea of an "abyss," replacing earlier associations with exotic travel, which had been appropriate in an age of imperial expansion. But the new image has a deeper significance, as Keating points out:

You don't journey to an abyss: you descend or fall into it. It is all very well claiming that a Dark Continent lies at one's doorstep but... what may walk out of an African rain forest is one thing, what *climbs* out of an abyss is quite another. Its use also implies a change in class relationships with the explorer peering over the edge at, or climbing down to, the massed poor below.[7]

Jack London affirmed that he had borrowed the image from an H. G. Wells story, "In the Abyss," and it was also used by General Booth, founder of the Salvation Army and author of *In Darkest London and the Way Out* (1890).[8] Orwell employs it too—but in a somewhat different sense. His aim is not to peer over the edge but, as we have seen, to "submerge" himself. Burma had left him with the conviction that the oppressors are always wrong, and he now transferred this belief from the injustices of imperialism to the class distinctions closer to home. But there is a paradox in Orwell's desire for escape from the company of oppressors, for his own words reveal him still operating very much from within the framework of his own class as he explains what this submersion meant to him: "Once I had been among them and accepted by them, I should have touched bottom" (*Wigan Pier*, 131), he writes. This awareness of social distance stayed with Orwell even after his experiences "down and out," for in relating, in *Wigan Pier*, how he partially overcame his revulsion against working-class male bodies Orwell says: "when you have shared a bed with a tramp and drunk tea out of the same snuff-tin, you feel that you have seen the worst and the worst has no terrors for you" (115).

Taking a far more critical look than Keating's at "social explorers," Peter Beresford has noted the role they tend to play in a society of established classes:

Ostensibly acting as a bridge between rich and poor; middle and working class, it [social exploring] is as much a symbol and reinforcer of the gulf between them. It trades in the lack of communication and contact between the two. The social explorer who puts on tramp's clothing and spends the night in a doss house is news; the thousands whose home it is, are unremarkable. Social explorers report to a "public" they never seem to imagine extending to the subjects of their exploration.[9]

Beresford observes that social exploration "has always been a genre with literary pretensions. This has not only increased its claim to importance, but also means that literary demands have had an important effect on its presentation of its subject." And he cites Orwell's own words to the effect that "nearly all" of *Down and Out* is true.[10]

Vagrancy (which is the focus of the London section of *Down and Out*) "has provided perhaps the most picaresque of subjects for the social explorer's attention,"[11] Beresford states, and in considering the usual suggestions made for solving this problem (Orwell proposed that workhouses should run small farms),[12] he observes that such recommendations reveal the narrowness of social explorers' analyses and their tendency "to share the assumptions of a social control perspective. This may explain why they are so often fêted by the establishment they seem to attack":

The predictable outcome of their twin loyalties to a social control perspective and their ostensible aim of improving the condition of their subjects, is their tendency to sentimentalise. In their company we encounter "unfortunates" and oddities, rather than people like ourselves. They offer excuses for people's predicaments rather than damning the order that engenders it. Although great importance is attributed to social explorers like Orwell, they seem to have little direct effect in changing policy or improving conditions, a connection between the two is more often assumed than sought or found. Instead they seem to serve more as the occasion for an emotional hiccup that gives a specious sense of action and concern. Although it has not shared the same significance in curricula, the government report [on casual wards, put out by the Ministry of Health in 1930] did more to improve conditions than "Down and Out in Paris and London" whose benefits largely seem to have been restricted to its author.[13]

Beresford's critique sheds considerable light both on the narrative technique (and its implications) utilized by Orwell in *Down and Out* and on the critical reaction to that book, which tends to get lost somewhere between praise for Orwell's supposed objectivity as a narrator and admiration for the man who took on this great hardship. In both kinds of responses, the assumptions of social distance, the upper-class perspective presumably shared by reader and author, go unnoticed. But Beresford's comments apply to the two parts of Orwell's book in quite different ways, for there is an essential discontinuity between the Paris and the London sections of *Down and Out*, perhaps explained by the fact that the London segment was added later, following the rejection of the Paris segment—at that time tentatively titled "A Scullion's Diary"—by Jonathan Cape.[14]

Narrative Tone. Orwell's style in *Down and Out* has frequently been praised for its "objectivity" and "neutrality," and he is thought to have successfully effaced his own personality in order to focus on the reality he describes. It seems to me that such judgments arise from great conceptual confusion. It is, of course, true that Orwell does not dwell on his own physical discomforts, but his silence on this point—consistent with his manly posture—makes his narrative neither objective nor neutral. Early reviewers[15] commended Orwell for the "quiet, level voice"[16] in his book and for his lack of sentimentality,[17] which suggests that readers had grown tired of being assaulted by emotional appeals on behalf of the poor and found Orwell's narrative stance a welcome contrast. But the absence of such appeals does not add up to "calm objectivity" (Granville Hicks's words in a later review),[18] for Orwell is neither calm nor objective about the sensations and textures of poverty. What he does contrive to do, however, is to distance his criticism to the point where the privileged reader need not feel any personal responsibility and blame for the conditions described. He accomplishes this result in two ways: by emphasizing revulsion at the smells and sights of poverty rather than horror at the very existence of poverty; and by serving up individual instances as "curious" tales (beginning in exotic Paris) with which to entertain the reader. Responding to both strategies, the reader feels encouraged to ignore the reformist intentions that occasionally break into the narrative and concentrate instead on the picturesque detail.

A few contemporary reviewers seem to have been sensitive to the possible inauthenticity of Orwell's account. *Down and Out* "fails to carry conviction," one reviewer states. "Down, certainly, but out?" the reviewer asks, answering: "Throughout the book the reader is forced to the belief that the author, though undoubtedly living and working with the very poor, had a sufficient reserve either of money or influence to kill fear for the future."[19] Some later critics also have expressed reservations about Orwell's narrative posture and its implications.[20] By far the larger number, however, have argued along the lines evident in Jenni Calder's comments about Orwell's "unbiased detachment" and lack of attention to himself: "He does not intrude. He becomes 'one,'"

Calder writes, "a generalised being whom he is regarding along with the other details, a useful vehicle for describing how one tries to get rid of bugs. It is personal experience viewed with scrupulous detachment. The result of this detachment is that when Orwell comes to make a subjective statement we accept it without thought." [21] However, not being provided with personal information about the narrator merely means that specific information is withheld while the reader nonetheless absorbs the narrator's values and identity. No one, for example, could ever mistake the narrator of *Down and Out* for an actual poor person or one lacking education (even before he reveals that he has been at Eton). Social distance permeates Orwell's narrative, but it is not the remoteness of an objective or absent narrator. Instead, it is of one speaking in a distinct upper-class ("cool") tone.

In making so much of Orwell's detachment or objectivity in *Down and Out*, critics tend to overlook the central feature of the Paris segment of the book (which takes up nearly two-thirds of the text): the sheer exuberance and sense of wonder brought by the young Orwell to his new experience of pauperization. *Down and Out* is very much a young man's work. It is not only high-spirited and wide-eyed but also excessively literal-minded, revealing a writer still unsure of his own abilities and apt to be distrustful of his reader's intelligence. Examples of these tendencies abound. When recounting the episode about writing for a Russian "secret society," the narrator spoils a good story by explaining what has become obvious: "And that was the last we ever heard of the secret society. Who or what they really were, nobody knew. Personally I do not think they had anything to do with the Communist Party; I think they were simply swindlers, who preyed upon Russian refugees by extracting entrance fees to an imaginary society" (45).[22] Attempting to evoke the work routine at Hotel X where he was employed as a *plongeur*, Orwell resorts to a kind of metawriting as he confesses his frustrations at being unable to do justice to the scene: "I wish I could be Zola for a little while, just to describe that dinner hour. . . . I could write pages about the scene without giving a true idea of it." Of the collisions, shouting, and quarrels in the kitchen, Orwell says, "—they pass description" (58). These breathless claims of ineffability illustrate his problem at that time: A would-be writer, he had to seek out a subject of sufficient inherent interest so that description alone, or even rapid allusion, would hold a reader's attention. He found such a subject in his adventures down and out.

Orwell chose to begin *Down and Out* by introducing his Paris neighbors as curious types rather than as individuals. "It would be fun to write some of their biographies, if one had time. I am trying to describe the people in our quarter, not for the mere curiosity, but because they are all part of the story. Poverty is what I am writing about, and I had my first contact with poverty in this slum. The slum, with its dirt and its queer lives, was first an object-lesson in poverty, and then the background of my own experiences (9)." [23] Employing a tough-sounding, staccato style, Orwell relates several of the men's adventures. First there is Henri, who never speaks. Because of his silence we cannot know the source of the story Orwell relates about Henri and his unfaithful girl friend, who loved Henri more passionately the more he brutalized her. There is no narrative perspective on this story; it is not attributed to Henri. It is, instead, presented in the foreground as a "fact." Orwell writes: "On being kicked the girl fell desperately in love with Henri. . . . As soon as she had been stabbed the girl fell more in love with Henri than ever" (8). Henri's story clears the way for the longer set piece about Charlie, this one in Charlie's own words, which Orwell renders in what appears to be a fairly literal translation from French, thus giving the reader a whiff of local color. Charlie's tale about the happiest day of his life—when he went to a brothel and bought and raped a terrified peasant girl—seems designed to sound both extravagant and entertaining. Both stories, in fact, are typical adolescent tales of male prowess, dominance, and brutality,[24] and Orwell clearly relishes them since he either invented them or chose them from among his notes or memories for these attention-grabbing early pages.[25] He ends Charlie's story with a characteristic comment: "He was a curious specimen, Charlie. I describe him, just to show what diverse characters could be found flourishing in the Coq d'Or quarter" (14).

Orwell's upper-class attitudes seep into the narrative in revealing ways, often giving a meaning to a passage quite obviously at odds with the point Orwell is trying to make. The most striking example of this occurs early in the book as Orwell describes his first encounter with poverty and hunger: "Mean disasters happen and rob you of food. You have spent your last eighty centimes on half a litre of milk, and are boiling it over the spirit lamp. While it boils a bug runs down your forearm; you give the bug a flick with your nail, and it falls, plop!, straight into the milk. There is nothing for it but to throw the milk away and go foodless" (16). Again, while describing the "odious job" of washing up in a restaurant, Orwell comments: "It is dreadful to think that some people spend their whole decades at such occupations" (62). Not only his inexperience but also a certain lack of imagination show through when, upon returning to London, he encounters old-age pensioners: "Till meeting them I had never realised that there are people in England who live on nothing but the old-age pension of ten shillings a week" (119). While this remark could be viewed as a device by which Orwell seeks to win the reader's sympathy for the point he is trying to make, such an intention hardly explains the clear tone that emerges in his reply to an Irishman with whom he was tramping, who asked him if he could do with some tea: "I should think I could," Orwell answered (125). And once he is in the spike (the casual ward), sharing a cell with another man, he exclaims in surprise: "But I say, damn it, where are the beds?" (130). This man made homosexual advances toward him during the night, and Orwell comments in relating the episode, "of course it was impossible to go to sleep again" (131). Even when Orwell does not write "of course" or "there was nothing for it but to . . .," these examples allow us to discern the class perspective he brought to his experience and its eventual narration. I suggest that a reader not of Orwell's own class would find this narration neither "objective" nor "neutral" but would see in it constant indications of the class background of the narrator.

This characteristic is evident also in Orwell's frequent use of "high culture" words, usually Latin or French (a practice he was later to deplore), which constantly jar with the reality he describes. A quarrel is "some silly *casus belli*" (170); there is a prejudice that "every tramp, *ipso facto*, is a blackguard" (178); and so on. One of the most embarrassing instances of this habit occurs when Orwell returns to the spike after working in the kitchen and finds the men there too bored even to talk. "The room stank of *ennui*" (175), he writes. The owners of common lodging houses would, he says, be opposed "*en bloc*" to any improvement in their facilities (188). Less blatant but equally telling is the social distance implicit in Orwell's constant use of "one" as he discusses his changing perceptions; for instance, "When one has realised that the usual attitude taken toward tramps is unfair, one begins to put oneself in a tramp's place and understand what his life is like" (180). The very laboriousness of this explanation suggests the gulf still separating him, and his presumed readers, from the reality he is evoking. But I do not believe that Orwell is intentionally emphasizing or displaying this gulf. He seems genuinely unaware of it, just as he seems unconscious of the condescension evident in so much of his account.

Orwell creates a semifictional *I* in *Down and Out*, a naive and literal-minded but sincere narrator who is tireless in his effort to convey the sensations of poverty to readers of a higher social class. With these readers he strikes a bargain: He will not play upon their sympathies or guilt. The narrative sticks to the bargain: Little is made of the routine inferiorization of the poor,[26] of the links between their poverty and the wealth of the rich. Rather, the poor are either presented as queer and interesting cases or turned into caricatures. What they all have in common, the situations that led them into poverty, is not explored. Real passion enters the narrative only in the description of smells, as *I*'s sensitive nose is intensely revolted by the "subfaecal stench of the spike" (132), the "horrible hot reek of urine" (141), the "slimy roller towels," and the unforgettable "reek of dirty feet" (129). For the rest, he adopts a tone of slight bemusement. While in Paris, *I* is in a state of perpetual excitement as strange and odd tales are unfolded of the spectacle of poverty at its most picturesque. We learn little of what habitual poverty is like for those who have no choice. The class barrier remains intact: *I* is an intermediary, a guide leading the rich on a walking tour among the poor. Yet *I* prides himself as well on being at one with the destitute, whom he embraces as *we*, in the conviction that his own reactions and those of real tramps are identical.[27]

Orwell repeatedly raises serious questions about the poor—beggars, tramps, dishwashers who work seventeen-hour days (as he himself did for ten days)—then proceeds to trivialize them in his answers. The problem "Why are there tramps?" is thus transformed into the quite different question of "Why do tramps tramp?"—easily answered by referring to vagrancy laws that made it illegal for tramps to obtain relief while staying in one place. Orwell knows that tramps think of spikes as potential prisons, but he does not ask why society employs this particular form of social control. He wants to rid his reader of common prejudices and misconceptions concerning the poor but never considers the function of such misconceptions as key elements in an ideological mystification that allows economic exploitation to continue. Quite possibly the popularity of *Down and Out* is linked to this refusal to play on the reader's guilt as a member of the exploiting class. Similarly, in *The Road to Wigan Pier*, as we shall see, Orwell's criticism of the exploiters will be deflected into an attack on crankish socialists. In short, while urging his readers to change their attitudes toward the poor, he treats these attitudes as disembodied ideas, without suggesting a concomitant change in the social structures that explain such attitudes and give them their significance.

The effect of Orwell's habit of ostensibly abstracting himself from his narrative is to endow the world he portrays with an inevitability that fundamentally misrepresents it. Deceiving the reader about the actual conditions under which he experienced poverty and withdrawing a genuinely critical consciousness from his observations lead to other distortions of which the reader remains in ignorance. Mrs. Cecil Chesterton, by contrast, whose book *In Darkest London* (1926) describes her experiences as a destitute woman in London, provides us not only with her motive—to go penniless from her comfortable home in order to learn at first hand how an impoverished woman could survive—but also with her prism. She does not attempt to conceal, behind a pseudonaturalistic screen, her own self coming to judgments about her experiences. By giving us the circumstances of her social descent,[28] she trusts us to try to break through our own comfort and imagine ourselves in the position of others, or to consciously refuse to do so. Orwell does none of this. Behind the fiction of transparence lies a lack of challenge to the reader, an unwillingness to call the author's, and therefore also the reader's, social status into question. He thus leaves the reader in the position of a passive witness to an inevitable, unpleasant, and remote reality. The poverty of which he writes is a literary object, served up as if there could be no alternative to his educated voice mediating between the distasteful features of the story—for it is "a story"—and ourselves as readers, as male readers, of course.

Invisible Women. Orwell's poor are largely male loners;

there are no children in this world and almost no women.[29] Even in the Paris sections of *Down and Out* women appear primarily as sex objects or background figures and only occasionally as co-workers. They are not important to the narrative. Nonetheless, Orwell seems to find his few comments about women interesting, and he no doubt believes them to be profound. In relating his return to England, he notes: "I find this entry in my diary for that day: 'Sleeping in the saloon, twenty-seven men, sixteen women. Of the women, not a single one has washed her face this morning. The men mostly went to the bathroom; the women merely produced vanity cases and covered the dirt with powder. Q. A secondary sexual difference?' " (112). What is significant here is that Orwell considered these thoughts worth repeating in his book. Such "observations," invariably comparing women negatively with men, are always a prominent feature in Orwell's writings.

The beginning of *Down and Out*, with its emphasis on the ugly screaming of two women, is typical of the kind of attention Orwell bestows on women (and the negative characterization of their voices is another constant of his work), as are his passing descriptions—such as of a church congregation one weekday, "mostly stringy old women who reminded one of boiling-fowls" (162). When not remarkable for some disagreeable feature, women tend to be invisible to Orwell. This is apparent in his treatment of workers in the Hotel X in Paris. He introduces the job hierarchy at the hotel, mentioning the pay of every member of the staff except "laundresses and sewing women," who are listed without salary information. He observes that "Different jobs were done by different races" (64), but, though all the higher-paying positions were, by his own description, performed by men, he fails to notice or comment on this fact. He then relates some hoary stereotypes —no doubt meant as enlightened rejections of even older prejudices—for example, that men cooks are preferred to women because of their punctuality "and not for any superiority in technique" (68). As an explanation of why women are kept from certain kinds of work, however, this falls apart, and on the very next page he discusses the *plongeur*'s job—with no prospects, no required skills or interest, "the sort of job that would always be done by women if women were strong enough" (69). The sexual hierarchy at work is further exemplified in Orwell's description of the *plongeurs*' pride in being known as *débrouillards* who can manage to do the impossible and constantly flaunt their tough-ness: "You will often hear *plongeurs* boast, '*Je suis dur*'—as though they were soldiers, not male charwomen." Orwell concludes: "Thus everyone in the hotel had his sense of honour" (70).

The most compelling example in *Down and Out* of the narrowing and damaging effect of his misogyny on Orwell's per-ception of reality occurs in relation to the sole woman tramp he encounters on his expeditions. One would expect a "social ex-plorer" to pay special attention to such an oddity, but Orwell merely introduces this woman as an occasion for asserting his own superiority, thus situating her in such a way that she cannot fail to fulfill her "natural" female function of providing a nega-tive contrast to men and masculinity. He describes her as follows: "She was a fattish, battered, very dirty woman of sixty, in a long, trailing black skirt. She put on great airs of dignity, and if anyone sat down near her she sniffed and moved farther off." In reply to one tramp's friendly words, she bitterly says, " 'when I want to get mixed up with a set of *tramps*, I'll let you know.' " Orwell comments: "I enjoyed the way she said *tramps*. It seemed to show you in a flash the whole of her soul; a small, blinkered, feminine soul, that had learned absolutely nothing from years on the road. She was, no doubt, a respectable widow woman, become a tramp through some grotesque accident" (172). These remarks are all the more revealing in the light of Orwell's very different reaction immediately thereafter to a young male tramp of similar preten-sions. He was, Orwell tells us, "superior," a carpenter, on the road because he had no tools with which to work. He too holds him-self aloof from the others, believing that all tramps are lazy and should not be encouraged by being given decent food. Having argued with him to no avail, Orwell analyzes why this man disso-ciates himself in an "interesting" and "subtle" way from " 'these here tramps.' " Making no reference to this man's small mascu-line soul, Orwell simply says, "I imagine there are quite a lot of tramps who thank God they are not tramps" (176). This is a case in point of Orwell's tendency to treat men as individuals and women as mere representatives of the inferior female sex. Not even on the road are all people equal. On the contrary, in the tramping culture, where ideas of conventional masculinity stamp men simultaneously as failures (in terms of economic power and its concomitant control over women) and as embodiments of manhood (as free and unencumbered adventurers), hostility toward women could be anticipated as the norm rather than the exception.

Orwell was not, however, ignorant of the difference between individual negative characterization and generic attacks. This is apparent in his 1946 comments on George du Maurier's novel *Trilby*: "There is no question that the book is antisemitic," he writes, noting "the fact that Svengali's vanity, treacherousness, selfishness, personal uncleanliness and so forth are constantly connected with the fact that he is a Jew" (CEJL, 4:252). Of course, Orwell himself had employed such stereotypes about Jews in his own books many times before he became more enlightened (slowly—as the war against Hitler wore on); the point, however, is that Orwell was capable of analyzing the technique of the generic slur but chose not to question his own use of this technique in relation to women. Nor did the passage of time improve this blind spot.

Equally revealing of Orwell's androcentrism is the fact that he broaches the issue of destitute women only in the context of expressing dismay at the "second great evil of a tramp's life" (the first being hunger): "that he is entirely cut off from contact with women" (*Down and Out*, 180). It is curious that in all of *Down and Out*, only in relation to the numbers of men and women who are destitute does Orwell cite statistical information. He seems to have felt, at least in that instance, a need to justify his neglect of women throughout his account. His statistics allow him to conclude that "at the charity level men outnumber women by something like ten to one," a point that must, however, be placed in perspective. Vagrants are themselves only a tiny fraction of the very poor; the argument of statistical insignificance used by Orwell to justify disregarding vagrant women could therefore be used as well to prove that the fascination with vagrancy is out of all proportion to its relatively low incidence.[30]

Orwell's explanation of the paucity of destitute women on the road is itself of interest: "The cause is presumably that unemployment affects women less than men; also that any presentable woman can, in the last resort, attach herself to some man" (181). Although he comments that "women's lodging-houses are said to be generally worse than the men's" (186), he does not ask whether this condition, or the general absence of lodging places for women, might have something to do with the small number of female vagrants. He also altogether ignores the fact that in the time of which he writes women in the British population outnumbered men by about 16 percent, and this excess of females over males was (along with the declining birthrate) an often-mentioned problem.[31] In addition, Orwell's complacency about women's job prospects[32] is contradicted by the experiences of Mrs. Cecil Chesterton who, having heard it said that a woman could always find a job, tried to do so "with nothing but my personality between me and starvation,"[33] only to discover that without references or connections it was "tragically impossible" to get any sort of work.[34] Her account, In Darkest London, provides ample evidence of the marked lack of facilities for destitute women at that time. Mrs. Chesterton notes, pointedly, that in one of the few casual wards to which women were admitted, the men had hot tea every morning, and "the women have the dregs of their teapots an hour later."[35] She also calls attention to the contrasting public responses to destitute men and women: "Dirt, in a man, not infrequently suggests romance—in a woman it implies degradation, neglect and an obstinate refusal to undertake the obligations of her sex."[36] Describing her difficulty in buying food or drink from street stalls even when she did have a few pennies to spend, she notes that a woman, especially a woman alone, is not welcome, whereas "the most abject specimen of man is quite welcome if he has the price to pay for his refreshment. But in the case of women there is the rooted belief that they must be bad lots or they would have a home; if they are not thieves they are prostitutes, and either way a commercial connection with them might cause trouble with the police."[37]

Without, of course, employing our vocabulary of "gender roles," Mrs. Chesterton observes that a woman vagrant is considered more of a deviant from conventional femininity than a man vagrant is from masculinity—an issue Orwell never addresses. The "romance of the road" is a purely masculine mystique, suggesting manly independence—a notion that has even crept into critical reaction to Orwell and his social exploration, as evidenced by comments such as, "Down and out, he had become a free man."[38] But a "free man" is a cultural image solely of masculinity. One cannot say a "free woman" and evoke any comparable resonance. Indeed, in order to give Dorothy Hare similar experiences in *A Clergyman's Daughter*, Orwell had to exculpate her by means of amnesia. Wandering off and living down and out would not, from the conventional point of view, reflect a taste for freedom or adventuresomeness in a woman.[39] Had Orwell not been predisposed generally to ignore women, his one encounter with a woman on the road might have stirred curiosity or compassion in him rather than derision. As we shall see again in *The Road to Wigan Pier*, the whole problem of female poverty is one Orwell largely suppresses.[40]

He does, however, remember women when deploring the tramps' lack of access to them. His concern here is with the "degradation worked in a man who knows that he is not considered fit for marriage." "No humiliation could do more damage to a man's self-respect," Orwell writes, than being cut off "from the whole race of women" (181), for women are necessary to satisfy men's sexual hunger, and thus, so Orwell explains, a masculine society of tramps suffers from its isolation. But if men deprived of women feel degraded and humiliated (like cripples and lunatics, Orwell says), it must be because something in the relationship between men and women allows men as a class to feel superior. By their mere presence and inferiorized social identity, women bestow superiority on men. Hence what at first glance seems only physical deprivation—sexual starvation—assumes moral significance. None of this is mentioned by Orwell, though it is implicit in his account. It is, indeed, "sexual starvation" that he has in mind, as is clear in his comments about the homosexuality and "occasional rape cases" that result from this sexual isolation. Orwell in effect equates voluntary homosexual relations with the violence against another individual that rape signifies and sees both from the curious perspective solely of the men who practice them.

Why did Orwell not simply say that his direct experience down and out was limited to men because he, as a man, had easier access to other men or because he was much more interested in men than in women? I think the reason is that to make such an admission is to acknowledge that there *is* another reality, that the androcentric model of the world is not a sufficient one. It would have been too much of a challenge, too close to an awakening, had he openly acknowledged that his work, however interesting, had relevance only to men. For someone unwilling to make this admission, the ideologically sounder tactic is simply to ignore any definition or perception of reality that might, however mildly, challenge the "naturalness" and completeness of the androcentric status quo. By implication (and even, as we have seen, explicitly on a few occasions), Orwell's focus reverses the truth, which is that women in western capitalism are at every level of society poorer than the men of that level. But to acknowledge this truth would have forced him either to extend his moral commitments or to recognize their narrow limits.

Down and Out in Paris and London does not project the self-righteous persona Orwell was later to develop. Especially when one compares it with *The Road to Wigan Pier*, written only five to six years later, the simplicity of Orwell's attitudes in the earlier book is refreshing. He reveals his prejudices without making banners of them, as if innocently unaware that they might be objectionable to others (How else can one explain his coarse comments about foreigners and Jews?). Possibly this is what makes *Down and Out* Orwell's "nicest" book of reportage.

Henry Miller was "crazy about" *Down and Out* and considered it to be Orwell's best book, "a classic." [41] It is easy to see why; the book lacks that self-conscious moral fervor that Miller in particular did not appreciate, while it overflows with masculinity of a characteristically adolescent kind—something Miller himself seems never to have outgrown. Most likely Miller recognized a kindred spirit in the Orwell of *Down and Out*—a man with neither ties nor responsibilities, going against the conventions of his class, acting out as a pauper and a tramp one ideal of masculine freedom.

THE ROAD TO WIGAN PIER

Orwell tended to mix literary forms in his writings. His works of fiction contain essays (Goldstein's book in *Nineteen Eighty-Four*), bits of playwriting (the Trafalgar Square scene in *A Clergyman's Daughter*), and monologues (Gordon's harangues against the money world in *Keep the Aspidistra Flying*). But his two books about poverty and working-class life reveal a division of a more extreme kind. In *Down and Out in Paris and London*, as we have seen, two rather different stories are united by the theme of poverty. But in *The Road to Wigan Pier*, parts 1 and 2 seem to stand as entirely separate books. Part 1, based on Orwell's seven-week investigation[42] of unemployed and working men's lives in the north of England, is a detailed, apparently factual account of some of Orwell's experiences in February and March 1936. Part 2, on the other hand, includes a violent diatribe against socialist cranks in the guise of an explanation of why the "average thinking person" and "genuine working man" is put off by socialism, as well as some extremely illuminating autobiographical sections. By 1936, when he composed *Wigan Pier*, Orwell had come to enjoy a certain reputation, which perhaps made it easier for him to speak directly about his own life. But he also had a clear stake now in promoting a polemical image of himself, and he contributed to this image in the way he presented his past life.

Wigan Pier, for all that, is not fundamentally a split book. At a deeper level it is united by Orwell's gender ideology. This ideology appears again and again as he discusses working-class life in northern England, recounts his experiences in the mines, offers discourses on the working class's purported smell, and finally expresses his fears about socialism and his anger at "cranks." It is Orwell's preoccupation with manhood that provides the logical thread tying this apparently odd assortment together. Part 2 of *Wigan Pier* gained Orwell considerable notoriety in his time; for us, it provides a clear example of his increasingly coercive discourse. The self-righteous and denunciatory tone (already evident in *Burmese Days* and *Keep the Aspidistra Flying*) had finally escaped the bounds of fiction. It was to accompany Orwell for the rest of his life.

Visible Men and the Working-Class Family. Orwell went to the north of England to examine the conditions of the working class at a time of severe unemployment.[43] He studied housing, diets, miners, and life on the dole. All these subjects he approached from a middle-class-male point of view. Showing a journalistic taste for sensationalism, he begins his book with a description of the repulsive Brooker household, turning next to a dramatic depiction of his descent into the mines. Only after these two set pieces does he focus in a more general way on the questions he went north to investigate.

Orwell treats the Brookers' house, "a beastly place" (5), as "fairly normal" (15), though it was recognized by local people as an atypical, filthy house.[44] Perhaps because the house is so "beastly," it provides the occasion for Orwell to make some observations on the difficult lives of women, as in his description of Emmie, the fiancée of one of the Brookers' sons, an "unhappy-looking girl who worked at one of the mills for some starvation wage, but nevertheless spent all her evenings in bondage at the Brookers' house" (11). Mrs. Brooker is "too ill" to work, though Orwell specifies that he suspected "her only real trouble was over-eating" (6–7),[45] and Mr. Brooker therefore prepares most of the food. Orwell describes him peeling potatoes with an "air of brooding resentment. You could see the hatred of this 'bloody woman's work,' as he called it, fermenting inside him, a kind of bitter juice" (11).

On a few other occasions Orwell expresses sympathy for the women he observes. In describing the overcrowded and inadequate houses he saw, he comments: "In such places as these a woman is only a poor drudge muddling among an infinity of jobs" (52); a woman in a caravan dwelling had "a worn skull-like face on which was a look of intolerable misery and degradation. I gathered that in that dreadful pigsty, struggling to keep her large brood of children clean, she felt as I should feel if I were coated all over with dung" (56).[46] But in both these instances (as also in the famous episode of the young woman kneeling by the waste pipe),[47] Orwell's contacts with women are limited to viewing them at some distance. He does not speak to them, does not explore their lives or possibilities as he does the men's. Perhaps he feels that in noting their miserable living conditions he has said all there is to be said about their lives, but as a result he makes no comments at all about women's employment opportunities in the towns he visits or about the effects of unemployment on women wage earners.[48]

The limited visibility of women to Orwell is even more striking in *Wigan Pier* because by his own account among insured workers in Wigan nearly 20 percent were women. Orwell tells us that the population of Wigan at the time was close to 86,000. Of these, about 36,000 were insured workers (26,000 men and 10,000 women). Having learned enough by then to realize how deceptive statistics are, Orwell estimated that the number of people living on the dole in Wigan would have been above 30,000, not just the 10,000 who were unemployed in early 1936. He criticizes the official figures, which in general reflect only heads of families on the dole and not their dependents, but he himself then goes on to treat the problem of unemployment exclusively as a man's problem, with no mention of the situation of women with dependents, which would have revealed even greater economic problems than those faced by men. In discussing the plight of unmarried unemployed men, he notes the advantageous position of married men who, even when unemployed, still have a home (72).[49] Echoing the official categories of "typical family" and "single man," Orwell adopts the administrative view of reality in which women appear primarily as "wives." One of the very few occasions on which Orwell notes status distinctions between men and women occurs as he discusses how unemployment affects a working-class family's division of household labor.

In a working-class home it is the man who is the master and not, as in a middle-class home, the woman or the baby. Practically never, for instance, in a working-class home, will you see the man doing a stroke of the housework. Unemployment has not changed this convention, which on the face of it seems a little unfair. The man is idle from morning to night but the woman is as busy as ever—more so, indeed, because she has to manage with less money. Yet so far as my experience goes the women do not protest. I believe that they, as well as the men, feel that a man would lose his manhood if, merely because he was out of work, he developed into a "Mary Ann." [72–73]

Orwell did his duty; he on occasion helped clear the dishes. Beyond this, he tells us that the "deadening, debilitating effect of unemployment" is greater upon men than upon women (73). Largely blind to the reality of women, Orwell has hardly a word to say about infant mortality or maternal mortality; not a word about the importance of proper nutrition for pregnant women (though he several times mentions the difficulty for undernourished *men* of producing healthy offspring); almost no discussion of the double day of wage-earning women or of their much lower wages.

In 1935 the average full-time earnings of men in all industries were about fifty-six shillings a week, in comparison with about twenty-seven shillings for women. In addition, the higher the men's rate of pay, the greater the difference between those rates and what women earned in the same industry.[50] Viewed in terms of Seebohm Rowntree's already minimal "Human Needs of Labour" standard, established in 1936 from his survey of poverty in York, the *average* earnings of women workers were below

Rowntree's minimum (thirty-one shillings a week), and nearly half the adult male workers earned less than Rowntree's fifty-three shillings a week for a man, wife, and three children.[51] Thus both men and women workers lived in conditions of extreme economic hardship—not, however, to the same extent, and it is this additional distinction that Orwell fails to see, simply because he too considers women largely in terms of a family unit in which the husband is the presumed wage earner.

Elizabeth Wilson has noted that "The unemployed men of the Depression survived on the dole, eking out an apathetic existence," and were in effect bought off by the dole. "But these men were the visible part of an iceberg; sunk below them were millions of toiling, downtrodden women, their lives the picture of the most dreadful neglect." Discrimination against women continued everywhere, and especially in the two vital fields of employment and welfare, Wilson states.[52] Such information helps us to see that Orwell is ignoring a deep and pervasive problem. By implication, he treats women's poverty as ancillary to men's and remediable by improving men's economic situation; that is, he sees women's situation purely as a function of their relationship to men. Although he cites Sir John Boyd Orr on the estimated underfed population of England, Orwell never mentions—not even in a chapter devoted exclusively to diet—the common division of food within working-class families, which often left wives even more undernourished than their husbands. This was not an unknown phenomenon in the thirties, as a number of researchers had already called into question the notion that all members of a family have the same standard of living.[53] Orwell's disregard for the unequal situation of women within the working class cannot be considered an accidental omission. From passing comments in his other works, we know that he had at least some residual awareness of the routine sacrifice of women's interests to those of men, as we see, for example, in his description of the relationship between Gordon Comstock and his sister Julia in Keep the Aspidistra Flying. Since it seems unlikely that Orwell would have denied the existence of such inequalities in the working class, I suspect that it is something he simply did not want to see, and though he expresses sympathy for the working-class woman's lot, he is not prepared to raise the more threatening issue of women's position vis-à-vis men's.[54]

Although women as a group are largely invisible to Orwell, there is one respect in which they regularly appear in his writing, and that is as scapegoats on whom to focus anger or disdain. Several times in *Wigan Pier* Orwell uses the "old ladies in Brighton" as symbols of exploitative people with benighted attitudes toward the working class. This is all the more striking when we consider just what it is these "old ladies" represent, which Richard Hoggart explains as follows: "The 'old ladies living in retirement in Brighton' are representative figures for a great many more, for politicians and businessmen and writers and *rentiers* and university lecturers. It was to these above all that Orwell was speaking." [55] Hoggart of course overlooks the interesting transference to women of largely masculine roles in the world. The misogyny may be considered rhetorically effective, however, in that it is indeed likely to arouse in the average male reader a desire to distance himself from these "old ladies." Equally likely, on the other hand, is that the distance and misogyny conveniently locate guilt and responsibility on another, and "outside," group—the usual function of scapegoats. Such a strategy is also evident in Orwell's comment, early in *Wigan Pier*: "Ideally, the worst type of slum landlord is a fat wicked man, preferably a bishop, who is drawing an immense income from extortionate rents. Actually, it is a poor old woman who has invested her life's savings in three slum houses, inhabits one of them, and tries to live on the rent of the other two—never, in consequence, having any money for repairs" (50). Alex Zwerdling sees this passage as Orwell's corrective of the Marxist propaganda of his day, with its fat, greedy capitalist in a top hat,[56] and Orwell may indeed be right to observe that women, who are concentrated at the bottom of each economic class, may well be more typical owners of slum housing (on a small scale, of course) than are wealthy entrepreneurs. But this substitution of a female image for a generally more accurate male model of a capitalist is inadequate, once again eliciting stereotypes rather than understanding.

With precisely the same effect, Orwell several years later repeatedly used the image of women in their Rolls-Royces as symbols of everything he opposed in English society. The classic statement of the stereotype occurs early in "The Lion and the Unicorn" (1941). What answer can one give to the man who says he would be no worse off under Hitler, Orwell asks, "while common soldiers risk their lives for two and sixpence a day, and fat women ride about in Rolls-Royce cars, nursing pekineses?" (CEJL, 2:87). Orwell's call for a revolution in England (without which, so he argued, the war against Hitler could not be won) seems to rely substantially upon the assumed desire to overthrow these feminine types and the general softening of life in England for the sake of a tough, masculine version of socialism. As in *Wigan Pier*, here too the typical capitalist is converted into an old lady. Orwell writes: "Once check that stream of dividends that flows from the bodies of Indian coolies to the banking accounts of old ladies in Cheltenham, and the whole sahib-native nexus . . . can come to an end" (2:100). He even goes so far as to proclaim: "The lady in the Rolls-Royce car is more damaging to morale than a fleet of Goering's bombing planes" (2:90).

Orwell's insensitivity to certain facets of reality provides a telling reflection of his interests and selective perception. One of the most striking aspects of *Wigan Pier*—all the more impressive since it does not overtly relate to his chosen theme of working-class poverty and unemployment—is Orwell's fascination with the miners, about whom he becomes lyrical. Just as he selected the Brookers' rather extreme household as a "typical" lodging house, so he chooses mining as the "typical" working-class line of work. Far from being typical, however, it is a striking example because of the atypical dangers and demands of this (by then) exclusively masculine trade. Mining and quarrying together occupied only 4.22 percent of the work force in 1937, as opposed to, for example, 5.89 percent engaged in agriculture and forestry or—what would have been typical—33.13 percent in manufacturing.[57]

Orwell's fascination with the miners is apparent also in his extensive descriptions of the dangers of accidents in the mines, while devoting fewer pages to the less dramatic problem of chronic threats to their health.[58] Peter Stearns, in discussing changes in the concept of manhood that resulted from industrialization, cites "The dark shaft of a coal mine" as "one of the real tests of nineteenth-century masculinity."[59] As we shall see, Orwell was afraid of a society that might make such "tests" obsolete in the future. George Woodcock has remarked on the "peculiar intensity" in Orwell's description of the miners, but only when they are underground: "It is the miner in the mine who excites Orwell."[60] The scene in the mine as described by Orwell is like a dimly lit socialist realist painting. In the "frightful, deafening din" Orwell makes out "the line of half-naked kneeling men . . . driving their shovels." He feels "a pang of envy for their toughness," for the "dreadful," "almost superhuman" job they do (*Wigan Pier*, 20). They "look and work as though they were made of iron," and, indeed, to Orwell they really do look like "hammered iron statues." In the mine, "you realize what splendid men they are"; small, "but" with "the most noble bodies; wide shoulders tapering to slender supple waists, and small pronounced buttocks and sinewy thighs, with not an ounce of waste flesh anywhere." They form an unforgettable "spectacle . . . driving their huge shovels under the coal with stupendous force and speed" (21). The mine itself is also dramatic, with girders that "have buckled into fantastic curves" and "mysterious machines" and tools in evidence (23). The coal tumbles out in "monstrous boulders," and "monstrous 'dirt-heaps,' like hideous grey mountains," are later formed on the surface (28). Toward the end of this chapter, Orwell evokes the outside world that depends on these miners, and here he could not resist including an image calling up a contrasting—and to him visible—reality. We must have coal in order that, among other things, "the Nancy poets may scratch one another's backs" (30); all of us, you and I and the "Nancy poets" owe the amenities of our lives to these "poor drudges . . . driving their shovels forward with arms and belly muscles of steel" (31). Orwell experiences humiliation watching the miners work (31) and later on returns to this subject, saying: "If there is one type of man to whom I do feel myself inferior, it is a coal-miner" (102). Once the miners are dressed and away from the pit, however, they look ordinary, for "their thick ill-fitting clothes hide the splendour of their bodies" (32).

In contrast to his experiences with the tramps, Orwell now notes the insuperable distance that divides the journalist or social explorer from the working class. Once again, unquestioningly assuming his own centrality and placing the "working class" in the position of "other," he asks; "But is it ever possible to be really intimate with the working class?"—and concludes that it is not. In an intriguing display of lack of awareness of his own biases, Orwell tells us, "I have seen just enough of the working class to avoid idealizing them" (102–3), and then proceeds to do precisely that. Orwell's idealization of working-class family life develops from a declaration that the working class is much more manly than the middle class. Taking an astonishingly distorted view of education and work, he sets them up as opposing poles, with the working class "seeing through" the fraud of an "education" useless for a strapping youth who prefers the more manly task of "real work" (103–4). In considering the kind of attention Orwell gives to "work," it is worth noting that when he refers to "working people" or "working class" he in fact has in mind men, and it is only men's work that he envisions. Not the girl who does repetitive and boring factory work, for example, and who has left school to pursue this womanly fate of "real" work. Not even the boy who follows such a path.

In adopting this image of work rather than analyzing the gender ideology that gives rise to it, Orwell engages in a blatant romanticizing of what for the most part was routine, dull, dreary, and health-threatening stultifying activity. Identifying himself with the stereotype of the working-class view of manhood, Orwell writes passages hypostatizing the working-class youth who, at eighteen, is a "man" while his public school counterpart is still a "baby." He concludes: "There is much in middle-class life that looks sickly and debilitating when you see it from a working-class angle" (104). His concentration on the miners allows Orwell to so describe "work" that it necessarily evokes traditional images of masculinity, while his admiration takes the form of a humble declaration of the inferiority of his own class. But we must recognize that what he admires is not the working class's ability to survive in adverse conditions (had this been his focus, women's lives as "managers" of nearly nonexistent incomes would have caught his attention) but, rather, the inherent manliness, as he sees it, of working-class men's way of life. And Orwell's picture of the miners' lives, after all, is very much a positive one; he even persuades himself that their work is health-building rather than health-destroying, in contrast to the debilitating effects of book learning, which has no masculine connotations.

His argument develops from an admiration for physical labor and the tough, manly men who undertake it to an admiration for the kind of family life in which Father and his job are at the center of reality. Orwell writes that the manual worker, when employed and earning good wages, "has a better chance of being happy than an educated man. His home life seems to fall more naturally into a sane and comely shape." He crowns this idyllic image with an oft-quoted though banal passage evoking the ideal working-class interior:

Especially on winter evenings after tea, when the fire glows in the open range and dances mirrored in the steel fender, when Father, in shirt-sleeves, sits in the rocking chair at one side of the fire reading the racing finals, and Mother sits on the other with her sewing, and the children are happy with a pennorth of mint humbugs, and the dog lolls roasting himself on the rag mat—it is a good place to be in, provided that you can be not only in it but sufficiently *of* it to be taken for granted. [104; Orwell's emphasis]

The essential point about this scene, Orwell is quick to underscore, is that its "happiness depends mainly upon one question—whether Father is in work" (105). But the reader notices another point: This genre scene complements Orwell's earlier passage stressing that in a working-class home "it is the man who is the master and not, as in a middle-class home, the woman or the baby" (72–73). To Orwell's eyes, this patriarchal image gives the working-class home its "naturally" more "sane and comely shape," and "easy completeness." It allows him to create a myth of "perfect symmetry" (104) and to ignore the fact of domestic inequalities.

The distinction between working-class and middle-class life in terms of men's authority and power recurs in Orwell's subsequent novel *Coming Up for Air*, whose narrator, George Bowling, empathizes with the lot of men (like himself) who live in the suburbs, in "semi-detached torture-chambers where the poor little five-to-ten-pound-a-weekers quake and shiver, every one of them with the boss twisting his tail and the wife riding him like the nightmare and the kids sucking his blood like leeches. . . . I'm not so sorry for the proles myself. . . . The prole suffers physically, but he's a free man when he isn't working" (14). Noting the rigidifying of gender roles that accompanied industrialization in the nineteenth century, Peter Stearns has analyzed it as a reaction on the part of threatened men to diminishing control over their livelihoods.[61] Richard Titmuss observes that women's increased economic dependency after the shift from domestic to industrial production also led to changes in the psychological subtleties of relationships between the sexes. "Authoritarian patterns of behavior, sanctioned in the factory, were carried into the home," he writes.[62]

To move from Orwell's admiration for the miners' splendid bodies to his idealized image of working-class life is not, however, to change subjects. Rather, drawing these aspects of the book together helps us to see the ideological continuity in Orwell's vision. Similarly, his nostalgia for the Edwardian age, in which family scenes such as his fantasized one were, in his view, more common (*Wigan Pier*, 104), must be seen as a function of his longing for the days when men were real men. Like all believers in golden ages, Orwell imagines that people in his own time exhibit signs of physical degeneracy when compared to past specimens of manhood and exclaims: "Where are the monstrous men with chests like barrels and moustaches like the wings of eagles who strode across my childhood's gaze twenty or thirty years ago?" (88). What makes this question interesting is, first of all, that it conflicts with our knowledge that, by almost every standard of measurement, health and nutrition in England improved between the wars, and this despite the very real hardships imposed by the Depression.[63] Second, we see in Orwell's nostalgia a desire to stop time at a particular point—and that point is, not incidentally, precisely the moment before the extreme gender polarization embodied in working-class male views of masculinity began to be seriously undermined. Orwell's protests against industrialization, it must be realized, are only against the "unmanning" effects of its second (modern) phase. He does not protest the existence of coal mining and factory production. These belong to his stylized image of the Edwardian age, with which he contrasts the filthy past (Middle Ages) and the sterile (utopian, he calls it) future.

One might well ask: What is the basis of Orwell's knowledge of the working class before the war? He was eleven when the Great War started and by all accounts did not have much contact with working-class families. What he seems to be offering the reader is a childhood image, an unconscious idealization; hence the "monstrous men" of his "memory." Orwell describes a class, a world, in much the same terms adults use in recalling a building or street that seemed immense in childhood.

If Orwell's ideal of family life depends on Father and his job at the center of reality, what about Mother? Richard Titmuss has calculated that up until about 1911 the typical working-class mother had approximately ten pregnancies and spent a total of about fifteen years in a state of pregnancy and in nursing a child during its first year of life. By 1950, when Orwell died, the typical mother spent approximately four years in this way.[64] Titmuss writes that, as women's health care and life expectancy have increased,

the number and proportion of mothers worn out by excessive childbearing and dying prematurely . . . from diseases . . . are but a fraction of what they were fifty years ago. Above all, the decline in the size of the family has meant, in terms of family economics, a rise in the standard of living of women which has probably been of more importance, by itself, than any change since 1900 in real earnings by manual workers. Nor would it be hard to argue that this factor was far more influential up to the Second World War than any additional benefits derived from the expansion of the social services and improvements in medical care.[65]

Is it any wonder, in view of this, that Orwell later lists "birth-control fanatics" (Wigan Pier, 190) among the detestable cranks who are giving socialism a bad name? He is, of course, right in perceiving a change since the days of his childhood, but he cannot properly name this change—which has to do, above all else, with the altered position of women as they become free of perpetual pregnancies.[66]

Working-Class Smells and Orwell's Homophobia. Part 1 of Wigan Pier is strong on description. But when the time comes for analysis, we get instead the diatribe against socialists in part 2. Rather than examining the significance of what he has observed, Orwell switches to a meditation on attitudes—as if these could explain either the material conditions or the family relations of the working class.

Appreciation of the miners and of idealized family scenes does not, of course, exhaust Orwell's response to the working class. Equally revealing are his notorious remarks on the issue of smell. When Orwell was attacked for saying that the working class smelled, he defended himself by pointing out that he was only describing a belief held by members of his own class, not a fact, and on several occasions he denied having written that the working class did, indeed, smell. But his text reveals a constant shift in narrative focus which, not surprisingly, generates a good deal of ambiguity.

He begins by declaring that in his childhood it was often said that "*The lower classes smell*" (his emphasis). "That was what we were taught," he explains, and then discusses the special force that "a *physical* feeling" has, as opposed to other likes or dislikes. And it is here that he introduces ambiguity, for it will be noticed in the following passage that he is no longer explaining what he was taught but describing different kinds of people as *they are* and how this affects *us* (himself and his readers, presumably):

Race-hatred, religious hatred, differences of education, of temperament, of intellect, even differences of moral code, can be got over; but physical repulsion cannot. You can have an affection for a murderer or a sodomite, but you cannot have an affection for a man whose breath stinks—habitually stinks, I mean. However well you may wish him, however much you may admire his mind and character, if his breath stinks he is horrible and in your heart of hearts you will hate him. [112]

Note that there is no mention here of *belief*, but rather of the *fact* of stinking. He then returns to the theme of the damage done to the average middle-class person by being brought up to believe that the working classes are dirty, affirming that this was precisely what his own class was taught:

Very early in life you acquired the idea that there was something subtly repulsive about a working-class body; you would not get nearer to it than you could help. . . . And even "lower class" people whom you knew to be quite clean—servants, for instance—were faintly unappetising. The smell of their sweat, the very texture of their skins, were mysteriously different from yours. [112–13]

Once again in this last passage Orwell has shifted from inculcated belief to apparently factual representation of the servants' bodies.[67]

Far more important than the debate about Orwell's own attitudes subsequently generated by these lines is the phrase that introduces this entire discussion. Again situating himself and his class at the center of reality, Orwell proclaims that the belief that the lower classes smell is "the real secret of class distinctions" (112). This is an extraordinarily depoliticizing reduction of a complex phenomenon to a single physical and, as we shall see, exciting (to Orwell, that is) detail. Such a reduction perhaps captures perfectly Orwell's childhood perspective, but it is an astonishing thing for a grown man to be setting out as the key to class antagonism. Even if he holds this to be true, it should at least cause him to question the ideological function of such a belief, so effective in placing the onus on the exploited rather than the exploiters. But no such analysis is forthcoming. Instead, Orwell engages in a sensationalistic depiction of this purportedly widespread attitude, in his most assertive voice-in-the-wilderness style. This episode thus provides another instance of his tendency to ask an important question only to answer it tangentially, directing the reader's attention away from the key issues. In this case, a potentially serious discussion of middle-class ideology is channeled into a consideration of the question of working-class smells.

Orwell had earlier united the aesthetically appealing and the repulsive in his discussion of the peculiar kind of ugliness he finds in an industrial town. "Look at it from a purely aesthetic standpoint and it may have a certain macabre appeal. I find that anything outrageously strange generally ends by fascinating me even when I abominate it" (Wigan Pier, 97). These words, written in the context of his visual sense, can also be applied to his sense of smell, and in Wigan Pier we find the stress not only on the splendid and powerful physiques of miners but also on the issue of the smell of working-class men. It seems to me that these two themes, usually treated separately, need to be joined to illuminate the characteristically Orwellian ambivalence about the working class. More specifically still, I suggest that Orwell's revulsion from the odor of working-class men should be viewed as intricately related to his fascination with their strong bodies. The one is the negative aspect of the other, the attraction offset by the aversion. This is apparent, in Orwell's discussion of smells, in his quasi-erotic description of a childhood recollection:

You watched a great sweaty navvy walking down the road with his pick over his shoulder; you looked at his discoloured shirt and his corduroy trousers stiff with the dirt of a decade; you thought of those nests and layers of greasy rags below, and, under all, the unwashed body, brown all over (that was how I used to imagine it), with its strong, bacon-like reek. [112]

Nor is it only *smells* that evoke this kind of reaction; rather, it is any sort of intimate physical contact. Orwell recalls traveling on a train in his adolescence and being revolted at the sight of a quart bottle of beer being passed around among some working men: "I cannot describe the horror I felt as that bottle worked its way towards me. If I drank from it after all those lower-class male mouths I felt certain I should vomit" (115). Orwell's habitual androcentrism usually keeps him from noting that he is speaking specifically about men; he routinely generalizes his perceptions—so that in describing working-class *men*, for example, he seems to believe he has described working-class *life*. This makes it all the more significant that, in reporting his reaction to the working class, he carefully specifies that his physical aversion was to males only. After the above passage, for example, he writes: "I still don't like drinking out of a cup or bottle after another person—another man, I mean; with women I don't mind —but at least the question of class does not enter" (115). It is in this context that Orwell makes the comment cited in chapter 2, about his lack of physical revulsion from Burmese men: "I felt towards a Burman almost as I felt towards a woman" (124). I commented, earlier, on the significance of this transformation of Burmese males into social females. It needs to be recalled here, in the context of the distinction Orwell is drawing between his aversion to men—especially manly men, the ones he most admires—and his acceptance of physical intimacy with women.

But Orwell's rather unclear discussion of the issue of smell makes it hard to focus on the importance of his words. His own account purports to explain middle-class antagonism toward the working class. He notes, for example, his revulsion at the sight of sweating British soldiers in Burma and chalks this down to pure prejudice, "For a soldier is probably as inoffensive, physically, as it is possible for a male white person to be. . . . But I could not see it like that. All I knew was that it was *lower-class* sweat that I was smelling, and the thought of it made me sick" (125; Orwell's emphasis). Orwell's belief in the revulsion felt by members of his own class for the working class on account of its alleged smell ignores the fact that cross-class relations of the most intimate kind were in fact the norm rather than the exception throughout the Victorian period and no doubt continued in his own time. Of course these relations, typically involving upper-class males and working-class females, constituted a routine, if not generally discussed, feature of life. Even Winston Smith, in *Nineteen Eighty-Four*, has intercourse with an aging prole prostitute. However, in specifying that his aversion is solely to *male* smells, Orwell betrays that his analysis is not, in fact, of the olfactory class system but of something far more personal. What, then, does it signify?

It seems to me that Orwell's aversion to contact with

working-class male bodies is, for him, a necessary complement to his powerful attraction to the image of masculinity these men generate. He repeatedly stresses that working men in his youth were more belligerent, more manly, than in the postwar period and compares the "submissive" working class of the 1930s unfavorably with the "openly hostile" men of his boyhood (115). But by specifying that his revulsion was from working-class *male* odors only, Orwell reassures his readers (and himself): His adulation of brawny working men must not be misunderstood, for it exists within the context of his fundamental commitment to heterosexuality. This also makes sense of his emphasis on the effeminacy of the Burmese manservant whom he allowed a level of intimacy intolerable with an English male. Certainly there is in Orwell's writings sufficient evidence of sexual and olfactory disturbances to warrant the attention of an expert in these fields.[68]

"Homophobia" has been defined as "the irrational fear or intolerance of homosexuality"—usually male homosexuality.[69] Orwell displays homophobia in this sense very clearly. Throughout his writings he seems to feel that in order to discredit individuals and groups it is sufficient to attach to them the label of "Nancy boy" or "pansy"—two terms specifically designating the passive partner in a male homosexual dyad. But it seems to me that Orwell's homophobia is revealed more fully by his complex reactions of attraction to and revulsion from working-class males. The concept of homophobia, as elaborated by Gregory Lehne, should not lead to its use as another tag, replacing the label of "pansy" with that of "homophobic." Rather, the term is intended to help us focus on some of the stresses and lines of fault that emerge in a culture in which gender roles cease to be merely expressions of sexual preference and instead become polarized along hierarchical lines, with manly men situated at the top and forever required to defend their positions. Lehne sees homophobia as a constellation of social and political attitudes rather than as an individualized fear of homosexuality and notes that in homophobia the real threat is not homosexuality but a change in the male sex role. Since a homosexual may be "latent," any man is constantly under suspicion, and hence proof of "manhood" must go on continuously. In this way homophobia is used to control all men, not only homosexuals, and to maintain male roles.[70]

In understanding the pressures of the male gender role, homophobia provides us with an important conceptual aid. *Wigan Pier* offers us a nearly perfect expression of the constellation of anxieties and longings generated by the commitment to "masculinity" in a time of rapid social change. Orwell's homophobia is manifest not primarily in the ease with which he attached the label of "pansy" or "Nancy boy" to men he perceived as opponents. By itself, this verbal tic should not, I feel, be made too much of. Nor is it evident only in his comments on male smells.[71] More significant is the deep revulsion he expresses in regard to effeminate or otherwise "unmanly" men—a revulsion focusing specifically on these men's buttocks. I mentioned in chapter 2 the portrait in *Burmese Days* of Mr. Macgregor who, in his tight khaki shorts that outline his buttocks and reveal his dimpled knees, reminds Flory of a homosexual scoutmaster. To the disdainful Flory, this man is one type of detestable sahib. But Macgregor makes a fascinating reappearance in *Wigan Pier*, converted now into the typical socialist and brought in to exemplify Orwell's contention that wherever socialists are gathered there is a prevalence of cranks:

One day this summer I was riding through Letchworth when the bus stopped and two dreadful-looking old men got on to it. They were both about sixty, both very short, pink, and chubby, and both hatless. One of them was obscenely bald, the other had long grey hair bobbed in the Lloyd George style. They were dressed in pistachio-coloured shirts and khaki shorts into which their huge bottoms were crammed so tightly that you could study every dimple. Their appearance created a mild stir of horror on top of the bus. [152]

The man next to Orwell commented, "Socialists," and Orwell decides he was probably right since the Independent Labour Party's summer school was just then being held at Letchworth. The importance of this scene on the bus for Orwell is that it bears out his notion that "decent people" are alienated by socialists. As he puts it just before introducing the episode of the two men, "One sometimes gets the impression that the mere words 'Socialism' and 'Communism' draw towards them with magnetic force every fruit-juice drinker, nudist, sandal-wearer, sex-maniac, Quaker, 'Nature Cure' quack, pacifist, and feminist in England" (152). He also mentions vegetarians ("food-cranks" [153]) "and all that dreary tribe of high-minded women and sandal-wearers and bearded fruit-juice drinkers who come flocking towards the smell of 'progress' like bluebottles to a dead cat" (160).[72] And, as if the reader had not been sufficiently browbeaten, Orwell later affirms:

We have reached a stage when the very word "Socialism" calls up, on the one hand, a picture of aeroplanes, tractors, and huge glittering factories of glass and concrete; on the other, a picture of vegetarians with wilting beards, of Bolshevik commissars (half gangster, half gramophone), of earnest ladies in sandals, shock-headed Marxists chewing polysyllables, escaped Quakers, birth-control fanatics, and Labour Party backstairs-crawlers. [190]

Socialism, in Orwell's view, is in danger of being diluted into "some kind of pale-pink humbug even more ineffectual than the parliamentary Labour Party" (194). As Orwell sees it, the problem is this: "You have got to attract the man who means business" (195). The problem for Orwell, as I see it, is how to make socialism "manly." [73]

Manhood versus The Machine: Socialism and Softness. Orwell's attack on socialism in the second part of *Wigan Pier* proceeds along two main tracks. First, he characterizes socialists as cranks and lavishes considerable attention on examples of their crankishness. Second, he accuses socialists of being machine worshipers and invokes a vision of the menace of mechanization. In each case there are major assumptions not themselves clearly formulated: (1) that socialists are, typically, as Orwell describes them; (2) that this is the cause of socialism's lack of popular support among the working class; (3) that socialists do indeed worship the machine and see it as the solution to all human problems. Orwell's strategy for avoiding serious discussion of these assumptions is itself of interest. He weights his arguments in his favor by continually referring to "honest people," "decent people," "intelligent people," "thinking people," "sensitive people," all of them presented as sharing his own perceptions—a good example of his use of coercive discourse. In contrast to these good citizens are the superficial, thoughtless cranks who value labor-saving devices and worship the machine; these are repeatedly caricatured as "little fat men" addicted to a "fat-bellied" idea of progress—not at all, Orwell specifies, the "Men like Gods" of H. G. Wells's misguided utopian imagination.[74]

I propose to take seriously Orwell's catalogue of socialist cranks and examine it in conjunction with his imagery evoking the evils of the machine. This will help lay bare the underlying logic linking parts 1 and 2 of *Wigan Pier*. My objective in examining Orwell's imagery is not to defend the advent of the machine (defense and attack seem to me rather beside the point at this stage) but to note what Orwell's language tells us about his way of construing the "problem" posed by the machine.

"People know that in some way or another 'progress' is a swindle," Orwell states (168), and he will show us why this is so; he will reason where "people" usually feel by "instinct." In our age, "we can actually *feel* the tendency of the machine to make a fully human life impossible" (167; his emphasis), Orwell affirms, without asking for whom this is true. His meaning, however, emerges from the subsequent pages: To be fully human is to display those qualities that "we" admire in "human beings" (170). Again Orwell avoids specifying who "we" are and what serves as his model of a "human being," matters that I shall return to in a moment. The qualities themselves are spelled out by Orwell: We admire physical courage, which is a response to danger, and physical strength (as well as "loyalty, generosity, etc.," about which Orwell has nothing else to say in this book). But the machine world will be one "in which *nothing goes wrong*" since mechanical progress moves toward greater and greater efficiency (169; his emphasis). In other words, "The truth is that many of the qualities we admire in human beings can only function in opposition to some kind of disaster, pain, or difficulty" (170). This is the argument that must be dealt with, the serious objection to socialism that Orwell had earlier promised to get to. Let us take it apart and examine its premises.

First of all, Orwell's suggestion that mechanical progress will eventually lead to a world in which "nothing goes wrong" is clearly untenable. It is interesting that this is how he viewed the machine, for in our time a far more serious problem is generated by our awareness of how much can go wrong with "the machine" —whether the machine is an electrical generator or a nuclear power plant. Besides this, things "go wrong" in human life for emotional and personal reasons unrelated to prevailing levels of technology; these are constraints with which any utopia must deal—and writers like William Morris, in his *News from No-*

where, attempted to take such aspects of reality into account. But Orwell is not saying that he is objecting to a sterile vision of utopia (one that many utopian writers would themselves object to); instead, he seems to believe he is objecting to the real conditions that socialists, wedded to the machine, are trying to bring about. But let us disregard this problem; let us grant that indeed things might never go wrong. Is Orwell correct in his argument that the qualities we admire can exist only in response to the challenge of disaster, pain, or difficulty? Specifically, are physical courage and strength—the features he is concerned with—qualities of this kind, always valued as they battle against danger and difficulty? Are they, in short, characteristics "naturally" admired wherever they occur? The answer is clearly no, as a simple example demonstrates. Men, not women, are generally admired for physical strength and courage. These qualities are not only devalued but even criticized in women (a six-foot-tall, powerful woman is not generally admired for her strength but rather pitied or ridiculed for her departure from the ideal of femininity). Have women in the past been admired as they labored in fields, hauled water, beat laundry under primitive conditions, or spent fourteen-hour days working in a factory? Even when women routinely face pain and death—that is, when they give birth, when they are indeed in labor—they have not generally been admired for this; instead, it has been considered merely an inevitable part of the female lot in life. Are *all* men, in fact, necessarily admired for *all* feats of strength and endurance? The point is clear: These qualities are not valued in themselves, contrary to what Orwell believes. They are valued above all in men and only in specific circumstances, because an ideology is at work here that grants the accolade of manhood to certain admired qualities in certain circumstances yet fails to recognize these qualities when they occur elsewhere. Orwell does not see that he is giving expression to this ideology, which channels and cuts off his vision. His discussion of what "we" admire in "human beings" is thus exposed as a conventional expression of what he (and others in his society) admires in men. The traits admired by Orwell clearly derive their meaning from the culture in which they are embedded. Even in Orwell's own time other qualities could replace these physical ones as guarantors of manhood—for example, wealth or political power. Men have decided what counts as significant tokens of achievement, and women in general have simply not been admitted as contenders for these supposedly "human" qualities.[75]

But if the admiration for these qualities in "human beings" is in fact culturally determined, then Orwell is wrong also to argue that something of inherent value would be destroyed by mechanical progress as it deprives men of the occasion for prowess. For just as Orwell's society established a hierarchy of values, and the gender to which they could be applied, so a mechanical world, even were it to exist in the extreme form Orwell fears, would be equally capable of generating its own cultural values. We might not, now, be able to foresee what these values would be, but they would evolve, just as Orwell's particular scale of values clearly reflects a conventional view of manhood evolved by his society. Orwell's full meaning becomes evident as his argument continues, for he drops the pretense that he is talking about what "we" admire in "human beings" and states explicitly what he has been hinting at all along: "The tendency of mechanical progress is to make your environment safe and soft; and yet you are striving to keep yourself brave and hard" (170). Who is "you" in this passage? Obviously not a woman of Orwell's society. It turns out that Orwell is again talking exclusively about the changes that would affect *men* in a mechanized civilization.

Orwell's argument concludes: "In tying yourself to the ideal of mechanical efficiency, you tie yourself to the ideal of softness. But softness is repulsive; and thus all progress is seen to be a frantic struggle towards an objective which you hope and pray will never be reached" (172). This is the conflict that Orwell sees as inherent in socialism—which, let us recall, he has identified with a fully mechanized world. A human being, Orwell tells us, needs work: "Above the level of a third- or fourth-grade moron, life has got to be lived largely in terms of effort" (173), and this effort must, in his view, be motivated by necessity. Thus, there is no escape in discussing "creative work" as a substitute for the necessary work of the nonmechanized world. One cannot voluntarily forgo technology, Orwell believes. It is absurd to imagine a citizen of Utopia, he says, coming home from his day turning a handle in the tomato-canning factory and doing some pottery glazing or handloom weaving, for "No human being ever wants to do anything in a more cumbrous way than is necessary," and "to put silly little difficulties in your own way, would be a piece of dilettantism" (175–76). This passage merely demonstrates that Orwell does not understand the concept of play—which depends upon the creation of gratuitous difficulties (a subject to which I return in chapter 8, in discussing the gamesmanship apparent in *Nineteen Eighty-Four*). Mechanical progress, Orwell concludes, frustrates the human need for effort and creation. Again one may ask what human being he is referring to. Surely not the woman who spends her day bent over a laundry tub. A man who sweats all day and goes home with aching muscles is not likely to be more satisfied at an otherwise alienating job than someone who pushes a button in Orwell's much-dreaded machine civilization— except (and this is the point) when society tells the former he is doing a "man's" job while it devalues the latter. For Orwell, difficulty equals hardness equals opposite of softness equals masculinity. And the logic of these equations is assumed, not demonstrated. Difficulty has nothing inherently to do with hardness understood as an antonym of softness. Orwell confuses the issue by identifying difficulty with what-men-do-which-requires-courage-and-strength, and even here it is an essential part of his definition that it be what *men* do, not what *women* do, since women's displays of "courage" and "strength" are not viewed in the same light. Thus, Orwell cannot proceed to the more important part of the argument, which should focus not on "difficulty" but on the diverse causes of satisfaction in work.

This reduction of arguments against socialism is not, as should now be clear, entirely separate from his criticism of socialists. His cranks and oddballs turn out, on inspection, to generally present a challenge to or a deviation from traditional sex roles. Such is the logic of his catalogue: The vegetarians, sandal wearers, feminists, pacifists, birth control fanatics, fruit juice drinkers—all these disparate cases of crankishness threaten the predetermined and contrasting roles and modes of behavior habitually assigned to men and women. At times it is hard to see the logic of Orwell's imagination. Why, for example, should he be hostile to birth control, given his own description of overcrowded houses? But birth control frees women from their biology and allows them to enter the world outside the family circle; in this respect it is an incipient form of freedom from patriarchy. And why ridicule hygiene? Perhaps Orwell thinks there is something "feminine" about concern with one's body. Let us recall his own habitually shabby

and baggy suits, the cigarette hanging from his mouth, all suggesting a studied neglect. He misunderstands vegetarians as motivated
by the (to him contemptible?) desire to prolong their own lives
and cannot discern as a possible motive for vegetarianism a respect for animal life. So the two aspects of Orwell's argument—
the more superficial attack on socialists as cranks and the view of
socialism as leading to a mechanized and hence repulsively soft
and degenerate future—come together as expressions of Orwell's
anxiety about manhood. As Orwell puts it: "The implied objective of 'progress' is—not *exactly*, perhaps, the brain in the bottle,
but at any rate some frightful subhuman depth of softness and
helplessness" (176; his emphasis). The machine, in Orwell's view,
is like a succubus, depriving men of their power: "The oftener
one surrenders to it the tighter its grip becomes. You have only to
look about you at this moment to realize with what sinister speed
the machine is getting us into its power" (178–79). The thinking
person, in Orwell's vision, veers away from the socialist fold upon
observing both "the dullness of individual Socialists and the apparent flabbiness of Socialist ideals" (185). This is why socialism
must rid itself of its cranks: "If only the sandals and the pistachio-
coloured shirts could be put in a pile and burnt, and every vegetarian, teetotaller, and creeping Jesus sent home to Welwyn Garden
City to do his yoga exercises quietly!" (195–96).

In a letter dating from the same period in which Orwell
was writing *The Road to Wigan Pier*, he again comments on the
typical middle-class socialists who, he says, give him the creeps:
"And then so many of them are the sort of eunuch type with a
vegetarian smell who go about spreading sweetness and light and
have at the back of their minds a vision of the working class all
TT, well washed behind the ears, readers of Edward Carpenter or
some other pious sodomite and talking with BBC accents" (CEJL,
1:216). Toward the end of *Wigan Pier*, Orwell again returns to the
issue of smell, this time in a different context: "Socialism, at least
in this island, does not smell any longer of revolution and the
overthrow of tyrants; it smells of crankishness, machine-worship
and the stupid cult of Russia. Unless you can remove that smell,
and very rapidly, Fascism may win" (190). What is most interesting about this passage is that, coming as it does right after one of
Orwell's catalogues of socialist cranks, it reveals his desire to redeem socialism as a manly adventure, to dissociate it from those

things he regards as despicable. The nasty smell was first associated with the working class, then became an unsexed "vegetarian smell," and is finally transferred to socialism itself. The task at hand is announced in terms of freeing socialism from this odor.

In the last few pages of the book, Orwell attempts to rehabilitate socialism—which he identifies with "justice and liberty"—by briefly combating his own earlier arguments. It does not matter, he says, if socialists are cranks; that is no reason to reject socialism. And, as far as the machine goes, it is here to stay and there is no point railing against it. Significantly, Orwell devotes far less attention to dismissing his own charges than he did to building them up, with the result that his affirmation of socialism as England's only hope (which means, he specifies, "the overthrow of tyranny" [195]) sounds vague and unconvincing. What is most likely to stay with the reader is not Orwell's "formal" adherence to socialism, expressed in a few abstractions, but his more detailed and vivid attack on it. This is why critics such as Frank Gloversmith conclude: "The assumed debater's role with Orwell's offering to be devil's advocate in sketching a case against Socialism, converts into a total position, and there is an attack in earnest, sustained, unopposed." [76] It is simply inadequate for Orwell to attempt to correct the impression that he is attacking socialism by the occasional affirmation that he is *for* socialism. The burden of proof rests with his analysis itself, which is very far from being a careful examination of a political movement he deeply values. Pretending to be typical, Orwell is in fact eccentric and often near hysteria himself. His approach, in addition, is fundamentally ahistorical. As in *Down and Out*, though more overtly political at this point in his life, Orwell is still essentially a critic of manners, not of politics. He treats all socialists as of one type, not as people with diverse interests and pursuing a number of different strategies. Communications theory teaches us that redundancy in a message is a means of reducing the possible alternative interpretations while affirming the basic message. In part 2 of *Wigan Pier* such redundancy clearly occurs in Orwell's attacks on socialism and its adherents.

Orwell has little interest in how mechanization affects the organization of work, and even less in the question of ownership of the means of production or the economic inequalities between owners and employees. Rather, his critique of the machine proceeds almost entirely upon moral grounds: He is worried about the *qualities* demanded by work in a highly mechanized age and, not surprisingly, he polarizes those qualities along the lines of hardness/softness. This is of a piece with his idealization of the miners. The notion that a man must face challenges lies behind much of Orwell's rhetoric about work. As in so many other cases, however, he never focuses on his own assumptions here, never asks why he holds these particular views about manhood and labor. Instead, the association is assumed and unquestioned, while it controls in every detail the argument that Orwell elaborates. He simply affirms what "a man" wants to be and needs to do and proceeds from there, failing to distinguish between biological and cultural needs and between needs and norms.

A comment in Orwell's last notebook reveals that in 1949, more than ten years after writing *Wigan Pier*, he still held the same views of the relationship between a "hard" life and masculine strength and vigor. He writes: "Greater and ever-increasing softness & luxuriousness of modern life. Rise in the standard of physical courage, improvement in health & physique, continuous supersession of athletic records. Qy. how to reconcile?" (CEJL, 4:515). The obvious answer to Orwell's query is "better nutrition," something he may have been unwilling to grant given his antagonism toward industrialism and its products. His tendency to discuss the physical only from the point of view of its moral implications may explain his ignorance of the dynamics of material life. The masculine mystique in Orwell's thinking made it impossible for him to recognize and value the simple material changes that better nutrition and the "easier" life were bringing about.

In contrast with Orwell's idealization of the miners, socialism, in his sexually polarized view of life, appears as female—it is soft, enveloping, emasculating. Although the machine may be conceived of as glass, steel, impersonal, the world Orwell thinks it will bring about is an effeminate world. Orwell's sensitive, decent, thinking man will become like a stereotyped woman, soft and helpless, and since femininity is in fact an imposed social role, why indeed could it not be imposed on men as well? Against this nightmarish vision (which foreshadows the world of *Nineteen Eighty-Four*) the coal miner stands like a colossus. No wonder Orwell did not, at this time, wholeheartedly consider himself a socialist. It was to take Spain, and the manly solidarity of the trenches, to turn him into one.

The Road to Wigan Pier is an eloquent example of just how hard-won and precarious an acquisition a masculine gender identity is. One cannot help but be struck by the pathetic quality of Orwell's fear of softness—this, rather than poverty, is the abyss constantly waiting to swallow him up. His imagery presents femininity, in its conventional sense, as a kind of mucilaginous condition from which masculinity must ever strive to separate itself or, should it cease to do so, be engulfed and lost. Orwell's anxieties are evident in his use of sinking or submerging imagery: on the one hand, the fear and revulsion of sinking into softness; on the other, the desire to sink into failure, to touch bottom by going down and out (while still retaining a distinctly masculine identity). At the end of Wigan Pier he imagines the middle class sinking down into the working class where it belongs. Here he reconciles his fears—the submersion offset by the masculinity of the working class. Orwell's adulation of the miners, his homophobia, his fear of socialism as soft and hence repulsive, all bear witness to the fact that manhood is an achieved identity, not a "natural" state; hence no male can feel "like a man" unless he is constantly manifesting his masculinity. Eternal vigilance, Orwell seems to be saying, is the price of manhood.

Judged as an analysis of the ills of socialism and the machine, the second part of The Road to Wigan Pier is exceptionally unclear and weak—as was noted long ago by Victor Gollancz in his introduction to the Left Book Club edition. But when the entire book is looked at from the point of view of Orwell's imagery and emotional tone, its unity and simplicity emerge with great clarity. There is a certain transparency in Orwell's writing—not, however, that usually assumed by the critics: a prose so clear that it lets us "see through" to the object described. Orwell's writing, in my view, displays quite a different kind of transparency, that of prose so emotionally laden, full of associations of such obviously personal significance, that it lets us see clearly not the purported object of this prose but the man who composed it.

Four

Masculine/Feminine

in the Early Fiction

Gender enters a narrative in many different ways. We are not, after all, brains in bottles—that image of the future that so repelled Orwell. We write as we read, with our bodies. But though we are born male or female, we become masculine and feminine only through a laborious and never-ending training. We bring this training with us to all our activities, even those we like to envision as pure acts of imagination, for these are acts of *our* imaginations and so return us to the centrality of gender in our sense of identity.

What would a text be like that did not begin with assumptions deriving from our society's differential treatment of males and females? Can we even imagine a novel without gender hierarchy as its fundamental premise? Of course such a novel would have no narrative innuendos appealing to male readers' complicity, no displays of contempt for women, no parodies of the language attributed to a despised sex, no assumptions about character dependent merely upon having been born male or female.

In rapid succession in 1934 and 1935 Orwell wrote two novels, one with a female protagonist, the other with a male. He did not write these books from the perspective of a neutral or neuter narrator; nor can we read them with neutrality, for like all our narratives they not only speak differently of men and women, they also speak differently to men and women. Taken together, these two novels, *A Clergyman's Daughter* and *Keep the Aspidis-*

tra Flying, enable us to study Orwell's gender ideology and its constraints on him as a writer of realistic fiction.[1]

A CLERGYMAN'S DAUGHTER

The very title of Orwell's second novel at once induces the reader to take a particular perspective on his protagonist. She is to be viewed not as an individual in her own right but rather in terms of her relationship to a man, a clergyman, her father. This is the only one of Orwell's novels to have such a title, one that refers to the main character and at the same time identifies this character through a relationship to someone else. Dorothy Hare is not even *the* clergyman's daughter, which would give her a more specific identity, but merely *a* clergyman's daughter, a generic, or rather paradigmatic, being. Orwell thus communicates to us that Dorothy's ascribed social identity (derived through male lineage only) is the salient fact about her. But he is also writing in a tradition of works with such titles—specifically, D. H. Lawrence's early short story "Daughters of the Vicar" (in Lawrence's volume entitled, by way of contrast, *The Prussian Officer* [1914]), and Flora Macdonald Mayor's subtle and moving novel, *The Rector's Daughter* (1924). It may be, then, that Dorothy Hare is rightly seen as "a clergyman's daughter"; perhaps her life will, as it turns out, be circumscribed by this fact. Can we, therefore, expect the text to evoke for us the world of this woman and encourage us to quit the world of male centrality we have found in Orwell's other writings?

When a male writer focuses on a female character he has, in principle at least, a unique opportunity: to project a female consciousness, to verbally create life from a female point of view. Other narrative stances, however, are also possible. The character can, for example, be seen from a purely external point of view, especially consistent with a third-person narrative, and can even be judged and commented on by a masculine narrative voice. If no realistic narrative can be without gender, writers nonetheless utilize this fact with different degrees of sensitivity. Once the matter has been placed in this perspective, we notice a central characteristic of Orwell's second novel. Far from taking advantage of his own choice of a female protagonist as an occasion to distance himself from his routine masculine perceptions, Orwell resolutely resists this opportunity and confines himself to narrative strategies that must fail to create, for his character, any authentic presence within the novel. Other critics have noted the result; Raymond Williams, for example, mentions that Dorothy Hare has no "*sustained* identity."[2] But Williams does not examine why this is the case in comparison to Orwell's other protagonists.

Although Orwell frequently had difficulty creating characters in his fiction (even in *Nineteen Eighty-Four* it is Winston Smith's situation, not his character, that successfully emerges from the text), the special failure of *A Clergyman's Daughter* is, I believe, the result of Orwell's willful evasion: He must remain on guard not to enter a female world view. When the novel first appeared, critics frequently referred to Dorothy Hare's "breakdown," the incident ostensibly accounting for her loss of memory and subsequent descent into another social class. But Dorothy does not suffer a breakdown; she suffers from a creator, Orwell, who, having invented a female protagonist, does not know how to get her out of the house and into the street where he wants to place her. As it happens, what is most notable about Dorothy, in contrast to Orwell's other protagonists, is the extent to which Orwell molds her into a cipher.[3]

Of the novel's five chapters, three are entirely devoted to Orwell's own adventures in the early thirties. When asked by Harper and Brothers to provide information about the book, to be used for publicity in connection with its American publication, Orwell himself, in a letter to his agent (May 2, 1936; LL), stressed this: "All I can say abt the sources of it is that the passages relating to hop-picking & to nights spent in Trafalgar Square were drawn directly from my own experience, & that the part abt the third-rate girls' school was imaginatively reconstructed from my own experiences in third-rate boys' schools." He does not mention the theme of Dorothy's loss of faith—which, indeed, seems superimposed on the narrative in an effort to make the book something more than a fictional successor to *Down and Out*. If one compares the novel's hop-picking episode with Orwell's autobiographical account of his weeks hop picking in Kent (in CEJL, 1:52–71), it becomes clear that Dorothy is conceived of not as a genuine character at all but as a puppet that the puppet master Orwell can animate with his own consciousness. On the level of language, this is evident in his constant abandonment of the narrative framework and of Dorothy as the center of consciousness, and in his utilization of the pronoun *you*—actually a substitute for *I*, that is, Orwell.[4] The present tense and editorializing comments in the hop-picking and schoolteaching episodes are another way of abandoning the pretense of fiction for the here-and-now of journalism. And the sub-Joycean Trafalgar Square drama, of which Orwell was inordinately proud at the time, is an extreme example of the use Orwell makes of his protagonist as a mere lens devoid of identity.

Not surprisingly, Dorothy Hare is Orwell's least articulate protagonist. While purporting to depict her inner life, especially as it relates to her religious faith, Orwell constantly places her in situations in which attention is diverted from Dorothy to some more colorful and far more vocal character. As we shall see, Orwell deprives Dorothy not only of her memory (and hence a personal history) but also of sexuality, so hard is it for him to allow himself to adopt, even in imagination, a "female" awareness. But failures are as revealing as successes in fiction. As long as we disregard Orwell's resistance to thinking as a female, we cannot understand the particular defects of this novel or its lack of cohesion and depth.

Misogyny and Narrative Voice. Orwell's bias invades the novel at its very beginning. Immediately following the first sentence, "As the alarm clock on the chest of drawers exploded like a horrid little bomb of bell metal, Dorothy . . . awoke . . ." (5), the narrator comments, "The alarm clock continued its nagging, feminine clamour, which would go on for five minutes or thereabouts if you did not stop it." Gender thus intrudes into the narrative as an appeal to not clearly articulated stereotypes about women; this is the level of everyday misogynistic banality, something Orwell does not shun. Of course, he does not pretend to be confining himself strictly to the consciousness of his female protagonist; rather, Orwell utilizes what is conventionally called an "omniscient narrator," a narrative voice that, like the godhead image from which it derives, turns out on inspection to be male. Once the reader removes her automatic assent from such common narrative devices, it becomes clear that what we are witnessing is the author's personal process of association of ideas. In Orwell's case, the words seem to have simply escaped him, as words will; nothing within the narrative requires the clamor of the alarm clock to be seen as nagging and feminine. In fact, there is much (such as the female protagonist who is purportedly the center of consciousness of the novel) that makes such a description especially inappropriate and jarring. However unintentional, the phrase is effective in conveying something to the reader: the narrator's gender allegiance. If the book's title prepares us for a narrative about a woman, the novel's second line reveals that this woman and her story will be judged from a conventionally biased masculinist perspective.

But it is not only in these inadvertent intrusions that Orwell's misogyny is displayed. In the main, his characterizations of women tend toward the ridiculous or the grotesque. He shows far greater indulgence to his male characters: Mr. Warburton may be a philanderer, but he is also a good-natured scoundrel, while the scandal-mongering Mrs. Semprill or the pathetic and distasteful Mrs. Pithers (these female caricatures always carry evocative names in Orwell's texts) have no such redeeming features, and Mrs. Creevy, the owner of the wretched school in which Dorothy teaches for a time, is depicted in far more negative terms than is Dorothy's father, the rector. Although the clergyman is certainly the object of Orwell's satire, he is portrayed without the venom that marks Orwell's depiction of Mrs. Creevy; and this despite the fact that, as Dorothy's father, he is far more culpable in his treatment of his daughter than is Mrs. Creevy in exploiting her employee. Orwell even faults Mrs. Creevy for being petty in her avarice, instead of the "bold, grasping type who will ruin you if he can, but who never looks twice at twopence" (192). This type of belittling criticism of women—denying them even the imagination to have grand defects—also recurs in Orwell's other work.

Orwell's different tone in characterizing males as opposed to females is apparent even in the novel's secondary characters. Victor, for example, is a "restless, intelligent little creature, and only happy when he was quarrelling with somebody or something" (59), whereas Miss Foote is "a tall, rabbit-faced, dithering virgin of thirty-five, who meant well but made a mess of everything and was in a perpetual state of flurry. Mr Warburton used to say that she reminded him of a comet—'a ridiculous blunt-nosed creature rushing round on an eccentric orbit and always a little behind time'" (70). Dorothy's companions in the hop-picking episode also undergo such differential descriptions. While Nobby is depicted in great detail (clearly based on Orwell's pal Ginger [CEJL, 1:52–71]), Flo, "a silly-looking, plump creature" (83) is described in almost exclusively negative terms. She is lazy and, while on the road, blubbers all night "in the most intolerable manner," our judgmental narrator states, "and by the morning she was in a state of semi-collapse. Her silly fat face, washed clean by rain and tears, looked like a bladder of lard, if one can imagine a bladder of lard contorted with self-pity" (97).

Even the postmistress, an insignificant character, is brought to life by a rapid appeal to the reader's presumed innate misogyny: She is "a woman with the face of a dachshund and a bitter contempt for all hop-pickers" (123). Orwell likes to recall characters to the reader's mind by repeating one dominant trait, but he typically takes a slightly more complex view of male characters than of female. Thus the "dog-faced postmistress" (124) can be contrasted with Deafie, one of the hop pickers, "a queer old man and a poor companion after Nobby, but not a bad sort. . . . He was also an exhibitionist, but quite harmless" (127). The original model for Deafie appears in Orwell's piece on hop picking (CEJL, 1:68), where he is again described as a "decent old man, really," despite his tendency to expose himself to women and children.

The masculine narrative stance, ever ready to rely on misogynistic stereotypes, is apparent again in Orwell's treatment of Dorothy's adventures in London. Her landlady there is "a drabby old creature with remarkably thin hair and face so emaciated that it looked like a rouged and powdered skull. Her voice was cracked, shrewish, and nevertheless ineffably dreary" (130–31). Looking for work, Dorothy is "interviewed by women of every conceivable type—large, chubby, bullying women, thin, acid, catty women, alert frigid women in gold *pince-nez*, vague rambling women who looked as though they practised vegetarianism or attended spiritualist séances" (134). As they reject her, mystified by her good accent, they turn "the prying, feminine glance from her face to her damaged hands, and from those to the darns in her skirt" (135). Later, Dorothy and two other women are arrested for begging "off a nasty old lady with a face like a horse, who had promptly walked up to the nearest policeman and given them in charge" (166). Sometimes the contrast between Orwell's depiction of males and females is evident in a brief sentence: "he was an alert-looking greengrocer with a dried-up, shrewish wife" (204). In fact, the characteristic Orwellian approach to description in this novel is disdainful judgments about women and more subtle and detached descriptions of men. When a male character is satirized, as in the case of Dorothy's cousin, Sir Thomas Hare, the portrait is drawn with humor rather than loathing, even when Orwell relies, as he often does, on animal analogies: "Sir Thomas Hare was a widower, a good-hearted, chuckle-headed man of about sixty-five, with an obtuse rosy face and curling moustaches" (169), which give him the appearance of "a well-meaning but exceptionally brainless prawn" (170).

Mr. Warburton, too, is used by Orwell to inject disdain for women into the novel. Warburton refers to the "hags" who have been gossiping about Dorothy (238) and asks her to marry him because "I'm sick of these disgusting women I've spent my life with, if you'll forgive my mentioning them, and I'm rather anxious to settle down" (247). Conveying an image of feminine psychology that seems derived primarily from W. H. Auden's poem about Miss Gee, a spinster whose childlessness resulted in cancer, he announces that "women who don't marry wither up—they wither up like aspidistras in back-parlour windows" (249). He paints a bleak picture of Dorothy's future, possibly as a companion to "some diseased hag who will occupy herself in thinking of ways to humiliate you" (249). In Orwell's world view, it is not women's limited options that create the problems but the sheer nastiness of other women; this is the net impact on his readers of all his negative portrayals of women. Nowhere in Orwell's writings is friendship between women depicted. Gissing's *Odd Women* (a novel that Orwell clearly drew on—it is mentioned in passing in *A Clergyman's Daughter*) features a number of such friendships, but for Gissing's complex network of relationships among women Orwell substitutes an isolated female protagonist suffering from the inherent beastliness of other women.

If Orwell borrowed from Gissing some awareness (only touched on) of women's lack of material options, often resulting in poverty and loneliness, he took far more from D. H. Lawrence's story "Daughters of the Vicar," and a comparison of these two works will allow us to see clearly the particular limitations of Orwell's approach. Orwell's characterization of Dorothy Hare is meager compared to Lawrence's evocation, in far fewer pages, of the vicar's wife and daughters. Though Lawrence is, as always, preoccupied with masculine power, both moral and sexual (embodied in two separate male characters in his story), he shows both sympathy and depth in his representation of women. If he describes a narrow and bitter woman, he also, in only a few lines, suggests the reasons for this. Instead of blanket condemnation, he appeals to context, having a keen sense of people in the process of "becoming." [5] Even the minor characters in Lawrence's story receive sympathetic attention. Unable to quicken our imagination, Orwell feeds us judgments—his own—expressed in the form of labels and pejorative tags, and his novel thus tells us more about his attitudes than about his characters. Not satisfied with having the narrative itself reveal his disdain for women, Orwell must attribute this sentiment even to his female protagonist, as he will later do to Julia in *Nineteen Eighty-Four*. It should not be thought that by making Dorothy reject sexual relations with men, Orwell is suggesting that she rejects male domination. She does not, nor does she dislike men: "On the contrary, she liked them better than women. Part of Mr Warburton's hold over her," the narrator explains, "was in the fact that he was a man and had the careless good humour and the intellectual largeness that women so seldom have" (75). Given such a view of women, it is not surprising that Orwell experiences great difficulty evoking a woman's consciousness, which in turn makes it hard for him to move her through his own experiences. This problem he simplified for himself by depriving Dorothy of three vital human characteristics: memory, consciousness, and sexuality.

Memory, Consciousness, Sexuality. Late in the novel, after Dorothy has regained her memory and resumed her usual life, Orwell causes her to reflect that all that had happened to her had "no real importance": "The truism that all real happenings are in the mind struck her more forcibly than ever before" (240). "It is the things that happen in your heart that matter," she muses (258). Thus, her loss of religious faith alone counts; and even this is quickly set aside as she finds that "doing what is customary, useful and acceptable" blurs the distinction between having faith and not having faith (261). This theme, that physical hardship does not really matter, is reiterated in *Keep the Aspidistra Flying*. Only in *Nineteen Eighty-Four*, when Winston and Julia painfully discover that reality is *not* inside the head, that what happens to the body has profound effects on an individual—only then is this theme laid to rest. However, if Dorothy Hare's adventures do not matter, why has Orwell spent 150 pages on them? Orwell himself recognized that his novel is episodic and disjointed.[6] Dorothy cannot turn her adventures into literature—she is not a writer—so Orwell has them simply fall away from her. This point is underscored at the novel's end by Dorothy's denial of the validity of her experiences. In a remarkable repetition of Orwell's judgment of the sole woman tramp depicted in *Down and Out*, Dorothy reveals that she has learned nothing whatsoever from what had happened to her. Through both her timely amnesia early in the novel and her final denial of the significance of her experiences, Orwell turns Dorothy into the mere lens he needs to make use of his adventures as they impressed him, without ever asking himself how such events would affect a woman like Dorothy.

In *Nineteen Eighty-Four* Orwell protests against the distortion and suppression of memory, but he readily resorted to this device when it was necessary to his fictional purposes in *A Clergyman's Daughter*. Apparently he could think of no other way of removing this sheltered woman from her environment of genteel poverty. Actually, the problem of Dorothy's lack of authentic consciousness runs through the novel, even before, and again after, her amnesia. Unlike Orwell's male protagonists, who are capable of endless reflection on their condition, Dorothy's characteristic reaction is to assail herself with uplifting exhortations: "Come on, Dorothy, up you get! No snoozing, please!" (5), and, at the novel's close, "Come on, Dorothy! No slacking, please!" (261).

It seems to me that the loss-of-memory device does more than merely place Dorothy where Orwell wants her to be. It is also a loss of perspective from which to reflect on one's experiences. In reporting on his own adventures, Orwell clearly brought a fully formed self to his episodes down and out. And in *A Clergyman's Daughter* he wants to continue to bring this self to bear on Dorothy's adventures in that same world. But he can do so only by first emptying her, depriving her of any personal history, in order then to filter his own views, memories, perspectives through her. Compare Dorothy with the protagonist of *Keep the Aspidistra Flying*, Gordon Comstock, who brings a fully elaborated ideology to his position as a rebel; or with George Bowling, whose story in *Coming Up for Air* is a quest for his past; or with Winston Smith in *Nineteen Eighty-Four,* functioning in a society in which historical memory undergoes constant violation. Even Winston brings personal consciousness to his experiences, to an extent that far exceeds Dorothy's throughout the novel of which she is the heroine.

Yet after Dorothy's memory has returned Orwell still allows her to respond only in a semiconscious mode. Her rejection of Mr. Warburton's proposal of marriage is the result not of reflection but of her aversion to sex. Incapable of acting as a free individual, she has gone from her sheltered and servile life in the rectory, through hardship and hunger, to the still servile but far less sheltered world of Mrs. Creevy's school, and finally back to the rectory. But Dorothy cannot compare her different experiences or reflect upon them. Each incident in her wretched life is presented as a self-contained episode. And this is precisely the cause of the novel's failure; its whole structure is an artifice on which to hang these experiences. Even Dorothy's supposed loss of faith is a minor, because insufficiently explored, theme. The book's real focus is on these adventures as the continuation of Orwell's life as a social explorer. Orwell's personal identity unites these episodes, not Dorothy's.

Dorothy is even less able than Orwell's other passive (usually passive-aggressive) protagonists to act, or even to think, rebelliously. One wonders whether Orwell could have imagined a male character so totally passive, such a perfect victim, as Dorothy. The amnesia—the loss of identity, of her past—is generally overlooked when critics see Dorothy as yet another of the fictional protagonists in Orwell's novels of the thirties who try unsuccessfully to escape from societal constraints. It is no accident that this most passive, least conscious, of Orwell's heroes is also his only female protagonist. Living in a perpetual present, Dorothy is truly a person without a memory. Her acquaintances, her experiences down and out, simply pass from her with no apparent aftereffects except for the loss of faith that is proclaimed but then rapidly found to have made little difference. Orwell merely restores her to her original setting, completing the circle by placing her once again among the costumes and the gluepot.

But Dorothy Hare is not the only one of Orwell's characters, though she is the only one of his protagonists, to be deprived of a critical consciousness. It is characteristically difficult for Orwell to attribute a full consciousness like his own to people he assigns to the category of "other" in his scheme of things. These "others" occur in three different forms in Orwell's writings, according to race, class, and sex. We have seen (chapter 2) in "Shooting an Elephant" how Orwell attributes genuine awareness only to that narrative's *I*, the white British imperialist, thus undermining his own critique of imperialism. His other writings share this characteristic. In his 1939 essay "Marrakech," Orwell asserts that the black soldiers are unaware of their own potential power. Every white man, he writes, shares one thought when he sees a black army march past: "How much longer can we go on kidding these people? How long before they turn their guns in the other direction?" But this thought, Orwell states, "was a kind of secret which we all knew and were too clever to tell; only the Negroes didn't know it" (CEJL, 1:393). Failing to think deeply about inferiorization and its outward results, or about the types of mechanisms for coping with it that an individual might develop, Orwell settles for an easy belief in the whites' deeper awareness. In *Nineteen Eighty-Four* Orwell shows how a white man attempts to think independently about a complex totalitarian machine; but he could not conceive of a black man thinking independently of his white "superiors" and thus makes no distinction between what he superficially observes and what lies behind it.

Similar confidence in (undefined) white male superiority occurs in a wartime diary Orwell kept from 1940 to 1942. Writing in April 1942, Orwell wonders how Indians would be treated if the Russians took over India. As "natives," he concludes, adding: "It's very hard not to, seeing that in practice the majority of Indians *are* inferior to Europeans and one can't help feeling this and, after a little while, acting accordingly" (CEJL, 2:419; his emphasis).[7] In his early sketch on hop picking, another such generalization occurs (omitted when this material was incorporated into *A Clergyman's Daughter*). Describing the poor wages hop pickers earn, which he sees as inevitable until there is a pickers' union, Orwell comments: "It is not much use to try and form a union, though, for about half the pickers are women and gypsies, and are too stupid to see the advantages of it" (CEJL, 1:63). As in *Burmese Days*, here too we see race and sex working together in such a way that only white males are exempted from the reductive generalization.

A variation on this theme occurs in several of Orwell's most famous texts containing epiphanies, moments of illumination in which the humanity of people he has hitherto viewed in terms of dehumanizing generalizations suddenly breaks through, and Orwell's perception is jarred as he understands, with a shock, that these are people like himself. These texts are usually appreciated for their sensitive and humane awareness, but what is normally overlooked is that this awareness is always preceded by the assumption of the narrator's superior perception. In the early sketch entitled "A Hanging" (1931), Orwell describes how his idea of what it means to kill a man is altered by the Hindu prisoner's gesture of stepping aside to avoid a puddle on the way to the gallows. What the text reveals, however, is that the prisoner at first looks to Orwell like a mere insignificant object. Into this scene, well defined in terms of the prisoner's already marginal existence, breaks the unexpected gesture, making Orwell (or the Orwellian narrative persona) realize that the prisoner is alive, just as he is (CEJL, 1:44–48). This chronicle is generally interpreted along the lines Orwell lays down, as the revelation of the barbarity of execution, but its primary meaning, I believe, is another. An inferiorized human being has for an instant become a genuine person in the eyes of one of the masters. That this master is the proper model of human life and authentic awareness goes without saying.

A similar situation is described in *The Road to Wigan Pier*. On a cold March day, as his train carries him out of town, Orwell catches a glimpse of a young woman kneeling on the ground behind a house, poking a stick up a blocked waste pipe. Orwell notes her exhausted face, testimony of miscarriages and drudgery,

and it wore, for the second in which I saw it, the most desolate hopeless expression I have ever seen. It struck me then that *we* are mistaken when we say that "It isn't the same for them as it would be for us," and that people bred in the slums can imagine nothing but slums. For what I saw in her face was not the ignorant suffering of an animal. She knew well enough what was happening to her—understood *as well as I did* how dreadful a destiny it was to be kneeling there in the bitter cold, on the slimy stones of a slum backyard, poking a stick up a foul drain-pipe. [*Wigan Pier*, 16–17; emphasis added]

The usual Orwellian ambiguity is present in this passage—the desire to convert the reader (assumed to be a person who thinks as

Orwell does) to a more humane perception, but at the same time the egocentric assumptions: the discovery that the young woman has awareness, unlike a suffering animal; the implication that Orwell and his class are the measure of true sensitivity to poverty; the praise ultimately bestowed on this woman for having a consciousness like his own.

This tendency to see the "other" as devoid of real consciousness (always modeled on his own) is present in Orwell's work over many years. It does not belong merely to one phase of his life—say, his first experiences with individuals of a different class or race. Despite their implications, these epiphanies show at least an effort on Orwell's part to communicate a breakthrough in routine judgments and to incite a similar discovery in his readers (though never by actually challenging the ideological functions of their comfortable illusions). The scene with the young woman and the drainpipe is unusual for Orwell, as it is one of the very few moments in all his writings in which *his* level of awareness is attributed to a woman. In *A Clergyman's Daughter* no such effort is made.

If Dorothy's amnesia provides Orwell with one way of evading a confrontation with a female character different from himself, there remains another problem. Orwell assumes the heterosexuality of all his characters (except, of course, of those males caricatured for their homosexuality or effeminacy—one of these, the "epicene youth" named Ralph, pronounced Walph, appears in *A Clergyman's Daughter*). Dorothy may have no memory and little consciousness for most of the novel, but she is still a woman. As a heterosexual woman rapidly turning into an old maid, she would have required rather more attention to her inner life and desires than Orwell was prepared to bestow. Some imaginative intimacy with the character would have been necessary (think of Flaubert saying "Madame Bovary, c'est moi!"). How does Orwell handle this problem? In a manner remarkably similar to his handling of Dorothy's personal memory: by wiping out this aspect of her life.

He accomplishes this by assigning the label "abnormal" to Dorothy and informing us that she had, ever since childhood, a "horror of *all that*" (76; his emphasis), a profound aversion to any kind of sexual contact with men. This is explained by means of a weak allusion to certain "dreadful scenes between her father and her mother" (77), witnessed when Dorothy was nine. Saved once again from having to think as a female, Orwell projects his homophobia onto Dorothy, but now with the convenient label—because she is a woman—of "disability" and "abnormality." Orwell writes: "Like all abnormal people, she was not fully aware that she was abnormal." But he then overdetermines his argument by adding: "It is, moreover, a thing too common nowadays, among educated women, to occasion any kind of surprise" (77). Thus Dorothy's horror of sexual intimacy, and what this might have to do with her sense of her own self and her life, becomes simply another example of the horrors of modern life. Orwell's own thoughts about chastity become clear in his characterization of Mrs. Creevy, who, the narrative informs us (from a perspective that could not possibly be Dorothy's), spends her spare time

restitching some bloomers of harsh white linen of which she had pairs beyond number. They were the most chilly-looking garments that one could possibly imagine; they seemed to carry upon them, as no nun's coif or anchorite's hair shirt could ever have done, the impress of a frozen and awful chastity. The sight of them set you wondering about the late Mr Creevy, even to the point of wondering whether he had ever existed. [192]

If Dorothy Hare is never seen acting as anything other than a passive female (when, that is, she is not merely a conduit for Orwell in recounting his own adventures), her options are nonetheless determined by her status as a woman. She can return to her father, in which case the scenario outlined by Mr. Warburton, of her future spinsterhood, is likely to take place. Or she can transfer from her father's house to Mr. Warburton's domain by marrying him and thus acquire both social status of a sort and greater material comfort. These are her only choices, it appears, and, significantly, they are spelled out for her by Mr Warburton, who is granted the superior insight that Dorothy lacks. Her own life with the hop pickers, or on the streets of London, or even at her wretched job as a schoolteacher, freed her from this status as the ward of a father or husband. But because Orwell deprives her of any critical consciousness, the issue of her autonomy is never articulated, nor does she turn her attention to this particular dimension of her experience as she contemplates returning to her father's house. Orwell limits her so severely that she cannot even take a critical look at the restrictions imposed on her, cannot begin to exercise her human freedom. Thus her "decision" to stay with her father is presented as the result of her uncontrollable revulsion at the thought of sexual contact with Mr. Warburton; no alternative is open to her. And, once home again, she is unable to compare her current situation with her former life. Her return is not even motivated by a sense of obligation to her father—that too is made clear—but is born out of a passivity that, given her rejection of marriage, makes it impossible for her to contemplate other options.

The last image we have of Dorothy is of the clergyman's daughter faithfully returned to her task of making paper armor for a church pageant. Who will wear this armor? Presumably little boys imitating grown men of times past. So the novel ends on a note that strikes me (if not Orwell's implied ideal readers) as ironic. Dorothy is busily at work helping to reproduce in children the very source of her oppression, the sex-role polarization that makes women into mere servants to men. Used by her father within the world of the novel, Dorothy is used also by her creator, Orwell, who cannot grant her even the limited authenticity of his other protagonists. In raising the issue of women's service to men at the cost of their own personalities and lives, Orwell would seem to be indirectly pointing an accusing finger at himself. But by emphasizing Dorothy's passive return to her old habits, and her apparent absorption in them, this theme is deflected at the novel's end, and the inevitability of Dorothy's fate as a clergyman's daughter is affirmed. Thus does the text endeavor to contain the tensions produced by its own contradictions.

KEEP THE ASPIDISTRA FLYING

What happens to Dorothy Hare once she ventures beyond the rectory is, as we have seen, largely accidental. By contrast, what happens to Gordon Comstock, protagonist of *Keep the Aspidistra Flying*, is full of purpose. These two opposing life stories reflect Orwell's consistently gender-typed approach to male and female existence. They are matched by other details in the novels. Gordon never thinks about anyone except himself; he talks incessantly, imposing his egocentric and self-pitying views on others; he manipulates virtually every conversation, and the reader learns early in the novel to recognize his characteristic whine (so often resembling Orwell's own letters from this phase of his life and again raising the complex question of Orwell's attitude toward his unattractive protagonists).[8] Although *Aspidistra* relies on the same "omniscient" narrative technique as *A Clergyman's Daughter*, Gordon is overwhelmingly the center of consciousness of the novel, and no other character comes close to impinging on his space in the novel. While once again using his protagonist as a conduit for his own recent experiences (working in a bookshop; getting arrested; living on the periphery of the fashionable literary world), Orwell can integrate these experiences into his male protagonist's life in a way he was not able to do with Dorothy Hare's adventures. At the end of *Aspidistra,* Gordon returns to his "good" job at the advertising agency, marries (as Orwell was to do shortly thereafter), and eagerly anticipates the birth of his child; that is, he embraces, however ambiguously, the social responsibilities and privileges implicit in being a dominant male. In many respects, then, Dorothy and Gordon stand diametrically opposed to one another, acting out the consequences of their respective gender roles.

Functional Misogyny. Gordon Comstock is a small, frail, moth-eaten thirty-year-old poet who has declared war on the money god. He has quit his job in an advertising agency and, over a two-year period, sunk into the grim depths of poverty—the descent that so fascinated Orwell. The novel, though in the third person, is one long diatribe against the overwhelming power of the money world whose corrupting tentacles reach into all areas of life.

Aspidistra is a far better book than *A Clergyman's Daughter*. It is much livelier, and if Gordon Comstock is neurotic and pathetic in his self-pitying obsession with money, at least he is also comical and a curiosity. In addition, in this novel Orwell on occasion expresses a sympathetic attitude toward women, especially in relation to Gordon's sister, Julia. And, most important, Gordon's girl friend, Rosemary, Orwell's only really positive female character (in all his books), is portrayed in several respects as an admirable and independent person. In the presence of these unusual qualities, it is fascinating to see how Orwell nonetheless introduces gender hierarchy and stereotypes into the text and does so in a way that constantly reverses his basic characterizations.

Even a superficial reading of the novel reveals that repeated pejorative characterizations of women occur in *Aspidistra*, as they do in *A Clergyman's Daughter*. Because Gordon Comstock is so much the center of the book, however, and because he is depicted as a thoroughgoing misanthrope, such comments, capable of being taken as part of the characterization rather than as authorial intrusions, are not as jarring in this novel. Though the usual stereotypes of feminists and virgins appear, more important in this book than passing misogynistic comments is Orwell's technique of derailing the reader by carefully positioned remarks about women. Thus even petty misogyny can be set to work within a text, establishing alliances between writer and (presumably male) reader and performing redemptive or cleansing operations on otherwise questionable male characters. In this way it functions as a technique for containing the contradictions within the text.

An interesting example of this technique occurs in a scene between Gordon and Rosemary. We know very little about Rosemary (though her "small" size is commented on dozens of times); she is not important enough for us to be provided with insight into her ambitions and desires or her own background; references to her family occur only when she contemplates their reaction to her pregnancy. It is this pregnancy that will provide Gordon with the pretext for returning to the money world at the novel's end. While resisting his war on society, Rosemary is shown as consistently generous and caring in her response to Gordon, preoccupied with his decay and sympathetic to his desire to be a poet, but also healthily impatient with his diatribes. Gordon has only one other friend in the novel—the wealthy Ravelston (modeled on Orwell's friend Richard Rees), publisher of the "middle- to high-brow" socialist monthly *Antichrist*. After losing his carefully sought "bad" position in the bookshop as a result of a drunken spree, Gordon stays with Ravelston for some time, sponging off his friend and hating himself for this but making little effort to find a new job. Rosemary visits Gordon at Ravelston's apartment, at a moment in the narrative when Gordon's self-pity has begun to weary the reader. Orwell has stressed Gordon's *nostalgie de la boue*, the desire to hit bottom, and, with his characteristic ambivalence toward this creature so like himself (but without his ability to work hard at his writing), has begun to make Gordon sound downright silly. The narrative itself, however, makes no criticism of Gordon; indeed, we see things from his point of view. He knows he is in some sense loathsome, but at the same time he believes that he is fighting for a principle. By the time Rosemary appears, Gordon is on the verge of losing the reader's sympathy. How does Orwell deal with this situation?

First of all, through Gordon's eyes we see that his encounter with Rosemary is once again the occasion for a struggle between them. It is she who must make the first move toward him. Her interest in and concern for him are thus a sign of his victory at having made her come to him but also of his deep alienation. He is, above all, bored, as he constantly repeats. Rosemary then verbalizes what the reader has known all along: that Gordon can in fact get work by returning to the New Albion, the ad agency at which he used to work, where his talent for copywriting had been noted. The reader of course remembers this detail, which has the effect of distancing us from Gordon as he carries on about his inevitable demise. We know, after all, that he is not genuinely poor but is embracing this condition voluntarily and exulting in his "failure." Rosemary expresses this awareness, so Gordon must do battle with this truth. Orwell has perhaps pressed his point too far, and there is danger at this stage that the reader will simply lose patience with both Gordon and the novel.

Just when the reader may be tempted to dismiss Gordon and his melodrama altogether, an interesting diversionary tactic enters as the "omniscient" narrator makes judgments about Rosemary that place her before the reader not as an individual but as a typical example of her sex. The ground of the discussion suddenly shifts, and instead of an argument to be worked out between the two protagonists, we find the narrator intervening to protect Gordon's position by individualizing it, while trivializing Rosemary's by referring to her reactions as those "any woman" would have (211). She is helpless in the face of Gordon's refusal to return to the agency: "After all, it was no use. There was this money-business standing in the way—these meaningless scruples which she had never understood but which she had accepted merely because they were his. She felt all the impotence, the resentment of a woman who sees an abstract idea triumphing over common sense" (212). By this apparently slight shift of focus, Gordon is let off the hook, for the reader would not want to be consigned, with Rosemary, to uncomprehending and benighted womanhood, incapable of appreciating abstract principle or lofty scruple.

As their discussion continues and Rosemary makes a perfectly logical point, the narrative informs us that she was "changing her ground with feminine swiftness" (213). In fact, she has simply drawn an inference. Gordon has stated that earlier he was out looking for a job, and she comments that he had not even shaved that day, a relevant point. But the narrator has usurped our independent judgment and replaced it with his own, adding to it another generalization about the female sex. Gordon's very weak position has (apparently) been redeemed by being contrasted with the even less tenable attitudes of the female sex. Orwell's positioning of these stereotyped comments serves an important function in this scene; they are neither accidental nor incidental but an essential element in his strategy which, though ambivalent toward his character, requires that character to retain at least a minimum of the reader's credence and sympathy. This is achieved by diminishing Rosemary in the reader's eyes, so that their disagreement begins to take on the appearance of a lone individual's struggle for principle against the uncomprehending pettiness of females-in-general.

This male/female contrast is reinforced in the novel by the other couple: Ravelston and his girl friend, "that bitch Hermione Slater," as Gordon refers to her. Hermione is repeatedly drawn as a superficial, rich, and spoiled young woman who interferes with Ravelston's socialistic (or merely charitable) impulses: woman as temptation, luring a good man from the path of social justice, just as Rosemary tries to lead Gordon away from his commitment to principles. The narrative at one point describes Hermione as she leans against Ravelston: "The woman-scent breathed out of her, a powerful wordless propaganda against all altruism and all justice" (110). This is in keeping with a major theme of the novel, articulated by Gordon as follows: "it's the women who really believe in the money-code. The men obey it; they have to, but they don't believe in it. It's the women who keep it going. The women and their Putney villas and their fur coats and their babies and their aspidistras" (125). Rosemary reminds Gordon that women did not invent money, and he replies:

It doesn't matter who invented it, the point is that it's women who worship it. A woman's got a sort of mystical feeling towards money. Good
and evil in a woman's mind mean simply money and no money. Look at
you and me. You won't sleep with me, simply and solely because I've got
no money. Yes, that *is* the reason. . . . It's not because you're mercenary.
You don't want me to *pay* you for sleeping with me. It's not so crude as
that. But you've got that deep-down mystical feeling that somehow a man
without money isn't worthy of you. He's a weakling, a sort of half-man—
and that's how you feel. Hercules, god of strength and god of money—
you'll find that in Lemprière. It's women who keep all mythologies going.
Women! [126; Orwell's emphasis] [9]

As ridiculous as Gordon's comments sound in their evasion of
any serious consideration of women, men, and money, they are
given some plausibility by the narrative focus, which allows Gordon to speak while giving Rosemary no serious argument in return. She simply laughs at him in a conciliatory and good-natured
way. Orwell's own position in all this is ambiguous. He seems to
accept Rosemary's judgment that Gordon's ranting is "palpable
nonsense" and therefore unworthy of reply; but, if this is so, why
expound this nonsense at such great length? And why show Rosemary eventually capitulating to this blackmail? Orwell further
disarms any serious feminist critique by the editorial comment:
"Gordon's diatribes against women were in reality a kind of perverse joke; indeed, the whole sex-war is at bottom only a joke. For
some reason it is fun to pose as a feminist or an anti-feminist according to your sex" (126).

Yet the narrative reveals that beneath the "joke" of the sex
war and beneath the purported seriousness of Gordon's war on
money, lies the old equation: Male control of money equals male
control of women, an equation that Gordon has turned on its
head and Orwell never attempts to set right.[10]

Money and Male Power. To be moneyless is to lack (masculine) vitality, to have nothing to "spend." Gordon's rebellion
against the money god is, in this sense, a rebellion against the
demands of a male gender identity. Eager as he is, however, to descend into the soft belly of poverty and failure, where no effort
need be made, Gordon does not want to relinquish his masculine
prerogatives. Though Gordon himself makes the money/vitality
connection, his rejection of the demand that he "be a [conven-

tional] man" does not extend beyond the apparent rejection of money.

Chapter 6, in the center of the novel, is a perfect expression of Gordon's androcentric vision. It begins with Gordon's musings:

This woman business! What a bore it is! What a pity we can't cut it right out, or at least be like the animals—minutes of ferocious lust and months of icy chastity. Take a cock pheasant, for example. He jumps up on the hens' backs without so much as a with your leave or by your leave. And no sooner is it over than the whole subject is out of his mind. He hardly even notices his hens any longer; he ignores them, or simply pecks them if they come too near his food. He is not called upon to support his offspring, either. Lucky pheasant! How different from the lord of creation, always on the hop between his memory and his conscience! [113]

He continues to reflect about women, and as his thoughts wander from Rosemary to "women in general" (113) and back to Rosemary again, it is clear that she is simply the particular embodiment of the category "woman" with whom he is involved. He desires "a woman's body," not an individual, and his rebellion seems to be fueled in large part by anger that among human beings sexual behavior has social consequences. He lives in a society in which men are expected to take some responsibility, if only financial, for their offspring.

Although Gordon fantasizes about a "free" male sexuality, family structure within the novel is paradoxically presented as a purely masculine affair. In *Aspidistra*, as in *A Clergyman's Daughter*, "family" means male lineage only. Chapter 3, devoted to the history of the Comstock family and their loss of "vitality" (signaled by the lack of offspring among any of the remaining relatives),[11] is in fact a history of the male line. In keeping with this bias, we are given almost no information about Gordon's mother, or even his paternal grandmother—though we are told that Gran'pa Comstock was "a tough old scoundrel" who "plundered the proletariat" and "begot twelve children" (43). The novel's final line, as Gordon presses his head against Rosemary's pregnant belly, affirms this constricted and self-serving masculinist view of life: "Well, once again things were happening in the Comstock family" (268). Thus what men do, say, decide, fear, and want are made to appear as the forces that move and shake the world. At the same time, the novel's subtext presents the female corollary to this view: A woman's intervention in a man's life comes through her submission. When Rosemary tries to reason or argue with Gordon, she gets nowhere; but when she "gives in," she gets what the novel assumes she must want: a baby and a husband with a "decent" job.

Gordon asserts that money alone provides a man with "a hold" over a woman (114), a view that, in its odd way, is accurate: It is money that allows a man "to pick and choose" (115), but Gordon, typically, considers the problem strictly from a man's point of view. His rebellion is only against the infringement of his rights, the assault on his ego, of having to have money in order to exercise his masculine prerogatives. Interestingly, early in the chapter Gordon expresses his hatred for a particular pub, with its sights, sounds, and smells "all so blatantly and offensively male" (113). Gordon does not want the all-male society of the pub, or its one "barmaid with her lewd smile which seemed to promise everything and promised nothing" (113). The more basic structure that is "offensively male" and that so narrows the range of this novel —the virtual exclusion of women from direct access to money—is never looked at in terms of the gender hierarchy. Still less, of course, is there in the novel a critique of capitalism that would explain both Gordon's fury at the money world and women's position within that world.

With money or without, Gordon continues to assert his status as a male at the center of reality: It is his desires, his wishes, his needs that count, and Rosemary must bend to them. The language of their sexual encounters, always presented from his point of view, makes this explicit: He "wanted to *have had* her" (151; Orwell's emphasis) and urges her to "be nice" to him, which he defines as "Let me do what I want with you" (153).[12] Orwell was especially inept at handling love scenes, and Gordon's patronizing words to Rosemary in their scene in the country are embarrassing: " 'Take your clothes off, there's a dear,' he whispered" (153). But Gordon's sexual desire is constantly sabotaged by the recollection that he only has eightpence in his pocket. This particular episode is brought to a sudden halt when Rosemary realizes Gordon has not brought any contraceptives. To Gordon, mention of such a detail turns their love scene into something "squalid and ugly," and he self-righteously proclaims: "You don't think I go in for that kind of thing, do you" (155), after which he launches once again into his antimoney diatribe, for in his view it is only his lack of money that makes Rosemary worry about pregnancy. This attitude is in keeping with Gordon's admiration for the "lower classes," who are not afraid to live, as expressed earlier in the novel: "How right the lower classes are! Hats off to the factory lad who with fourpence in the world puts his girl in the family way! At least he's got blood and not money in his veins" (51).[13]

But Gordon's struggle with Rosemary is not primarily about sexual domination; it is her moral submission to him that he demands and finally gains when, at his lowest point, she goes to his room and out of "pure magnanimity" (240) gives herself to him (the words are appropriate for this particular scene), without pleasure, without passion even on his part. The encounter signifies her capitulation to his vision of the world: He does not have to marry her; she will not worry about birth control. Rosemary acts the part of a sacrificial lamb, and "love," in a woman, presumably explains this sort of "sacrifice." On a man's part, however, at least judging by Orwell's characters, "love" implies nothing of the kind, indeed, hardly anything that could even remotely be considered as a giving of oneself, let alone a sacrifice.

Rosemary's consequent pregnancy—the result of this one joyless sexual encounter—is what leads to the novel's resolution, for Gordon can now be saved from himself: He will behave in the traditionally honorable way, marry Rosemary, and return to the money world via the promised "good" job at the ad agency. Orwell makes it explicit that Gordon was looking for a way out of his tedious rebellion, and the pregnancy/marriage scenario (only a slight variation on what E. M. Forster refers to as "the idiotic use of marriage as a finale")[14] provides the occasion for Gordon's return. "After all he did not lack vitality, and that moneyless existence to which he had condemned himself had thrust him ruthlessly out of the stream of life" (258); but a different kind of thrusting has now returned him to it. Perhaps because Gordon resolutely declares he will now "sell his soul" (259) by going back to advertising,[15] critics have seen the novel's end as a defeat for Gordon, engineered by Rosemary.[16] Not only does the sex war indeed exist within the novel; it also exists outside of it and helps us to understand such a response, which reveals critics identifying themselves with Gordon's battle against money (and the demand that men provide economically for women) and ready to lay the blame on women for this state of affairs.

What needs to be noted, however, is that Gordon is the prime mover of virtually everything that happens in the novel, in precise contrast to Dorothy Hare, ever incapable of acting on her own behalf. His passive-aggressive behavior is still a carefully chosen form of behavior. Rosemary may choose to "give herself" to Gordon, to allow him this moral victory in a last effort to save him (instead of herself), but she lets her man make all the decisions, including whether she should have an abortion, or marry, or return home pregnant and unmarried, or pregnant, married, and abandoned by her husband. She abdicates any and all her own rights for the sake of his demand for absolute freedom. His dignity, his needs, are the constant yardstick against which all their interactions are measured.

Gordon's sudden shift from rejecting to embracing masculine "responsibility" is unmatched by any shift in his view of Rosemary. While "his baby" accounts for his newfound "decency," nowhere is there evident a comparable concern for Rosemary in her own right; her significance in his life has increased merely because she is the container of this new life that he has created. He will change roles, from that of infant making demands of an ideal mother to that of husband making demands of an ideal wife/mother. At the novel's end, then, the sex-role reversal that has prevailed—with Gordon dropping out and into passivity and Rosemary earning her own income and living alone —is finally "righted," as Gordon assumes the responsibility and pressures that accompany male supremacy.

There is a striking continuity between *Aspidistra* and Orwell's early short story "The Slack-bob" (see chapter 1), though the former was written when Orwell was about thirty-two years old and the latter when he was an adolescent. Both texts protest against the control supposedly wielded by females; both respond with anger and shame to the demands that a man measure up; and both link these attitudes to disdain for women. In a sketch in his last notebook, Orwell elaborates on the subject of women's presumed attitudes toward men. He evokes the impressions a young boy gathers from overheard conversations between his female relatives and "their feminist friends" that implied that "women *did not like men*" (Orwell's emphasis) and got no plea-sure from sexual intercourse.[17] However uncertain Orwell may have felt as a child about the desirability of being a male (if this passage is autobiographical), Orwell's work as an adult shows him fully integrated into his society's gender hierarchy. It is facile to conclude that his misogyny may be linked to an essential feeling of inferiority and its resultant pain and anger, but this psycholo-gizing does not help us to see precisely how that misogyny is tied to a masculine gender identity. Orwell's writings reveal the rescue operation constantly performed by misogyny in a sexually polar-ized society—an operation solely benefiting men. Although the desperate quality in both Gordon Comstock's protest against the demands of manhood and his desire for a relationship not medi-ated by money suggests a potential on Orwell's part to see further into the problem, this potential is deflected by the habit of blam-ing women instead of analyzing their position within either an individual household or an entire society. The same tendency to blame is at work in Orwell's bitter recollection of his life as a schoolboy at St. Cyprian's, "Such, Such Were the Joys," an essay never published in his lifetime, in which Mrs. Wilkes (called "Bingo" in the essay) emerges as the very model of a castrating woman terrorizing little boys.[18]

In *Aspidistra* there is no such evil mother figure; there are, however, the various shopgirls, cashiers, and servants onto whom Gordon projects his feelings of inferiority and hence his hatred.[19] Nowhere in the novel is there any consideration of the respective positions of these women in comparison with Gordon himself. For all his self-criticism, Gordon never begins to acknowledge his total egocentricity; indeed, self-criticism and even self-hatred become redeeming features, the marks of genuine sensibility and charac-ter! Gordon, for example, knows it is hateful to borrow money from his sister, "poor Julia," a born spinster; he realizes that her interests have all her life been sacrificed to his. But he does not reflect on what the narrative reveals: that his worst job, inten-tionally taken at his nadir, still brings him a salary equal to Julia's after her six years of constant labor in a teashop. He voluntarily descends; she struggles to ascend, without the option of a "good" job from which she can walk away for principle's sake. But Orwell has nothing to say about this theme. In addition, women's lack of options in a man's world does not come clearly into focus because

Orwell introduces personal elements that again derail the reader. Thus we are given an explanation for the mere ten-shilling raise that Julia receives after six years: "The horrible ladylike lady who kept the teashop was a semi-friend as well as an employer, and thus could sweat and bully Julia to the tune of 'dearest' and 'darling' " (55). This friend, in other words, is not so different from Mrs. Creevy in *A Clergyman's Daughter.* Thus other women can be blamed for the miseries of working women's lives.

Why does Gordon consider it humiliating to borrow money from his rich friend Ravelston, to let Rosemary pay her own way, but not to take money from his sister who is far worse off than he is? The maintenance of male prestige and power is at stake here, necessarily an element in Gordon's relationships with Ravelston and with Rosemary. But power does not enter into his relationship with Julia, his sister—or, rather, not in the same way, for it had long ago been established that he was the important member of the family. Thus, when Julia sacrifices herself still further by giving him money out of her inadequate salary, she is merely continuing to acknowledge his superior status and her own insignificance. In each case Gordon can maintain his position by slightly different behavior. The importance Gordon attributes to money in his relation to Rosemary is underscored by his sexually demanding and imposing behavior the night he has ten pounds in his pocket, having finally sold a poem. In earlier scenes, not having enough money "unmanned" him. With money in his pocket he is once again "manned" and sexually aggressive.

Orwell's narrator declares that "no woman will ever understand" a man's refusal to settle into the prison of a "good" job. "Serve the money-god, or do without women—those are the only alternatives" (116), we are told. Since the novel never questions this equation, the reader (like Gordon) is not encouraged to consider the matter from a woman's point of view, and the interlocking themes of Gordon's rebellion against the money god and his anger at women can never be disentangled.

Orwell's critique of the money/power system and the demands it imposes on men does not come into clear focus in *Aspidistra* because he refuses to address the issue of gender as it relates to power, and instead portrays women as money-grubbing, preying on men. But just as the protest against money never becomes an argument for socialism, so the protest against male financial "responsibilities" never becomes an argument for women's equal participation in these and other arenas. Instead, Gordon Comstock, like Flory in *Burmese Days*, remains caught in a contradiction he is not able to confront and unravel, because to do so would require recognition of the injustice and exploitation of women that are the concomitants of male supremacy— and it is this supremacy, above all, that Orwell's texts cannot challenge. Unlike Flory, however, Gordon does not die at the end of the novel: He rejoins the living, as a social as well as a biological male, head of the family and thereby with the right, so well displayed on the novel's last few pages, to impose his will on Rosemary.

If this restoration to his male prerogatives has involved Gordon's capitulation to the money world, what has it meant for Rosemary? Her autonomy is even more threatened than Gordon's —or would be if she had ever emerged as a character whose fate, like Gordon's, mattered. In the last few pages she is transformed, before our eyes, into the stereotypical female, existing by virtue of her relationship to a man (as was implicit in Orwell's treatment of her throughout the novel). We see her serving Gordon coffee in fulfillment of his dream of conventional family life and relinquishing her ability to make decisions about her own fate. This latter point is underscored by the arguments Gordon repeatedly wins, the last of which results in the ironic purchase of the long-hated aspidistra, emblem of lower-middle-class tenacity and decency.

Orwell, however, offers no critique here of the loss of autonomy that conventional marriage implies for both partners (a theme he will elaborate in *Coming Up for Air*, though treating it once again from a masculine point of view). Rather, he seems to be mechanically playing out a conventional notion of middle-class marriage, with Gordon, who carries this model in his head, aspidistra and all, calling the shots. The descent into a different mode of being is implied by this last scene. Rosemary, who will give up her job before the baby is born, will surely have two babies to care for, Gordon and the newborn child. Her fate, however, was never the issue, never even raised as an issue, throughout the novel, because in Orwell's world view only a man's decisions are important, and the kind of life one is to lead is a moral dilemma only for a man. A woman's life, according to the model Orwell sets out in this novel, is dictated by her biology. Therefore, the fact of conceiving a child carries as an inevitable consequence an entire way of life in which Rosemary ceases to be a person with choices. That she connives in this fate is hardly surprising. Orwell could not have imagined it otherwise, and he never succeeded in creating an autonomous female character. Unable to envision the possibility of a different kind of female fate, Orwell devotes an entire novel to the problem of male destiny alone—as if these were not the interlocking halves of every social whole.

Five

Rites of Manhood, I:

Homage to Catalonia

and the War Myth

As long as war is seen as heroic, men will expose themselves to being killed and will kill others. As long as participation in war constitutes a claim to respect, the myth of war as heroic will endure. Orwell contributed to the war myth in two ways: first, by giving an ambivalent account of his participation in the Spanish Civil War—ambivalent because, while showing that war-is-hell, his description also conveys the impression that war is a hell through which every man should go; second, because "wounded in Spain" became the standard epithet accompanying every mention of Orwell, on jacket blurbs for his books, in biographical captions over his articles. Orwell's participation in the Spanish Civil War was, and continues to be, held up as an object for our admiration. Although he was to declare in 1948 that war, while it may sometimes be necessary, "is certainly not right or sane" (CEJL, 4:413), he did not attempt to analyze the role of the war myth in the apparently futile effort to keep the peace.

Homage to Catalonia, Orwell's book on his experiences in Spain, was published in April 1938. It is a compelling account of his political education and his growing commitment to socialism and violent hostility to Communism. Orwell had gone to Spain in December 1936 to help defend the Republic against fascism. By his own account, he intended at first to do this through journalism. But when he witnessed the revolutionary atmosphere then prevailing in Barcelona, where class distinctions and social hierarchies seemed to have disappeared, he was so impressed that, he says, "I recognized it immediately as a state of affairs worth fighting for" (9). Largely by chance, Orwell found himself with the militia of the POUM (Partido Obrero de Unificación Marxista, the United Marxist Workers' Party), a political unit that was later suppressed.

The conflict among the Republicans ostensibly had to do with the best strategy for winning the war. But in Catalonia, a true socialist revolution was taking place, and the POUM, like the anarchists, viewed it as inseparable from the larger struggle against the fascists. However, the Republican government, supported by the Communists (who, with Soviet military aid, were far better equipped than the POUM and the anarchists), took the position that the revolution was a distraction from the main purpose of defeating the fascists. After fighting broke out in Barcelona in early May 1937, government propaganda accused the anarchists and the POUM militia of being in league with the fascists. The roundup of members began, and revolutionary socialism in Catalonia was effectively crushed by its supposed allies, the Communists. Orwell's detailed description of this civil war within the civil war is the part of his book that has received the most attention. His anger at the censorship, fabrications, and distortion in both Spanish and British accounts of these events led him by stages to a view of politics that was to be fully articulated later, in *Nineteen Eighty-Four*. Lies, manipulation, attacks on the very notion of truth and objective reality, destruction of the past by rewriting history—these themes, later so important to Orwell, all appear first in *Homage to Catalonia*.

But to my mind there is a deeper significance to Orwell's book. Out of the experience of his four months at the Aragon front he fashioned a *war narrative* so structured, weighted, and colored as to allow the personal meaning of war for Orwell to emerge. Orwell often deplored war in his writings. He went through an antimilitarist phase in the two years before the Second World War (this is discussed in chapter 6). Even when he became a highly vocal patriot during World War II it was with the conviction that war was the lesser of two evils and fascism the greater. But there is more to be said about his responses to war, and this chapter will attempt to explore the subject further. In raising this issue—the importance of war in Orwell's life—I am of course not urging that his political allegiances or his critical comments on war in general be disregarded. I believe, however, that the imagery and emotional tone he created for *Homage to Catalonia* reveal another dimension of Orwell's war experience, one that has been consistently overlooked. Orwell's admirers have sensed (though they have not analyzed) the masculinist ideology that he affirms, and many have joined in a chorus of praise for his performance as a warrior.[1]

THE MAKING OF A WARRIOR

The usual explanation of Orwell's voyage to Spain is that he shared with many other leftists in the 1930s the view that a stand had to be made in Spain against "fascism." Perhaps the mood of the time is best suggested by the title of one study of intellectuals and the Spanish Civil War: *The Last Great Cause.*[2] Great Causes will, of course, appear as long as war continues. At critical moments Orwell embraced Great Cause ideology and an ethic of "just" wars. But *Homage to Catalonia*, as we shall see, reveals the extent to which the "justice" of a particular war, however defensible it seems, ceases to be a factor as the goal of action takes on a life of its own.

Carl von Clausewitz's famous dictum "War is merely the continuation of policy by other means"[3] was intended to urge that the political aims of war remain primary. But precisely because war is a different *kind* of policy, Great Cause ideology is a necessary part of it. This ideology does not arise from a void. Orwell's integration into it occurred in his youth, as his earliest published poems reveal.

When Orwell was eleven years old, in 1914, a patriotic poem of his entitled "Awake! Young Men of England" appeared in a local newspaper:

> Oh! give me the strength of the lion,
>   The wisdom of Reynard the Fox,
> And then I'll hurl troops at the Germans,
>   And give them the hardest of knocks.

> Oh! think of the War lord's mailed fist,
>   That is striking at England today;
> And think of the lives that our soldiers
>   Are fearlessly throwing away.

> Awake! oh you young men of England,
>   For if, when your Country's in need,
> You do not enlist by the thousand,
>   You truly are cowards indeed.[4]

Many of the key elements of Great Cause ideology and the war myth in general are evident in this poem: the hypostatized enemy, the glorification of death, the patriotic appeal, the emotional blackmail of the label of coward. At this time Orwell was attending St. Cyprian's; years later he was to describe such schools as perpetuating a tradition in which "the duty of dying for your country, if necessary, is laid down as the first and greatest of the Commandments" (CEJL, 2:70). In a boys' school geared to producing ruling-class men, the Great War must have intensified the already aggressively masculine atmosphere.

At the age of thirteen, Orwell published a second poem, this time on the death of Kitchener, the war hero who had been brought out of retirement in 1914 to become secretary of war:

> No stone is set to mark his nation's loss,
> No stately tomb enshrines his noble breast
> Not e'en the tribute of a wooden cross
>   Can mark this hero's rest.
>
> He needs them not, his name ungarnished stands,
> Remindful of the mighty deeds he worked,
> Footprints of one, upon time's changeful sands,
>   Who n'er his duty shirked.
>
> Who follows in his steps no danger shuns,
> Nor stoops to conquer by a shameful deed,
> An honest and unselfish race he runs,
>   From fear and malice freed.[5]

Thirty years later Orwell wrote: "I am not able, and I do not want, completely to abandon the world-view that I acquired in childhood" (CEJL, 1:6). Although he probably did not have in mind the childhood indoctrination into the glories of war, his words nonetheless apply to this side of his education. Not only his rediscovery of an intense patriotism in August 1939 but also his experiences in Spain suggest the continuity in Orwell's life of the war myth learned in childhood. In "My Country Right or Left," a 1940 essay, Orwell deals with this issue first by trying to sort out from among the later accretions the impressions the Great War had made on him while it was occurring. He describes the indifference toward the war that he and the other boys at school felt. A pacifist reaction has already set in: "The young officers who had come back, hardened by their terrible experience and disgusted by the attitude of the younger generation to whom this experience meant just nothing, used to lecture us for our softness. Of course they could produce no argument that we were capable of understanding. They could only bark at you that war was 'a good thing,' 'it made you tough,' 'kept you fit,' etc etc. We merely sniggered at them" (CEJL, 1:537). At the time, "1914–18 was written off as a meaningless slaughter, and even the men who had been slaughtered were held to be in some way to blame." Belatedly, however, Orwell came to recognize the role of war in initiation into manhood:

But the dead men had their revenge after all. As the war fell back into the past, my particular generation, those who had been 'just too young,' became conscious of the vastness of the experience they had missed. You felt yourself a little less than a man, because you had missed it. I spent the years 1922–7 [in Burma] mostly among men a little older than myself who had been through the war. They talked about it unceasingly, with horror, of course, but also with a steadily growing nostalgia. You can see this nostalgia perfectly clearly in the English war-books. [1:537–38] [6]

In considering the sources of this ideology, Orwell notes that "even the 'just too young' had all been trained for war. Most of the English middle class are trained for war from the cradle onwards, not technically but morally." He recalls political slogans as well as material incentives:

At seven years old I was a member of the Navy League and wore a sailor suit with "HMS *Invincible*" on my cap. Even before my public-school OTC [Officers Training Corps] I had been in a private-school cadet corps. On and off, I have been toting a rifle ever since I was ten, in preparation not only for war but for a particular kind of war, a war in which the guns rise to a frantic orgasm of sound, and at the appointed moment you clamber out of the trench, breaking your nails on the sandbags, and stumble across mud and wire into the machine-gun barrage. I am convinced that part of the reason for the fascination that the Spanish civil war had for people of about my age was that it was so like the Great War. [CEJL, 1:538] [7]

Despite his recognition of the role of childhood training in the formation of adult ideologies (a theme he returned to in *Nineteen Eighty-Four* with its child spies), Orwell a few years later was writing nostalgically about the toys of his youth. In a newspaper column in December 1945, he laments the lack of toys available for Christmas in an England still experiencing shortages of all kinds: "One of the greatest joys in my own childhood were those little brass cannons on wooden gun-carriages.... The largest were six or eight inches long, cost ten shillings and went off with a noise like the Day of Judgment. To fire them, you needed gunpowder, which the shops sometimes refused to sell you, but a resourceful boy could make gunpowder for himself if he took the precaution of buying the ingredients from three different chemists." Normal, healthy children, Orwell states, enjoy explosions. "One of the advantages of being a child thirty years ago was the light-hearted attitude that then prevailed towards firearms. Up till not long before the war you could walk into any bicycle shop and buy a revolver, and even when the authorities began to take an interest in revolvers, you could still buy for 7s.6d. a fairly lethal weapon known as a Saloon rifle. I bought my first Saloon rifle at the age of ten, with no questions asked." [8]

Orwell's disappointment was intense when he first heard the sound of artillery fire in Spain: "It was so different from the tremendous unbroken roar that my senses had been waiting for for twenty years" (CEJL, 1:538).[9] Given the image of war implanted in his childhood, it is not surprising that the Spanish Civil War struck Orwell as merely a bad copy of 1914–18, as he says in "My Country Right or Left" (1:538). But he was to have a second chance at war, for the moment arrived, he goes on to say in this essay, when, just before the Nazi-Soviet pact in August 1939, he stopped opposing the horror of the coming war and recognized the "real state" of his feelings. These were revealed to him in a dream in which he realized that he would be "simply relieved when the long-dreaded war started" (1:539) and that he was "patriotic at heart." Despite all the pamphlets he had written and the speeches he had made against war with Germany, he now knew that he would not "sabotage or act against my own side, would support the war, would fight in it if possible" (1:539). Yet he acknowledges that his change of heart had no connection with the need to resist nazism: "What I knew in my dream that night was that the long drilling in patriotism which the middle classes go through had done its work, and that once England was in a serious jam it would be impossible for me to sabotage."

Instead of analyzing the war training to which he, like most young boys, had been subjected, however, Orwell now drops this theme and treats this war as uniquely meritorious. "My Country Right or Left" begins as an analysis of how men in a given society are infected with war fever and ends as an expression of patriotic commitment to the Second World War. In thus pressing home the importance of patriotism in 1940, Orwell disregards the evidence of his own experience. His desire to fight in Spain had had nothing to do with patriotism. The nostalgia for the Great War, felt by the veterans he met in Burma, and the fascination of the "just too young" generation for the Spanish Civil War had clearly been manifestations not of patriotism but of something else. But Orwell gives up trying to understand this "something else" as his discussion veers toward his feelings for his country.

At the same time, Orwell's experiences in Catalonia provided him with a model to be applied to England, and he repeatedly argues that socialism is a necessity if Hitler is to be defeated. In "The Lion and the Unicorn," his major essay of this period, Orwell asserts that only a socialist nation "can fight effectively" (CEJL, 2:67). Raising strong echoes of Catalonia, he writes: "The war and the revolution are inseparable" (2:90); "We cannot win the war without introducing Socialism, nor establish Socialism without winning the war" (2:94); "Either we turn this war into a revolutionary war . . . or we lose it, and much more besides" (2:103).

"My Country Right or Left" ends with a remarkable passage in which Orwell valorizes the patriotic and militaristic training of his childhood and transforms it into the necessary precondition of a socialist revolution in England: "It is exactly the people whose hearts have *never* leapt at the sight of a Union Jack who will flinch from revolution when the moment comes" (CEJL, 1:540; Orwell's emphasis). This, Orwell concludes, proves "the spiritual need for patriotism and the military virtues, for which, however little the boiled rabbits of the Left may like them, no substitute has yet been found." In Orwell's version of history, socialist revolution is the manly culmination of childhood training in patriotism and militarism. This is a most intriguing shift.

Without comment, Orwell has proceeded from the exposé of boyhood training in militarism to the affirmation of patriotism as a self-evident virtue. As patriotism is introduced into his discussion, the analysis ceases, as if a short circuit had occurred. But the Germans were patriotic too, and it is not clear why Orwell thinks patriotism a special virtue when he finds it in himself or among the British.[10] Orwell's response to war is much more simply explained by his adherence to the myth of the warrior, which makes military prowess an essential part of the conventional notion of manhood and therefore something men want and need.

One senses this myth at work in "My Country Right or Left," in the relief Orwell felt once he was again able to commit himself to a military cause and dissociate himself from the "boiled rabbits" on the left. Disappointed and distressed that he was not in fit health for military action against the Nazis (a misfortune he often lamented), Orwell sought paramilitary means by which to participate. He became active in the Home Guard, about which he wrote extensively during this period. One can imagine how frustrated he would have been on the sidelines had he not had the experience of the Spanish war behind him, for it is not the spirit alone, or the eagerness, that matters in the ritual. The trial by fire is the part that counts.

The war in Spain went on for nearly two years after Orwell departed the front, in poor health, recovering from a throat wound, and in danger of being imprisoned as a member of the suppressed POUM militia. His part in the war had been played out. If the POUM had simply faded into insignificance, what kind of a book would Orwell have written? As it was, he was able once more to take on one of his preferred roles, but this time Goliath was a world press determined—as he saw it—to keep the news of what he took to be the Communists' real goals (to destroy the revolution that had begun in Spain) from reaching the public. Anti-Communism was Orwell's new crusade, and it was to stay with him to the end of his life and provide the occasion for his two most famous books.

MALE AND FEMALE ROLES

In his detailed study of the Spanish Civil War, Hugh Thomas writes: "Spain gave British intellectuals a sense of freedom, the thought of rubbing shoulders with the dispossessed in a half-developed country, above all the illusion that their 'action' could be effective." [11] As *Homage to Catalonia* opens, Orwell is in the Lenin Barracks in Barcelona. It is clear that he conceives of his presence in Spain as a gesture of human solidarity, for it involves crossing national and linguistic boundaries and recognizing strangers as comrades. He therefore begins with a story about an Italian militiaman to whom he was instantly drawn. What is interesting about this description, however, is that it is thoroughly conventional. The militiaman is depicted in an abundance of masculine imagery: He is tough-looking; he has powerful shoulders; his cap is pulled fiercely over one eye; his face is that of a man "who would commit murder and throw away his life for a friend" (7). But he is not only tough, he is also ignorant, probably illiterate, and Orwell depicts the man's pathetic reverence for his supposed betters. Orwell hardly spoke a word to this man; they had no common language but that of mutual recognition. Indeed, Orwell states that he knew he could retain his first impression only if he did not see this man again. The Italian's presumed ignorance is therefore matched by Orwell's willful ignorance. But what if Orwell's image of him were false? He would then have to revise this idealization of a "natural" man in whom tough and aggressive manhood combines with lack of intellectual development. Orwell preferred not to know, and he acknowledged this preference.

Should we take this passage as a warning to the reader, a subtextual indication that this is the kind of contact Orwell would be making with Spain throughout the book? Orwell invites this view, for he follows up with a rather weak justification, "One was always making contacts of that kind in Spain" (7), and further explains: "With his shabby uniform and fierce pathetic face he typifies for me the special atmosphere of that time. He is bound up with all my memories of that period of the war" (8). This Italian militiaman, as we shall see, reappears five years later in Orwell's essay "Looking Back on the Spanish War."

In describing Barcelona in late December 1936, with the anarchists in control and revolution in full swing, Orwell seems swept along by events and eager to relinquish the distance necessary for reporting. Though he stresses the apparent unity of the struggle, his text reveals that there were still typical divisions, typical oppositions: "There were perhaps a thousand men at the barracks, and a score or so of women, apart from the militiamen's wives who did the cooking. There were still women serving in the militias, though not very many. In the early battles they had fought side by side with the men as a matter of course. It is a thing that seems natural in time of revolution" (11). Orwell here affirms that a revolution provides a break with everyday life, and within that context such things as greater equality between the sexes may seem natural. But this equality was not of long duration: "Ideas were changing already, however. The militiamen had to be kept out of the riding-school while the women were drilling there because they laughed at the women and put them off. A few months earlier no one would have seen anything comic in a woman handling a gun" (11).[12] Despite these drastic alterations in women's status in the militias, Orwell reveals a startling lack of curiosity about the revolution's effect on women. What emerges is his limited definition of political equality, which includes equality among classes, appreciation of the lack of rank and salary distinctions within the POUM militia, but no awareness of these same issues as they relate to women.[13] Once again, and in even more unusual circumstances than in *Down and Out in Paris and London* and *The Road to Wigan Pier*, Orwell restricts his focus to men and thus limits his work.

Orwell's autobiographical writings reveal his pride at his soldiering, yet he rarely simply admits to feeling pride. This is something very fundamental with him, consistent with his presentation of himself in an understated, low-key way. He does, however, admit to feeling humiliation, and these admissions occur in interesting situations. One such situation arises early in *Homage to Catalonia*: "It was rather humiliating that I had to be shown how to put on my new leather cartridge-boxes by a Spanish girl" (17). In this and other instances, humiliation is caused by needing help; to need help is, for Orwell, to have a wedge driven into his autonomy. How could he not know how to put on cartridge boxes? How could a woman know this better than he? Such a breach of sex roles challenges the idea that war is *naturally* a man's business; it brings the existence of sex roles as socially conditioned performances too close to the surface.

Although Orwell makes a distinct effort not to present himself heroically (even overdoing this), he remains stuck within a limited and conventional notion of what it means to be a man, and his words reveal to us how fragile such a conception of manhood must be if it is so easily threatened. This is apparent also in another moment of humiliation, one that occurs when he first experiences machine-gun fire: "Petty though it was, the whole experience was very interesting. It was the first time that I had been properly speaking under fire, and to my humiliation I found that I was horribly frightened." This statement, like many of Orwell's "confessions," is quickly followed by an explanation/generalization, a favorite device of his: "You always, I notice, feel the same when you are under heavy fire—not so much afraid of being hit as afraid because you don't know *where* you will be hit" (44; Orwell's emphasis).

Within the POUM militia, gradations of manhood are observed, as we learn when Orwell describes one member of the militia, a half-witted "little beast of fifteen," called by everyone *maricón*, which Orwell translates as "Nancy boy." The militamen also use this label to underline the distinction between "us" and "them" as they shout *Fascistas-maricones* at their enemies. This show of bravado, however, does not reassure Orwell, who remains convinced that "we were not real soldiers" (22), so far are the militiamen from his image of authentic fighters.

INACTION / IN ACTION

When Orwell arrives at the Aragon front, he realizes with "a shock of dismay" that his image of trench warfare, based on reports of the Great War, will find no confirmation in reality. Instead of being fifty or one hundred yards away, as he expects, the fascists are seven hundred meters away. He feels "indescribably disappointed" (24). It is phrases such as this that convey the underlying hope and excitement with which Orwell approached combat. "Now that I had seen the front I was profoundly disgusted. They called this war!" (24), he writes. The structure of this sentence is of special interest, for the word "war" occupies the syntactic position of a desired, elevated, longed-for object against which "this" experience does not measure up. Orwell explains shortly thereafter: "I ought to say in passing that all the time I was in Spain I saw very little fighting" (25). Thus the reader who has great expectations, like Orwell's, is forewarned that disappointment may lie ahead. At the same time Orwell here anticipates events, mentioning that he was later "wounded and disabled," thereby holding out some promise of "action" to come.

Many pages later, in describing one particularly "vile job" that he and some other men did (dragging sandbags into position as a barricade to enemy fire), he writes: "I remember feeling a deep horror at everything: the chaos, the darkness, the frightful din, the slithering to and fro in the mud, the struggles with the bursting sand-bags—all the time encumbered with my rifle, which I dared not put down for fear of losing it. I even shouted to someone as we staggered along with a bag between us: 'This is war! Isn't it bloody?' " (93). There is a curious ambiguity to this passage. Until we get to the words Orwell shouted we feel his horror at the situation; but these words reintroduce the mythic image of war. Of course it's bloody (in both senses). Were it not bloody, frightful, and horrible, men would not feel tested by it. In contrast to his earlier disgust, expressed in the phrase "They called this war!" (24), Orwell's words now ring out as a not-so-subtle expression of pride. And, indeed, shortly thereafter he writes: "Now that we had finished wrestling with those beastly sand-bags it was not bad fun in a way; the noise, the darkness, the flashes approaching, our own men blazing back at the flashes" (94). These images of war as "fun" recur a number of times throughout his account.

Orwell's eagerness for action was such that for a time he was attracted to the more "efficient" Communists who "were getting on with the war while we and the Anarchists were standing still" (62). By February, he writes, "I was sick of the inaction on the Aragon front and chiefly conscious that I had not done my fair share of the fighting. . . . When I joined the militia I had promised myself to kill one Fascist—after all, if each of us killed one they would soon be extinct—and I had killed nobody yet, had hardly had the chance to do so" (70). "Fascists" now appear not as other human individuals but as some generic evil that must be exterminated, and in order to better participate in this extermination Orwell later planned to transfer to the International Brigade in Madrid from the Independent Labour Party (ILP) contingent that he had joined late in January 1937.

Using military images, Orwell validates the "heroism" of dying in battle—as when he makes it clear that his verbal attacks on the Communists are aimed only at the "people higher up," not at the rank and file and "least of all against the thousands of Communists who died heroically round Madrid" (67). And in railing against the lies and propaganda reported in the left-wing press, Orwell angrily makes the point that this was done, "as usual, by people who were not fighting and who in many cases would have run a hundred miles sooner than fight" (64). He stresses that people who make up atrocity stories never fight: "It is the same in all wars; the soldiers do the fighting, the journalists do the shouting, and no true patriot ever gets near a front-line trench, except on the briefest of propaganda-tours" (65). Orwell naturally dissociates himself from such timid writer-types.[14] Thus the accolade of manhood, in a war situation, is not awarded equally to all: The men in military action are more manly than those outside of it; within warfare the fighters are more manly than, say, the journalists who may be present briefly; and, among the fighters, those who take part in the heaviest fighting are the most manly of all—to be outranked, perhaps, only by the dazzling aggressive recklessness of certain individuals whose feats will be recounted to young boys someday as part of their indoctrination into war ideology.

Orwell's account of the "bloody pantomime," as the English would-be fighters called the war, is tinged with regret: "we were hardly under direct fire," "the only danger was from stray bullets" (71). Again and again he complains that "nothing happened, nothing ever happened" (71): "And still nothing happened, nothing ever looked like happening. 'When are we going to attack? Why don't we attack?' were the questions you heard night and day from Spaniard and Englishman alike. When you think what fighting means it is queer that soldiers want to fight, and yet undoubtedly they do. In stationary warfare there are three things that all soldiers long for: a battle, more cigarettes, and a week's leave" (73). In noting, rather than exploring, this condition, Orwell does not hesitate to speak for all soldiers, so unvarying is the war experience in his mind.

But action comes in a number of different forms. During a six-week period, the only military exercise that the POUM engaged in was the attack on a lunatic asylum that the fascists had turned into a fortress, an action that was "mucked up, as usual." The captain who led the attack, Orwell writes, was of doubtful loyalty. "Either from fright or treachery he warned the Fascists by flinging a bomb when they were two hundred yards away. I am glad to say his men shot him dead on the spot," Orwell concludes (74). Far from acknowledging regret or ambivalence at this loss of life, Orwell reveals satisfaction at the immediate retribution against the captain—the two possible causes of his behavior apparently being equally unacceptable to Orwell.

When Orwell does criticize the "glory of war" illusion it is not in relation to the heroics of killing or dying but rather in relation to problems of hygiene, such as lice: "In war *all* soldiers are lousy, at least when it is warm enough," he writes (75). But quite possibly he is missing the point, for part of the "glory" of war is precisely the stories one can later tell, of hardships such as lice and ice-water baths and discomforts of all kinds. It is not only because they do not kill that noncombatant men are despised by soldiers but also because of the "soft" life they lead in comparison with the soldiers.

In *Homage to Catalonia*, Orwell's descriptions of finally being involved in "action" are important indications of the meaning of war to him. It is perhaps because of these passages that Hugh Thomas refers to Orwell's narrative as "a better book about war itself than about the Spanish War." [15] In a "beautifully planned" move in April, Orwell writes, just after he came back from spending ten days in a "so-called hospital" because of a poisoned hand, the line advances to within 150 yards of the fascists. All through the night the militiamen construct trenches and parapets in silence. Orwell devotes several pages of description to the new situation that ensues. Four paragraphs in a row begin with "And then . . . .," which is also repeated within the paragraphs. The abundant use of present participles further helps create an intensely dramatic and poetic mood:

And then the dawn coming up and the Fascists suddenly discovering that we were there. . . . Then a vicious swirl of bullets. . . .

And then, next night, waiting at Torre Fabián for an attack. . . .

And then waiting fifty or sixty yards from the Fascist parapet for the order to attack. A long line of men crouching in an irrigation ditch with their bayonets peeping over the edge. . . .

And then, for many mornings to follow, the sound of the Anarchist attacks on the other side of Huesca. Always the same sound. Suddenly, at some time in the small hours, the opening crash of several score bombs bursting simultaneously—even from miles away a diabolical, rending crash—and then the unbroken roar of massed rifles and machine-guns, a heavy rolling sound curiously similar to the roll of drums. [80–82]

Although these passages also depict the death of some men (including "wretched children" from the POUM youth league), the overall effect is a lyrical one. This is war in the grand style, with the endless waiting finally rewarded, and it quite possibly at last approaches Orwell's expectations.

In the passages differentiating the sounds of the guns there is a sensuous quality to Orwell's description, almost a loving detail and pleasure, in comparison with which the human element recedes in importance. And, indeed, he does not risk eliciting the reader's critical reaction to the pain and suffering that is inflicted by these weapons. When he describes casualties, it is in rather clichéd terms that evoke a touch of sympathy while blocking off any deeper awareness—as in his reference to the "wretched children" unable to escape as the unit pulls out (82). There is a notable effort here to understate the human drama of war while expressing the fascination with war technology. Orwell does not tell us about any of his comrades as individuals; they are interchangeable men doing their jobs. But he does tell us that "as the days went on the unseen but audible guns began each to assume a distinct personality." Not the actions of men but the individualized weapons take on moral attributes as Orwell describes the "evil sound," the "devilish metallic crash" (83), the "evil little shells" making a "doubly diabolical noise" (84). Among all this imagery, the "poor devils" who are victims cease to be significant.

The quality of dramatic expectation, the orientation toward action and the task at hand, are evident as Orwell describes the volunteer mission that he, among fifteen men, undertook:

I cannot convey to you the depth of my desire to get there. Just to get within bombing distance before they heard us! At such a time you have not even any fear, only a tremendous hopeless longing to get over the intervening ground. I have felt exactly the same thing when stalking a wild animal; the same agonized desire to get within range, the same dreamlike certainty that it is impossible. And how the distance stretched out! I knew the ground well, it was barely a hundred and fifty yards, and yet it seemed more like a mile. [87]

In the imaginative immediacy created by this narration, distance is abolished as Orwell tries to situate the reader within this physical space, sharing in that intense desire. His humane values may make him want to undermine war and certainly not present it as longed-for and exciting; yet these qualities permeate his imagination, contaminating his narrative not only when he depicts his emotional reactions but also in the very description of events. For Orwell's fear, frustration, eagerness, are not independent personal characteristics but the result of the interplay of different texts: the text in his mind and the "text" being played out before him, which eventually becomes a text for the reader, the text that we read.

Orwell does not address the problem of language created by the very existence of war. Uncritically adopting the vocabulary of efficiency in killing, he complains that after three weeks at the front he has fired "just three shots at the enemy .... at this rate it would be twenty years before I killed my first Fascist" (42). Without irony he depicts weapons as bad, better, the best, and speaks of a bomb "worth throwing." The complete reversal of moral standards involved in transgressing the prohibition against killing one's fellows is inevitably accompanied by these distortions in language,[16] which Orwell unthinkingly duplicates as he praises weapons, partakes of the pleasure of a job "well done," and feels frustrated and angry when he cannot get on with the job of destruction. While not consciously glorifying the military hero, Orwell's very language affirms the values of war, for it does not allow an entry into the analysis of this peculiar kind of efficiency measured in terms of men's abilities to kill one another. Taking the terms of war ideology very much for granted, Orwell reproduces them, and the problem becomes not how to prevent wars but how to locate or ensure better weapons that would be "worth" fighting with.

The drama of fighting episodes is also conveyed in the choice of verbs: Men run, shout, fall wounded, leap to their feet, dash up slopes, fling bombs, and so on (89). Of course war *is* action, and as long as men define themselves by action understood as force applied in opposition to some countervailing force, it will constitute a lure even for such relatively nonviolent individuals as Orwell. War promotes the fantasy of an encounter with "the enemy," the measuring of strength. In "The Lion and the Unicorn," Orwell states: "War, for all its evil, is at any rate an un-answerable test of strength, like a try-your-grip machine. Great strength returns the penny, and there is no way of faking the result" (CEJL, 2:79). In *Homage to Catalonia*, he writes: "I took it for granted that there would be a Fascist waiting for me at the top. . . . I seemed to feel in advance the sensation of our bayonets crossing, and I wondered whether his arm would be stronger than mine" (89). The indoctrination of his youth now comes back to him as he lunges for the man just out of reach: "my mind leapt backwards twenty years, to our boxing instructor at school, show-ing me in vivid pantomime how he had bayoneted a Turk at the Dardanelles" (90).

But Orwell's desire for action is still not satisfied: "When we went on leave I had been a hundred and fifteen days in the line, and at the time this period seemed to me to have been one of the most futile of my whole life. I had joined the militia in order to fight against Fascism, and as yet I had scarcely fought at all, had merely existed as a sort of passive object, doing nothing in return for my rations except to suffer from cold and lack of sleep. But now that I can see this period in perspective I do not altogether regret it" (101). And he goes on to report, just as he did at the end of *Down and Out in Paris and London*, in a school-boy's didactic manner, that this period "taught" him many things.

Orwell describes the revolutionary environment as a fore-taste of the socialism to come: "One had breathed the air of equal-ity. . . . For the Spanish militias, while they lasted, were a sort of microcosm of a classless society" (102). Curiously, this part of Orwell's text falls oddly flat, no doubt because he does not de-scribe the state of equality with anywhere near the detail he de-votes to his military experiences (even the time when "nothing was happening"). And he does not deal with the important ques-tion, to which we will return later, of how a foretaste of the class-less society can occur in an all-male environment.

In retrospect Orwell finds special value in this phase of his life, for it has "taken on the magic quality which, as a rule, be-longs only to memories that are years old" (103). Yet what Orwell most of all seems to remember is not the classless atmosphere of either Barcelona in December 1936 or life in the trenches but rather his months on the line, which he has just described almost exclusively in military, not social, terms. He becomes nostalgic as he explores the "magic quality" of his memories of this time: "It was beastly while it was happening, but it is a good patch for my mind to browse upon. I wish I could convey to you the atmosphere of that time. I hope I have done so, a little, in the earlier chapters of this book. It is all bound up in my mind with the winter cold, the ragged uniforms of the militiamen, the oval Spanish faces, the morse-like tapping of machine-guns, the smells of urine and rotting bread, the tinny taste of bean-stews wolfed hurriedly out of unclean pannikins" (103). Lyricism reappears as Orwell relives incidents "that might seem too petty to be worth recalling," all conveying a sense of physical intimacy, difficulty, danger, embarrassment over fear, and finally even the bonding of men at war regardless of which side they are on: "As the yellow dawn comes up behind us, the Andalusian sentry, muffled in his cloak, begins singing. Across no man's land, a hundred or two hundred yards away, you can hear the Fascist sentry also singing" (104).[17]

WAR AS A MASCULINE INITIATION RITE

Toward the end of April 1937, Orwell went on leave to Barcelona, where his wife, Eileen Blair, was working at the ILP office: "And after that the trouble began" (*Homage to Catalonia,* 105). At this time Orwell wanted to go to Madrid, where the "action" was, and therefore decided to transfer into the International Brigade, for which he needed a recommendation from a member of the Communist Party. But the desire for a week's rest and certain chance events prevented him from making immediate arrangements, and as a result he happened still to be in Barcelona when the fighting broke out there on May 3. Orwell rather dryly reports his experiences of the street fighting in Barcelona. On occasion again adopting an antiheroic tone, he makes frequent criticisms of these events, admitting the sheer boredom, frustration, and discomfort he felt.

When Orwell later describes the atmosphere of Barcelona during the last few weeks he spent there, with the Communists in power and able to impose their version of the war, he again and again uses the word "evil": "there was a peculiar evil feeling in the air—an atmosphere of suspicion, fear, uncertainty, and veiled hatred"; "there was a perpetual vague sense of danger, a consciousness of some evil thing that was impending" (186); "It was as though some huge evil intelligence were brooding over the town" (189). No one, reading his account, could possibly want to have an experience of fear and intimidation such as Orwell felt in Barcelona. His evocation of the mood of those days is unambiguous and makes it all the more striking that in his depiction of fighting on the Aragon front Orwell does not ultimately convey a negative impression to the reader. In addition, only when he comes to discuss the reporting of the Barcelona events in the Communist and international press, does Orwell's tone become one of real anger. Why is Orwell angry?

The answer may lie in the vital role that war reporting plays in the war myth. Without the possibility of heroic reports, would men still engage in those heroics? This is the important question raised by Nancy Huston in an essay called "Tales of War and Tears of Women." Huston argues that "it is much less significant that men's History is made of wars than that men's wars are made of stories." The need to transform the events of war into a story, Huston writes,

constitutes one of the most salient differences (there are others, of course) between human and animal violence. Specifically *in order that* human violence not be reducible to animal violence, it is imperative for men to establish a narrative sequence; to show how a given series of incidents resulted in the outbreak of armed conflict, to show how in the course of confrontation certain individuals or groups were distinguished by their courage while others were dishonored by their cowardice; to show what spectacular reversals took place in the positions of the protagonists; to show what curve was described by the escalation of aggressions, up to and including the obligatory *dénouement* consisting of peace treaties, calculation of losses, and "definitive" distribution of the terms Conqueror and Conquered.[18]

Heroic narrative, as Huston says, thus describes "two forces who are disputing the right to use the first-person triumphant.... what counts is the capacity to kill the triumphal narrative of the Enemy."[19] This means that fighting men are dependent upon positive reports of their actions, at least from their own side. Lies or distortions about those actions threaten to make one's "sacrifice" meaningless. The Communist attack on the integrity of the POUM and the anarchists, the propaganda asserting that they were betraying the Republican side and were in fact in league with

Franco, strip them of the record of their deeds. Their history, and thus the reality of their commitments and dedication to the Republic, is in effect wiped out. Orwell may be willing to die in Spain, but he does not want his death reported as that of a stooge for Franco. His account of his reaction to the suppression of the POUM in June 1937 suggests that Huston is right in her emphasis on war stories, whatever form they take. "In the whole business," Orwell writes, "the detail that most sticks in my throat, though perhaps it is not of great importance, is that all news of what was happening [the suppression of the POUM and the arrest of its members and supporters] was kept from the troops at the front" (198). The attack on Huesca was beginning, and Orwell thinks it was probably feared that if the POUM militia had been informed of what was occurring in Barcelona they might have refused to fight. "Actually nothing of the kind happened when the news arrived. In the intervening days there must have been numbers of men who were killed without ever learning that the newspapers in the rear were calling them Fascists. This kind of thing is a little difficult to forgive" (199). Orwell here acknowledges (in that understated way he uses at times, which induces the reader to give him special credence) the importance of war narratives in men's commitment to their cause. Accurate reporting is the essence of "making history." *Homage to Catalonia* was written to set the record straight, and the issue of rewriting history became a major theme in *Nineteen Eighty-Four*.

But it is important to remember that if Orwell had not had these brushes with lies and fabrications he would in all likelihood still have written a war narrative, and it would still have utilized the "first-person-triumphant." This term, with which Nancy Huston has enriched our language, has applications beyond the monopoly of history accorded to the winner.[20] Orwell's ambivalent narrative shows how difficult it is to write any war memoir without recourse to the first-person-triumphant. "Triumphant" may refer not only to the outcome of a particular war but also to a man's successful participation in a masculine rite of passage. Orwell's personal triumph stands regardless of the outcome of the war in which he fought, in a sense regardless of his own limited experience of war.

In a letter dated August 20, 1937, to Victor Gollancz, his publisher, Orwell protests the Communist Party's "campaign of

organised libel ... against people who were serving with the
P.O.U.M. in Spain," and threatens to take legal action. He especially objects to attacks against him in the *Daily Worker* which,
he says, contain "the implied suggestion that I did not 'pull my
weight' in the fight against the Fascists. From this it is only a
short step to calling me a coward, a shirker etc., and I do not
doubt these people would do so if they thought it was safe." Not
only what Orwell actually did but what he is thought to have
done matters, and the record can be set straight only by composing his own account.[21] Despite the restrictions and unsatisfactory
conditions in which he found himself in Spain (restricted and unsatisfactory relative to large-scale heroic deeds), Orwell nonetheless creates a first-person-triumphant narrative, structured as an
initiation rite in which his separation from his own society, his
initiation into warfare, killing, and being wounded, all emerge as
clearly marked stages, now permanently recorded.

The term "rite of passage" describes the pattern of separation, transition, and incorporation (return) that is characteristic of
important stations in the lives of primitive peoples.[22] Though the
details of such rites may vary considerably, in traditional male
initiation rites involving the passage from boyhood to manhood
the idea of death and resurrection is fundamental. The boy must
face pain and possible death; he must, in fact, be prepared to die.[23]
Initiation rites in primitive societies are highly structured traditional procedures that aim at the ultimate integration of the individual into a group. But any kind of rite presupposes a social
group that validates it and gives it meaning, and a rite must thus
be seen as an aspect of the social life of the group.

In initiation rites, a basic change in existential condition
occurs; the novice, in effect, has become *another*.[24] Initiation also
establishes a distinction between the initiated and the noniniti-
ated,[25] and, for this reason, it is a secret rite. War has served as
such a rite for men, and it is secret in the sense that women are
excluded from it—which may be one reason why there is such
hostility in many societies to the idea of women soldiers. The exclusion is an important part of the ritual; without it, war could
not serve as a marker of manly status.

The pattern of an initiation rite is observed in Orwell's
account of his experience of war. First the separation—the departure from one's usual life, the travel; then the seclusion with

people of one's own sex in a special place (barracks, trenches), with special preparations and with the use of special implements (weapons). The transition involves the experience of fighting (this is another reason why those who do not fight, even when they participate in another mode, are often seen as being less "proven" than the fighters). And death or being wounded rounds out the rite. Orwell acknowledges this conclusion to the trial by gunfire when he is finally wounded after four and a half months in action: "Not being in pain, I felt a vague satisfaction. This ought to please my wife, I thought; she had always wanted me to be wounded, which would save me from being killed when the great battle came" (*Homage to Catalonia*, 177–78). If one is lucky enough to survive, the rules of this particular rite affirm that one can now leave the war with a fortified sense of manhood.

This pattern is repeated in Orwell's later novel *Coming Up for Air*, in which the narrator's active participation in the Great War ends once he has been wounded. That the war continues, that the political problem has not been solved, is a separate issue and in a sense no longer relevant. Within the ongoing war so many personal destinies, each expressed in terms of the myth of the warrior who has undergone his trial by fire, are worked out. The men replace one another as interchangeable parts, each convinced of his own heroism or lack of it, each an actor of a scene in a drama which he has not helped to write but which could not take place without his participation. Women are not immune from these myths, and indeed they, too, may define their men according to the categories made available by the war myth. And they too are vulnerable to the excitement (so it is considered) of war. Eileen Blair's comments about her visit to her husband in the trenches reveal this too: "I never enjoyed anything more." [26] But, for her, war is not a ritual, and she can express her reaction in the much less weighty language of mere adventure. The war ended for Orwell when he departed, and thereafter his writings deal not so much with the ongoing situation in Spain as with what truly interested him: the way it was reported in the British press.

Men may believe that war releases something "natural" in man—his combative "instincts" [27]—but, in fact, like other initiation rites (and is it accidental that warriors are drawn from the very young?), participation in it marks a passage *into* culture; the initiate, if he survives, becomes a full-fledged member of his society. How true this is can be judged by the embarrassment often felt by men who, for one reason or another, did not participate in war. Like Orwell's "just too young" generation, they are thought to have missed something important, and their status, in comparison to that of combatants, is low.

This age-old ritual, which has been supported by the war myth handed down from generation to generation first in the form of oral poetry, then in the form of written narratives, now may well be in transition, for the forms of war and the ways of reporting it are altering drastically. In our own time, however, as both books and films show, the traditional initiatory structure is still being transmitted to the young.

Perhaps the foremost function of myth, as Mircea Eliade states, is "to reveal the exemplary models for all human rites and all significant human activities." [28] But in order to understand how myths can go on having significance to individuals in highly differing societies, we need to recognize that "primitive" and "modern" are both structures that can exist anywhere at any time.[29] As a result, it is not only in traditional agricultural societies that myth continues to be a powerful ideological tool.

Homage to Catalonia, by participating in the war myth, helps make the myth intellectually respectable even among people who would not ordinarily consider themselves vulnerable to unexamined and wholly traditional notions of aggressive manhood. In a column he wrote in 1945, arguing for the importance of telling the truth, Orwell comments that "genuine progress can only happen through increasing enlightenment, which means the continuous destruction of myths" (CEJL, 4:37). But myths should not be understood in this limited sense of "lies" as opposed to "truth"; rather, they should be seen to involve deeply held beliefs and particular ways of construing the world and human beings' roles and potentialities within it. In the larger sense, Orwell's observation, even though he did not apply it to many of his own beliefs, is correct.

Orwell's war experience is a time outside of time, a reality not limited to a particular geographical space, as indicated by his reactions to Spain once he has his discharge papers. Admiring the patterns of swallows' nests in the cornices of crumbling buildings, he comments: "It was queer how for nearly six months past I had no eyes for such things. With my discharge papers in my pocket I felt like a human being again, and also a little like a tourist. For almost the first time I felt that I was really in Spain, in a country that I had longed all my life to visit" (*Homage to Catalonia*, 194). To be in a war is thus to be involved in a special sort of time and place that separates one from everyday reality; and to be a soldier is to play a special sort of role that reduces one's perspective. And now, in a comradely sort of way, he can even lament with a waiter that war is "such a pity!" (195), which again makes Orwell feel like a tourist, that is, feel distanced from his own recent experiences. The war will go on for other people, but Orwell will return to England, lamentably without the beautiful oak wine jugs he would like to buy but that are not available. And nowhere in these transformations he undergoes is there any critical awareness that war involves men in the acting out of a role, in participating in a mythic image of man-as-warrior.

Mircea Eliade has generalized from his study of primitive and traditional societies' myths and come up with what he terms "primitive ontology." For the archaic mentality, he writes, whether ancient or modern, the value of an act is a result of its participation in a reality that transcends it. Human acts achieve meaning and value through "their property of reproducing a primordial act, of repeating a mythical example," which Eliade calls a "paradigm." Such acts are meaningful because they were "consecrated in the beginning . . . by gods, ancestors, or heroes." [30] Men "repeat these exemplary and paradigmatic gestures ad infinitum" and, in this way, contemporary events are assimilated into earlier mythic patterns.[31] In Orwell's account the very structure of the book gives this away, for Orwell is participating in a pattern much older than he; he is perpetuating the genre of war narratives, and he cannot help but glorify war as he does this. The *situation* counts for more than his own consciousness; perhaps this is why there is a break in the book between his analytic chapters, devoted to party politics and expressing his typical concerns and outraged judgments, and the description of his experience at the front, in which lyrical passages occur that could apply to any war, all wars, with only the technology and materiel (or, in this case, lack of it) to differentiate between this account and others.

George Woodcock is one critic who recognizes the war myth at work in Orwell's book. In *The Crystal Spirit*, Woodcock writes:

There is a certain archaic grandeur about the setting of Orwell's experiences in *Homage to Catalonia*, and even about the actors. For, by the accident of history, he has entered a small, simplified society dominated by a few broad ethical concepts which gain value because of the material primitiveness of existence. These badly armed militiamen, guarding their mountaintops with very little but their ideals, seem a great deal nearer to the men who fought at Thermopylae and Marathon than to the great mechanized armies of modern times. It was doubtless this sense of living in a world snatched out of history and validated by myth that made Orwell recollect it immediately afterwards as something which had "the magic quality" of "memories that are years old." [32]

But, in fact, this "accident of history" is not necessary for the war myth to be perpetuated. In our society men are trained to relate to war in a way that approximates Eliade's "primitive ontology." The significance of present events is found through their participation in and duplication of the mythological past. Myth arrests time, "the event becomes 'eternal': it happens now and always, and operates as a type." [33] Myths also have another important function, and that is to help people overcome doubts concerning an undertaking by assuring them that what they are about to do has already been done in one form or another. [34] In this way the fear of war is allayed, and the urgency of participating in it is reinforced. For myth also codifies belief and lends support to a traditional way of doing things, and human freedom is thereby reduced to an acquiescence in "destiny."

Roland Barthes has written extensively about the ideological function of myth:

Myth does not deny things, on the contrary, its function is to talk about them; simply, it purifies them, it makes them innocent, it gives them a natural and eternal justification, it gives them a clarity which is not that of an explanation but that of a statement of fact. ... In passing from history to nature, myth acts economically: it abolishes the complexity of human acts, it gives them the simplicity of essences, it does away with all dialectics, with any going back beyond what is immediately visible, it organizes a world which is without contradictions because it is without depth, a world wide open and wallowing in the evident, it establishes a blissful clarity: things appear to mean something by themselves. [35]

The myth of war identifies war activity as an essential rite of manhood and keeps us from focusing on the contradiction between the conventional deploring of war and the glorification of it. War simply becomes something a man-must-do, and we are not invited to analyze who is this "man" and what is the meaning of this "must." Orwell not only employs this myth in *Homage to Catalonia*, he also utilizes the technique of myth in his dream-discovery of his patriotism in 1939. There is no pretense here of analyzing political events and coming to a rational conclusion; instead, patriotism is "revealed" in a dream; the commitment to fight is "discovered." They preexist the individual's encounter with them; they are, to Orwell, essences—and this despite his recognition of childhood indoctrination. This is what Barthes means by calling myth "depoliticized speech." [36]

Understanding the ideological function of myth (among its many other functions) helps us to see why Orwell, with his discharge papers in his pocket, "felt like a human being again" (*Homage to Catalonia*, 194) and why it is only *now* that he is able to really see Spain. Until this point, his time in Spain has been not his own personal time, to which he could bring his own individual perspective, but rather that eternal time of war in which men-warriors, as long as they are brought up in this tradition, will participate. Orwell's own account allows us to understand the way the mythic mode works, but it is significant that he could not stand back and describe his participation in terms that would help prevent other young men, in the future, from seeing his account too as part of the mythic past. To the very end of his book Orwell holds to a traditional notion of the heroic. He believes in the significance of a heroic death in battle—and contrasts this with "meaningless" death in lesser circumstances. Being wounded makes him angry. He does not want to leave this world, he tells us; this world suits him, after all; and then too: "The stupid mischance infuriated me. The meaninglessness of it! To be bumped off, not even in battle, but in this stale corner of the trenches, thanks to a moment's carelessness!" (178). But he is not resentful toward the fascist who shot him and even fantasizes that, had the man been taken prisoner, "I would merely have congratulated him on his good shooting" (179). War is sport, with sportsmanship as the prevailing ethic, Orwell here suggests, forgetting for the moment what a fraud this is: Orwell might have been shot by chance; it might not have been "good" shooting at all in the sense of taking aim and hitting one's target. The whole interaction is turned into a sporting encounter, by which Orwell is able to demonstrate that he too is a good player and bears his opposite number no ill will for his own possible demise. Curiously, the thought of dying in this pointless way (instead of "in battle") is infuriating but not humiliating, for by being wounded he is acting out his role of soldier, even if the circumstances are less than glorious.

Far more disturbing to Orwell is the death of Bob Smillie, reportedly of appendicitis, in a Spanish jail. Orwell describes this vigorous young man who fought fascism "with faultless courage and willingness" and whose utterly pointless death "is not a thing I can easily forgive.... To be killed in battle—yes, that is what one expects; but to be flung into jail, not even for any imaginary offence, but simply owing to dull blind spite, and then left to die in solitude—that is a different matter. I fail to see how this kind of thing . . . brought victory any nearer" (206–7).

Orwell here seems to be suggesting that certain ends (victory) justify certain sacrifices (such as dying in battle) and that the unheroic death that does not further the cause is meaningless. But what would one then make of all the deaths that, once victory has been attained (by only one side, obviously), cease to have meaning since they contributed not to victory but only to defeat? If the ends justify the means—and only those ends (victory) justify the means (the sacrifice of life)—it follows that the side that loses the war must see its sacrifice as meaningless. Since this side did not achieve its ends, the sacrifices, it could be argued, were pointless. But to prevent a clear perception of the inevitable pointlessness (to at least one side) of the disruption and destruction of life brought on by war, a curious reversal of the ends-justify-the-means formula occurs. A metaphor develops that sees the means themselves as somehow valuable and positive. This is what the language of sports contributes to war ideology, for in playing a game winning is not the only thing; playing well counts too. Orwell's uncritical adherence to the mystification involved in applying such a view to war is apparent in his own use of game imagery and in his sporting attitude toward the man who shot him. The very rhetoric of "sacrifice" also contributes to the mystification imposed by the war myth. Quite a different response might be possible if a term existed that signified a totally wasteful, pointless, violent destruction with neither honor nor virtue in it. The absence of such a word, like other significant absences in our language, is in its way eloquent. Meanwhile, "sacrifice" does its work.

The rite of passage that war represents, the affirmation of manhood, the idea that war is a proving ground, a crucible (clichés with obvious power on men's self-perception)—all these are a way of separating the means from the ends they are supposed to attain and making the means themselves repositories of value and significance.

Orwell's tendency to valorize death-in-warfare as in itself a mark of masculine honor comes through with disturbing clarity in the wartime diary he kept between 1940 and 1942. In late May 1940, just before the fall of France, when it looked as though the British Expeditionary Force then in France would be trapped there, Orwell wrote: "Horrible though it is, I hope the BEF is cut to pieces sooner than capitulate" (CEJL, 2:340). Equally extreme is Orwell's comment, a few weeks later, about the prospects of German conquest not only of England but also of the United States: "If the USA is going to submit to conquest as well, there is nothing for it but to die fighting, but one must above all die *fighting* and have the satisfaction of killing somebody else first" (2:349–50; Orwell's emphasis).[37]

In "Why I Write," Orwell describes himself as a small child constantly weaving a continuous story in which he was "the hero of thrilling adventures" (CEJL, 1:2). There is still something of this ongoing narrative at work in his account of Spain, and it perhaps explains his frequent judgments on his actions. He is examining how both he and the war measured up. The tendency to overexplain is evident as Orwell describes how he and his wife decided to leave Spain: "I was extremely weak, my voice was gone, seemingly for good, and the doctors told me that at best it would be several months before I was fit to fight. I had got to start earning some money sooner or later, and there did not seem much sense in staying in Spain and eating food that was needed for other people" (*Homage to Catalonia*, 190–91). Orwell seems to fear that the apparent altruism of this last comment might strain the credulity of his reader, for it is at once followed by a complete change in reasoning—the "confession" that is a characteristic part of Orwell's narrative voice: "But my motives were mainly selfish. I had an overwhelming desire to get away from it all; away from the horrible atmosphere of political suspicion and hatred, from streets thronged by armed men, from air-raids, trenches, machine-guns, screaming trams, milkless tea, oil cookery, and shortage of cigarettes—from almost everything that I had learnt to associate with Spain" (191).

Words that would have seemed supercilious if written early in his sojourn in Spain have quite a different ring when admitted after several months in the front line and a bullet in the throat. Now they bespeak a justified exhaustion with the war. Once again, we are in the presence of a ritual. One needs to "earn" the right to express dislike of war, and one earns it by exposing oneself to danger and by showing willingness to kill. Then the experience is complete and one can withdraw from it honorably. Being wounded, however, is a necessary part of the rite, for we cannot imagine Orwell writing the above paragraph without having first earned that particular credit extended to those who have undergone the trial by fire. But it is one thing to admit to being fed up with war and quite another to admit to fear. Orwell's ambivalence toward the traditional demands of masculine courage emerge again when he says: "Being wounded had spoiled my nerve for the time being—I believe this usually happens—and the prospect of being under fire frightened me horribly" (192). Here we have a confession swaddled in a disclaimer and a generalization.

On only a few occasions does Orwell break through his conventional assumptions about the significance of war and come close to recognizing that it forces individuals into fixed roles that come prepackaged with meanings. One such moment occurs when he goes to see the commander of his battalion, George Kopp, who had been jailed after the suppression of the POUM: "[Kopp's] plump fresh-coloured face looked much as usual, and in that filthy place he had kept his uniform neat and had even contrived to shave. There was another officer in the uniform of the Popular Army among the prisoners. He and Kopp saluted as they struggled past one another; the gesture was pathetic, somehow" (208). Under prison conditions of the worst sort, without a context to imbue the gesture with authenticity and meaning, the insistence upon continuing one's role (which suddenly appears as a mere role) is of course "pathetic."

A more telling example of breaking through the conventional frame of war is recounted by Orwell in his 1942 essay

"Looking Back on the Spanish War." Going forth one morning to snipe at the fascists outside of Huesca, Orwell saw a man jump out of the fascist trench (as Orwell refers to it):

He was half-dressed and was holding up his trousers with both hands as he ran. I refrained from shooting at him. It is true that I am a poor shot and unlikely to hit a running man at a hundred yards, and also that I was thinking chiefly about getting back to our trench while the Fascists had their attention fixed on the aeroplanes. Still, I did not shoot partly because of that detail about the trousers. I had come here to shoot at "Fascists"; but a man who is holding up his trousers isn't a "Fascist," he is visibly a fellow creature, similar to yourself, and you don't feel like shooting at him. [CEJL, 2:254]

In discussing this and four other writers' examples of "acts of kindness" in war, Michael Walzer writes that an enemy "alienates himself from me when he tries to kill me, and from our common humanity. But the alienation is temporary, the humanity imminent. It is restored, as it were, by the prosaic acts that break down the stereotypes in each of the five stories." [38] But, of course, the "enemy" views "me" in precisely the same terms. In these situations of frame breaking, something happens that threatens the ordinary definition of the situation. Most of what takes place in war situations—and this is surely the point of military training—depends on a failure to question the particular frame one has been thrust into. Orwell especially appreciated (though it also irritated and angered him) the lack of hierarchy and traditional discipline among the POUM militia, but at the same time he did not question the war myth. He believed, as soldiers always believe, that the "enemy" was out there, threatening him, and he placed himself in a situation in which this became true. What is of interest is why more episodes of frame breaking do not occur. The war myth, which prevents recognition that a man's self-realization, his initiation into manhood, is to come about through the deaths of other men, perpetuates this state of affairs.

Orwell's efforts to resist the view of war as glorious, by his mock-heroic touches[39] and his emphasis on the filth and discomfort, are self-contradictory. However well-intentioned, they provide an interesting example of what Roland Barthes terms "inoculation." Inoculation plays an important part in the maintenance of myth, for in this way one "immunizes the contents of the collective imagination by means of a small inoculation of acknowledged evil; one thus protects against the risk of a generalized subversion." [40] Because Orwell presents himself as an innocent narrator whom we can trust (in part due precisely to his warnings that we should not trust him too much), the emergence of a romantic image of war in Orwell's narrative has much more force than were he to openly champion such a view. We can see the inoculation technique at work in Orwell's description of the train taking him to a hospital as it passes a troop train full of Italians from the International Brigade: "It was like an allegorical picture of war; the trainload of fresh men gliding proudly up the line, the maimed men sliding slowly down, and all the while the guns on the open trucks making one's heart leap as guns always do, and reviving that pernicious feeling, so difficult to get rid of, that war *is* glorious after all" (*Homage to Catalonia*, 184; Orwell's emphasis). By admitting, apparently with heavy heart, that this feeling is pernicious and difficult to get rid of, Orwell affirms the underlying truth of the very thing he is ostensibly denying and in abandoning this subject without further analysis, he suggests that the romantic image of war is so fundamental as to be beyond understanding, beyond question. This image takes on the status of truth, all the truer for being grudgingly admitted. By the technique of inoculation Orwell ultimately affirms that the war myth, if not wholly correct and despite all reservations, is at least irresistible.

THE SPANISH LEGACY

Homage to Catalonia draws to a close on a rhapsodic note, once again recalling the feel of the months at the front; above all, the faces of the Spanish militiamen. And Orwell now validates the experience by saying: "This war, in which I played so ineffectual a part, has left me with memories that are mostly evil, and yet I do not wish that I had missed it.... Curiously enough the whole experience has left me with not less but more belief in the decency of human beings" (219–20). In his essay "Looking Back on the Spanish War," written five years after his experiences in Spain, Orwell initially takes a much harder and less romantic view of his months at the front and describes the smell of the latrines, the discomfort, and the stupidity of war. But once again this apparent attack on war is abandoned as memories come back to him of war-as-camaraderie. Although he sees this as a by-product of the revolution, stories of male bonding in war are in fact common and have nothing to do with the politics of the situation. Characteristically, Orwell claims that the intelligentsia is always bought off by fascists whereas the working class is not. He does not reflect, in this connection, on the popularity of Hitler and Mussolini. Instead, he claims that the most reliable enemy of fascism is the working class.

Toward the end of this revealing essay, Orwell recalls the Italian militiaman who appeared at the beginning of *Homage to Catalonia*. The memory of his face reassures Orwell "that there was at any rate no doubt as to who was in the right" (CEJL, 2:264). Once again Orwell appeals to mystical comradeship, giving it political significance, and he forgets that such comrades, and no doubt such faces, existed also on the other side. "This man's face, which I saw only for a minute or two, remains with me as a sort of visual reminder of what the war was really about. He symbolises for me the flower of the European working class, harried by the police of all countries" (2:264). The essay draws to a close with a lyrical defense of the common man, which, in Orwell's view, is what the Spanish war and the Second World War are about, and ends with a poem in memory of the Italian militiaman:

> The Italian soldier shook my hand
> Beside the guard-room table;
> The strong hand and the subtle hand
> Whose palms are only able
>
> To meet within the sound of guns,
> But oh! what peace I knew then
> In gazing on his battered face
> Purer than any woman's!
>
> .   .   .   .
>
> Your name and your deeds were forgotten
> Before your bones were dry,
> And the lie that slew you is buried
> Under a deeper lie;
>
> But the thing that I saw in your face
> No power can disinherit:
> No bomb that ever burst
> Shatters the crystal spirit.
>
> [2:266–67]

The last verse of this poem is the most quoted one, and it contains in brief the full meaning of first-person-triumphant narrative: One does not die while such poems celebrate one's existence. "Mere" physical death matters little as long as "the crystal spirit" survives. This is the war myth in full force. But the poem is interesting also for other reasons. Not only is there a close resemblance to Orwell's poem on Kitchener's death written when he was thirteen (and little improvement in the writing); there is also a distinct similarity in the mood. From the death of the famous Kitchener to that of an unknown militiaman, the emotions evoked in Orwell have not changed, nor have the romantic/heroic associations. Orwell does not, in fact, know that the militiaman died, but he needs to conceive of him as dead in order to elicit the maximum of heroic pathos. Of special significance in this poem, however, is its vision of the brotherhood-at-arms and the totally conventional contrast between this male bonding and the lesser existence of women, disdainfully disposed of in the second verse. Here again we have part of the appeal of war: the band of brothers who affirm one another's manhood.

In the case of the Spanish Civil War, especially, the idea of the band of brothers played a significant part in attracting young British intellectuals to the Republican cause. Julian Symons, in his book on the 1930s, describes these British volunteers in Spain: "One unconscious motive behind their action was the wish to obtain that contact with the working class which was denied to them in their ordinary lives." [41] He does not hesitate to conclude: "The most satisfying experiences in Spain undoubtedly belonged to those who went out to fight. The others, who stayed on the fringe, made speeches and attended Congresses, felt, in the reluctance to fight, something vitally true to their own characters, yet were at the same time ashamed." [42] Along similar lines, George Woodcock describes Orwell's time in Spain as "the most meaningful and possibly—in spite of everything—the happiest experience of his life," [43] presumably because it provided Orwell "for the first and last time the kind of acceptance into a casteless comradeship of workingmen which he had always desired." [44]

In a letter written to Cyril Connolly on June 8, 1939, shortly before his return to England, Orwell says: "I have seen wonderful things & at last really believe in Socialism, which I never did before" (CEJL, 1:269). Orwell was perhaps referring to the apparently classless society of Barcelona that so impressed him on his arrival in Spain as well as to the organization of the militias, but even in this letter he goes on to discuss his military experience, not the social revolution. "A pity you didn't come up to our position & see me when you were in Aragon. I would have enjoyed giving you tea in a dugout," his letter concludes— once again striking the note of war as "fun." War undoubtedly promotes, on each side, solidarity created by an extreme and shared threat, and Orwell must have thought of this later, when he depicted, in *Nineteen Eighty-Four*, the Party's effective manipulation of an entire people by propagating an atmosphere of threat, a never-ending war. There are many other examples of joint endeavors in life when the habitual divisions between people are for one reason or another suspended. But with all its artificial constraints, how can a war situation possibly provide a model of a human society? How can such lofty redemptive qualities be found in it? An all-female society under extreme duress would never be held up as a model of any kind of "society." But just as the male is conventionally regarded as the representative of the human species, so all-male groups count as the generally human. In addition, war has penetrated our consciousness as a virtually unavoidable part of life. Thus it does not immediately strike us as absurd to talk, as Orwell does, of the Spanish militias as "a sort of microcosm of a classless society" (*Homage to Catalonia*, 102).[45]

But precisely in the reduction of humanity to a group of fighting men lies the explanation, I believe, of Orwell's conversion to socialism at this time. We need to recall how much of his attack on socialism in *The Road to Wigan Pier* was based upon its association, in Orwell's mind, with an efficient industrialized society in which softness would reign supreme while the manly virtues of strength and courage would atrophy. In contrast to all this, what Orwell has experienced in Spain is the association of socialism with an archetypal masculine historical moment: war. So the former image of socialism as leading to repellent softness, which haunted Orwell, is now replaced by an image of socialism as manly, as something to fight for and to die for.

When Orwell states that it is the ideal of equality that makes men willing to risk their skins (102), he seems to have things backward: It is risking their skins in war that temporarily gives men the feeling of equality, at least when they are all equally at risk. In a life-threatening situation, men learn to help and trust each other, and the competition of their daily existence is deflected by the unity of interests which sets them clearly against another group labeled "the enemy."[46] But Orwell forgets that men are fighting and dying on the other side too and that to valorize the ethics forged by this fighting and dying is to promote a destructive ideal of manhood rather than the humane ideal of socialism. In Spain, as *Homage to Catalonia* reveals, Orwell experiences life largely in a masculine vacuum. Can it be a coincidence that in this book there occur few of the typical misogynist comments one finds in Orwell's other books? It is the fascists who take on the role of Other, to be inferiorized, to be labeled *maricones*. Among the militiamen there are no irritating vegetarians, sandal wearers, birth control advocates, or pansy poets to undermine masculine solidarity. This is the context of Orwell's only experience of a "classless society."

Homage to Catalonia ends with Orwell traveling back to England and finding it difficult, as the train passes through southern England, "probably the sleekest landscape in the world" (220), to believe "that anything is really happening anywhere" (221). The book's closing sentence is a long, poetic evocation of a peaceful, soft, slow-moving country and its inhabitants, "—all sleeping the deep, deep sleep of England, from which I sometimes fear that we shall never wake till we are jerked out of it by the roar of bombs" (221). After examining Orwell's ambivalence toward the war experience, however, one cannot read this lyrical ending without hearing in it strains of a meaning quite the opposite of its overt one. Is it really "fear" that Orwell feels as he gazes on this landscape? Is there not in this passage a desire to bring this country, this sleeping beauty, back to life? The image of sleep can be a negative one, after all. Orwell was already sensitive to this when, at the age of eleven, he wrote his first patriotic poem "Awake! Young Men of England." More than twenty-five years later, in "The Lion and the Unicorn," he again represents England in negative images of sleep, needing to be roused (CEJL, 2:58, 66, 103). Far, then, from appreciating the beauty and peacefulness of the English countryside, Orwell seems to be suggesting a lack of consciousness, lack of life, against which the "roar of bombs" may seem like life itself, indeed life on the heroic, because dangerous and intense, scale. And is the "roar of bombs" that Orwell "fears" as he returns to England totally unrelated to the "tremendous, unbroken roar that my senses had been waiting for for twenty years" (CEJL, 1:538)?

Orwell experienced Spain in the long shadow cast by the First World War, just as participants in the Great War had imagined that conflict in terms of still earlier wars of which they had heard.[47] In this way a chain of interwoven experiences and texts is created, with the latter constantly reinforcing a paradigm of manhood against which men must ever measure themselves. The war narrative, whether as poetry, fiction, or journalism, is the vital link in this chain.

Six

Rites of Manhood, II:

Flight into Masculinity

His baptism by fire behind him, Orwell was able for a brief time between 1937 and 1939 to reject war as a solution to the threat posed by Germany. Building on the antiwar sentiments occasionally surfacing in *Homage to Catalonia*, he moved toward a pacifist position. Orwell's most important work during this phase was the novel *Coming Up for Air*, written in the winter of 1938–39 in Marrakech, where Orwell and Eileen Blair had gone because of his poor health. In a letter to his agent dated April 25, 1939, Orwell describes the novel as "more or less unpolitical, so far as it is possible for a book to be that nowadays, but its general tendency is pacifist" (LL).[1]

Coming Up for Air, Orwell's only novel utilizing an I-narrator, recounts George Bowling's failed attempt to recapture the good old days of his Edwardian childhood. The book elaborates some of Orwell's already familiar themes: the longing for an apocalyptic end, by means of bombing,[2] to modern civilization—a wish first articulated in *Keep the Aspidistra Flying* and then hinted at, as we have seen, in the closing pages of *Homage to Catalonia*; the nostalgia for an idealized past, already familiar to us from *The Road to Wigan Pier*; the love of nature combined with anger at its destruction by sprawling suburban mediocrity. These subjects have been much examined by other critics, but the major theme linking *Coming Up for Air* and *Homage to Catalonia* has routinely been ignored: The novel continues to explore masculine initiation rites. Working backward from the rite of passage represented by war, Orwell now turns to those peacetime rituals that mark his protagonist's passage from childhood to boyhood and to young manhood. These stages are explicitly named in the novel, and their significance is stated. For George Bowling, growing up represented a flight into masculinity, and it is this flight that he will attempt to re-create as, fat, forty-five, with a new set of false teeth and a windfall of seventeen pounds won on a horse, he contemplates his life and plans a temporary escape, his "coming up for air."

"BEFORE THE WAR"

As George Bowling tells his own story, he structures it along two axes, one spatial, the other temporal. The spatial axis takes him, in the novel's last part, back to Lower Binfield, where he grew up. The temporal axis (occupying nearly half the novel) involves a recollection of his life up to the present. Of this remembrance, the most important part by far is the seventy-five-page depiction of life "before the war." In other respects, too, the novel is organized around the break in the narrator's life made by the First World War. Looking back on his past from the vantage point of the year 1938, Bowling sees his life in three segments: the first twenty-one years, up to the war; his service in the army; and the following twenty years of his life ("after the war"— much more summarily described). In terms of the novel's structure, the centrality of the war is again emphasized by the location of the brief chapter devoted to Bowling's war experiences precisely in the middle of the novel.

The very language Orwell puts on Bowling's lips reproduces the sense of discontinuity between the time before and the time after the war. The novel's first twenty-five pages, focusing on Bowling's present, are laden with nonspecific descriptions relying heavily on vague phrases like "one of those," "a sort of," "a kind of," and "the type that." These formulations, which characterize much of Orwell's writing, seem to me to indicate an anxiety about the validity of what is being said, as if Orwell— and here Bowling—must defend the right to make assertions either by stressing their typicality, and hence their claim on our attention, or by wrapping the observations in a reassuring vagueness, perhaps to ward off challenges.[3] *Coming Up for Air* contains more of these awkward constructions than any of Orwell's other works; for example, Bowling describes himself as having "one of those bricky-red faces" and "those kind of pudgy arms" (7); he is "the active, hearty kind of fat man" (8) who is "the type that people automatically slap on the back" (21). Trying to establish the point that Bowling *is* a type, Orwell does not seem to trust his readers to reach this conclusion on their own.

Once Bowling's remembrance of the past is jogged by a name on a poster, however, the description of things and events suddenly turns concrete and specific, suggesting that these memories are much more real to him than his actual present as a forty-five-year-old fat man. But the shift in language also points to another aspect of Bowling's world view: His memories of Lower Binfield evoke a time when everything was in its place, as is apparent in the litany that closes part 1 of the novel:

I'm back in Lower Binfield, and the year's 1900. Beside the horse-trough in the market-place the carrier's horse is having its nose-bag. At the sweet-shop on the corner Mother Wheeler is weighing out a ha'porth of brandy balls. Lady Rampling's carriage is driving by, with the tiger sitting behind in his pipeclayed breeches with his arms folded. Uncle Ezekiel is cursing Joe Chamberlain. The recruiting-sergeant in his scarlet jacket, tight blue overall, and pillbox hat, is strutting up and down twisting his moustache. The drunks are puking in the yard behind the George. Vicky's at Windsor, God's in heaven, Christ's on the cross, Jonah's in the whale, Shadrach, Meshach, and Abednego are in the fiery furnace, and Sihon king of the Amorites and Og the king of Bashan are sitting on their thrones looking at one another—not doing anything exactly, just existing, keeping their appointed places, like a couple of fire-dogs, or the Lion and the Unicorn. [34]

Even those elements that might be thought of as chaotic in this passage (the drunks) are all part of a world in which everything is in its "appointed place" and life is reassuring. Bowling's own time, by contrast, is one in which certainty, clarity, and precise assignment to places have ceased to exist.

Part 2 of *Coming Up for Air* elaborates Bowling's memories of life "before the war" and includes his later judgments on this life. In the chummy male tone pervading the novel, Bowling tells his imaginary listener:

Christ! What's the use of saying that one oughtn't to be sentimental about "before the war"? I *am* sentimental about it. So are you if you remember it. It's quite true that if you look back on any special period of time you tend to remember the pleasant bits. That's true even of the war. But it's also true that people then had something that we haven't got now.

What? It was simply that they didn't think of the future as something to be terrified of. It isn't that life was softer then than now. Actually it was harsher. People on the whole worked harder, lived less comfortably, and died more painfully. [106; Orwell's emphasis]

I have already discussed how notions about the "harshness" of the past shape Orwell's thinking. In *Coming Up for Air* such ideas are part of what makes the past precious to Bowling. After describing the rigors of the old days—poverty, inadequate housing, bankruptcy, illness, drunken husbands, "girls ruined for life by an illegitimate baby," and other "ghastly things," Bowling defines what it is that people did possess in former times: "A feeling of security, even when they weren't secure. More exactly, it was a feeling of continuity. All of them knew they'd got to die, and I suppose a few of them knew they were going to go bankrupt, but what they didn't know was that the order of things could change. Whatever might happen to themselves, things would go on as they'd known them" (107). In those days people "didn't feel the ground they stood on shifting under their feet" (108). It is the passing of this fixed order that Bowling most laments, and, as if words themselves no longer knew their place, he lists the horrors of contemporary life by giving their hyphenated names: food-queues, out-of-works, stream-lined bullets, hire-purchase payments, down-trodden pen-pushers, mowing-machines, garden-rollers. In short, Bowling's adult life is everything that Gordon Comstock in *Keep the Aspidistra Flying* most dreaded, all his worst expectations come true.

Although critics have made extravagant claims for reading Bowling as everyman (perhaps responding to Orwell's invitation to do so), his life story is far from paradigmatic. Needless to say, *Coming Up for Air* is not an accurate historical portrayal of social and political changes between 1900 and 1938. What the novel does represent is an idealized notion of an Edwardian boyhood.[4] The stability of the pre-World War I epoch in this narrator's eyes may well be the result of his status within that world: He was a child, successfully negotiating important developmental tasks. And, as we shall see further on, it is these tasks, a boy child's rites of passage, that the novel most lovingly elaborates.

Bowling's own description of his safe passage through these rites allows us to understand his dissatisfaction with the present. At the same time, the meaning of these rites can be grasped only against the background of the domestic world from which they are designed to break away.

WOMAN'S DOMAIN

What was life like as George Bowling was growing up? Bowling provides us with a series of tableaux of moments in his past, many of them accompanied by editorializing comments asserting the typicality of his life and urging the reader to draw on his own comparable experience—a tactic I shall analyze later in this chapter.

Bowling's account begins with an image of the two separate worlds occupied by his father and his mother: his father's seed shop and the family's home dominated by the figure of his mother in the kitchen:

The very first thing I remember is the smell of sainfoin chaff. You went up the stone passage that led from the kitchen to the shop, and the smell of sainfoin got stronger all the way. Mother had fixed a wooden gate in the doorway to prevent Joe and myself (Joe was my elder brother) from getting into the shop. I can still remember standing there clutching the bars, and the smell of sainfoin mixed up with the damp plastery smell that belonged to the passage. It wasn't till years later that I somehow managed to crash the gate and get into the shop when nobody was there.... This must have been when I was about six. [35–36]

Having alluded to his confinement to the domestic sphere as a child, Bowling launches into lyrical descriptions of his slowly enlarging world, complete with characteristically Orwellian catalogues: things to be picked and to be eaten, candies in the sweet shop, most of them no longer available, and so on.[5] These were all part of the life that is lost, "killed stone dead" by the war (39). But what most clearly emerges in this chapter is Bowling's negative depiction of women in positions of control and the satisfaction he seems to take from their eventual downfall. In describing Katie, the twelve-year-old girl who took George, then aged five, and Joe, his seven-year-old brother, for their walks, Bowling twice mentions that she dragged him by the arm and called him "Baby" (38, 39) but also comments that "her mental level wasn't very different from ours." Although at this stage of their lives she had some authority over the boys, "so far as conversation went we were almost on equal terms" (38). The chapter's final paragraph is a sharp break with the narrator's happy memories:

Poor Katie! She had her first baby when she was fifteen. No one knew who was the father, and probably Katie wasn't too certain herself. Most people believed it was one of her brothers. The workhouse people took the baby, and Katie went into service in Walton. Some time afterwards she married a tinker, which even by the standards of her family was a come-down. The last time I saw her was in 1913. I was biking through Walton, and I passed some dreadful wooden shacks. . . . A wrinkled-up hag of a woman, with her hair coming down and a smoky face, looking at least fifty years old, came out of one of the huts and began shaking out a rag mat. It was Katie, who must have been twenty-seven. [41]

A similar description occurs much later in the novel when Bowling returns to Lower Binfield and runs into Elsie, his first lover. What is important for us to note at this point is that his description of Katie's fate appears as an integral part of his nostalgic recollection of the past. Katie's life story is an apparently necessary aspect of the happy stability of life "before the war."

Bowling's family, as he portrays it, is a model of the sexual division of both labor and the world at large. Each parent is remembered in a typical activity, his father standing behind the counter of his shop, his mother in her kitchen: "I never remember her without an apron" (47) or "when she wasn't cooking" (48). Bowling's portrait of his mother inseparably links her positive presence in his life to her limitations, as he conflates childhood and adult perspectives in his description:

I used to like to watch Mother rolling pastry. There's always a fascination in watching anybody do a job which he really understands. Watch a woman—a woman who really knows how to cook, I mean—rolling dough. She's got a peculiar, solemn, indrawn air, a satisfied kind of air, like a priestess celebrating a sacred rite. And in her own mind, of course, that's exactly what she is. . . . When you saw her cooking you knew that she was in a world where she really belonged, among things she really understood. Except through the Sunday papers and an occasional bit of gossip the outside world didn't really exist for her. Although she read more easily than Father, and unlike him used to read novelettes as well as newspapers, she was unbelievably ignorant. I realized this even by the time I was ten years old. She certainly couldn't have told you whether

Ireland was east or west of England, and I doubt whether any time up to the outbreak of the Great War she could have told you who was Prime Minister. Moreover she hadn't the smallest wish to know such things. [48–49]

Bowling of course does not situate these recollections in their proper social context, which would have to include the detail that his mother, like all British women of her time, did not (and would not for two decades more) have the right to vote. Instead, as in the description of Katie, the point is to differentiate the growing boy from these limited women. Father appears as an individualized person, a man who may or may not find his work suitable (as it happens, he does not). Mother, however, is simply Woman. Unchanging womanhood resides in her, constricted but priestesslike within her narrow domain. Her specifically feminine fate is not set against the background of social expectations pressing on her. Instead, there is an implicit criticism in the portrayal of the smallness of this woman's world perfectly symbolized by her confinement to certain parts of the house. We are told that she herself is to blame for this, as her willful insistence on this state of things makes any other sort of life impossible: "Her job, 'the woman's work,' was to look after the house and the meals and the laundry and the children. She'd have had a fit if she'd seen Father or anyone else of the male sex trying to sew on a button for himself" (49–50).[6]

At the same time, Mother was firmer than Father (who "was really much too weak with us" [50]), and Bowling remembers her "as something vast and overflowing, with her yellow hair and her beaming face and her enormous bosom, a sort of great opulent creature like the figure-head of a battleship" (100). The same image occurs in another description. In 1916 his mother travels to see him because he has been wounded in the war: "I'd known her as a great splendid protecting kind of creature, a bit like a ship's figurehead and a bit like a broody hen, and after all she was only a little old woman in a black dress. Everything was changing and fading. That was the last time I saw her alive" (114).[7] But if Bowling's mother was, from his child's-eye perspective, a formidable protectress, she was also a fearful and superstitious figure who tried to control her sons by imposing her anxieties on them. "According to Mother, everything that a boy ever wants to do was 'dangerous.' Swimming was dangerous, climbing trees was dangerous, and so were sliding, snowballing, hanging on behind carts, using catapults and squailers, and even fishing" (51). The world outside her home was a scene of violence and murders, which had "a terrible fascination" for her: "as she often said, she just didn't know how people could *be* so wicked" (52; Orwell's emphasis). Throughout these descriptions of Bowling's mother, there is apparent an enormous, if indirect, condescension, missing from his depiction of his father. Without offering much comment on Mother's tastes and ideas, Bowling presents them in such a way as to make them appear ludicrous. And yet, like Katie, the figure of Mother is part of Bowling's nostalgic evocation of the superior past.

Toward the end of his reminiscences, some sixty pages later, Bowling recalls his return (after a three-year absence during the First World War) to Lower Binfield for his mother's funeral: "Well, there was the house where I'd been a child and a boy and a young man, where I'd crawled about the kitchen floor and smelt the sainfoin and read 'Donovan the Dauntless.' . . . It had been as permanent to me as the pyramids, and now it would be just an accident if I ever set foot in it again" (115–16). To understand this clear delineation of phases in his development, we must in each instance apprehend what it is that Bowling was leaving behind as he moved from one stage to the next. The process of becoming a boy—no longer a sexually undifferentiated "kid"—will involve a separation from the female world with its restrictions and taboos. But for such a separation to be effective and free of guilt, this world must stay in its appointed place. In thinking back upon his life, therefore, Bowling must emphasize the contentment and continuity of his parents' lot. In a scene reminiscent of the working-class interior evoked by Orwell in *The Road to Wigan Pier*,[8] Bowling pictures the past for us:

I can see them now. A Sunday afternoon—summer, of course, always summer—a smell of roast pork and greens still floating in the air, and Mother on one side of the fireplace, starting off to read the latest murder but gradually falling asleep with her mouth open, and Father on the other, in slippers and spectacles, working his way slowly through yards of smudgy print. And the soft feeling of summer all round you, the geranium in the window, a starling cooing somewhere, and myself under the table with the *B.O.P.* [*Boy's Own Paper*], making believe that the tablecloth is a tent. [46]

Bowling is relieved that his parents did not live to know "that everything they'd believed in was just so much junk" (109). His father, never realizing he was ruined, died in early 1915 before actually going bankrupt. Bowling's mother died not long afterward:

Mother never lived to know that the life she'd been brought up to, the life of a decent God-fearing shopkeeper's daughter and a decent God-fearing shopkeeper's wife in the reign of good Queen Vic, was finished for ever. Times were difficult and trade was bad, ... but you carried on much the same as usual. The old English order of life couldn't change. For ever and ever decent God-fearing women would cook Yorkshire pudding and apple dumplings on enormous coal ranges, wear woollen underclothes and sleep on feathers, make plum jam in July ... with the flies buzzing round, in a sort of cosy little underworld of stewed tea, bad legs, and happy endings. [108]

This revered and defunct past is the antithesis of the dismal present, as the description early in the novel of George Bowling's adult life makes clear. Given Orwell's knowledge of French, his choice of "Ellesmere Road" as Bowling's residence is a not-too-subtle indication that Bowling now lives in a world in which things have so far lost their "appointed place" that the female sphere is no longer confined to the kitchen. Bowling describes his neighborhood for his reader: "Just a prison with the cells all in a row. A line of semi-detached torture-chambers where the poor little five-to-ten-pound-a-weekers quake and shiver, every one of them with the boss twisting his tail and the wife riding him like the nightmare and the kids sucking his blood like leeches" (14). In this hyphenated and emasculated world, men like Bowling imagine that they own their houses, but this illusion is all part of "a huge racket called the Hesperides Estate, the property of the Cheerful Credit Building Society" (15). Sounding ever more like Gordon Comstock, Bowling suggests that the Hesperides Estate should be "surmounted by an enormous statue to the god of building societies. It would be a queer sort of god. Among other things it would be bisexual. The top half would be a managing director and the bottom half would be a wife in the family way" (15). Bowling contrasts men like himself with the "prole" who, he says, "suffers physically, but he's a free man when he isn't working" (14). What can this mean but that, unlike proletarians, middle-class men are "controlled" by their wives and children (a point already made by Orwell in *The Road to Wigan Pier* and discussed in chapter 3, above)?

Bowling's resentment of what he sees as control by women is also apparent in his disappointment when he returns to Lower Binfield. Far from retrieving the past, he finds that this past no longer exists; in every particular it has been destroyed, as underscored by the description of some of Bowling's childhood landmarks. The George no longer bears the familiar sign, "a crude kind of picture, with St George on a very thin horse trampling on a very fat dragon"; instead, the new sign is "kind of artistic-looking. You could see it had been painted by a real artist. St George looked a regular pansy" (181). The family's corn and seed shop and the parlor of their home have metamorphosed into "Wendy's Teashop," and it too is "dolled up." Sitting almost at the very spot where his father's armchair used to be, Bowling is served weak tea (186)—another object of Orwell's scorn.[9] The world, in short, has become effeminate, and not even by returning to his childhood haunts can Bowling bring back the past. Here, I think, lies the explanation for Orwell's ambivalent use of bombing imagery, in this as in his other books: Along with genuine horror at the prospects of a brutal future, he expresses a frustrated child's pleasure in destruction. If life cannot be as it was in Bowling's idealized boyhood, let the bombers come!

In the old days a woman such as Bowling's mother knew her place and clung to it; but by the time of his own marriage, as we shall see, things had changed. The perspective in either case is the same: What does the woman's way of life mean for *men*, for *me*? No protest is made in the name of rights or principles against this clearly hierarchical and sexually polarized world, although Orwell frequently objected to inequality and hierarchy directed against other groups. This self-interested omission leads to another oversight: a lack of awareness that hierarchy within the family is a concomitant of hierarchy in society as a whole. Thus Bowling's nostalgia for the past is never able to connect that past to the future it engendered—a future of apocalyptic fears and fantasies. Instead, Bowling's vision remains static, with past and present portrayed as separable blocks in time, one valued, the other abhorred and leading to a dreaded future. But how, in fact, did Bowling as a child react to the life he now so longs for? What was his relation to the world of women, confined but contented, represented by his mother?

MORE MASCULINE INITIATION RITES

Boyhood. For George Bowling, growing up meant escaping from his mother's petty domain. The stability and continuity she provided also imposed a series of separations from the outside world, the world of men, which her two sons had to enter. She was not only a "beaming face" and "enormous bosom"; she was also "something vast and overflowing" (100). Although Bowling's image of her as a battleship's figurehead is impressive, it calls to mind that the real actors are the men manning the ship. This was the lesson that Bowling, as a child, had to learn; and, by his own account, he learned it in stages.

The first stage involved his crashing through the barrier his mother had erected separating her kitchen from the world beyond—his father's seed shop. This he accomplished when he was six years old. His father's shop was not yet the world; however, it connected the outside world to the domestic one, both physically and metaphorically. Appropriately, Bowling's mother "very seldom" (49) went into the shop, had no knowledge of it (or of the family's finances), and instead abided by the geographical and social divisions limiting her role.

After depicting the stable maternal scene of his childhood in chapter 2 of part 2, Bowling, in chapter 3, focuses on one particular day when, at the age of eight, he was accepted into his brother's gang. Marking his transition from being just a "kid" to being a "boy," this event is described in the novel as both an initiation into boyhood and a further separation from the world of women. The gang, which boasts the sinister name of "Black Hand," goes fishing. Fishing is something George's ever-fearful mother forbids. On this particular day, however, George decides to follow along. He is not easily accepted by the older boys, and only after he has withstood a beating by his brother do the other members decide to let him stay. From his adult perspective, Bowling lyrically describes the experience of fishing, utilizing the biblical style also used by Orwell in his evocation of fighting in Spain. The unmistakable sensation of getting his first bite (61) further parallels the experience, in *Homage to Catalonia*, of a shot going "home." Although Bowling knows his mother will give him a hiding for having cut school, he spends the rest of the day with the gang. They had not decided "whether I was really a member yet, but for the time being they tolerated me" (62). Even their walk on this day is something special, "a long, meandering, scrounging kind of walk, the sort of walk that boys go for when they're away from home all day, and especially when they're away without permission. It was the first real boy's walk I'd had, quite different from the walks we used to go with Katie Simmons" (62–63). The boys then take shots at birds with their catapults, shout obscenities (George is jeered at because he knows only three), and talk about where babies come from.

All these activities can be understood to be part of a rite of passage for George. The boys, having fun, are engaged in the specifically male behavior of their society: They "play" by throwing stones at birds and doing "taboo" things like shouting obscenities which, in turn, bring to mind sexual activity and their ignorance of the facts of life. But in their apparent defiance of the adult world they are not behaving in antisocial ways; instead, they are acting out recognizable male patterns in a society in which male behavior is often aggressive and destructive and thus clearly differentiated from the nurturing activities associated with women. Later the boys get filthy digging about in a rubbish dump and shoot stones at some half-grown chicks they find in a thrush's nest: "There were four of them, and we each had one to stamp on" (64), Bowling recalls. On their way home (driven there by hunger), the boys chase a rat with sticks and trample on old Bennet's beloved onion bed.

The significance of the day's experience is not left to our imagination:

I'd walked ten miles and I wasn't tired. All day I'd trailed after the gang and tried to do everything they did, and they'd called me "the kid" and snubbed me as much as they could, but I'd more or less kept my end up. I had a wonderful feeling inside me, a feeling you can't know about unless you've had it—but if you're a man you'll have had it some time. I knew that I wasn't a kid any longer, I was a boy at last. And it's a wonderful thing to be a boy, to go roaming where grown-ups can't catch you, and to chase rats and kill birds and shy stones and cheek carters and shout dirty words. It's a kind of strong, rank feeling, a feeling of knowing everything and fearing nothing, and it's all bound up with breaking rules and killing things. The white dusty roads, the hot sweaty feeling of one's clothes, the smell of fennel and wild peppermint, the dirty words, the sour stink of the rubbish dump, the taste of fizzy lemonade and the gas that made one belch, the stamping on the young birds, the feel of the fish straining on the line—it was all part of it. Thank God I'm a man, because no woman ever has that feeling. [64–65] [10]

Differentiation between men's experiences and women's is the essential feature of this day's events, for it gives to the adventure its specific meaning as a rite of passage. Such a rite always involves an act of exclusion, in this case separation from still younger males (and one's own younger self) and, more importantly, from women, a permanently uninitiated group. Although the final comment in the paragraph just cited is Bowling's adult formulation of this differentiation, the feeling itself is attributed to the original experience. But separation is not the only thing taking place. Another aspect of the day's events is that they bind him to the world of men. The "rules" being broken are social rules, imposed by women (mothers)—and it is normal for males to break these rules; indeed, according to this rite, it is essential for growing boys to break them. Bowling situates himself comfortably within the community of males beyond the stage of being "kids," and he is labeling his experience as typical for males, who, unlike women, are fortunate enough to have such adventures.

But he is still, alas, only an eight-year-old child, small enough to be taken over his mother's knee—which is precisely what she does when he gets home. His initiation is in any case not complete, for the boys decide, the next day, that he must first go through an "ordeal" they have devised, which includes chewing and swallowing an earthworm. They further seek to humiliate him by making out his fish—he had been the only boy to catch one—to be smaller than it was. "But it didn't matter. I'd been fishing. I'd seen the float dive under the water and felt the fish tugging at the line, and however many lies they told they couldn't take that away from me" (65–66). Another important lesson here: The opposition to the world of women does not automatically create male solidarity; there may be unity-against-women, but this does not eliminate competition among men, so that the initiation is merely the beginning of a continual struggle for status and recognition.

Summarizing the subsequent seven years, when "what I chiefly remember is fishing" (66), Bowling consolidates the meaning of being a boy in his description of his other activities:

> In early spring we went after squirrels with squailers, and later on we went birdnesting. We had a theory that birds can't count and it's all right if you leave one egg, but we were cruel little beasts and sometimes we'd just knock the nest down and trample on the eggs or chicks. There was another game we had when the toads were spawning. We used to catch toads, ram the nozzle of a bicycle pump up their backsides, and blow them up till they burst. That's what boys are like, I don't know why. [68]

In Bowling's account, part of what is so magical about this time of life is precisely that it is an in-between time, before the boys are again caught up in a world containing women. The impending change is hinted at in relation to Joe: "Joe was barely fifteen when he started going after girls, and from then on he seldom came out fishing, which he said was a kid's game" (71–72). Thus each new stage in a boy's life distinguishes him further as a man and separates him more profoundly from his past as a "kid." "Don't mistake what I'm talking about," Bowling says in his characteristically brusque tone. "It's not that I'm trying to put across any of that poetry of childhood stuff. I know that's all baloney.... The truth is that kids aren't in any way poetic, they're merely savage little animals, except that no animal is a quarter as selfish" (73). This leads to an extraordinary passage: "A boy isn't interested in meadows, groves, and so forth. He never looks at a landscape, doesn't give a damn for flowers, and unless they affect him in some way, such as being good to eat, he doesn't know one plant from another. Killing things—that's about as near to poetry as a boy gets" (73–74). Not satisfied with equating "childhood" and "boyhood," Bowling here reduces "boys" to precisely the type of youngster he is describing, redefining an inherently problematic experience as a fact of nature requiring no further discussion. These and similar passages raise the question of whether Orwell might not be aiming at an exposé of a boy's initiation into manhood and protesting against so restricted a definition of masculinity. However, given the unremitting nostalgia expressed by Bowling and the continued evocation of these experiences as aspects of an idyllic past, such an interpretation would be difficult to support. Orwell presents this boyhood without a trace of irony. As Bowling says, recalling his day of fishing with the Black Hand: "It was as though they were in paradise and I'd got to join them" (59).

To my mind, the most intriguing aspect of Orwell's narrative is that it clearly depicts a brutalizing childhood training in masculinity while at no point calling into question the value or consequences of this training. Quite the contrary, it is valorized precisely for its function in forging a male identity in opposition to women. George Bowling does distance himself to some extent from his own experiences by letting his vision range across his past and depicting in great detail what this education in a male gender identity was like. Its brutality is not only clear, however, but also relished, as if there were no further stage of human maturity that might provide Bowling with a different vantage point on this experience. Hence it is no surprise that his adult idea of an enjoyable time consists in a return to this past in which he first affirmed his masculinity. Like that first time, this moment too must be stolen away from the world of controlling females.

Although Bowling's flight into masculinity can be understood substantially in terms of his own society's unequal attribution of value to distinct male and female activities and modes of being, the special emotional intensity of that flight, and its ritual reconstruction decades later, can be further elucidated. Nancy Chodorow is among the recent scholars to devote attention to the quite different dynamics of gender identity formation in boys and in girls. Women's mothering, Chodorow argues, "produces asymmetries in the relational experiences of girls and boys as they grow up, which account for crucial differences in feminine and masculine personality."[11] Mothers tend to experience daughters as similar to and continuous with themselves. The experience of being reared by a same-sex parent also contributes to a situation in which girls tend to "remain part of the dyadic primary mother-child relationship itself.... By contrast, mothers experience their sons as a male opposite.... A boy has engaged, and been required to engage, in a more emphatic individuation and a more defensive firming of experienced ego boundaries."[12] Thus, for boys but not for girls, "issues of differentiation have become intertwined with sexual issues."[13] Girls emerge from this process with a greater basis for "empathy" than do boys: "From this retention of preoedipal attachments to their mother, growing girls come to define and experience themselves as continuous with others; their experience of self contains more flexible or permeable ego boundaries. Boys come to define themselves as more separate and distinct, with a greater sense of rigid ego boundaries and differentiation." Chodorow concludes: "The basic feminine sense of self is connected to the world, the basic masculine sense of self is separate," and masculine personality thus "comes to be defined more in terms of denial of relation and connection (and denial of femininity), whereas feminine personality comes to include a fundamental definition of self in relationship." [14] According to Chodorow, "for boys the major goal is the achievement of personal masculine identification with their father and sense of secure masculine self, achieved through superego formation and disparagement of women." [15]

If one superimposes this scenario on Orwell's novel, with its large, powerful mother contrasted with a small, quiet father (45), the urgency of Bowling's desire to separate from the feminine world makes sense. Acting out the role of a boy eager to assume masculine prerogatives, Bowling learns to do so in part through disparagement of the feminine sphere and of women themselves. Had Orwell simply reproduced in this novel the sex-gender system in which, as Chodorow states, women's "primary social location is domestic," [16] he would be no more than an accurate observer of his society. But he does something else: Through his main character (who is in this respect like all Orwell's other narrative voices), Orwell valorizes this situation, as is apparent in the sentimental evocation of an idealized Edwardian age when women were safely at home while men forged bonds among themselves and acted on the "real" world, the world outside the home. It is this image, with its boyhood rituals and clearly demarcated gender boundaries, that George Bowling longs for. But the nostalgia diverts attention from the main beneficiaries—men —of a system that subordinates women even as it blames them for their submersion in the "cosy little underworld" of domesticity.

Young Manhood. A second important rite taking place in *Coming Up for Air*—that of sexual initiation—marks Bowling's rediscovery of the world of women and at the same time consolidates his distance from them, for at this stage he is in the role not of dominated son but of dominating lover.

After a boyhood spent primarily on fishing and reading, especially of boys' weeklies (the subject of one of Orwell's best-known essays),[17] Bowling at age fifteen goes to work for a local grocer and stays in this job for the next six years.[18] At this stage of the narrative Bowling telescopes time, shifting from scene to scene and suggesting an old-fashioned cinematographic image of calendar pages being pulled off the wall: "And time was slipping away. 1910, 1911, 1912" (99); "1911, 1912, 1913. I tell you it was a good time to be alive" (102). Now, reluctantly, Bowling introduces Elsie Waters: "I don't want to tell the story of myself and Elsie Waters, even if there was any story to tell. It's merely that she's part of the picture, part of 'before the war' " (102–3). Tell the story, however, he does.

Bowling's sexual initiation is recounted in the inept prose that characterizes Orwell's fictional treatment of sex in all his work. Though Elsie is two years older than George and already experienced, their affair is presented as a new occasion for a display of male mastery (however inexpert) over women. She is described as very feminine, and Bowling specifies that this means compliant: "As soon as you saw her you knew that you could take her in your arms and do what you wanted with her. She was really deeply feminine, very gentle, very submissive, the kind that would always do what a man told her, though she wasn't either small or weak. She wasn't even stupid, only rather silent" (103–4). Their first sexual encounter (as in *Aspidistra* and *Nineteen Eighty-Four*) occurs out-of-doors, near the carp-laden secret pool to which Bowling had for years planned to return, to fish. "I wanted her very badly, and wanted to take the plunge, only I was half-frightened" (105). But male fear is overcome by female submission: "In her black dress she looked—I don't know how, kind of soft, kind of yielding, as though her body was a kind of malleable stuff that you could do what you liked with. She was mine and I could have her, this minute if I wanted to. Suddenly I stopped being frightened" (105).

Although Bowling tells us that "I'm grateful to Elsie, because she was the first person who taught me to care about a woman. I don't mean women in general, I mean an individual woman" (103), nothing about his subsequent relations with women suggests that this is true. His affair with Elsie lasted for about a year and was interrupted by the war. After a few months in the army, he stops writing to her and later avoids returning to Lower Binfield because he does not want to see her. When he finally does see her again, during his futile expedition to Lower Binfield near the novel's end, what is most striking is the lack not only of concern but even of kindness in his response to her physical deterioration. Just as she had affirmed his masculine sexuality in his youth, so does she affirm his masculine superiority in middle age. Spotting a woman walking in front of him, Bowling follows her, noting that she is tallish, fattish, shabby: "All in all, she looked a bit of a slut" (203). He hears her talking with another woman, "their voices cooing away in one of those meaningless conversations that women have when they're just passing the time of day" (203). At last he recognizes her: "Yes, it was Elsie. No chance of mistake. Elsie! That fat hag!" (203). Feeling "a kind of horrible fascination," he follows her:

It was horrible, and yet I got a kind of scientific kick out of studying her back view. It's frightening, the things that twenty-four years can do to a woman. Only twenty-four years, and the girl I'd known, with her milky-white skin and red mouth and kind of dull-gold hair, had turned into this great round-shouldered hag, shambling along on twisted heels. It made me feel downright glad I'm a man. No man ever goes to pieces quite so completely as that. I'm fat, I grant you. I'm the wrong shape, if you like. But at least I'm *a* shape. Elsie wasn't even particularly fat, she was merely shapeless. Ghastly things had happened to her hips. As for her waist, it had vanished. She was just a kind of soft lumpy cylinder, like a bag of meal. [204; Orwell's emphasis]

This passage echoes Bowling's earlier words as he recalled his first initiation rite: "Thank God I'm a man, because no woman ever has that feeling" (65). Such static formulations of distinctions between males and females, always asserting male superiority without further examination, are typical of Orwell. In a short review written in 1940 of a "really vulgar" matinée called *Applesauce*, Orwell praises the "utter baseness" of comedians like Little Tich and Max Miller and argues that it is important for such actors to continue to exist. "They express something which is valuable in our civilisation and which might drop out of it in certain circumstances," he says. "To begin with, their genius is entirely masculine. A woman cannot be low without being disgusting, whereas a good male comedian can give the impression of something irredeemable and yet innocent, like a sparrow." [19]

Here again Orwell asserts, but does not analyze, sexual stereotypes and reveals that, like George Bowling, he believes masculinity itself to be the virtue that protects men from an evil fate,
whether physical or moral.

Not yet satisfied with his judgment of Elsie, Bowling must
examine her at close quarters and therefore follows her to a dingy
shop, where she serves him without recognizing him. Her face
gives Bowling "almost as big a shock as that first moment when
I'd recognized her." Again the passage is notable for its generalization as Elsie is portrayed not as an individual but as a type: "The
whole face had kind of sagged, as if it had somehow been drawn
downwards. Do you know that type of middle-aged woman that
has a face just like a bulldog? Great underhung jaw, mouth turned
down at the corners, eyes sunken, with pouches underneath. Exactly like a bulldog. And yet it was the same face, I'd have known
it in a million" (205). Bowling concludes, "It's queer how these
women go to pieces once they're married" (206), repeating an
observation made earlier in the novel about his own wife. Such
remarks are of course not intended to raise serious questions about
the effects of marriage on women of this class. Instead, they are
simply part of a systematic expression of distance from and superiority over women. Elsie's husband, also named George, is described in quite a different tone, without either the pejorative or
the generic characteristics ascribed to Elsie: "He was a small stout-
ish chap, in shirt-sleeves, with a bald head and a big gingery-
colored soup-strainer moustache" (206). The only expression of
possible feeling for Elsie occurring in this scene is compromised
by Bowling's complicitous appeal to his presumably male reader:

I watched old Elsie poking about among the litter [of the shop] and mum-
bling to herself. Do you know the kind of shuffling, round-shouldered
movements of an old woman who's lost something? No use trying to describe to you what I felt. A kind of cold, deadly desolate feeling. You can't
conceive it unless you've had it. All I can say is, if there was a girl you
used to care about twenty-five years ago, go and have a look at her now.
Then perhaps you'll know what I felt. [206]

Orwell's familiar assumptions are here: the universality claimed
for this experience, the unexplained decay of women, the lack of
any affection or tie that might make physical change acceptable
as a fact of life, the condescension implicit in the unspoken but

assumed male centrality from which such judgments about women are made, and the appeal to the reader as a fellow male with identical judgments, actual or potential.

There is a unity to Bowling's experiences as recounted in the novel: His first initiation into boyhood (the fishing episode) depends in large part on differentiation from the world of females; and now, in middle age, his own deterioration is ameliorated by the contrast with his first lover. His masculinity thus serves him well in the creation of a self-protective identity that allows him, at key points in his life, to assert his supremacy. And no other model of human relations is even hinted at throughout the novel. But lest his descriptions of Elsie prove too grim, Bowling now conjures up her singular good fortune in having found a husband, given her unconventional sexual behavior:

And, on the other hand, who'd ever have foreseen that Elsie would end up like this? She'd seemed the kind of girl who's bound to go to the devil. I know there'd been at least one other man before I had her, and it's safe to bet there were others between me and the second George. It wouldn't surprise me to learn that she'd had a dozen altogether. I treated her badly, there's no question about that, and many a time it had given me a bad half-hour. She'll end up on the streets, I used to think, or stick her head in the gas oven. And sometimes I felt I'd been a bit of a bastard, but other times I reflected (what was true enough) that if it hadn't been me it would have been somebody else. But you see the way things happen, the kind of dull pointless way. How many women really end up on the streets? A damn sight more end up at the mangle. She hadn't gone to the bad, or to the good either. Just ended up like everybody else, a fat old woman muddling about a frowsy little shop, with a gingery-moustached George to call her own. [207] [20]

Bowling is thus able to leave his encounter with Elsie content that he is a man and absolved of guilt. Next morning he decides to visit the secret carp-filled pool at Binfield House, near the spot where he had first "had" Elsie. In recounting his return to Lower Binfield, Bowling here reverses the sequence of his original initiation rites, so that he now moves from the phase of his life represented by Elsie to the still earlier phase in which fishing was his passion. But the pond, like Elsie, has decayed—it is now a rubbish dump—and the old grounds of Binfield House have been turned into "another of those sham-Tudor colonies" with "arty-looking houses" (212) inhabited by vegetarians, lady novelists, and psychic researchers (215) who imagine that by living there they have returned to nature. Bowling fulminates: "God rot them and bust them! . . . doesn't it make you puke sometimes to see what they're doing to England, with their bird-baths and their plaster gnomes, and their pixies and tin cans, where the beech-woods used to be?" (215). At last Bowling recognizes the futility of his effort to retrieve his boyhood world: "I'm finished with this notion of getting back into the past. What's the good of trying to revisit the scenes of your boyhood? They don't exist. Coming up for air! But there isn't any air. The dustbin that we're in reaches up to the stratosphere" (215–16). Although he is still determined to enjoy his remaining three days, even this simple ambition is not to be realized, for the ludicrous (and gratifying) accidental bombing of the town puts an end to his attempted return, just as the real war of an earlier period had finished off the world of his youth.

PACIFISM AND TALKING TOUGH

Two wars, one past (the Great War), the other imminent (the Second World War), are dealt with in *Coming Up for Air*, and George Bowling's scorn of military heroics against fascism is predicated on his experience in the Great War. As with Orwell, so with his protagonist: Past participation in war provides the ground for speaking against it—a paradox that makes a genuinely pacifist stance impossible. Though the First World War finally separates George Bowling from his life "before the war," his role in the fighting is not depicted in any detail in the novel. Having just written an entire book about this rite of passage in his own life, Orwell obviously did not feel the need to go into it again.

To explain Orwell's brief "pacifist" phase fully, we must also situate it in the context of his political involvements in the late 1930s. The Independent Labour Party had facilitated Orwell's trip to Spain in 1936, and it was through his connection, however tenuous at the time, to the ILP that Orwell had ended up in the POUM, the ILP's "sister party" in Spain, rather than in the International Brigade.[21] In June 1938, Orwell officially joined the ILP because, as he explained at the time, he considered it the only significant British party "which aims at anything I should regard as Socialism" (CEJL, 1:337). The ILP, as Bernard Crick points out, was "anti-militarist" rather than "pacifist," for while criticizing the impending war as an imperialist struggle over markets, it "in theory believed in being prepared to fight a revolutionary war." [22] Having rediscovered his patriotism just before the Nazi-Soviet pact in 1939 (see chapter 5, above), Orwell, apparently without conflict, broke with the ILP early in the war because of its continued "pacifism." [23]

While Orwell's politics in 1937–39 followed the ILP line, his rhetoric in discussing political commitments was characteristically his own. It is this rhetoric, and not his shifting views on the Second World War, that provides us today with the keynote to Orwell's thinking. Well before joining the ILP, Orwell's writings against a possible war with Germany exploited the language of masculinity. In August 1937, for example, Orwell praises the antiwar book *The Men I Killed* by Brig. Gen. Frank P. Crozier (whom one scholar has called "the most colourful and unlikely pacifist of the inter-war period")[24] because, he says, though the book is on the whole unconvincing, General Crozier is a "living contradiction of the widespread notion that every pacifist is a Creeping Jesus" (CEJL, 1:283). Orwell's slow acceptance of the term "pacifist" for his own position, as his letters of the time reveal, is accompanied by two characteristic moves: He identifies pacifism as the unfashionable cause needing to be defended against the biased big daily papers and the "possessing class" in general; and he labels the prowar faction as unmanly. In a May 1938 letter to the *New English Weekly*, responding to a critique of pacifism, Orwell deploys both strategies: "It is a question of mobilising the dislike of war that undoubtedly exists in ordinary decent people, as opposed to the hack-journalists and the pansy left" (1:332). Every manual worker inwardly knows, Orwell affirms in the very tone and vocabulary he would soon give to George Bowling, "that modern war is a racket." [25]

Six months later, in an article entitled "Political Reflections on the Crisis," Orwell castigates the Left in much the same vein for giving the false impression that the English people want war. By contrast, he says, French intellectuals, who have been taught by conscription what war is like, are not war-hungry; but the British intelligentsia who declare that we "must" fight (the very position he himself was to embrace eight months later) do not imagine that the war will affect them personally. "The type of person who writes articles for the political Left has no feeling that 'war' means something in which he will actually get hurt," writes Orwell, and he again blames the soft "pansy" life for creating war hunger:

Our civilisation produces in increasing numbers two types, the gangster and the pansy. They never meet, but each is necessary to the other. Somebody in eastern Europe "liquidates" a Trotskyist; somebody in Bloomsbury writes a justification of it. And it is, of course, precisely because of the utter softness and security of life in England that the yearning for bloodshed—bloodshed in the far distance—is so common among our intelligentsia.[26]

This paragraph, like Orwell's other writings of this period, strikes a strong note of "I've been there," an authority and confidence deriving from his own passage through the ritual of gunfire; he can write against war without having to fear the accusation that he is himself "soft." His virile rhetoric, accusing opponents of being less than real men, will only a short time later be aimed at those still embracing the antiwar position, as can be seen in Orwell's 1943 verse polemic with the pacifist writer Alex Comfort. Responding to Comfort's own verse "*Letter to an American Visitor*, by Obadiah Hornbrooke," Orwell writes:

> Your hands are clean, and so were Pontius Pilate's,
> But as for "bloody heads," that's just a metaphor;
> The bloody heads are on Pacific islets
> Or Russian steppes or Libyan sands—it's better for
> The health to be a CO than a fighter,
> To chalk a pavement doesn't need much guts,
> It pays to stay at home and be a writer
> While other talents wilt in Nissen huts;
>
> [CEJL, 2:299]

The poem goes on in full manly outrage, including Orwell's usual expressions of homophobia:

> Each little mob of pansies is a world,
> Cosy and warm in any kind of weather;
> In such a world it's easy to "object,"
> Since that's what both your friends and foes expect.

He contrasts this with his own behavior:

> At times it's almost a more dangerous deed
> *Not* to object; I know, for I've been bitten.

I wrote in nineteen-forty that at need
I'd fight to keep the Nazis out of Britain;
And Christ! how shocked the pinks were! Two years later
I hadn't lived it down; one had the effrontery
To write three pages calling me a "traitor,"
So black a crime it is to love one's country.
Yet where's the pink that would have thought it odd of me
To write a shelf of books in praise of sodomy?

[2:300]

Coercive discourse here assails the opponent's masculinity and this—it seems to go without saying—invalidates his political position.

To take another set of examples: In March 1939, in a letter to Herbert Read, Orwell discusses the "idealistic Hitler-fascists" and wonders whether their leader in England, Mosley, "will have the sense and the guts to stick out against war with Germany, he might decide to cash in on the patriotism business" (CEJL, 1:386). But as soon as his own position on the war has changed, Orwell's habitual slurs are cast in the other direction and pacifists become not only pansies and gutless but even "objectively pro-Fascist," which obliges him to point out "the overlap between Fascism and pacifism" (2:181) and to call pacifism a form of "power worship," like communism and fascism (3:8). In addition, Orwell now finds his opponents doomed to unmanly self-gratification. In western Europe, he writes in a wartime diary entry dated June 27, 1940, "Communism and Left extremism generally are now almost entirely a form of masturbation. People who are in fact without power over events console themselves by pretending that they are in some way controlling events." Further along in the same entry he also criticizes the ILP: "These people live almost entirely in a masturbation fantasy, conditioned by the fact that nothing they say or do will ever influence events, not even the turning-out of a single shell" (2:358). Whatever turn his commitments took, Orwell always made his changing opponents targets of the same accusations: of being cowards, of being soft, of acting in bad faith,[27] and of not having guts. Political alliances alter, patriotism wanes and waxes in Orwell, but the rhetoric stays the same.

In *Coming Up for Air*, George Bowling's trajectory as a warrior follows and brings to mind Orwell's own. In this sense, *Homage to Catalonia* functions as a shadow text informing our reading of Bowling's schematic account of war. Bowling's effective experiences of war are ended when he is slightly wounded by a shell in 1916. After his recovery, he goes to an officers' training camp; then, from 1917 through 1919, in a humorous example of bureaucratic bungling, he is forgotten on the north Cornish coast where he had been sent to guard a nonexistent food dump. During these years Bowling reads widely and becomes a narrator capable of serving as Orwell's alter ego when necessary. The main function of this entire war experience is that it bolsters Bowling's contention, realized in retrospect, that "the day I joined the Army the old life was finished. It was as though it didn't concern me any longer" (112). The hidden continuity between Bowling's old life and his war experiences, however, lies in war's consolidation of his masculine identity. But once the initial patriotism and pride in his uniform have worn off, Bowling finds war like an "enormous machine" that makes it impossible to either resist or assert one's own free will: "The machine had got hold of you and it could do what it liked with you" (112).

From his more cynical adult perspective, Bowling notes the importance of soldiers' illusions that jobs would be awaiting the survivors: "Of course, if ideas like that didn't circulate, no war would ever be fought" (125). Orwell's own behavior suggests that such logical explanations do not touch on the deeper reasons why men support war, for, as noted above in chapter 5, once his patriotism was revealed to him in a dream, Orwell found many rationales for supporting the war against Germany, including a belief that the war "will wipe out most of the existing class privileges," as he argued in "The Lion and the Unicorn" (CEJL, 2:78). But Bowling also depicts war as a necessary part of one's education: "If the war didn't happen to kill you it was bound to start you thinking. After that unspeakable idiotic mess you couldn't go on regarding society as something eternal and unquestionable, like a pyramid. You knew it was just a balls-up" (123). Bowling's conflation of personal and political history is apparent in his choice of words, for earlier he had described his parents' house in similar terms: "It had been as permanent to me as the pyramids, and now it would be just an accident if I ever set foot in it again" (116). The point of the earlier scene, however, was to show his innocence and youthful vanity, for during that last visit (to attend his mother's funeral) he had concentrated more on his officer's uniform than on the life that was disappearing. In other words, it is only in retrospect—from his position as a disgruntled forty-five-year-old man—that Bowling valorizes his youth and sees his life as a series of subsequent disappointments that can, in a general way, be traced back to "the war."

The most serious expression of antimilitarism in the novel occurs in a chapter satirizing a Left Book Club meeting. Proud of these pages, Orwell anticipated, perhaps with some glee, that they would annoy Victor Gollancz, founder of the club and still, at this time, Orwell's publisher. "I thought Gollancz might show fight," Orwell wrote to Moore, his agent, on April 25, 1939 (LL); but despite Orwell's predictions Gollancz published the book.

Orwell's scathing description of the "little" professional antifascist speaker deliberately "stirring up hatred" (145) no doubt foreshadows his later creation, in *Nineteen Eighty-Four*, of the Two Minutes Hate spectacles and Hate Week. But the articulation of antiwar sentiment in *Coming Up for Air* is hopelessly compromised by Bowling's "I've been there" posture and clear paternalism toward the young man who, after the lecture, asks him if he would not fight fascism. " 'You bet I wouldn't,' I said. 'I had enough to go on with last time.' " The young man presses him, arguing that "this time it's different," and asks Bowling if the Nazis don't make his blood boil. "I went off the boil in 1916," Bowling replies, alluding to the year he was wounded, again revealing the importance of the wound as a conclusion to the initiation rite of war, "And so'll you when you know what a trench smells like" (151). Bowling is sarcastic about the young man's commitments:

Felt as strongly as all that about the German Jews! But as a matter of fact I knew just what he felt. He's a hefty lad, probably plays rugger for the bank. Got brains, too. And here he is, a bank clerk in a godless suburb, sitting behind the frosted window, entering figures in a ledger, counting piles of notes, bumsucking to the manager. Feels his life rotting away. And all the while, over in Europe, the big stuff's happening. Shells bursting over the trenches and waves of infantry charging through the drifts of smoke. Probably some of his pals are fighting in Spain. Of course he's spoiling for a war. How can you blame him? For a moment I had a peculiar feeling that he was my son, which in point of years he might have been. And I thought of that sweltering hot day in August [1914] when the newsboy stuck up the poster ENGLAND DECLARES WAR ON GERMANY, and we all rushed out on to the pavement in our white aprons and cheered. [151–52]

Bowling tries to tell the boy that "you've got it all wrong. In 1914 *we* thought it was going to be a glorious business. Well, it wasn't. It was just a bloody mess. If it comes again, you keep out of it. Why should you get your body plugged full of lead? Keep it for some girl. You think war's all heroism and V.C. charges, but I tell you it isn't like that" (152; Orwell's emphasis). And he goes on to evoke the discomfort and misery of war. But, "of course," this argument makes no impression.

The antiwar sentiment Orwell puts in Bowling's mouth is ineffective because, as I argued in chapter 5, the authority of the old warrior's position as a proven male constantly reinforces rather than allays the young would-be warrior's need to experience this rite for himself. This self-defeating structure is not identified by Orwell in any of his writings. Given Bowling's own anxiety to escape from the world of women, why should he expect the young man to be receptive to the suggestion that he should keep his body "for some girl"? In fact, the antiwar argument in *Coming Up for Air* is further undermined by its position in a generally misogynistic scene, for Bowling's whole description of the Left Book Club meeting has another, ulterior, function: It affirms his superiority over his wife and her two friends. Hilda's stupidity and ignorance are stressed throughout the novel, and her alliance with these two women who jointly search for interesting things to do has been richly ridiculed by Bowling in the preceding chapter. Incapable of understanding anything, the three women go to Left Book Club meetings because they are held indoors and are free: "The three of them sit there like lumps of pudding" (142), Bowling says, and he repeats the description later on as they all listen to the antifascist speaker: "You could see by the look of Miss Minns's long thin neck that she wasn't feeling happy. Was this improving her mind, or wasn't it? If only she could make out what it was all about! The other two were sitting there like lumps of pudding" (146).

After the meeting, feeling the need for conversation and knowing that it is "hopeless trying to talk to Hilda" (153), Bowling visits his bachelor "pal" Porteous, a retired public schoolmaster always ready to talk and drink. As Bowling says: "When you live in a house like ours, more or less infested by women and kids, it does you good to get out of it sometimes into a bachelor atmosphere, a kind of book-pipe-fire atmosphere" (154). Though the two men share "dirty stories," Bowling criticizes his scholar friend for being "rather old-maidish about it" and always telling a story "in a veiled kind of way" (156). It is a foregone conclusion from this initial feminizing description of Porteous that the scene between the two men will simply end as a further indication of Bowling's superiority—and, indeed, he soon realizes that Porteous, though learned, really has a "dead mind" and is incapable of change.[28]

Having distanced himself from everyone around him, Bowling lets his narrative skip a few months and then resumes on a March morning when, worried about what will happen after the expected war and filled with a sudden love of life, he decides to return for a week to Lower Binfield, hoping that at least the place itself might be unchanged: "I only wanted to get my nerve back before the bad times begin" (168). Earlier, Bowling had envisioned spending the seventeen pounds he had won on a horse in quite a different way: "The alternatives, it seemed to me, were either a week-end with a woman or dribbling it quietly away on odds and ends such as cigars and double whiskies" (9)—that is, on his "masculine" pleasures. He has accepted, as he keeps reminding us, that "no woman will ever go to bed with me again unless she's paid to" (163–64; variation of this on p. 8), but all he wants now is to have a week of peace and quiet.

"Of course the fly in the milk-jug was Hilda" (168), and Bowling's good mood and pleasant expectations suddenly falter as he devotes nearly a page to an elaboration of her jealous nagging and accusations. "Sometimes she's been right about the woman and sometimes she's been wrong, but the aftereffects are always the same. Nagging for weeks on end!" He takes it as self-evidently pointless to try to explain to Hilda how he wants to spend the week: "If I explained till the Day of Judgement she'd never believe that" (169). Just as he could not explain to his mother why he wanted to go fishing with the other boys, so it is futile to explain to Hilda his "harmless" desire to return to his hometown. Women are uncomprehending opponents attempting to control and hold back their men. And a man's task, in childhood and in maturity, remains the same: to reject his ties to them and try to make good his escape, though he knows he will be found out in the end.

COMBAT IN THE DOMESTIC ZONE

Although Bowling's wife and his mother are to a certain extent conflated within the novel, there are important differences between them having to do with the different historical moments in which they live and the particular circumstances of their lives. These factors help explain why it is that Bowling needs to reenact his earlier flight into manhood.

Bowling's adult home life is an example of what one scholar, Rose Laub Coser, calls the "father-absent home." Given the husband's daily removal to a workplace no longer centered in or near the home, it is the wife who must perform tasks formerly undertaken by her husband. These tasks, such as dealing with merchants, schools, and other representatives of the world outside the home, help create a certain autonomy in women, even though they remain dependent on their husbands' income. Coser notes that, as a result, "in modern society men have lost some of their utility as necessary intermediaries between the family and the outside world, and women have become public even when they are domestic." [29] This is the shift we see between Bowling's father's generation and his own. Bowling's mother exemplifies that sort of postindustrial middle-class woman who was confined to the home and centered her attention on caring for her husband and children. At the same time, her contacts with the outside world were restricted due to her husband's very proximity: in the shop he owned, which was attached to the house. Bowling's wife, by contrast, is not nearly so confined as was his mother, for not only is Bowling away from home every day, he is also frequently absent on trips, thus necessitating further independence on Hilda's part. But, except for the desperate outings with her two friends that Bowling so smugly scorns, we know nothing about Hilda's life; she seems to have no interests, no ideas.

While Bowling's typical recollection of his mother is of a "priestess" rolling dough in her kitchen-shrine, his typical image of Hilda is of a disgruntled consumer constantly "glooming about money" (137). The former is an emblem of a "natural" social world; that is, a world a boy child could safely escape from. The latter is an emblem of an "unnatural" world in which Bowling's masculine supremacy is never securely established. He cannot even control his children, as is apparent in a scene in which Hilda tries to keep him from fishing: "And fancy you going fishing at your age!" she says. "A great big grown-up man like you. Don't be such a *baby*, George" (Orwell's emphasis). The children then get in on the act and dance around Bowling, chanting: "Farver's a baby! Farver's a baby!" Bowling comments: "Unnatural little bastards!" (87)

Bowling's desire to return to Lower Binfield is not, I think, a journey "back to the womb of the past," as one critic has called it.[30] The description of his contrasting present and past lives reveals that Bowling longs for the more drastically differentiated male and female roles of his childhood, in which he could both experience the safety of his mother's world and use it as a platform from which to make his escape via a series of masculine rites of passage. It is this he seeks to achieve by re-creating the flight from another woman, his wife. He is not running back to his mother—as his account of his childhood makes abundantly clear—but rather running back to the life that first allowed him to assert himself as a male, that gave him the thrill, so graphically described in the novel, of participation in the world of men. When he does return to Lower Binfield, he protests not merely its transformations but the particular direction of those transformations: The place has become effeminate and "modern." Not surprisingly, once there he can neither fish nor fuck. In short, none of his attempted repetitions of earlier rites now leads to success. Hence the bombing fantasy that ends his stay, which rips a wall off a grocer's shop and leaves the interior neatly exposed: "It was just like looking into a doll's house" (221). He has learned his lesson: "Fat men of forty-five can't go fishing. That kind of thing doesn't happen any longer, it's just a dream, there'll be no more fishing this side the grave" (222). And as he drives away he realizes that there is "no way back to Lower Binfield, you can't put Jonah back into the whale" (223). The belly of the whale, in this context, is that safe world in which Bowling affirmed himself as a boy, a youth, a man. It is an order of things that the technology, methods of warfare, and general "softness" of modern life threaten. The point of being Jonah, of course, is also to be able to get out of the whale and tell the story to a group of admiring listeners.

Orwell was to take on the role of admiring listener to one contemporary Jonah late in 1939 when he wrote his essay on Henry Miller, "Inside the Whale." George Bowling's rejection of warmongering and his desire merely to survive also exemplify the "quietism" that Orwell was to identify in Miller, and critics have tended to read *Coming Up for Air* in light of the later essay. In explaining Miller's "passive attitude," Orwell utilizes Jonah imagery again: Miller is "inside the whale," making no effort to alter or control the "world-process," an attitude Orwell now finds appealing and even redeeming. Observing that people habitually refer to Jonah in the *whale*, though in the Bible it is described merely as a great fish, Orwell interprets this transposition as a sign

of the hold that the Jonah myth has upon our imaginations. For the fact is that being inside a whale is a very comfortable, cosy, homelike thought. ... The whale's belly is simply a womb big enough for an adult. There you are, in the dark, cushioned space that exactly fits you, with yards of blubber between yourself and reality, able to keep up an attitude of the completest indifference, no matter *what* happens. A storm that would sink all the battleships in the world would hardly reach you as an echo. [CEJL, 1:521; Orwell's emphasis]

The echo here, however, is of Orwell's evocation in *Coming Up for Air* of Bowling's mother in her "cosy little underworld of stewed tea, bad legs, and happy endings" (108). As noted earlier, in his 1943 verse attack on pacifists Orwell again utilizes such imagery, even closer to his description of being inside the whale, but now in a tone of deep scorn:

> Each little mob of pansies is a world,
> Cosy and warm in any kind of weather.
> [CEJL, 2:300]

What is one to make of such similar imagery appearing in such differing contexts, now despised, now lamented? It seems to me that Orwell carefully structures every situation in which he allows the attractiveness of such imagery to appear. The positive aspects of Bowling's mother's world, after all, are embedded in the novel within the general celebration of Bowling's escape from that world. And even Orwell's account of Jonah stresses not primarily the connection to the whale but the separation from the world outside. Moreover, it is no accident that Orwell's most forceful praise of "quietism" occurs in the context of a discussion of Henry Miller, the most frenetically phallic writer of his time. In his essay, Orwell claims that Miller gives "you" (meaning men, of course) "the peculiar relief that comes not so much from understanding as from *being understood*. 'He knows all about me,' you feel; 'he wrote this specially for me' " (CEJL, 1:495; Orwell's emphasis; this passage, incidentally, remarkably foreshadows Winston Smith's feelings about O'Brien in *Nineteen Eighty-Four*). Orwell here chooses to treat Miller's obsession with his own sexuality as typical and thereby identifies himself with it. This is all the more intriguing given Orwell's reticence and awkwardness in writing about sex. I believe Orwell was trying to acquire some masculinity-by-association through this identification with Miller. There is no evidence, in fact, that Orwell saw all women as "cunts"—as Miller does; yet Orwell seems to want to pretend to have Miller's attitudes and desires and, further, attributes them to all men.[31]

The fantasy of passivity, of sinking into the belly of the whale and letting events sweep over one, can thus be expressed in utter safety. The obsession with sexual domination cultivated by Miller's fictional persona and Orwell's appreciation of Miller's toughness and typicality obviously ward off any charges of "unmanliness." Since, however, Orwell does not call attention to Miller's preoccupation with masculine sexual prowess or to his profound misogyny,[32] he fails to notice that what occurs in Miller's writing is a slight redefinition of manhood, now limited to the private sphere of sexual relations—a definition befitting an age of faceless power politics in which individual men feel helpless.

While Orwell's hero in *Coming Up for Air* does not imitate Miller's manic sexuality—though he makes it clear that he is "unfaithful" to his wife whenever he has the opportunity (138), apparently not too often given his obesity—his sense of identity is linked to both an escape from the world of women and disdain for them. *Coming Up for Air* can be read as Orwell's horror story of marriage in his time (adumbrated in *Aspidistra*)—half melodrama, half-farce—a marriage based on the economic dependency of an ever less satisfied female and the resentment and discontent of an ever more "henpecked" male. If Bowling rejects war on the international scene, he is perfectly willing to live with it on the domestic scene, with the two principals locked into a situation in which strategic attacks, defeats, and retaliations are the norm. However, it is crucial to note that Bowling is our sole source of information about Hilda (as about everything else in the novel), and so we never hear her side of the story. Most striking in Bowling's view of marriage is the complete absence of minimal consideration and respect, an absence that Bowling treats as inevitable. Hilda emerges as merely an antagonist, or, rather, an antagonist and a habit, nothing more. In virtually every description of Hilda, George Bowling's total lack of friendly feeling for her, and for "wives" in general, is apparent.

Bowling's account of his courtship and marriage reveals a pattern characteristic of the other relationships depicted in the novel: Like his mother, who shrank in his view as he grew older, like his pal Porteous, far better read than Bowling but ultimately shown to be a fool, Hilda, too, is first seen as his superior and then quickly put in her place. Indeed, Bowling specifies that a reversal has occurred in their relationship. Though he began as the social inferior, the representative of the "God-fearing shopkeeper class" and she came from "the poverty-stricken officer class" (133), a change took place in their respective positions over time: "in the last few years she's become much more definitely lower-middle-class, in outlook and even in appearance, than I am" (138).

Demonstrating his complete inability to see Hilda as more than one-dimensional, Bowling first explains her away by virtue of her status as the daughter of a genteel-poor Anglo-Indian family and later by virtue of her status as a "wife," a particularly dismal example of the species "woman," perhaps in unattractiveness matched only by the "old maid" stereotype, also evoked in the novel. Bowling explains: "Well, Hilda and I were married, and right from the start it was a flop. Why did you marry her? you say. But why did you marry yours? These things happen to us. I wonder whether you'll believe that during the first two or three years I had serious thoughts of killing Hilda. Of course in practice one never does these things, they're only a kind of fantasy that one enjoys thinking about" (135). Even in the initial pages of description of Hilda, her transposition into "woman" is apparent:

One gets used to everything in time. After a year or two I stopped wanting to kill her and started wondering about her. Just wondering. For hours, sometimes, on Sunday afternoons or in the evening when I've come home from work, I've lain on my bed with all my clothes on except my shoes, wondering about women. Why they're like that, how they get like that, whether they're doing it on purpose. It seems to be a most frightful thing, the suddenness with which some women go to pieces after they're married. It's as if they were strung up to do just that one thing, and the instant they've done it they wither off like a flower that's set its seed. What really gets me down is the dreary attitude towards life that it implies. If marriage was just an open swindle—if the woman trapped you into it and then turned round and said, "Now, you bastard, I've caught you and you're going to work for me while I have a good time!"—I wouldn't mind so much. But not a bit of it. They don't want to have a good time, they merely want to slump into middle-age as quickly as possible. After the frightful battle of getting her man to the altar, the woman kind of relaxes, and all her youth, looks, energy, and joy of life just vanish overnight. Here was this pretty, delicate girl, who'd seemed to me—and in fact when I first knew her she *was*—a finer type of animal than myself, and within only about three years she'd settled down into a depressed, lifeless, middle-aged frump. I'm not denying that I was part of the reason. But whoever she'd married it would have been much the same. [135–36; Orwell's emphasis] [33]

In the absence of any serious consideration of what might cause such a state of affairs, this portrait merely serves as a contrast with Bowling's frequent description of himself as a jolly fat man. Hilda's lack of joy in life (which he discovered after about a week of marriage) is explained by her origins: Decayed middle-class families, Bowling tells us, are like that; "all their vitality has been drained away by lack of money" (136). But even after offering this explanation (again contrasting with the greater vitality of his own shopkeeper class), Bowling depicts Hilda's "glooming" about money as something she rather enjoys; it merely becomes a token of her dismal character. Like Gordon Comstock in *Aspidistra*, while waxing eloquent on what is wrong with women, George Bowling makes no effort to enter his wife's reality. In his descriptions of their respective characters, Bowling of course does not consider the position of dependency of such a woman, with few choices and no means of earning money. The "frightful battle" to get her man to the altar and the dreary marriage that follows appear to Bowling as things that women do to men.

What is most striking in the description of Hilda is that it is satirical: She is reduced to a few simple traits presented in a grotesque light; for example, "She loves getting into a panic because something or other is 'serious'" (137). When Hilda is first mentioned, early in the novel, it is in similar terms, which, characteristically, trivialize her concerns: "Old Hilda was glooming behind the teapot, in her usual state of alarm and dismay because the *News Chronicle* had announced that the price of butter was going up, or something" (10). And: "She's one of those people who get their main kick in life out of foreseeing disasters. Only petty disasters, of course. As for wars, earthquakes, plagues, famines, and revolutions [the vital "real world" disasters presumably occupying Bowling's own mind], she pays no attention to them" (11).

The function of these descriptions is easy to discern: The rather boring George Bowling appears, by contrast, as a worldly, lively, and free spirit, however constrained by domestic miseries. He is also, it goes without saying, of superior intelligence, hence capable of judging Hilda in all respects: "like all jealous women she'll sometimes show a cunning you wouldn't think her capable of. Sometimes the way she's caught me out would have made me believe in telepathy, if it wasn't that she's often been equally suspicious when I didn't happen to be guilty" (138). Why do they stay together?

There've been times when I've thought of separation or divorce, but in our walk of life you don't do those things. You can't afford to. And then time goes on, and you kind of give up struggling. When you've lived with a woman for fifteen years, it's difficult to imagine life without her. She's part of the order of things. I dare say you might find things to object to in the sun and the moon, but do you really want to change them? Besides, there were the kids. Kids are a "link," as they say. Or a "tie." Not to say a ball and fetter. [139]

After the ludicrous description of Hilda's two friends, Mrs. Wheeler and Miss Minns,[34] Bowling engages in a type of confessional display: "Well, that's Hilda. You see what she's like. Take it by and large, I suppose she's no worse than I am. Sometimes when we were first married I felt I'd like to strangle her, but later I got so that I didn't care. And then I got fat and settled down"; now he has become "just a poor old fatty with nothing ahead of you this side the grave except sweating your guts out to buy boots for the kids" (142). The effect of Bowling's confession is, of course, to deny what it affirms, for, following directly upon the long and ridiculous portrayal of Hilda and her two friends, it further raises the narrator in the reader's esteem and serves to increase the distance between Bowling and his wife. He now appears not only as insightful but also as agreeably modest and truthful—not to mention self-sacrificing, as the last line quoted affirms. Whatever limitations there may be in Bowling's character, they are redeemed by the contrast he creates between himself and his account of his frumpy, gloomy, nagging wife.

It would be tedious to trace Bowling's further carping comments about Hilda; the preceding examples are entirely representative in their tone and content. What is more interesting is to note the critics' rush of identification with Bowling, evident in almost all commentaries on the novel, as if Orwell has, in this text, tapped a deep reservoir of communal misogyny—not the abstract antiwoman diatribes of Gordon Comstock, but the far more specific antiwife, long-suffering-husband routine of the Donald McGill comic postcards.[35] Orwell was not able to analyze the ideology of gender roles depicted on McGill's postcards (he instead chose to believe that some subjects are inherently funny); nor is he able to see beyond the given awfulness—from Bowling's point of view, of course—of Hilda Bowling. Critics typically celebrate Bowling's oft-stated zest for life and commitment to going on, which allows them to see him as a hero and a symbol. But their ingenuous identification with Bowling and their constant reiterations of his own view of himself as a man much tried by a dreadful world and a dreadful wife suggest other things at work. In my view, Bowling is no "perfect emblem for the English people," as John Wain has chosen to see him,[36] but, rather, a spokesman for a misogyny ever more frantic in the face of changes threatening men's sense of being in control.

Orwell deals with the personal and the political in such a way as to affirm the conventional gender division of the world. Bowling, that is to say, is politically involved, out "in the world," visionary of the bad times that are coming; his wife, meanwhile, is at home and will remain absurdly preoccupied with the price of butter as the bombs descend (225). We are meant to despise her and applaud him, which is precisely what most critics have done, forgetting that Bowling is of course the hero of his own story. Because Orwell's portrait of Bowling is not idealized in the obvious sense (he is fat and middle-aged, has false teeth, sells insurance), readers perhaps find it easier to absorb his version of reality, to herald him as a man confronting his historical moment, to accept his self-characterization and not question his judgments. In an androcentric world the overtly political (that is, as conventionally defined: concerns with wars, rulers, international conflicts) is granted a significance and level of discussion not usually accorded the covertly political (the power structures governing individual households and individual lives). It is probably this that allows critics to appreciate Bowling's "decency"— as if rejecting warmongering and the "hate world" of politics on the large scale were a token of decency in everyday life.

But it is not enough to read *Coming Up for Air* in terms of nostalgia for the past, prescient fear of the future, and stoic acceptance of wifely bitchiness. On its own terms, the novel demands a very different reading, as I have shown in the preceding sections. If one examines the ideology implicit in George Bowling's view of life, it becomes impossible to celebrate his "soul" [37] or to see him as the embodiment of Orwell's socialism[38] (a bizarre socialism, if true). How, then, can one explain critical reaction to this novel?

MALE BONDING AS A NARRATIVE TECHNIQUE

Coming Up for Air presents the reader with different problems than did Orwell's earlier novels, in large part because of Orwell's choice of narrative technique. In *A Clergyman's Daughter* we saw Orwell maintaining a rigid distance from his female protagonist and failing to create an authentic female character. In *Coming Up for Air* we are at the other extreme of narrative: the first-person novel. Orwell himself was later to describe I-narrative as a form of daydream that is easy to write but has serious disadvantages (CEJL, 4:511–12).[39]

The tough masculine tone adopted by George Bowling is introduced in the first lines of the novel when he describes how "I'd nipped out of bed and got into the bathroom just in time to shut the kids out" (7). While shutting out his family, Bowling appeals to an imaginary listener, an implied reader who is his silent counterpart. Bowling's narrative voice calls this particular kind of reader into being by causing the actual reader to step into the mental set of the reader who is being addressed. Though Bowling identifies this reader as a person of his own class, a man like himself,[40] the reader whom he evokes is required to be capable of ironic distance, of appreciating the sensitivity and awareness, as well as the humor and toughness, in Bowling's descriptions of his life. Thus, on the novel's first page: "It was a beastly January morning, with a dirty yellowish-grey sky. Down below ... I could see the ten yards by five of grass, with a privet hedge round it and a bare patch in the middle, that we call the back garden" (7). "We" may call it the back garden, but Bowling and his reader are assumed to know better. At the heart of Bowling's repeated claim to ordinariness lies the counterclaim: that in his awareness of his environment, in his ironic self-criticism, he is in fact superior to that environment—and the reader will understand and appreciate this since he too has this superior kind of awareness. In a sense, then, while purportedly presenting Bowling as the average lower-middle-class chap, Orwell is appealing to the reader's sense of social superiority.

Within the world of the novel, the character who most embodies lack of awareness, who is truly submerged and unable to come up for air, is George Bowling's wife, Hilda. From the beginning of his narrative Bowling invites the reader to unite with him against Hilda, to form an alliance that will continually redound to his (and the male reader's) credit. Bowling's generalizations about men are repeatedly presented as celebrations of what it means to be a man, whereas his generalizations about women are almost always derogatory and demeaning (his mother in her kitchen is the sole exception, and even there, as we have seen, Bowling expresses considerable ambivalence). But, not content with this, Bowling also appeals to his implied reader in a more blatant way, making it clear that he himself is very much a man's man. For example, he gruffly "confesses" to the reader that nothing he has ever done "has given me quite such a kick as fishing. Everything else has been a bit of a flop in comparison, even women. I don't set up to be one of those men that don't care about women. I've spent plenty of time chasing them, and I would even now if I had the chance. Still, if you gave me the choice of having any woman you care to name, but I mean *any* woman, or catching a ten-pound carp, the carp would win every time" (80; Orwell's emphasis).

Bowling repeatedly addresses the implied reader in a *mon semblable, mon frère* tone. In fact, the most characteristic phrase in the novel is "you know how it is" or some variation of this, invariably appealing to exclusively male perspectives and experiences. George Bowling's "humanity" and even his desire for intimacy become evident to his readers only within the framework of this male bonding, for these traits are notably lacking in his reaction to any other person in his life. Not only in relation to Hilda and Elsie but even in the description of his father's decline (Who would guess that the phrase "A small shopkeeper going down the hill is a dreadful thing to watch" [101] is a description of the narrator's father?), Bowling uses situations merely for the sake of making generalizations, for sounding off about the world. In short, this character cannot maintain any sort of personal relationship with other people, and the novel is a story of his attempt to redefine his separateness and to affirm his masculinity to one person, one only, and that one conveniently abstract: the reader.

The scenes that stir Bowling's emotions in the novel are the rituals of his youth; even the five minutes of worked-up sentiment when he thinks his wife might be dead or ill (a scene apparently contrived by Orwell purely for the sake of showing us that Bowling's gruff exterior conceals some "genuine" feeling for Hilda) pale in comparison. It is evident from Orwell's other fiction that the inability to depict real relationships is part of Orwell's inadequacy as a novelist. I do not think, however, that this should be viewed only as a literary problem; the disinclination to understand relationships, the desire to substitute caricature for character, to use monologue instead of dialogue, all suggest a felt need to cultivate distance. From this point of view George Bowling may well be Orwell's most successful creation, for here at last is a character who need forge one relationship only—with the male reader—and, to judge by critical response, has done this successfully enough to be affirmed as "everyman." Critics have failed to examine this entire narrative strategy, though their job is, one would think, to analyze, not merely join in; and they thus continually affirm their solidarity with Bowling and their opposition to his shrewish wife.[41]

While talking endlessly to his reader, Bowling talks almost not at all, by his own account, to his wife. Instead, at the novel's end, when she confronts him with his deception (she assumes he was with another woman), he plays the role of inexpressive male, viewing his wife as an opponent and refusing to speak openly to her while appearing to the reader as victim.[42] In a scene early in the novel Bowling bites into a frankfurter, which is then turned into a symbol of the modern world: "The thing burst in my mouth like a rotten pear. A sort of horrible stuff was oozing all over my tongue. But the taste! For a moment I just couldn't believe it. Then I rolled my tongue round it again and had another try. It was *fish!* A sausage, a thing calling itself a frankfurter, filled with fish!" (26–27; Orwell's emphasis). One critic has noted that this is a "perverse phallic image"[43] but without commenting on the further implications of the passage. The scene places Bowling in the position of a passive homosexual; he is deprived of his own phallic power. In his last scene with Hilda, what is to prevent Bowling from being finally cast into a passive role from which not even critics' heroics could rescue him? The tactic is quite simple: It is within the context of his presumed superiority to his wife that Bowling plays the role of downtrodden husband. But it is only that, a role, successfully "seen through" by the critics. Bowling's appeal to the reader's sense of male solidarity helps bring about such an outcome:

And Gosh! what I could see ahead of me! You know what it's like. The weeks on end of ghastly nagging and sulking, and the catty remarks after you think peace has been signed, and the meals always late, and the kids wanting to know what it's all about. But what really got me down was the kind of mental squalor, the kind of mental atmosphere in which the real reason why I'd gone to Lower Binfield wouldn't even be conceivable. That was what chiefly struck me at the moment. If I spent a week explaining to Hilda *why* I'd been to Lower Binfield, she'd never understand. And who *would* understand, here in Ellesmere Road? Gosh! did I even understand myself? The whole thing seemed to be fading out of my mind. Why had I gone to Lower Binfield? *Had* I gone there? In this atmosphere it just seemed meaningless. Nothing's real in Ellesmere Road except gas-bills, school-fees, boiled cabbage, and the office on Monday. [231; Orwell's emphasis]

George Bowling must create in his reader the person who will understand and judge, and the reader must take Bowling's word for it that Hilda would "never understand," without asking why or what her version of this marriage, these events, and "modern life" would be. Bowling appeals to the reader's sympathy by evoking "our" knowledge of female stereotypes—"you know what it's like" with its implication that all of us have had to put up with such scenes. Bowling cannily whispers into the reader's ear and thus brings us close to him. If, that is, we are male readers or females reading-as-males.[44] The women in the novel are all outsiders; among Bowling's mother, wife, and the few other caricatured women, there is not much for a female reader to choose. She finds herself, in other words, required to assent to a narrative that works against her (as Judith Fetterley has put it, in another context).[45] Unless she resists, she is coopted by the narrative's ascription of a negative sign to femaleness and a positive sign to maleness. If this problem is only implicit in Orwell's earlier novels, which utilized a third-person narrative, here it becomes explicit as George Bowling in effect calls into being a reader who is a fellow male sharing his assumptions about the good life of the past, the modern horrors just around the corner, and, of course, the miseries of marriage.

For Bowling, the "mental squalor" he detests naturally exists outside himself. Everything is blamed on externals—the world and the wife he cannot control. Nowhere is there a recognition of his own responsibility even in the private sphere: "Nothing remained except a vulgar low-down row in a smell of old mackintoshes" (232). And by these very words he dissociates himself from this scene. Repeatedly describing his efforts to reason with Hilda as "one more try," his attempt in fact consists of telling her she is wrong (230–32) and finally giving up when she counters that he has lied all along. He does not stop her short by saying, "You're right. I did lie." This is the issue that is evaded in the novel's conclusion, in which Bowling presents himself yet again as a long-suffering husband. Finally he resolves: "No use playing injured innocence any longer. All I wanted was the line of least resistance"; he will let Hilda think he was with a woman and "take my medicine" (232). This further lie will exonerate him from what he has done. She is angry about the wrong thing; hence, once again, wrong. Her position has not altered, which in an ironic way serves to verify Bowling's status as master in this scene. His superior understanding, contrasted with her eternal wrongheadedness, is thus displayed to the bitter end.[46]

The male struggle to control the private sphere, if only in this perverse form, is an essential part of the androcentric ideology at the heart of this novel. It is the counterpart to Bowling's recognition of his lack of control in the public sphere. No relationship is drawn between these two spheres except in terms of Bowling's despair over "modern life." Bowling may not be able to reproduce the escape from women that he experienced in his youth; there are no more rites of passage for him to go through. But he will take his medicine, like a man, as he did years earlier when, though his mother spanked him, the real victory was his. He returns from Lower Binfield with nothing to show for his effort to recapture the past except his superiority to an old lover and his continuing gratitude that "Thank God I'm a man." Only this attitude remains as a permanent defense and consolation as he confronts his wife. But he is not alone, for even in this final scene he is aided by the reader who can be counted on to know, understand, and applaud.

Seven

Political Fiction and

Patriarchal Fantasy

In his essay "Marrakech," Orwell elaborates on the perception that came to him, during his stay in Morocco, that "All people who work with their hands are partly invisible." Describing the file of "very old women," each bent beneath a load of firewood, who passed by his house every afternoon for several weeks, he comments: "I cannot truly say that I had seen them. Firewood was passing—that was how I saw it" (CEJL, 1:391). One day he happened to be walking behind the firewood and finally noticed "the human being underneath it"—a woman. By contrast, he writes, his awareness of the mistreatment of animals was immediate: "I had not been five minutes on Moroccan soil before I noticed the overloading of the donkeys and was infuriated by it." Orwell then describes the small Moroccan donkey, a faithful and willing worker, in the anthropomorphic terms he was later to use for Boxer, the immense and hardworking cart horse in *Animal Farm*, and concludes: "After a dozen years of devoted work, it suddenly drops dead, whereupon its master tips it into the ditch and the village dogs have torn its guts out before it is cold" (1:392). In a fascinating example of his tendency to generalize from personal reactions, Orwell states: "This kind of thing makes one's blood boil, whereas—on the whole—the plight of the human beings does not. I am not commenting, merely pointing to a fact. People with brown skins are next door to invisible. Anyone can be sorry for the donkey with its galled back, but it is generally owing to some kind of accident if one even notices the old woman under her load of sticks" (1:392). The woman, Orwell had earlier explained, "accepted her status as an old woman, that is to say as a beast of burden" (1:391). Rebellion is not a possibility for her, any more than for the Negro soldiers (very visible to Orwell, however) described later in the same essay as unaware of their potential power (see chapter 4).

Orwell explained the genesis of *Animal Farm* in a 1947 preface to the Ukrainian edition of the book. For a decade he had "been convinced that the destruction of the Soviet myth was essential if we wanted a revival of the Socialist movement."

On my return from Spain I thought of exposing the Soviet myth in a story that could be easily understood by almost anyone and which could be easily translated into other languages. However the actual details of the story did not come to me for some time until one day (I was then living in a small village) I saw a little boy, perhaps ten years old, driving a huge cart-horse along a narrow path, whipping it whenever it tried to turn. It struck me that if only such animals became aware of their strength we should have no power over them, and that men exploit animals in much the same way as the rich exploit the proletariat.

I proceeded to analyse Marx's theory from the animals' point of view. To them it was clear that the concept of a class struggle between humans was pure illusion, since whenever it was necessary to exploit animals, all humans united against them: the true struggle is between animals and humans. From this point of departure, it was not difficult to elaborate the story. [CEJL, 3:405–6]

In Morocco, Orwell perceived the cruel labor of donkeys more readily than that of brown-skinned women. Though he abstracts himself from his description and attributes his reaction to all people ("merely pointing to a fact"), this is a characteristic perception for Orwell. We see it duplicated in his account of how he came to write *Animal Farm*. For when Orwell was ready to think in terms of exploitation that transcends economic class, he blindly leaped from class to species without pausing to consider the question of gender. It was apparently easier for Orwell to identify with the animal kingdom, exploited at the hands of "humans," than to note that buried in class and race divisions in the human world lay the issue of gender oppression.

The animals' perspective adopted by Orwell as the starting point for his fable leads him to a conclusion—that the class struggle among humans is "pure illusion"—which is itself an illusion. Although humans have been united in their exploitation of animals, this does not mean that they are united in all other respects. There can exist both a class struggle and a general exploitation of animals. Only this gross simplification, however, enabled Orwell to write *Animal Farm*; in fact, the choice of allegory allowed Orwell to turn his penchant for generalization, one of his fundamental weaknesses as a writer, into a strength, for, as Gay Clifford points out, "allegory invites its readers . . . to see the particular narrative as being also a series of generalized statements, and demands that concepts be identified simultaneously in their fictional and ideological roles." [1] Clifford goes on to state that both *Animal Farm* and *Nineteen Eighty-Four*, like other modern allegories, "require a single act of translation (fiction to history for example) and then can be read as straight narratives whose moral significance is obvious. Indeed, without that clearly delimited act of translation they lose half their force." [2]

Allegory, like myth, presupposes an audience that will respond in certain ways.[3] This is one reason, Northrop Frye has observed, that critics dislike allegory, for it restricts the freedom of their commentary by prescribing its direction.[4] In Clifford's words: "The idea that there are as many ways of reading a work of literature as there are readers is anathema to allegory." [5] This observation is borne out by Orwell's anxious concern that *Animal Farm* be read "correctly." After the manuscript's rejection by Dial Press in New York in 1944, on the grounds that "it was impossible to sell animal stories in the USA," Orwell was "not sure whether one can count on the American public grasping what it is about," as he explained in a letter to his agent (CEJL, 4:110); and he even suggested that "it might be worth indicating on the dust-jacket of the American edition what the book is about" (4:111). Orwell need not have worried. When published in the United States in 1946, *Animal Farm* was the Book-of-the-Month Club main selection, and an unprecedented special letter was sent by the club's president to its members urging them to choose *Animal Farm* rather than an alternative title. It sold over half a million copies (4:519) in the club edition alone. Far from not being understood, it was immediately put to work as an anti-Communist text and to this day is taught in American schools, apparently for this purpose.[6]

PATRIARCH PIGS, MATERNAL MARES,
AND OTHER ANIMALS

The psychological appeal of the animal fable is easy to understand: By projecting human conflicts onto animal characters, readers can avoid feeling threatened or overwhelmed by the real-world problems they encounter in this simplified and in many respects charming form.[7] Neither the author nor the readers, however, are magically freed from their own prejudices by this displacement. On the contrary, a fable such as *Animal Farm* relies considerably upon engaging the reader's preconceived ideas. The author's particular concerns can be more clearly set in relief against a background of familiar and nonchallenging elements. In his fable, Orwell evokes not only our sympathy for certain animals but also our possible distaste for pigs, fear of barking and biting dogs, and awe at the size and strength of horses. But even in the early stages of his story he does not merely portray the animals as united in their animalness against the species *Homo sapiens;* nor, as the story develops, does he simply elicit "anti" feelings for the pigs and "pro" feelings for the other animals without further distinctions.

To be effective, an animal fable must maintain a delicate balance between the evocation of the animals' human characteristics and their recognizable animal traits. The reader must use both perspectives, the human and the animal, simultaneously, if the allegory is not to become ludicrous.[8] Orwell provides a poignantly humorous example of this in describing how the animals went through the farmhouse after the revolution: "Some hams hanging in the kitchen were taken out for burial" (22). Even Snowball's writing down of the Seven Commandments of Animalism is endearing: "It was very neatly written, and except that 'friend' was written 'freind' and one of the 'S's' was the wrong way round, the spelling was correct all the way through" (23). Descriptions such as this occur at many points in the text, and their emotional appeal clearly comes from the childlike quality of the details. At this stage of the proceedings the reader sees nothing sinister in the pigs' newfound literacy. Again and again Orwell attributes childlike tastes and habits to the animals, their love of singing their anthem, "Beasts of England," many times over, for example. This feature also explains why the book can be read with pleasure by children, who no doubt identify more intensely than adults with the animals and their lack of total command of adult human skills. At the same time, the flattened characterizations suitable for animal allegory neutralize some of Orwell's special difficulties as a writer of fiction. He has at last found a framework in which authentic relationships between characters and insight into human beings—ordinary requirements of the novel—are simply not important.

Orwell's animal challenge to Marxism presupposes a unity among the animals (as among the humans) that is purely imaginary. Katharine Burdekin, in an extraordinary feminist novel entitled *Proud Man*, published in 1934 under the pseudonym "Murray Constantine," depicts British society from the vantage point of an evolved self-fertilizing "person" who refers to the rest of us as "subhumans." Burdekin's narrator states the matter in plain language: "A privilege of class divides a subhuman society horizontally, while a privilege of sex divides it vertically."[9] Burdekin also discusses the problem of failed revolutions (which was later to preoccupy Orwell) and labels them "reversals of privilege." She relates these to the human preoccupation with the idea of importance, exacerbated in males due to their biological limitations—"womb envy," in short.[10] In *Animal Farm*, however, Orwell does not address the vertical division of society—by sex—on which patriarchy rests. Of course, we know that his aim was to satirize "dictatorship in general"[11] and the Russian Revolution in particular; but displacing his political message onto animals did not allow Orwell an avenue of escape from the messy business of the gender hierarchy. On the contrary, it is carefully reproduced in *Animal Farm*.

Although *Animal Farm* is mentioned in scores of studies of Orwell,[12] no critic has thought it worth a comment that the pigs who betray the revolution, like the pig who starts it, are not just pigs but boars, that is, uncastrated male pigs kept for breeding purposes. Old Major, the "prize Middle White boar" (5) who has called a meeting to tell the other animals about his dream, is initially described in terms that establish him as patriarch of this world: "He was twelve years old and had lately grown rather stout, but he was still a majestic-looking pig, with a wise and benevolent appearance in spite of the fact that his tushes had never been cut" (5–6). In contrasting his life with those of the less fortunate animals on the farm, Major says: "I am one of the lucky ones. I am twelve years old and have had over four hundred children. Such is the natural life of a pig" (10). Orwell here repeats the pattern we have seen in his other fiction, of stressing paternity as if the actual labor of reproduction were done by males. Authority comes from the phallus and fatherhood, and the sows, in fact, are hardly mentioned in the book; when they are, as we shall see, it is solely to illustrate the patriarchal control of the ruling pig, Napoleon. Leaders, then, may be good (Major) or bad (Napoleon)—but they must be male and "potent."

Contrasting with the paternal principle embodied in Major is the maternal, embodied in Clover, "a stout motherly mare approaching middle life, who had never quite got her figure back after her fourth foal" (6). Clover is characterized above all by her nurturing concern for the other animals. When a brood of ducklings that had lost their mother come into the barn, Clover "made a sort of wall round them with her great foreleg," and they nestled down inside it (7). Though Clover works along with Boxer— the enormous cart horse "as strong as any two ordinary horses put together" (6) whom Orwell uses to represent the working class, unintelligent but ever-faithful, to judge by this image—she is admired not for her hard labor but rather for her caring role as protector of the weaker animals.[13] Orwell here attributes to the maternal female dominion over the moral sphere but without any power to implement her values. As in *Nineteen Eighty-Four*, this "feminine" characteristic, though admirable, is shown to be utterly helpless and of no avail. In addition, this conventional (human) division of reality restricts the female animal to the affective and expressive sphere and the male to the instrumental.

I noted in chapter 6 that Orwell at times utilizes the same imagery in opposing ways; imagery relating to passivity, for example, is presented as attractive in "Inside the Whale" and repulsive when associated with pansy pacifists. This ambivalence is demonstrated as well in Orwell's use of protective maternal imagery. Clover's protective gesture toward the ducklings, viewed positively in *Animal Farm*, is matched by Orwell's ridicule of a similar image in his verse polemic with Alex Comfort in 1943, about half a year before Orwell began composing *Animal Farm*. Falling into his familiar tough-guy rhetoric, Orwell angrily defended Churchill against pacifist gibes:

But you don't hoot at Stalin—that's "not done"—
Only at Churchill; I've no wish to praise him,
I'd gladly shoot him when the war is won,
Or now, if there were someone to replace him.
But unlike some, I'll pay him what I owe him;
There was a time when empires crashed like houses,
And many a pink who'd titter at your poem
Was glad enough to cling to Churchill's trousers.
Christ! how they huddled up to one another
Like day-old chicks about their foster-mother!

[CEJL, 2:301]

The protective environment must (as in *Coming Up for Air*) be rejected if manly status is to be preserved. But the protective gesture itself, in its inevitable futility, is admired in *Animal Farm*,[14] and it is through Clover that Orwell expresses the sadness of the failed revolution after the "purges" occur, as the stunned animals huddle around her:

As Clover looked down the hillside her eyes filled with tears. If she could have spoken her thoughts, it would have been to say that this was not what they had aimed at when they had set themselves years ago to work for the overthrow of the human race. These scenes of terror and slaughter were not what they had looked forward to on that night when old Major first stirred them to rebellion. If she herself had had any picture of the future, it had been of a society of animals set free from hunger and the whip, all equal, each working according to his capacity, the strong protecting the weak, as she had protected the last brood of ducklings with her foreleg on the night of Major's speech. [75–76]

Clover is here contrasted with Boxer, who is unable to reflect on these matters and simply resolves to work even harder than before (74). Though Clover too "would remain faithful, work hard, carry out the orders that were given to her, and accept the leadership of Napoleon" (76), she has the moral awareness to know that "it was not for this that she and all the other animals had hoped and toiled" (76). But she lacks the words to express this awareness and instead sings "Beasts of England."

Clover stands at one of the poles of Orwell's conventional representation of female character.[15] The other pole is represented by Mollie, "the foolish, pretty white mare who drew Mr Jones's trap" (7) and is shown, early in the book, to have a link with human females. When the animals wander through the farmhouse, Mollie lingers in the best bedroom: "She had taken a piece of blue ribbon from Mrs Jones's dressing-table, and was holding it against her shoulder and admiring herself in the glass in a very foolish manner" (21–22). A less important female character is the cat who, during Major's speech, finds the warmest place to settle down in and does not listen to a word he says (7). Both Mollie and the cat, we later learn, avoid work; and Mollie is the first defector from the farm after the revolution, seduced by a neighboring farmer's offerings of ribbons for her white mane and sugar.[16]

Orwell's characterizations of old Major, Boxer, Clover, Mollie, and the cat all appear, clearly packaged and labeled, in the book's first three pages. The animal community thus forms a recognizable social world, divided by gender. This world is presented to us complete with stereotypes of patriarchal power, in the form of male wisdom, virility, or sheer strength, and female subordination, in the form of a conventional dichotomy between "good" maternal females and "bad" nonmaternal females. It is difficult to gauge Orwell's intentions in making use of gender stereotypes in *Animal Farm*. Given the evidence of his other texts, however, it seems unlikely that the possibility of a critical, even satirical, account of gender divisions ever crossed his mind. Perhaps he simply incorporated the familiar into his animal fable as part of the "natural human" traits needed to gain plausibility for his drama of a revolution betrayed. But in so doing he inadvertently reveals something very important about this barnyard revolution: Like its human counterparts, it invariably re-creates the institution of patriarchy.

SEXUAL POLITICS ON THE FARM

Not only does Orwell's satire of a Marxist ("Animalist") revolution fail to question gender domination while arguing against species domination, it actually depends upon the stability of patriarchy as an institution. This is demonstrated by the continuity between Mr. Jones, the original proprietor of the farm, and Napoleon (Stalin), the young boar who contrives to drive out Snowball (Trotsky), the only competing boar on the premises, and assumes Jones's former position as well as that of Major, the old patriarch.

In her study of feminism and socialism, Batya Weinbaum attempts to explain why socialist revolutions have tended to re-establish patriarchy. Describing this pattern in the Russian and Chinese revolutions, Weinbaum utilizes the terminology of kin categories: father, daughter, brother, wife. These categories allow her to point out that revolutions have expressed the revolt of brothers against fathers. Though her analysis relies on a Freudian model of sexual rivalry, agreement about motivation is not necessary in order to see the value of the kin categories she proposes. While daughters participate along with brothers in the early stages of revolution, they are increasingly left out of the centers of power once the brothers realize they can occupy the positions formerly held by the fathers, thus gaining privileged access to the labor and services of women.[17]

It is intriguing to note how closely this scheme fits *Animal Farm*. Although Orwell describes a generalized revolt of the animals, inspired by a wise father's message of freedom, this revolt against the human exploiter Jones is quickly perverted into a struggle between two of the brothers, each eager to occupy the father slot and eliminate his competitor. Orwell makes it explicit that the struggle goes on between the only two boars among the pigs. The male porkers (castrated pigs) are not contenders for the father role. There is even an especially nasty portrayal of Squealer, the public relations porker who, in keeping with Orwell's other slurs against the press, is depicted as devoid of masculinity (in Orwell's terms): He stays safely away from the fighting. Once Napoleon wins out over Snowball, we see just what the father role means in terms of access to females. As the sole potent male pig on the farm, Napoleon is of course the father of the next generation of elite pigs: "In the autumn the four sows had all littered about simultaneously, producing thirty-one young pigs between them. The young pigs were piebald, and as Napoleon was the only boar on the farm, it was possible to guess at their parentage" (96).

In addition, the relations among the sows, competing for Napoleon's favor, are hinted at near the story's end, when Napoleon is on the verge of complete reconciliation with the human fathers, the neighboring farmers. Orwell informs us that the pigs (males) began to wear Mr. Jones's clothes, "Napoleon himself appearing in a black coat, ratcatcher breeches, and leather leggings, while his favourite sow appeared in the watered silk dress which Mrs. Jones had been used to wearing on Sundays" (115). Perhaps because these details seem to be beside the point in terms of the allegory, they are all the more intriguing as instances of Orwell's fantasy at work. Intentionally or not, Orwell has re-created the structure of the patriarchal family. As in human families, power among the pigs is organized along two axes: sex and age.

Though we are told that the pigs as a whole exploit the other animals (by keeping more and better food for themselves, claiming exemption from physical labor because they are doing the "brainwork" of the farm, and finally moving into the farmhouse and adopting all the formerly proscribed human habits), it is only the male pigs whom we see, in the book's closing line, as indistinguishable from human males: "The creatures outside looked from pig to man, and from man to pig, and from pig to man again; but already it was impossible to say which was which" (120). Piggish adaptation to the human world involves not only the general class discrimination evident in the rewritten Commandment: "All animals are equal but some animals are more equal than others" (114).[18] It also appears more specifically in the gender hierarchy that culminates in this last scene, so different from the account of the revolution itself in which virtually all the animals and both sexes had participated.

Even as the animal allegory duplicates Orwell's gender assumptions, it also liberates him to some extent from the confines of his own androcentric framework. This is apparent in the unfolding of old Major's speech early in the book. He begins with general comments about the animals' lot: "No animal in England knows the meaning of happiness or leisure after he is a year old. No animal in England is free. The life of an animal is misery and slavery: that is the plain truth" (8). But as he continues to speak, his emphasis shifts slightly:

Why then do we continue in this miserable condition? Because nearly the whole of our produce is stolen from us by human beings. There, comrades, is the answer to all our problems. It is summed up in a single word —Man. Man is the only real enemy we have. Remove Man from the scene, and the root cause of hunger and overwork is abolished forever.

Man is the only creature that consumes without producing. He does not give milk, he does not lay eggs, he is too weak to pull the plough, he cannot run fast enough to catch rabbits. [8–9]

Here, for the first and only time in his writings, Orwell recognizes female reproductive labor as part and parcel of a society's productive activities and as a form of labor that gives females the right to make political and economic demands. In old Major's speech, it is this female labor, specifically, that becomes the most dramatic focal point. The passage quoted above continues:

Yet he [Man] is lord of all the animals. He sets them to work, he gives back to them the bare minimum that will prevent them from starving, and the rest he keeps for himself. Our labour tills the soil, our dung fertilizes it, and yet there is not one of us that owns more than his bare skin. You cows that I see before me, how many thousands of gallons of milk have you given during this last year? And what has happened to that milk which should have been breeding up sturdy calves? Every drop of it has gone down the throats of our enemies. And you hens, how many eggs have you laid this year, and how many of those eggs ever hatched into chickens? The rest have all gone to market to bring in money for Jones and his men. And you, Clover, where are those four foals you bore, who should have been the support and pleasure of your old age? Each was sold at a year old—you will never see one of them again. In return for your four confinements and all your labour in the field, what have you ever had except your bare rations and a stall? [9]

In this passage Orwell is finally able to make the connection between "public" and "private"—between the male's (typical) work of production and the female's (typical) work of reproduction. He sees that both forms of labor can be expropriated and that the "private" sphere in which relations of caring and nurturing go on is very much a part of the overall system of exploitation that old Major protests. Thinking about animals, Orwell notices that females are insufficiently rewarded for the labor stolen from them by men.

As the revolution decays, there occurs an episode in which Napoleon forces the hens to give up more of their eggs, so that they can be used for export to a neighboring farm. At first the hens sabotage this plan by dropping their eggs from the rafters of the barn. But they are quickly brought into line by the cessation of their rations (the acquisition of food still not being under their direct control). After holding out for five days, the hens capitulate (66–67). This increased expropriation of the hens' products is viewed by Orwell in precisely the same terms as the increased labor time extracted from the other animals. In contrast, when

Orwell wrote about the human working class, he never noticed the economics of reproduction or objected to women's exclusion from direct access to decent livelihoods—an exclusion justified by reference to their status as females and supposed dependents of males. It is as if, since his farm animals are not divided into individual family groupings, Orwell was able to break through the ideology of "typical family" that had earlier blinded him to the reality of women's work and position in capitalist society.

In *Animal Farm*, furthermore, Orwell touches on the problem of political expropriation of female reproductive capacity. Napoleon provides himself with a secret police force by separating a litter of newborn puppies from their mothers and rearing them himself, and these puppies, when grown up, drive out the rival brother, Snowball, and inaugurate Napoleon's reign of terror. Orwell here seems to protest against the breakup of the "natural" pattern by which the pups are suckled and raised by their mothers. This theme is reiterated when Napoleon seizes the thirty-one young pigs—his offspring—and appoints himself their instructor, so as to prepare the continued domination of pigs over the other animals in the future. Such "unnatural" expropriations stand in sharp opposition to the traditional patterns of family life so strongly supported by Orwell. The same sort of "state" interference in family life occurs, in more detailed form, in *Nineteen Eighty-Four*.

Although his fiction suggests a strong distaste for these examples of state expropriation of female reproductive labor, Orwell was actually urging the adoption in England of population policies that, if put into practice, would have openly treated women as mere vehicles for fulfilling state priorities. In "The English People," written in 1944 (that is, shortly after *Animal Farm*) though not published until 1947, Orwell, in the throes of a panic about the dwindling birthrate, exhorts the English to have more children as one of the necessary steps in order to "retain their vitality" (CEJL, 3:31). Interpreting the declining birthrate primarily as an economic problem, he urges the government to take appropriate measures:

Any government, by a few strokes of the pen, could make childlessness as unbearable an economic burden as a big family is now: but no government has chosen to do so, because of the ignorant idea that a bigger population means more unemployed. Far more drastically than anyone has proposed hitherto, taxation will have to be graded so as to encourage child-bearing and to save women with young children from being obliged to work outside the home. [3:32]

In addition to economic and social incentives, Orwell says, a "change of outlook" is needed: "In the England of the last thirty years it has seemed all too natural that blocks of flats should refuse tenants with children, that parks and squares should be railed off to keep the children out of them, that abortion, theoretically illegal, should be looked on as a peccadillo, and that the the main aim of commercial advertising should be to popularise the idea of 'having a good time' and staying young as long as possible" (3:32).

In brief, what the English must do is, among other things, to "breed faster, work harder, and probably live more simply" (3:37), a program ominously reminiscent of Napoleon's exhortation to the other animals: "The truest happiness, he said, lay in working hard and living frugally" (Animal Farm, 109). In Orwell's concern with socially adequate human breeding there is no more consideration for the choices of women than Napoleon shows for the desires of the hens or bitches whose eggs and puppies he removes. Orwell seems to assume that the "natural" desires of women will precisely coincide with the lines he sets out—if, that is, he has paused to look at the matter from their point of view at all. Several years later, Orwell still viewed the "population problem" in the same terms. In a newspaper column in 1947, he voices alarm that, if England does not quickly reach an average family size of four children (instead of the then existing average of two), "there will not be enough women of child-bearing age to restore the situation." He worries about where future workers will come from and again recommends financial incentives.[19] Though Orwell was hardly alone in expressing such concerns at that time, it is instructive to note the limited perspective he brings to the problem. And yet in Nineteen Eighty-Four he satirizes the Party's control over Outer Party members' reproductive behavior through the character of Winston's wife, Katharine, who chills Winston's blood with her commitment to regular sexual intercourse as an expression of "our duty to the Party." It seems obvious that Orwell's opinion of such state interference in sex and procreation has nothing to do with any sympathy for women as individuals but depends entirely upon his judgment of the merits of the state that is being served.

Nothing in Orwell's earlier writings reveals an awareness of the economic contributions made by women as reproducers, rearers, and caretakers of the labor force, not to mention as ordinary members of the work force. It is therefore all the more surprising that in letting his imagination translate human conflicts into animal terms this aspect of female roles at once sprang to his attention. At the same time, his female animals are still rudimentary in comparison with the more subtly drawn portraits of the male animals on the farm. The hens and cows, for example, appear primarily as good followers, prefiguring Orwell's description of Outer Party female supporters in *Nineteen Eighty-Four*. With the exception of the maternal Clover and, to a lesser extent, Mollie, the female animals are unimportant as individual actors in the fable.

The animals are differentiated not only according to gender but also by intelligence, the pigs being described as both intelligent and piggish even at an early stage in the revolution, when they appropriate the cows' milk for their own use. The other animals, with only a few exceptions, are generous, hardworking, and stupid by contrast. It is not power that corrupts the pigs; power simply provides them with the means to realize their "nature." The betrayal of the revolution in *Animal Farm*, though it occurs over a period of time, is not, in fact, described as a process. This is why *Animal Farm*, beyond what it has to say concerning Stalin and the Soviet Union, has a profoundly dispiriting message. Orwell presents a static picture of a static universe in which the notion of the pigs' animal nature explains what happens. The final tableau, with the pigs and the men indistinguishable, is the actualization of the potential inherent in the pigs from the beginning. Unlike what he does in *Nineteen Eighty-Four*, however, Orwell gives the pigs specific material motives for the exploitation of the other animals: better food, more leisure, and a privileged life, all acquired partly by terrorizing and partly by gulling the others into thinking that because the pigs are more intelligent they alone can manage the farm. The question of intelligence is a problematic one in this book, for Orwell associates this characteristic with exploitation. There is a suggestion here that generosity, cooperation, devotion are somehow incompatible with intelligence. The deeper question, of what power hunger is really about, is avoided, and the apparent answers Orwell provides in his animal fable are inconsistent and unsatisfying, for even among the pigs not all are shown to be corrupted by greed and the desire for power.

As the pigs duplicate the human model of social organization, they not only reproduce the pattern of patriarchy already familiar to the animals (judging by Major's status early in the book) but add to it those human characteristics that Orwell found most reprehensible—especially softness. They slowly adopt Mr. Jones's manner of living, complete with cushy bed and booze. This is contrasted with the heroic labor of the immensely strong Boxer, who literally works himself to death. Relations between the pigs and the other animals follow the patriarchal model also in that they are hierarchical and discipline-oriented; submission and obedience are extracted from the worker animals as the price of the supposedly indispensable pig leadership.

In addition to the touching solidarity evident among the worker animals, some individual relationships also emerge. One of these is the nonverbal "masculine" friendship between Boxer and Benjamin, who look forward to their retirement together. There is no female version of this friendship, however. Instead, Clover plays the role not only of maternal mare to the other animals but also of "wife"—to use Weinbaum's kin categories again —in that she has a heart-to-heart talk with Mollie. Cast in the role of the rebellious "daughter" who refuses to adhere to the farm's values, Mollie disbelieves in the communal cause and prefers to ally herself with powerful human males outside the farm, thus assuring her easier life as a kept and well-decorated mare. Orwell signals his disapproval of Mollie by showing her cowardice (39) as well as her vanity and sloth. Given the revolution's eventual outcome, however, Mollie's behavior, though egocentric, is not as misguided as it may seem. Orwell makes it explicit that under the rule of Napoleon the animals (except the pigs and Moses, the raven, who represents the church) have an even more arduous work life than animals on the neighboring (i.e., capitalist) farms. Mollie might better be viewed as having some spontaneous understanding of the rules of patriarchy, characterized by Weinbaum in these words: "Brothers may step across the line to become fathers; but daughters face a future as a powerless wife." [20]

ANIMAL FARM AS A FEMINIST FABLE

With astonishing ease and aptness, *Animal Farm* can be read as a feminist critique of socialist revolutions which, through their failure to challenge patriarchy, have reproduced patriarchal values in the postrevolutionary period. In this reading of the fable, the pigs would be the sole male animals, while most of the other animals are stereotyped females: compliant, hardworking drones brainwashed with the illusion that their work is done for themselves, surrendering the fruits of their productive and reproductive labor to their masters, who tell them that there never was hope of a different future.

As in the power relations between men and women, so in *Animal Farm* "science" is used to explain that pigs need better and bigger rations because they are "brain workers," an argument offering the additional message that the dependent animals could not manage on their own. These brainworkers take on the "hard" work of supervising the political and economic life of the farm, consigning the rest to the "less important" tasks of physical labor and maintenance of the farm/home. By also assuming the burden of "international" relations (with neighboring farms), the pigs keep the others pure from any contaminating contact with the outside world—again, an uncanny parallel to the public/private split of ordinary patriarchal society. Whether the individual nonpig animal is big and strong like Boxer or small and weak like the hens, it is held in check by an ideology of its own ignorance and dependence, subjected to violence and intimidation, and urged to sacrifice itself. Such an animal is not likely to rebel. But, as Orwell himself pointed out, the book does not end on a totally pessimistic note. For in the recognition that pigs and men are identical lies the spark of knowledge that can lead to liberatory action.

It would be absurd, of course, to suggest that Orwell intended such a feminist reading of his text. Everything he ever wrote shows that he took the patriarchal family to be the proper model of society. In "The Lion and the Unicorn" he complained only that England was like "a family with the wrong members in control,"

a rather stuffy Victorian family, with not many black sheep in it but with all its cupboards bursting with skeletons. It has rich relations who have to be kow-towed to and poor relations who are horribly sat upon, and there is a deep conspiracy of silence about the source of the family income. It is a family in which the young are generally thwarted and most of the power is in the hands of irresponsible uncles and bedridden aunts. Still, it is a family. It has its private language and its common memories, and at the approach of an enemy it closes its ranks. [CEJL, 2:68]

Of course, Orwell's version of just who is in control itself indicates his habitual misreading of the status of women in his own society. It seems to me that Orwell's complaint was on behalf of the brothers alone, as evidenced by his lack of awareness of the real disunity inherent in the patriarchal family.[21]

It is fascinating to see Orwell describe the betrayal of the animals' revolution in terms so suggestive of women's experience under patriarchy. It is women who, more than any other group and regardless of the race and class to which they belong, have had their history obliterated, their words suppressed and forgotten, their position in society confounded by the doublethink of "All men are created equal," their legal rights denied, their labor in the home and outside of it expropriated and controlled by men, their reproductive capacities used against them, their desire for knowledge thwarted, their strivings turned into dependence—all of these under the single pretext that they are not "by nature" equipped to do the valued work of society, defined as what men do. When read as a feminist fable, however, *Animal Farm* has another important message. The origins of the Seven Commandments of Animalism lie in Major's warnings against adopting Man's ways: "And remember also that in fighting against Man, we must not come to resemble him. Even when you have conquered him, do not adopt his vices" (11–12).

Orwell knew that something was missing from his political analysis, however, as is apparent in one of his "As I Please" columns dating from November 1946, in which he examines the front page of a daily newspaper and deplores the typical disasters it records. Long recovered from the quietist mood of "Inside the Whale" but now deeply pessimistic, he writes: "I think one must continue the political struggle, just as a doctor must try to save the life of a patient who is probably going to die. But I do suggest that we shall get nowhere unless we start by recognising that political behaviour is largely non-rational, that the world is suffering from some kind of mental disease which must be diagnosed before it can be cured" (CEJL, 4:248–49). As we shall see in chapter 8, Orwell's next novel, *Nineteen Eighty-Four*, can help us to understand the nature of this illness.

Eight

Gamesmanship and Androcentrism
in Nineteen Eighty-Four

Orwell's most important contribution to dystopian literature—fictional visions of "bad places"—is generally taken to be his analysis of power in *Nineteen Eighty-Four*. The major twentieth-century dystopian novels produced before *Nineteen Eighty-Four* depict societies dominated by "reason," eugenics, and the production process. Eugene Zamiatin's *We* (1924) and Aldous Huxley's *Brave New World* (1932), probably the best-known examples, are similar in their views of mechanized societies whose citizens are deprived of freedom through physical and psychological conditioning. The rulers of these societies justify their power by moral arguments; that is, they consider their pursuit of power a means to a socially desirable end.

Early utopian fiction repeatedly uses a kind of ethnographic model to explain the workings of the utopian society: Through long dialogues between a "native informant" and a representative of the familiar old society, the reader is exposed not only to impressions of the new society but also to a closely reasoned presentation of its inner logic. The dystopian literature that begins to be abundantly produced toward the end of the nineteenth century varies this formula: Now there is typically a scene in which the key authority figure explains the logic of domination to the rebellious protagonist. The pattern these dialogues follow owes much to the legend of the Grand Inquisitor in Dostoevski's *Brothers Karamazov* (1880). In a crucial scene set in Seville during the Inquisition, Christ, having reappeared, is taken into custody and brought before the Grand Inquisitor. Man, according to the Inquisitor, is weak and irrational and unable to deal with the burden of freedom. The church must therefore take this burden upon itself, providing its flock with happiness, security, and unity instead of freedom. In one way or another, this rationale for power also appears in Zamiatin's *We* and Huxley's *Brave New World*. But Orwell explicitly breaks with this pattern by presenting a vision of the immediate future in which no moral justification of any kind is offered for the control exercised by the Party.[1] It is, in fact, precisely this lack of moral justification that is the essential feature of Orwell's novel. Other twentieth-century dystopias, such as Jack London's *Iron Heel* (1907) and, especially, Katharine Burdekin's *Swastika Night* (1937; published under the pseudonym "Murray Constantine"), also explore the fascination with power, but *Nineteen Eighty-Four* is unusual in its apparent rejection of the moral justification for the exercise of power while failing to provide any substitute rationale.

In this chapter I shall analyze the implications of this rejection and suggest that the Party's actions can best be understood as a game. The concept of play throws considerable light on O'Brien's behavior in *Nineteen Eighty-Four*, and a perspective borrowed from game theory clarifies Winston Smith's role. This approach helps us to recognize that both O'Brien and Winston are players operating from a common frame of reference, sharing fundamental values. Examining these values leads, in turn, to an analysis and critique of Orwell's androcentrism in *Nineteen Eighty-Four*. A comparison of *Nineteen Eighty-Four* with *Swastika Night*—an important but little-known antifascist dystopia from which Orwell may have borrowed—is instrumental in allowing us to note the particular constraints operating on Orwell's imagination. His unquestioning adherence to traditional definitions of masculinity continues to create obstacles and contradictions in his avowed commitments to social justice. Orwell's despair, in *Nineteen Eighty-Four*, is, I believe, the result of his inability to confront this problem.

O'BRIEN AT PLAY

In a variation on the Grand Inquisitor scene in other dystopias, Orwell has O'Brien explain to Winston Smith that the answer Winston has been seeking—the "why" of the Party's pursuit of power—lies in power itself. The means have become ends: Power is pursued entirely for its own sake. O'Brien spells out for Winston precisely what power involves: "power is power over human beings" (212). In a series of questions and answers like a catechism, O'Brien asks: "How does one man assert his power over another, Winston?" and Winston, after weeks of torture, knows the answer: "By making him suffer." O'Brien explains the implications of this: "Obedience is not enough. Unless he is suffering, how can you be sure that he is obeying your will and not his own?" (214). The Party will always have available to it this intoxication of power, the thrill of victory; the image of the future that O'Brien presents to Winston is of a boot stamping on a human face—forever (215), an image borrowed from London's *Iron Heel.*

If we disregard, for a moment, the content of the activity O'Brien is involved in and concentrate instead on its form, we find that the rejection of instrumentality—that is, of activities pursued as means to an end—is an important feature of utopian fiction. William Morris, for example, in his novel *News from Nowhere* (1890), depicts a simple society that has voluntarily rejected many of the questionable gains of technology for the sake of creativity and pleasure in work. This ideal is close to the Marxist one of creative, nonalienated activity, and it implies freedom from the realm of necessity. Even utopias that do not envision such an achievement seem to share in the ideal, as we can see from their goal of an ever-decreasing workday that allows the cultivation of leisure. The more that human beings are freed from the realm of necessity, the closer they can approach the ideal of an intrinsically valuable existence.[2]

In other words, play and not work characterizes the good life, but to understand this idea we need to go beyond the common view of play as an escape from or a compensation for the rigors of daily life, or of leisure time as the mere period of recovery that it becomes when labor predominates in life. One of the most fundamental features of games, as virtually all students of play agree, is gratuitousness or immanence. Games are ends in themselves. They are not means to further ends (except in certain ambiguous situations—for example, professional sports). One of the simplest and clearest ways to envision the lack of instrumentality in games is to focus on the constraints imposed by play—the rules of the game, in other words. Consider basketball: If the purpose of the game were merely to put balls through baskets, a ladder could be brought in or the basket could be lowered or made much larger. Clearly, the voluntarily accepted rules of the game impose difficulties or obstacles that are essential to its pursuit. The aim—to make baskets—is thus not sufficient to define this activity as play. This end can be pursued only within the framework of certain constraints that constitute the game; accepting this framework is what playing the game means. Similarly, if someone throws a ball into the basket to dislodge a knife that might fall and injure a player during the game, this act cannot properly be viewed as playing the game. The game is an activity that is intrinsically valuable and that is pursued for its own sake. But to say that games are gratuitous is not at all to say that they are without meaning. Much can be learned about a society through the study of its games, and the games played in *Nineteen Eighty-Four* are no exception.

Not all forms of play, of course, depend on contest or competition, as Roger Caillois shows in extending Huizinga's conception of play. In addition to contest or competition, which he calls *agon*, Caillois introduces three other categories of play: chance (*alea*), simulation (*mimicry*), and vertigo (*ilinx*).[3] In *Nineteen Eighty-Four* all four categories of play appear, but it is above all the competitive game of power that is pursued. When power is pursued for its own sake, it becomes a game, and clearly it must be a competitive game for, far from being an absolute or independent abstraction, power always consists in a *relation*. In other words, the obstacle or difficulty that makes the game of power possible is another human consciousness. But not just any other consciousness, and especially not a weak one. A weak opponent in the game of power produces the same unsatisfactory victory as a weak opponent in a game of chess: For the game to be relished, a relative equality between the players is needed. This requirement explains a great deal about O'Brien's relationship to Winston Smith.

The game analogy provides a model that helps us understand the interactions within *Nineteen Eighty-Four*, but in no way should it detract from the utter seriousness with which we should view the world Orwell projects in this novel. We need first of all to free ourselves of the conventional opposition between the realm of play and the serious concerns of "real" life.[4] Games can be serious—deadly serious—as the game-playing aspects of military combat and political machinations make abundantly clear and as Orwell's remarks on sports also reveal. In "The Sporting Spirit," an essay written in 1945, Orwell comments on the orgies of hatred generated by international sporting contests and discusses the competitive spirit in the sports that had grown most popular. He links this emphasis to the rise of nationalism, which he characterizes as "the lunatic modern habit of identifying oneself with large power units and seeing everything in terms of competitive prestige." When strong feelings of rivalry are aroused, Orwell says, "the notion of playing the game according to the rules always vanishes. People want to see one side on top and the other side humiliated, and they forget that victory gained through cheating or through the intervention of the crowd is meaningless. . . . Serious sport has nothing to do with fair play. It is bound up with hatred, jealousy, boastfulness, disregard of all rules and sadistic pleasure in witnessing violence: in other words it is war minus the shooting" (CEJL, 4:40–44). Thus, in *Nineteen Eighty-Four* we see work broken up by the "play" of Two Minutes Hate and Hate Week, which reverse Orwell's description, for they involve intense hatred without the sport or, in other words, reduce the sport to the spectator's emotional response.

O'Brien's statements to Winston about the Party's single-minded passion for power have a number of implications that need to be explored. First, and most obvious, in its pursuit of power the Party is not wholly independent, for it depends on a supply of opponents. Power requires resistance: We do not speak of power over others when resistance is not present. Lack of resistance may show that power has become institutionalized, has been transformed into authority, but mere authority is not what O'Brien is describing here. Habitual obedience, as he points out, is not enough. There must be resistance—so that the powerful, in overcoming it, can experience the thrill of their power. Second, it stands to reason that the greater the resistance, the keener the pleasure in overcoming it. The Party, therefore, must want vigorous opponents, not merely cowering conformists, in order to enhance the experience of its own mastery. Here too one can see the outlines of a game, a contest, taking shape. This provides a partial answer to Philip Rahv's criticism that the world of *Nineteen Eighty-Four* is psychologically implausible. In Rahv's view, Orwell failed to distinguish between psychological and objective truth. Rahv doubts that O'Brien could live with the naked truth of power pursued for its own sake, let alone that the pursuit of power could motivate generations of Inner Party members. Evil, Rahv says, needs pseudoreligious justification; without this justification, O'Brien's motivation remains psychologically obscure and implausible.[5] But once we see that O'Brien's pursuit of power is a game, it becomes not only more plausible but ironically appropriate as a utopian ideal. Orwell's earlier works, especially *The Road to Wigan Pier*, also reveal a marked ambivalence toward the utopian aim of freedom from labor, the realm of necessity, and it is not surprising that he satirized this ideal in the dystopian game playing of *Nineteen Eighty-Four*. In addition, game playing affords intimacy and absorption; and intimacy is not otherwise available in the world of *Nineteen Eighty-Four*. Thus, O'Brien's devotion to the task of breaking Winston has a psychologically plausible basis: The need for intimacy between men, a theme also developed in Arthur Koestler's *Darkness at Noon* (1941).

From O'Brien's point of view, life in Oceania may provide too few opportunities for experiencing power. The war hysteria— the banners and parades and public displays—is part of the status quo. One can imagine the particular pleasure Inner Party members derive from the exquisite timing of the Party's reality control. At the end of Hate Week, precisely when the delirious mass hatred of Eurasia is at its peak, it is announced that Oceania is in fact at war with Eastasia and that Eurasia is an ally. The timing is an essential part of the fun, since it heightens the Party's sense of unique domination. The proles' principal, perhaps sole, reason for living is the weekly lottery—and it is fitting, given their total lack of control over their fate, that the Party allots to them a game of chance, that is, a game that reaffirms the arbitrariness of life and the proles' lack of power. But the games pursued by the Inner Party must be more complex, for they must forever reaffirm the power of Big Brother.

The eternal wars among Oceania, Eastasia, and Eurasia, with constantly shifting alliances that have no fundamental effect on the wars, are clearly depicted as games—as activities engaged in for their own sake but without hope of resolution. The three societies want only to prolong the game, not to arrive at an end point. At the same time, however, these wars, which define so much of life in 1984, serve a social purpose, as Goldstein's book explains. The wars are fought both to use up surplus production in a socially useless way—that is, without raising the standard of living—and to justify the eternal need for an elite group that must bear the burden of conducting the war. There are, then, reasons for the war, but these do not negate its gamelike character. All is process; the wars will presumably go on forever. But precisely because the wars serve an ulterior purpose—because they seem to justify the Party's rule—they are not occasions for the absolutely free exercise of power. In addition, they are far-off and in some sense abstract; hence they cannot provide the immediate boot-in-the-face thrill of power that the Party seeks.

With every aspect of life controlled, at least for the 12½ percent of the population who are Outer Party members and who make up the group from which dissidents might arise (the proles, of course, do not count; they are so insignificant that they can be left more or less alone as they struggle to eke out an existence), the Party may in fact find itself frustrated in its exercise of power. The constant routine arrests of quickly terrorized or already converted people must be a starvation diet for those whose reason for living is the process of subjugation. It would seem that, while the Party has an ever-increasing need for strong new opponents—who alone permit the full enjoyment of power—the Party's total control of life makes such victims harder and harder to find.

A similar contradiction at the very heart of the Party's policies relates to the development of Newspeak. When the world of 1984 has evolved further, when Newspeak is perfected—as Syme, who works on the definitive Newspeak dictionary, explains—thoughtcrime will literally be impossible and there will be no thought at all in our sense of the word (44–46). When this comes about, will the Party feel its power? Or its powerlessness? The latter is the more likely outcome, for power requires the contrast, something pulling against it, an obstacle to be overcome. Since power over others is inseparable from domination, conflict is its necessary arena. How will O'Brien or his future counterpart feel powerful when there is no opposition at all, when no one can even conceive of opposition? The pursuit of power is thus a more delicate operation than O'Brien, and perhaps Orwell, imagines.

Can one speak of power when the people are all lobotomized, as in Zamiatin's *We*? Against whom will O'Brien test his power in the future, when no Winstons can possibly exist? In 1984 the Party already seems to have difficulty in finding worthy opponents. Most of Winston's acquaintances, for example, are ideal Outer Party members. If they are arrested—as are Syme the dictionary maker, Ampleforth the poet, and even Parsons the total Party sycophant (who is overheard in his sleep denouncing Big Brother and is turned in by his seven-year-old daughter)—these arrests apparently serve merely as daily doses of terrorism to keep the Party's appetite for power whetted.

But let us look more closely at Winston's development as an opponent of the Party. There is no written law in Oceania; no reason for arrest need be given and no specific act need be engaged in before one can be arrested. A wrong expression, a wrong thought—perhaps any thought at all—can provide the occasion. Yet the Party has played hard to develop Winston as an opponent. He has been watched for at least seven years, as O'Brien tells him; his very dreams are known to the Party and may, in fact, have been in some way planted or induced by the Party. The Party has engaged in theatrical play—with disguises and props—and has provided Winston and Julia with a meeting place, the room above Mr. Charrington's shop. For all we know, the shop itself was there solely for Winston, a Party offering that caters to his taste for the past. O'Brien himself, in predicting (erroneously, it seems) that the Party will always have victims, tells Winston: "This drama that I have played out with you during seven years will be played out over and over again generation after generation, always in subtler forms" (216).

O'Brien, it appears, has gone to a great deal of effort to turn Winston into a serious opponent. Even the clipping that Winston had accidentally received eleven years earlier, which provided him with the first concrete proof that the Party was falsifying history, may well have been planted by the Party.[6] We do not know the origins of Winston's hatred for Big Brother, but we do know O'Brien's important role in focusing and strengthening Winston's opposition. O'Brien initiates Winston in the probably nonexistent Brotherhood, provides him with a copy of Goldstein's book (and later tells Winston that the book was actually written by Inner Party members, including O'Brien himself), and supports Win-

ston's rebellion against the Party, falsely claiming to be a con-
spirator too. All this otherwise inexplicable deception, simply put,
is an elaborate entrapment through which O'Brien creates for
himself an opponent of a better quality than the run-of-the-mill
arrests provide. By contrast, in Zamiatin's *We* and in Huxley's
Brave New World there is no entrapment, no effort by the state
to stage situations that will provide occasions for displays of
power. Instead, the state considers its policies important for the
well-being of all, and it genuinely promotes a quiescent, stable,
and subdued populace. Without an ideology of power as an end
in itself, there is no reason to cultivate opponents.

A further contrast between *We* and *Nineteen Eighty-Four*
is that in Zamiatin's novel the protagonist is genuinely seduced
into rebellious acts by a woman who leads an opposition group.
In *Nineteen Eighty-Four*, however, it is not Julia who is responsible for such a seduction but rather O'Brien. Winston sees his sexual relationship with Julia, which she initiates, as a political act,
a strike against the Party. It is thus made to serve a political purpose—or, in other terms, it is corrupted by the Party's all-pervasive
control. Julia, in contrast to Winston, seeks sexual encounters
purely for pleasure. Winston's true alliances are clear from the
beginning of the novel: He hates, fears, and desires Julia and is
unambivalently drawn to O'Brien. The smallest expression of interest on O'Brien's part makes Winston blossom into a conspira-
tor, in full defiance of all common sense and caution. O'Brien's
role in all this is clear and rather easy to understand. In the dia-
lectic of power, as Hegel indicates, every master must have a
slave. The master's hidden need to have his superiority recognized
by the slave creates the peculiar emotional intimacy of their situation. The game of power cannot be played alone: O'Brien has to
want Winston Smith and has to call him into being as a suitable
opponent. Hence he waits; he waits while Winston's health im-
proves, as a result of the affair with Julia; he waits until Winston
has read some of Goldstein's book. It is easy to see why: The book
fortifies Winston's commitment to objective reality and truth. It
affirms that Winston is not insane. Above all, it gives him hope.
He is at a sufficient height, now, from which to fall. And the
harder the fall, the greater will be O'Brien's enjoyment of the
game and the more intense his awareness of his own power.

Given this situation, it is not surprising that much of the

novel depicts not the playing of the game itself (the encounter between Winston and O'Brien in the Ministry of Love occupies only about one-sixth of the novel) but the setting up of the conditions for play. The central encounter begins only when O'Brien and Winston appear as opposing players—when Winston discovers that he has been led into a trap and that O'Brien is his chief tormentor. Once O'Brien and Winston have been defined as opponents, the game is in full play. But what are we to make of the fact that Winston knew the truth all along—knew, that is, that O'Brien was not working for the downfall of Big Brother? Winston admits to this knowledge right after his arrest (192), and the subject is never alluded to again. We have examined O'Brien's role in the game, but how can we understand Winston's?

GAME THEORY AND *NINETEEN EIGHTY-FOUR*

At this point game theory can be helpful. But I should make clear that the idea of a game, in game theory, is quite different from—and in some respects the very opposite of—the game playing I have been discussing in relation to O'Brien. The play concept of games, as we have seen, has to do with activities that have intrinsic rather than instrumental value. But the emphasis of game theory is in some sense the reverse: Game theory aims at maximizing payoffs—that is, it is a highly abstract, mathematical way of determining the strategy most likely to result in the attainment of each participant's goals. Above all, game theory is of interest for its emphasis on rational decision making in interdependent situations, those situations in which two (or more) players find that the decisions of each depend in part on what the other does. It is difficult to use game theory in situations that have many variables and that offer less than perfect information about the players' motives and choices; in other words, game theory is difficult to apply in situations that are not highly controlled and carefully defined, that is, in most human situations of any complexity. But game theory provides an interesting vocabulary and helps us focus on some important issues.[7] The absolute pursuit of power, as outlined by O'Brien, is a kind of zero-sum game. A simple model of a zero-sum game is chess, a game frequently mentioned in *Nineteen Eighty-Four*.[8] It is a game of total conflict, in which whatever one player loses, the other gains. But zero-sum situations assume that gains and losses can be quantified, and measurements are hard to make in interactions of the kind pursued in *Nineteen Eighty-Four*. Still, it is easy to see that, for O'Brien, if there are no losers, there can also be no winners.

The implications of game theory for many fields are now being explored. One anthropologist, Walter Goldschmidt, has argued that game theory has a contribution to make to cross-cultural studies by providing us "with a way of looking at human behavior so as to find what the goals are. Put another way, game theory assumes the goals to be known and with this knowledge calculates the strategies. Social anthropologists examine the strategies and through these calculate the great unknown in exotic cultures: the values." [9] Game theory, in this view, can provide us with the conceptual apparatus for understanding the values that lie behind the selection of certain forms of behavior. Even if we eschew the formal application of game theory, with its matrices and game trees, the approach can still help us to focus on the details of an interaction.

Orwell's novel explicitly tells us what O'Brien's motives and values are—and the analysis presented above has involved fleshing out those motives to see how his actions further certain specified ends. With Winston, however, we have almost an opposite problem: We know his actions in far greater detail, but we do not have the overriding rationale that makes sense of them all. We do not know why he is initially drawn to O'Brien or why he enters into a game with him in which, as he repeatedly says, he knows he is doomed from the start or why he interacts with O'Brien in the particular way that he does, to the point of loving and indeed almost worshiping him, even after he knows he has been trapped. Game theory assumes the rational pursuit of strategies, that is, that people's choices are rationally consistent with perceived preferences. Can we infer some overall goal from the choices Winston makes at various points in the narrative?

Orwell describes O'Brien as "a member of the Inner Party and holder of some post so important and remote that Winston had only a dim idea of its nature" and as "a large, burly man with a thick neck and a coarse, humorous, brutal face" who nonetheless seems curiously civilized (12). Fascinated by O'Brien, Winston entertains the hope that O'Brien's political orthodoxy is not perfect. The same scene depicts Winston's antagonism toward Julia and his suspicion that she may be an agent of the Thought Police. In view of the novel's later development, this scene reveals Winston's incredibly poor judgment of character. After the Two Minutes Hate, Winston catches O'Brien's eye and imagines he *knows* that O'Brien is thinking the same things he is: "An unmistakable message had passed. It was as though their two minds had opened and the thoughts were flowing from one into the other through their eyes. 'I am with you,' O'Brien seemed to be saying to him. 'I know precisely what you are feeling. I know all about your contempt, your hatred, your disgust. But don't worry, I am on your side!' And then the flash of intelligence was gone, and O'Brien's face was as inscrutable as everybody else's" (17–18). Although we can interpret Winston's response as due in part to O'Brien's intentional deception, this explanation is not sufficient to account for Winston's special attraction toward O'Brien; for up to this time Winston knows nothing about him except that he has an unusually high status within the Inner Party. As the book unfolds, we encounter no one more powerful than O'Brien—except the mythical Big Brother himself (who is, incidentally, portrayed as of the same physical type).

We expect a contest to be provoked by the person who anticipates winning, and indeed it is O'Brien who first makes overtures to Winston by finding a pretext for having Winston come to his house. But this does not make Winston a purely passive instrument of O'Brien's will. What is of interest here is the precipitous response Winston makes to O'Brien's gesture (129): He feels as if he has been waiting for O'Brien's move all his life, and he is at once ready to throw himself entirely on O'Brien's mercy, to incriminate himself as an enemy of the Party. Of course, this feeling might be an indication of his heroic character and his desperation in combating Big Brother. But does the scene in O'Brien's apartment bear out such a reading? In this crucial scene, which James Connors discusses in an insightful analysis of Winston's character,[10] Winston readily agrees to cheat, forge, blackmail, corrupt the minds of children, distribute addictive drugs, encourage prostitution, disseminate venereal diseases, murder, and throw sulfuric acid in the face of a child—all for the sake of weakening the Party (141). Thus Winston has no grounds for differentiating himself from the Party, as O'Brien reminds him when Winston later expresses a belief in his own moral superiority.

For the moment, it is still unclear *why* Winston is willing to act as O'Brien asks. But what is clear is that he cannot be seen merely as O'Brien's innocent victim. Winston has agreed to use others as means to his own ends, causing pain and death if necessary, and he therefore has no moral basis from which to protest when he discovers that O'Brien, in turn, is using him. Winston's very words and actions, after all, have led him to this path; so he is, we must conclude, an active participant in the game the two men are playing. This argument is one answer to the possible objection (to which I return later) that Winston enters the game unwillingly—a circumstance that would seem to violate a fundamental rule of play. As we see, although he is not fully informed, he does bear responsibility for his presence in the game. Without this element of personal responsibility, the novel would not be interesting; it would merely be mechanical. But Winston is O'Brien's accomplice; he is thereby implicated in his own downfall, for he did accept O'Brien's terms—the rules of the game, as it were—and these same rules prevail at their subsequent encounter in the Ministry of Love. By his own words and actions in O'Brien's apartment, then, Winston has entered the game. His illusion about O'Brien, about the Brotherhood, marks this stage—and, indeed, the very word "illusion" means "in play" (*in-lusio*).

There is an important sense in which O'Brien does not deceive Winston. He depicts the Brotherhood in almost exclusively negative terms, as hopeless and ineffectual. He leaves Winston with no doubt that any opposition is doomed to failure, perhaps for as long as a thousand years, that Winston will be caught, will confess, and will then die. Here we have the irony of truth told for the sake of a grand deception. Yet Winston accepts the Brotherhood as his salvation, and he agrees to all the conditions and rules set down by O'Brien. Indeed, it is Julia who first rejects separation from Winston for the sake of the Brotherhood—it is she alone who dares to interrupt O'Brien's litany to assert the claim of personal feeling. Winston, then, does agree to the game—but without recognizing its genuine configuration. As in the eternal wars among the three powers, the means are always the same and the rules are agreed on; all that changes is the identity of the opponent.

It is as important for us to understand the "why" of Winston's behavior as it is for him to understand the "why" of the

Party's pursuit of absolute power. The second scene between Winston and O'Brien, in the Ministry of Love, helps to clarify Winston's motivation. We need to recognize, however, that O'Brien's total victory is not quite the foregone conclusion that he tells Winston it is. For one thing, if it were entirely predetermined, once again the pleasure of the victory would be diminished. O'Brien too is operating under some constraints. Resisters do, after all, die under torture; they do sacrifice themselves for others (as Winston knows from his own observations of women and their children), and they can even refuse to play. These options make us realize that although O'Brien can kill Winston at any time, having to do so before extracting full enjoyment from the situation would not give O'Brien his preferred outcome for the game. Winston hopes to escape with his life and his dignity. O'Brien wants his own power to be affirmed, but that goal gives him no special reason for killing Winston, and he does not care whether Winston lives or dies. Roger Caillois points out that "one does not play to win as a sure thing. The pleasure of the game is inseparable from the risk of losing." [11] For O'Brien, obviously, losing is a relative thing; the key issue is how much power and domination he can gain over Winston. After Winston passes through the first two stages of his "reintegration"—learning and understanding—he is restored to health, strengthened and fattened for the psychological kill of the third stage, which is acceptance. When Winston hopes for death, O'Brien assures him it will come eventually; were it to come too soon, it would deprive O'Brien of a full victory.

If Winston cannot induce his own death and end both his suffering and the game, what option does he have? There is one, although he never considers it: He can refuse to play. His choices are limited. He is being defeated level by level: His belief in objective reality has crumbled; his sense of his own moral superiority has been destroyed; his body has been broken. He knows that the Party denies the possibility of martyrdom—hence the purely private torture and the mere obliteration, later on, of all signs of the victim's existence. But this last detail also suggests that the Party is aware of ways (such as martyrdom) by which its domination could be nullified. Winston learns, concretely, about the ways of the Party only through his game with O'Brien. He does not know what the Party's aim is until O'Brien explains it to him. Does his attitude change, then, once he realizes he is involved in a game of power? Can he now figure out a way to stop the game? If so, losing would be a form of winning. An unresisting "mouse" deprives the "cat" of the fun of the game. Does Winston pursue such a strategy?

Quite the contrary. In a crucial scene O'Brien tells Winston that they have beaten him and asks him whether there is even one degradation that he has not undergone. Remarkably, instead of keeping quiet and retaining his belief in his inner world, Winston at once offers it up to O'Brien as a challenge. " 'I have not betrayed Julia,' he said" (220). At this point, if we assume the rationality of Winston's choices—that is, if we assume that his moves reflect an effort to achieve certain goals—the logic of Winston's behavior, from the novel's outset, comes into focus. It now appears that Winston cares more about winning O'Brien's recognition than about sustaining his own inner world. With this virtual challenge to O'Brien he sacrifices the latter to the former and also keeps the game going. However temporarily, Winston has gotten something out of O'Brien—recognition—and he is once again pathetically grateful for O'Brien's understanding. Winston himself acknowledges the shallowness of his rebellion against the Party (222). Now we see the role that his attraction to the powerful O'Brien has always played in Winston's choices. Winston has been a true opponent for O'Brien, persisting in the game partly because of his desire to partake of O'Brien's power by gaining the recognition that O'Brien alone can bestow on him. This desire explains Winston's emphasis on being understood—and it explains why he is more in O'Brien's thrall after the weeks and months of torture than before.

Since Winston undergoes no change of heart when he discovers (or, rather, acknowledges what he has always known) that O'Brien is not part of the Brotherhood, it has clearly not been the hope of participating in a rebellion that has motivated Winston from the beginning. His choices throughout the game reveal that what he is after is recognition and affirmation from O'Brien, the most powerful man he knows. If this were not so, Winston would have every reason to refuse to play, to distrust O'Brien and hope for nothing from him. That Winston, instead, continues to accord O'Brien respect and even love reveals that the two men are operating from within the same frame of reference, the same values.

Both respect power, both see persons in terms of power roles—where they differ is in the degree and type of recognition they require from others. O'Brien, who is powerful, wants the stimulation of a worthy opponent to make the game interesting; Winston, who is powerless, wants the recognition that he has been a tough opponent in his way, that he has held on to his inner world despite all odds. Not surprisingly, Winston feels that O'Brien's mind contains his own (206). At the heart of their apparent struggle is an agreement about values, despite their disagreement about the nature of reality, and this agreement is the corruption at the core of Winston's rebellion.

It is clear, then, that in some sense Winston deserves his fate, for he is drawn to O'Brien and admires him precisely for the power and domination that O'Brien will, of course, ultimately use against him. The subtext of the novel has to do with Winston's embrace of the wrong values. Although Winston is not himself a brutal, dominant man, he wants the recognition of such a man. This conclusion, which is hinted at throughout the novel, becomes unavoidable when we see Winston's final bid for O'Brien's recognition.

Orwell's handling of the interaction between the two men illustrates what Fredric Jameson, in another context, has called the "ideological double standard." Jameson applies this term to adventure stories that allow the reader vicariously to experience and satisfy a taste for violence, while they ostensibly criticize such violence on political and social grounds.[12] The term can be extended to cover situations in which a value system is in fact derived from the very values that are being criticized. In *Nineteen Eighty-Four* both these aspects of an ideological double standard appear, but, given that the torture scenes are not very convincing, it is the implicit adherence to a value system the book ostensibly criticizes that is the more pernicious. Curiously, Orwell was perfectly aware of this potential in literature, as his comments on Galsworthy's *Forsyte Saga* reveal: "Well, the thing that strikes one about Galsworthy is that though he's trying to be iconoclastic, he has been utterly unable to move his mind outside the wealthy bourgeois society he is attacking. With only slight modifications he takes all its values for granted" (CEJL, 2:205). We can make the same criticism of the way Orwell depicts Winston's interaction with O'Brien.

When Winston defiantly declares that after all he has not betrayed Julia, he makes that betrayal indispensable to O'Brien's victory and shows himself once again to be the intelligent opponent-participant whose defeat O'Brien could especially relish. The "place where there is no darkness," in which Winston always imagined he would meet O'Brien, thus turns out to be the illuminated playing field of the torture chamber in which Winston gives up the last vestige of his inner world.

The peculiar intimacy between Winston and O'Brien is typical of competitive situations. In a study of the psychology of competition, Stuart Walker writes: "In few activities other than competition can a participant find a similar opportunity to assert his unique significance and simultaneously attain approval from the people he most respects. For his competitors become the people who mean the most to him."[13] O'Brien and Winston, as we have seen, are locked together in their game, each requiring the presence of the other. It is important to realize, however, that all victories in the game of power are temporary. Mastery and domination over another human being cannot be permanent; rather, these must be continually reestablished. It is in the exercise of power that power comes into being. The eyes of the dead no longer express recognition of the superiority of the master; a corpse is merely a thing, unable to acknowledge defeat. Similarly, when the Party has finally succeeded in completely breaking— that is, converting—a human being, that person is of no further interest. This is why, once Winston has betrayed Julia, his torment is over and there are no further episodes with O'Brien.

At the end of *Nineteen Eighty-Four*, Winston is sitting alone at the Chestnut Tree Café. He is now in the position earlier occupied by the three purported Party traitors: people broken by the Party, shunned by others, playing eternal games of chess over eternal glasses of Victory Gin. The chess problem that Winston is absorbed in is an appropriate if obvious metaphor for his game with O'Brien, as Winston himself senses. He is still trying to reason, but his reasoning now leads him to conclusions that oppose his earlier ones. He notes that in an ideal chess game white always wins and white symbolizes the good, and he then inverts this observation and concludes that whatever wins must be the good, by virtue of its victory. Since Big Brother clearly always wins, as he has over Julia and Winston, Big Brother must be good.

Here Orwell applies the game metaphor to the entire society of *Nineteen Eighty-Four*: All its members are engaged in a game, and in this game Big Brother always wins against the individual player.

In a sense, Winston has been forced to agree that whatever is, is right. If life is merely a neutral game, then one must, as in other games, admire the winner, regardless of who or what the victor is and how the victory comes about. Here is the ultimate logic of Winston's conversion: The victory he desired over the Party and Big Brother is transformed into the only possible victory available under the circumstances—that over himself. And this is what the last line of the novel tells us: "He had won the victory over himself. He loved Big Brother" (240). In typical doublethink fashion, defeat is now called victory. This reversal is a logical result of Winston's acceptance of the Party's value system, which, as we have seen, underlay even his rebellion. He continues to operate according to Party models: Victory and winning are still what activity is about, but the enemy has been redefined. It is not O'Brien or Big Brother or the Party. It is Winston himself. If he cannot affect the outside world, then at least he can transform the way he thinks about it, thus achieving as much reality control as he can in the circumstances. In a world based on the idea of domination, Big Brother, being stronger, *is* always right, just as white always mates black in the ideal chess game. Winston has no choice but to worship this ultimate strength.

Orwell uses game imagery in one other important instance toward the end of the book. Winston's last memory in the novel, a memory he quickly decides is false or induced by a trick, is of a different kind of game, of play that was joy. He recalls an occasion when, as a child, he and his mother had played Snakes and Ladders (a game that also appears in one of Orwell's idealized hearth scenes; see above, chapter 6, n.8). They played eight games and won four each. Surely Orwell did not think this detail, positioned just before Winston's final capitulation, would be overlooked. Winston's recollection is of an almost idyllic time, when games were not rigged, when opposing players might take turns in winning.

But, in focusing on this episode, Orwell invites us to consider once again the distinctive aspects of the games played in his novel. In three major ways, Winston and O'Brien's interaction departs from what we usually understand as playing a game. First, Winston, despite his complicity, is not a fully informed player of the game; he is more like the victim of a confidence game. Second, his participation in the game is not purely voluntary, as his sudden arrest underscores. And, finally, he cannot truly win, although he can influence the extent of his losses. This imperfect fit points to a significant feature of the game pursued in *Nineteen Eighty-Four*. Like everything else in that world, it is a perversion —a perversion of a game, similar to the perversion of intimacy, of sexuality, of family life, of nationalism, of language, and of all facets of cultural life in Oceania. But what this characteristic reveals is that even O'Brien's pursuits are subject to the peculiar limitations and inauthenticity of life in Oceania; his pleasure can only be partial, since he cannot have a perfect game partner under the prevailing rules, any more than he can have a genuine sexual intimacy or friendship. Thus the very aims and rationale of the Party are necessarily undermined by Party policy. The ideology of domination carries within itself the seeds of its own failure; it is a paradox. Orwell can successfully evoke the inescapable oppressiveness of life in Airstrip One, but he cannot convincingly explain Oceania's inner dynamics, which tend toward entropy. In this respect Philip Rahv's criticism of the novel (although not directed to this feature) is correct.

Nothing I have said so far about *Nineteen Eighty-Four* adequately explains the despair one senses at the end of the novel. The novel itself, after all, may be viewed as a demonstration of the incredible coercive forces that need to be brought to bear upon human beings to reduce them to their worst possible selves: the constant spectacles of hysteria; the sanctioning of the intimacy of pain, fear, and hatred and the prohibition of the intimacy of friendship and love; the continual material deprivation; the impediments placed in the way of genuine thought. Orwell depicts all this in great detail, while also showing us how the games played and the roles assumed within a game have everything to do with the overall values of a given society. In Oceania children participate in youth organizations called Spies, and in playing at spying they learn their social roles. Orwell was perfectly aware of the importance of such conditioning. And yet, when it comes to the essential problem of power and domination, he offers not even a hint of an etiology and instead appeals to unexamined notions of human nature.

Orwell seems to have believed in the cogency of his vision; had he not done so, the novel would not end on such a desperate note of capitulation. In a sense, then, it appears that Orwell did not carry his analysis far enough. All the perversions depicted in *Nineteen Eighty-Four* are due to domination and the pursuit of power, and Orwell sees these not as a social possibility that requires explanation but as a mysterious fact of nature. He thus reduces the desire for power to the status of a biological instinct or an unavoidable innate characteristic forever marking human nature.[14] But the world of *Nineteen Eighty-Four* is not a world in which human nature is seen playing power games; it is specifically the story of two men committed to shared ideas of what it means to be a man and, as we have seen, dependent on each other's recognition. Only in a culture that habitually disparages the female and accepts the male as the model for the human species could it ever have gone unremarked that *Nineteen Eighty-Four* is above all the story of two men's interactions and that Julia, who is not a participant in the game of domination, presents an alternative mode of behavior.

WOMEN IN OCEANIA

In the previous section I show that the analysis of gamesmanship in *Nineteen Eighty-Four* reveals a weakness at the heart of Orwell's critique of power: a value system derived from the very thing Orwell is ostensibly criticizing. This weakness may be viewed as part of Orwell's strategy in depicting a totalitarian society, for it is unlikely that he intended Winston Smith to be viewed simply as a hero, a man not compromised by the society in which he lives. At the same time, as always happens in fiction, Orwell's text reveals his own implicit values. Although *Nineteen Eighty-Four* may indeed have been intended to warn of a possibility rather than to prophesy, as Orwell claimed (CEJL, 4:502), this does not alter its profoundly negative impact. What alternatives could possibly exist in a world in which domination and brutality cannot even begin to be analyzed, because they are taken for granted as part of an inevitable "human" drive for power?

In the world of *Nineteen Eighty-Four*, although men fear women because they may be spies, in general the assumptions of male centrality and female "otherness" survive intact. Julia's love for Winston makes him healthier, whereas O'Brien's attentions destroy him physically and mentally, but Winston's true alliance, as we have seen, is with O'Brien, who engages him in combat and recognizes him as a worthy opponent—a recognition that means more to Winston than Julia's love.

The romance between Julia and Winston is far less important in the novel, and occupies less space, than the "romance" between Winston and O'Brien. This is clear from the novel's beginning when Winston fears and hates (because he desires) Julia while admiring and being drawn to O'Brien. In addition, Orwell devotes far more space to the details of Winston's torture than to the details of his affair with Julia. This affair is quite possibly a concession on Orwell's part to popular literature, as well as a vehicle for setting Winston's halfhearted rebellion in motion; but Winston's true longing is for intimacy with O'Brien, the most powerful man he knows. While Winston is never depicted in serious conversation with Julia, the talks with O'Brien that accompany Winston's torture and conversion are at the heart of the novel.

The minor role attributed to women in the novel cannot be interpreted as part of Orwell's strategy of criticizing and laying bare the dynamics of totalitarianism. As readers with a different kind of sensibility, we may be aware that *Nineteen Eighty-Four* depicts a masculinized world, but Orwell did not see it this way and never made any sort of critique of the sex-role system. Although there exists within the novel a certain amount of specific information about the Party's control of sexuality and family life, there is also a wealth of detail that merely demonstrates Orwell's habitual disdain for women, evident in all his work. Thus any analysis of sex roles in *Nineteen Eighty-Four* has to begin by distinguishing between Party policy toward Party women (the proles are ignored), as articulated in the novel, and Orwell's own attitudes that inadvertently seep into the text.

In the general statements about the Party's attempt to control sexuality, Orwell adheres to a hydraulic model and believes that the Party, by suppressing sexual pleasure, can redirect the individual's energy and emotions into fanatical support of Big Brother and hatred of Oceania's enemies. Thus sex is prohibited except for procreation within marriage—and then it is supposed to be performed merely as "our duty to the Party," without love or joy. Although Orwell states that there are no laws in Oceania —so that anything and everything can be forbidden—he also notes that divorce is not permitted but separation is. Winston's marriage to Katharine—whom he considers to be the emptiest person he has ever known—was a constant trial to him, for though she had no sexual feelings she insisted on periodically performing her "duty to the Party" (109), which Winston would have preferred to ignore altogether. Since they had no children, they were permitted to separate after a time.

Certain members of the Junior Anti-Sex League (to which Julia belongs) encourage the total prohibition of sexual intercourse and the production of children purely through artificial insemination. These children would then be brought up in institutions. But this view has not (yet) become policy. Orwell comments not at all on the meaning of such a policy for women; he includes this detail as merely another illustration of the fanaticism of Party women who support such antifamily measures. The problem of controlling family affections and allegiances is a crucial one in any totalitarian society, but Orwell does not address it beyond these few sketchy details and the description of the Spies; the child informers. He does not consider the types of conflicts such children might experience, nor does he dwell on the nature of family life given these constraints. Instead, he takes it for granted that everything works according to Party plan. Similarly, since the proles are in essence like Orwell's familiar working class, with personal loyalties and "normal" sexuality (which includes prostitution), Orwell sees no reason to dwell on them.

Orwell reveals Winston's reaction to sexual frustration but deprives his character of any insight into himself. Instead, Winston's responses become part of Orwell's indictment against women:

Winston had disliked her [Julia] from the very first moment of seeing her. He knew the reason. It was because of the atmosphere of hockey-fields and cold baths and community hikes and general clean-mindedness which she managed to carry about with her. He disliked nearly all women, and especially the young and pretty ones. It was always the women, and above all the young ones, who were the most bigoted adherents of the Party, the swallowers of slogans, the amateur spies and nosers-out of unorthodoxy. But this particular girl gave him the impression of being more dangerous than most. [12]

Orwell here dislodges the general comments about Party women so that they are no longer attached to Winston's point of view but instead take on the form of reliable "facts." In addition, there is no analysis of this female fanaticism. Thus it is included not as an indication of what the Party has done to women but only as a negative comment about women themselves, presumably by "nature" susceptible to such fanaticism. And this despite the fact that in Julia we have a woman who is clearly not a fanatic but who pretends to go along with all Party manias in an effort to avoid arousing suspicion. In this way she gains a margin of freedom for her real rebellion against the Party. Julia's deviation from the stereotype of female fanaticism does not evoke Orwell's analysis because she is in fact serving another stereotype: that of the apolitical, private-minded, egocentric female. While Winston can find a sexual "outlet" (with prostitutes and with Julia) and still be political, single women in Nineteen Eighty-Four seem to be either apolitical hedonists or sexually frustrated fanatics. Despite Orwell's sensitivity, elsewhere, to the fact that language can inhibit thought and the consequent need to guard against one's own biases, his own language in the novel depicts women in a way that wards off analysis while encouraging a misogynistic nod of recognition of how women "are."

In addition, Orwell ignores what is likely to happen inside the home in a society in which women are still viewed as inferiors and hatred runs high. We can only guess that among the proles life is very similar to British working-class life, about which Orwell had such ambivalent feelings (hence Winston both admires and despises the proles). Do Oceanian men find a release of tension and temporary assumption of masculine power through wife beating and rape? We do not know. The "private" sphere, despite Orwell's statement that such a thing no longer exists in 1984, is still a sealed-off area. We do know that early in the novel Winston has fantasies of torturing, raping, and murdering Julia—showing that this form of "outlet" is still available in imagination at least. During the Two Minutes Hate, as Winston watches the sheeplike face of Goldstein, the official Party enemy, on the screen, he suddenly succeeds

in transferring his hatred from the face on the screen to the dark-haired girl behind him. Vivid, beautiful hallucinations flashed through his mind. He would flog her to death with a rubber truncheon. He would tie her naked to a stake and shoot her full of arrows like Saint Sebastian. He would ravish her and cut her throat at the moment of climax. Better than before, moreover, he realized *why* it was that he hated her. He hated her because she was young and pretty and sexless, because he wanted to go to bed with her and would never do so, because round her sweet supple waist, which seemed to ask you to encircle it with your arm, there was only the odious scarlet sash, aggressive symbol of chastity. [16; Orwell's emphasis]

Doublethink apparently has not totally altered thought processes in Oceania; or perhaps Winston, as the rebellious hero, is meant to display the thought processes of more "normal" men. In any case, this supposedly totalitarian society seems to produce men whose thoughts and reactions often run along recognizable lines.

One of the clearest examples of the seepage into *Nineteen Eighty-Four* of Orwell's attitudes toward women occurs in the consistently negative depiction of their voices. As we have seen, this is a recurring feature of Orwell's characterization of women and therefore cannot be taken as part of the exposé of Ingsoc's negative effects on individuals. Among other examples, in the novel Orwell depicts a woman giving "a squeak of mingled fear and disgust." Mrs. Parsons has a "dreary, whining sort of voice," and the exercise leader on the telescreen in the morning yaps and barks in a "piercing female voice." There is also the "silly feminine voice" that Winston hears in the canteen and the screeching of the woman on the telescreen when he gets home. Interestingly, one male, the hated enemy Goldstein, is depicted in Party propaganda films as having a sheeplike, bleating voice.

The women in Orwell's narrative by and large appear as caricatures: They are Party secretaries, Party fanatics, Party wives like Katharine or the stereotypically helpless housewife Mrs. Parsons. They are also antisex freaks or prole prostitutes. There is no woman character in the novel comparable to Syme or Charrington or O'Brien. Although Goldstein's book explains that the

Inner Party is not linked by blood and that no racial discrimination is practiced—"Jews, Negroes, South Americans of pure Indian blood are to be found in the highest ranks of the Party" (168)—no female Inner Party members are mentioned. When Winston sees a man and a woman in the canteen, he assumes that the woman is the man's secretary. In describing Julia's work in Pornosec (which churns out machine-produced pornographic literature for prole consumption), work that is assigned to unmarried girls because they are thought to be less vulnerable than men to the corrupting influences of pornography, Orwell includes the detail that "all the workers in Pornosec, except the heads of the departments, were girls" (108). Although Orwell reveals male dominance to be a continuing feature of life in Oceania, he does not treat this as worthy of analysis and does not raise the issue of its role in a totalitarian society. Women's options in a given society, what access they have to earning their own living and what kind of living that would be compared, for example, to becoming a man's economic dependent in exchange for housework and child-care services; how, in general, society structures women's life paths in comparison with men's—all this has everything to do with the shape of life in that society. But Orwell does not realize this, judging by his lack of attention to this problem in *Nineteen Eighty-Four*. Even Julia is a largely unexplored character, seen only in terms of her relationship with Winston.

In charting Julia's character, Orwell introduced an important deviation from several of the novels that are known to have influenced his composition of *Nineteen Eighty-Four*: Both Jack London's *Iron Heel* and Zamiatin's *We* have heroic female protagonists. But Julia, the only major female character in *Nineteen Eighty-Four*, though also a rebel, evokes yet another female stereotype. She is a rebel only "from the waist downwards" (128), as Winston comments; she is motivated by love of pleasure—sexual pleasure—and is totally uninterested in the political dynamics of the society that oppresses her. Orwell invites the reader to view Julia in a largely negative way and to contrast her lack of seriousness with Winston's heroic attempt to understand his society. And, indeed, most critics have faithfully echoed this view of Julia, so that in comments on the novel she is routinely described as egocentric and unintelligent. A slight variation of this criticism is the condescension of Irving Howe, who refers to Julia's "charming indifference to all ideologies."[15] Yet there are grounds for a more positive understanding of Julia's character: She does not take the Two Minutes Hate seriously, unlike Winston who gets genuinely caught up in it. She falls asleep while Winston reads to her from Goldstein's book and is skeptical about all official pronouncements. But these positive aspects of Julia's character emerge more despite Orwell's conception of her than because of it. Significantly, Julia, who is also opposing the Party, receives no attention from O'Brien. Her rebellion against the Party does not have an ideological or theoretical foundation; rather, it is grounded in her desire for pleasure and for the pursuit of a personal life. The three central characters in Orwell's novel form an interesting group, and the ways Orwell names them reflect their status within the novel. Julia has only a first name; she is an insignificant female, and Orwell in this respect follows his society's convention of considering a woman's last name a disposable, because changeable, element in an uncertain social identity. O'Brien, at the opposite pole, has only a last name, in typical masculine style. And Winston Smith, halfway between the powerless personal feminine and the powerful impersonal masculine, has a complete name, albeit an ironic one in that it combines the legendary with the commonplace.

Julia's aim is to have as much pleasure as she possibly can, which, given the oppressive world in which she must function, is no small feat. And she harms no one. O'Brien, in the key scene in his apartment, assumes that Winston speaks for both himself and Julia as he questions them about their willingness to commit all sorts of atrocities for the sake of destroying the Party. While Winston agrees to everything, Julia says nothing (she must find all this talk about throwing acid in the face of a child ridiculous)—until O'Brien asks if she and Winston are willing to be separated for the sake of destroying the Party. Only now does she break into the conversation, to say no (142). Here it is Julia who is revealing the commitment to purely private values that Winston so admires in the idealized maternal figures of the prole woman and his own mother, yet she is not held up for our admiration. In fact, Julia becomes yet another source of misogynistic comments. She hates her living arrangements in the hostel where she lives with thirty other women (Winston, for reasons unknown, has his own flat) and complains to Winston: "Always in the stink of women! How I hate women!" (107).

Throughout the novel the contrast is drawn between Winston's attempt to understand his society and Julia's purely practical orientation: She is cunning, capable, mechanically oriented (she works on the machines in Pornosec)—and hedonistic, unanalytical, opportunistic. Winston's strenuous resistance to O'Brien's torture is depicted in great detail, but we are told in passing that Julia had capitulated at once to O'Brien's methods: "She betrayed you, Winston. Immediately—unreservedly. I have seldom seen anyone come over to us so promptly. You would hardly recognize her if you saw her. All her rebelliousness, her deceit, her folly, her dirty-mindedness—everything has been burned out of her. It was a perfect conversion, a textbook case" (208), hence not worthy of either admiration or pity, unlike the tougher, more heroic (given the values of the novel) Winston. The Party's aim is to destroy men—and the more they resist, the greater the thrill of power for the Party. Julia obviously does not play this game.[16]

The British writer Stevie Smith knew Orwell and used him as a model for two characters in her 1949 novel *The Holiday*. In a letter written in 1967, she recalls that Orwell once said to her, "Girls can't play," and she understood from this that he was referring not to sports "but rather [to] rules in general . . . and that girls were a shade anarchic and did not know or care about rules at all, with the understanding, I fancy, that they did not 'play the game.' " [17] Though Julia describes herself as "good at games," she does not take them seriously. Instead, she puts up an elaborate front in order to more effectively pursue her own aims. She explains: "I always look cheerful and I never shirk anything. Always yell with the crowd, that's what I say. It's the only way to be safe" (100). She displays an "open jeering hatred" of the Party (101) and astonishes Winston by her coarse language, for Party members are not supposed to swear and Winston in general conforms to this. By adopting a narrative perspective on Julia that is largely negative, Orwell does not invite the reader to consider critically the nature of the game that is being played in *Nineteen Eighty-Four* or the implications of its rules.

Orwell's tacit assumption of a male center of gravity is evident throughout the novel in ways that reveal that it is not merely a logical consequence of his narrative focus—which is, of course, on Winston. This androcentrism is apparent even in Goldstein's book, in which the typical Party member under constant surveillance is clearly depicted as a male: "Nothing that he does is indifferent. His friendships, his relaxations, his behaviour towards his wife and children, the expression of his face when he is alone, . . . are all jealously scrutinized" (170). The same model occurs again, when O'Brien describes the world based on pain and hatred that the Party is creating: "No one dares trust a wife or a child or a friend any longer. But in the future there will be no wives and no friends" (215). And, of course, the very image of the future that O'Brien presents to Winston derives from a specifically male role—that of a soldier: "If you want a picture of the future, imagine a boot stamping on a human face—for ever" (215).[18]

This narrow perspective is reiterated in the account of the Party's control of sexuality. Prostitution, Orwell writes, is common among the proles:

It was dangerous, but it was not a life-and-death matter. To be caught with a prostitute might mean five years in a forced-labour camp. . . . And it was easy enough, provided that you could avoid being caught in the act. The poorer quarters swarmed with women who were ready to sell themselves. Some could even be purchased for a bottle of gin, which the proles were not supposed to drink. Tacitly the Party was even inclined to encourage prostitution, as an outlet for instincts which could not be altogether suppressed. Mere debauchery did not matter very much, so long as it was furtive and joyless and only involved the women of a submerged and despised class. [55–56]

Orwell here clearly has in mind male (hetero)sexuality only. Fanatical adherence to the Party is presumably enough of an "outlet" for Party women—Julia notwithstanding. In addition, the continual wartime economy of 1984 seems likely to induce constant prostitution of women. How does Julia get the black-market items she brings to Winston? Is she really sleeping around only for fun, or also for profit? Since Inner Party members (who seem all to be male) clearly have material advantages, it makes sense to assume that there is a hidden system of distribution that draws on their power and access to scarce goods. In depicting an economy similar to that of London in the 1940s, Orwell reproduces key features of the system of which he seems to be unaware—for example, the ways in which economics affects the relations between the sexes.

That Orwell conceives of women primarily as objects, rather than as subjects in their own right, also emerges in details about Julia's behavior. Cosmetics, perfume, and traditional feminine attire are forbidden to Party members. Julia manages to find some makeup and perfume, however, and applies these one day in the secret room. Winston hardly recognizes her, such is the "improvement" in her appearance: She has become prettier and far more feminine. Julia exclaims: "And do you know what I'm going to do next? I'm going to get hold of a real woman's frock from somewhere and wear it instead of these bloody trousers. I'll wear silk stockings and high-heeled shoes! In this room I'm going to be a woman, not a Party comrade" (117). Since Julia has no knowledge of the past or of how women used to look, the assumption seems to be that something in women's nature makes them want to decorate themselves in this way and that Julia is merely expressing her "femininity," which the Party, naturally, tries to suppress. To "be a woman" appears to involve preparing oneself as a sex object for a man. By denying such allures to women, the Party is trying to kill the sex instinct, or at least to distort and sully it. Orwell writes: "And as far as the women were concerned, the Party's efforts were largely successful" (56).[19]

Despite this emphasis in *Nineteen Eighty-Four* on the trappings of "feminine" appeal, Orwell is reticent on the subject of sexuality itself. Though we are told that Julia has had many affairs, not a word in the novel deals with the problem of contraception and abortion—surely vital necessities in a society as officially chaste as is Oceania. The only reference to the biological facts of reproduction occurs when Julia, very discreetly, cancels a meeting with Winston because "It's started early this time" (114). This delicate reference to menstruation, and the assumption that it prevents intercourse (apparently the sole object of Julia and Winston's meetings), is reiterated when Winston reflects that this "particular disappointment must be a normal, recurring event" in marriage (115).

Judging by his novels over a fifteen-year period, there is very little change or development in Orwell's literary treatment of sex. Winston, like many of Orwell's other protagonists, is frightened of attractive women, and this fear interferes with his sexual performance. Julia is described less as a person than as a "youthful body," the possession of which fills Winston with "pride" (99). Orwell's visions of the "golden country"—in *Nineteen Eighty-Four* as in *Coming Up for Air* and *Keep the Aspidistra Flying*—always involve the attempt at sexual "possession" of a woman and hence the affirmation of manhood. Orwell describes Winston and Julia's lovemaking in words familiar from his earlier novels: "He had pulled her down on to the ground, she was utterly unresisting, he could do what he liked with her" (99).

Winston accepts and adopts the Party's vocabulary of "purity" and "virtue," revealing an interesting inconsistency in Orwell's conceptualization of Newspeak and doublethink. The Party, it turns out, uses the labels of purity and virtue in precisely the same way as our own bourgeois society does (or did): Chastity is pure, lack of sex is virtue. Yet instead of questioning this association, Orwell has Winston and Julia merely embrace "corruption." Winston shouts: "I hate purity, I hate goodness! I don't want virtue to exist anywhere. I want everyone to be corrupt to the bones" (103). By reacting as he does, Winston fails to challenge the Party's hold on experience. This is also apparent in his desire to "break down that wall of virtue" that surrounds the "impregnable" Party women. Orwell does not seem aware that there is nothing either new or revolutionary in Winston's judgment that Julia's sexual promiscuity marks her as "corrupt." Thus, while situating Julia's rebelliousness in her sexuality, and in this respect going against the Party's program for women, Orwell nonetheless reproduces familiar stereotypes about women.

Countering the "corrupt" sexually active woman is the idealized maternal type, self-sacrificing and protective of her children. In *Nineteen Eighty-Four* several examples of this type appear, most notably in the portraits of Winston's mother and of the singing prole woman. Certainly Orwell views in what is for him a positive way both the prole woman, who is a vigorous and enduring breeder (whose body is repeatedly—and rhapsodically—described as "monstrous" from childbearing),[20] and Winston's mother, who is a self-sacrificing maternal figure. Winston even feels, at some points in the novel, that hope for the future resides in these women and the values they embody. As a result, some critics have argued that Orwell attributes to women a crucial role in the maintenance of human dignity.[21] But it is important to recognize that these female figures are not held up as the proper model for human behavior in general. Instead, they are part of Orwell's idealization of the working-class family, made up of strong, hardworking men and the maternal women who are their economic dependents. As such, these characterizations are part of the problem, not the solution.

Winston's more general statement that hope lies with the proles is undermined by the opposing view articulated in the novel, that there is no hope since the proles are unconscious. In various writings, as we have seen, Orwell attributed lack of consciousness to the oppressed: proles, natives, blacks, and women such as Winston's mother, with good hearts and limited intelligence. That Orwell idealizes women's roles within the traditional family does not contradict but indeed affirms his commitment to a society based on unequal and sexually polarized social roles. He is nostalgic for the idyllic world of conventional family life with its patriarchal power and maternal women, the world depicted in nineteenth-century American novels such as *Helen's Babies* and *Little Women*, two books Orwell especially admired (CEJL, 4:242–47). He lives in a mental space peopled largely by men, with women providing the domestic background for the activities of men, breeding and rearing the next generation, and of course valorizing the masculine role by embodying a contrasting and inferiorized "femininity." This much emerges even in the brief memories that Winston has of his mother in *Nineteen Eighty-Four*, which include a clear image of his own boyhood dominance within the family. Winston recalls how his mother sacrificed her bit of food for both her children, but Winston, unable to share, insisted on taking his little sister's portion too—and did so, forcefully.

Orwell touches on this theme of male prerogatives in his other novels as well. In *Keep the Aspidistra Flying*, as we have seen, Gordon has precisely the same sort of relationship with his sister. Orwell comments on the sacrifice of girls' interests to that of their brothers but seems to consider this merely a somewhat regrettable and unavoidable lack of fair play. He does not focus on the role such preferential treatment plays in boys' development. Similarly, in *Nineteen Eighty-Four*, Winston too has had this sort of training, and his mother's self-sacrifice and helpless protective gesture toward her starving little girl, which he apotheosizes as an instance of the old personal values that only the proles are keeping alive, can be seen negatively as an important element in the construction of a dominant masculine gender identity—that very identity that encourages not imitation of such selfless behavior but rather the abuse of one's male prerogatives against females. Hence Winston's sister, too, is to be sacrificed to his interests; this is the significance of his grabbing out of her hand the smaller piece of chocolate (less than her rightful share) that his mother had given to her.

From this memory Winston concludes not that male dominance and egocentricity need to be combated but instead that this sacrificial and helpless female behavior is an important value (For whom? one might ask) to be preserved for the future. These are clearly the patterns that continue to govern in *Nineteen Eighty-Four*, not subjected to any analysis or criticism on Orwell's part. Instead, they are duplicated, as when Julia too brings food (real food, not the ersatz stuff Winston has been eating) to one of her meetings with Winston. Women share, men monopolize, in these rituals. Or, when men do give, in Orwell's fiction, it is as an expression of power; this is what is revealed in a scene in *Keep the Aspidistra Flying* in which Gordon finally gets some money and forces his friends to have an expensive meal that they do not want. Women's giving is taken as either tenderness, love, or mere deference to men. Men's is an assertion of dominance. In this way simple acts reproduce their socially constructed ritual significance, and gender-related inequalities are reinforced rather than challenged.

It is ironically appropriate that in *Nineteen Eighty-Four* the offering of food and femininity—tributes to the past—are made by Julia in the old-fashioned room above Mr. Charrington's shop. For the room too is a fraud, not a haven but a trap for Julia and Winston. There is no safety in the past, no escape from the world of 1984, since it is that very past that has created the masculine gender role we see at work in Orwell's dystopia. His vision thus comes full circle: no hope for the future, no escape into the past. Although in his earlier writings he occasionally argued against mistaking power hunger for a biological fact, in this novel Orwell dissociates this power hunger from the social context that alone can hope to explain it. While his novel makes it clear that life for women in Oceania is in many respects similar to their life in Orwell's own society, this is not part of his critique. Orwell assails Big Brother's domination but never notices that he is the perfect embodiment of hypertrophied masculinity.

GENDER AND POWER IN DYSTOPIA

I focused above on women in *Nineteen Eighty-Four* because Orwell's portrayal of them, both advertently and inadvertently, helps us to understand the kind of society created in this novel. Men are everywhere in *Nineteen Eighty-Four*, yet as *men* they are invisible to Orwell. Although Orwell does not notice that the male behavior he objects to is *male* behavior, we have repeatedly seen him identifying negative characterizations of women as specifically *female* and generalizing to the entire sex. Sometimes, in fact, he does this so hastily that he misconstrues or misinterprets other writers' work. An example relevant to *Nineteen Eighty-Four* is a review that Orwell published in 1940 of Winifred Holtby's play *Take Back Your Freedom*.[22] The play is a rather superficial psychological study of the development of a British dictator, but it is not as simpleminded as Orwell's admiring review of it suggests. Orwell seems to respond favorably to the play because his version of it fulfills his prejudices: The dictator is a latent homosexual whose mother has dominated him for too long, and Orwell's review, sounding the old theme of "blame mother," provides an opportunity to refer to yet another character as a "miserable pansy." Orwell gives the impression that it is because the dictator's mother is, as he puts it, "enlightened" that she has brought him up wrong, whereas the play indicates that it is because of her own thwarted ambitions (she had ceased to work when she married). In fact, the play makes a strong feminist argument, entirely overlooked by Orwell, about women's creativity and need to do professional work. In case the audience misses the point in relation to the dictator's mother, it is reiterated in the character of another woman, a journalist who attempts to assassinate the dictator because he has deprived her of her profession and hence made her life meaningless. Orwell does not mention this character or this reiterated theme of the negative consequences of women's exclusion from professional work. Instead, he offers his own typically misogynist version of the play and then praises it as "so remarkable in its insight."

A more important example of how Orwell's misogyny affects his reading of other writers occurs in the famous 1944 essay "Raffles and Miss Blandish." Orwell calls James Hadley Chase's *No Orchids for Miss Blandish* "a header into the cesspool" (CEJL, 3:216) and then gives a curious misconstrual of the novel's conclusion, in which Miss Blandish, once her ordeal of rape and terror is over, commits suicide. Orwell comments: "By this time, however, she has developed such a taste for Slim's caresses that she feels unable to live without him, and she jumps out of the window of a sky-scraper" (216–17). In 1945 Orwell added this footnote: "Another reading of the final episode is possible. It may mean merely that Miss Blandish is pregnant. But the interpretation I have given above seems more in keeping with the general brutality of the book" (217). But the novel, although not providing clear details of her brutalization (unlike its treatment of male characters), does convey the depth of violence and terror experienced by Miss Blandish. She is described as dazed, drugged, cringing, unable to remember her name, with blank eyes, incapable of any gesture of resistance, terror-ridden, and, ultimately, unable to face her wealthy father. Earlier in the novel she tells Slim, her tormentor: "Why don't you get rid of me? Do you think I want to live? I don't, I tell you." [23] And she is repeatedly described as backing miserably away from Slim.

Even if Orwell had missed all these signs of her terror (though some are echoed in *Nineteen Eighty-Four;* for example, Slim tells her he once saw a woman taken out of the river—"The rats had eaten away half her face"—and promises not to let Ma Grissom do that to her [p. 109]), how could he have overlooked this passage, near the novel's conclusion, describing Miss Blandish's realization "that this was the end of the nightmare and the beginning of another one. . . . Her body, racked and yearning for the peace of drugs, did not belong to her any more" (pp. 199–200)? And to the very end she hopes Slim will shoot her (p. 200). Orwell's footnote, quoted above, seems to rest on Miss Blandish's final words: "He's not dead. He's with me now, I know he is—at first I thought I was wrong, but I know I've got him with me. He wouldn't leave me alone, ever—and he never will" (p. 205). But these lines, in conjunction with the repeated description of Miss Blandish's terror and blank eyes, reveal that what has occurred is a loss of self. She is marked not just in her body but in her soul, precisely as Winston Smith ultimately will be. Her four months as Slim's prisoner have deprived her of her self, her inner world. If Orwell had been able to imagine Miss Blandish as a person, he might also have been able to give a less banal interpretation of the novel.

Orwell's essay is of interest for several other reasons. First of all, he considers Chase's prose "in the American language" to be "a brilliant piece of writing" (CEJL, 3:217), when it is in fact full of trivial (and not always correct) clichés of American speech. This is perhaps explained by Brian Foster's observation: "In the mind of many a young Briton and his girl, American speech is the hall-mark of the tough guy and the he-man." [24] More important, in his essay Orwell protests against the power worship and sadism evident in a novel such as *No Orchids for Miss Blandish* and raises a crucial issue: "The interconnection between sadism, masochism, success worship, power worship, nationalism and totalitarianism is a huge subject whose edges have barely been scratched, and even to mention it is considered somewhat indelicate" (CEJL, 3:222). Orwell cannot begin to untangle this "subject," however, because he conceives of the political in a restricted sense, having to do primarily with rulers, state policies, and their overt interference in individual life. Not surprisingly, he also misses seeing the political dimensions of the gender roles apparent in *Nineteen Eighty-Four* for, while clearly depicting a world run by men preoccupied with power and domination, a world in which not a single woman is shown in a comparable role, he never addresses the issue of sex roles and gender stereotypes. *We* can see O'Brien and Winston involved in a competitive game in which affirmation of manhood is at stake, but Orwell cannot. As a result, Orwell's warning in *Nineteen Eighty-Four* seems curiously limited and off-center. The issue of gender roles lurks in the background of Orwell's text, seeping in without his apparent intention, waiting vainly to be brought forward and addressed.

Another writer in Orwell's time did address this issue in an early antifascist dystopia that in other respects strikingly foreshadows *Nineteen Eighty-Four*. In June 1937, twelve years before the publication of *Nineteen Eighty-Four*, *Swastika Night* was published in London under the male pseudonym "Murray Constantine." Its author, Katharine Burdekin, had published eight previous novels, six under her own name and two as Murray Constantine. *Swastika*

Night was reissued in July 1940 as a Left Book Club selection and became one of the very few works of fiction the club ever distributed to its members. Victor Gollancz, founder of the club and of the publishing house that bears his name, was also Orwell's first publisher, and *The Road to Wigan Pier* was itself a Left Book Club selection for March 1937. There is no direct evidence that Orwell was acquainted with Burdekin's novel; only the internal similarities between *Nineteen Eighty-Four* and *Swastika Night*— to be explained in a moment—suggest a connection.

Orwell, as we know, was an inveterate borrower, whose debt to writers such as Jonathan Swift, Rudyard Kipling, H. G. Wells, Jack London, Eugene Zamiatin, and James Burnham have been noted and studied by many critics.[25] But some of Orwell's other borrowings have gone undetected. In writing *Nineteen Eighty-Four*, he also seems to have borrowed from Jim Phelan's *Jail Journey*. Reviewing Phelan's book in 1940, Orwell focuses on what he judged to be the "truly important" feature of the book, its "straightforward discussion of the sex life of prisons." Orwell considers the life described in the book to be "genuinely horrible," with sex deprivation as the main form of punishment. In smug distaste, Orwell writes: "It is perfectly well known to anyone with even a third-hand acquaintance with prisons that nearly all prisoners are chronic masturbators. In addition there is homosexuality, which is almost general in long-term jails. If Macartney's *Walls Have Mouths* [another prison memoir] is to be believed, some prisons are such hotbeds of vice that even the warders are infected." [26]

While *Nineteen Eighty-Four* incorporates the notion that sex deprivation is at the heart of a totalitarian society, Orwell's main borrowing from Jim Phelan is along quite another line. The real importance of Phelan's book is his effective portrayal of a total institution, and a comparison of his account with Orwell's novel shows that the atmosphere of *Nineteen Eighty-Four* in fact owes much to *Jail Journey*'s depiction of prison life.[27] It is this prison atmosphere (and not, as Anthony West has argued, Orwell's experiences as a schoolboy at St. Cyprian's) [28] that Orwell projects onto the world at large in *Nineteen Eighty-Four*, but whereas Phelan, by cynically turning himself into a model prisoner, eventually wins his release, in Winston Smith's world no such escape is possible.

If Phelan, in *Jail Journey*, felt that the prison experience was designed to deprive him of his manhood, Burdekin's *Swastika Night*, which *Nineteen Eighty-Four* in so many respects resembles, makes the connection between masculinity and domination as elements in a socially constructed gender identity.[29] Burdekin envisions Germany and England in the seventh century of the Hitlerian millennium. The world has been divided into the Nazi Empire (Europe and Africa) and the Japanese Empire (Asia and the Americas), which are, lamentably (given the militaristic mentality that rules both spheres), in a state of perpetual peace due to their inability to conquer one another and their unwillingness to further deplete the supply of men. Hitler is venerated as a god, and a "Reduction of Women" has occurred, by which they have been driven to an animal-like state of ignorance and are now kept purely for breeding purposes. Rape is not considered a crime, since women's former "right of rejection" was an affront to masculine vanity. Burdekin thus sees that rape is fundamentally an assault on female autonomy. All books, records, and even monuments from the past have been destroyed in an effort to make the Nazi reality the only one while wiping out traces of earlier civilizations. The Reduction of Women and the exaltation of men have, not surprisingly, led to homosexual attachments among the men, although for the German men procreation is a civic duty. A type of feudal society is in force, with German Knights as the local authorities. Christians, having wiped out all Jews at the beginning of the Nazi era, are now themselves the lowest of the low and are considered untouchable.

Like literary eutopias ("good places"), dystopias provide a framework for leveling criticism at the writer's own historical moment. Extrapolating from his own environment, Orwell arrives at an urban society that is as shabby as postwar London, and onto this he grafts Nazi and Stalinist elements. Burdekin, however, extrapolates from the romantic and medieval longings of Nazi ideologues such as Alfred Rosenberg and hence imagines a totalitarian society in which a spurious Germanic mythology with its cult of masculinity governs life and sheer ignorance is combined with brutality to form the main instruments of control. But the similarities between these two novels extend far beyond their authors' utilization of the dystopian framework. Both books depict a totalitarian regime in which individual thought has been all but eliminated and, toward this end, all information about the past has been destroyed—much more thoroughly in Burdekin's novel than in Orwell's. In both books the world is divided into distinct empires in stasis (perpetual peace in *Swastika Night*; perpetual war in *Nineteen Eighty-Four*). There is a similar hierarchy in each novel with Big Brother and der Führer at the top and the most despised groups (proles; women) at the bottom and considered to be animals. And in both societies the upper echelons have material privileges denied to others.

Furthermore, in each novel there is a rebellious protagonist who is approached by a man in a position of power (O'Brien, the Inner Party member; von Hess, the Knight). This powerful man becomes the mediator through whom the protagonist's tendency to rebel is channeled, and in each case he gives the protagonist a secret book and hence knowledge. In both novels, also, a photograph provides a key piece of evidence about the past. The protagonists, Winston and Alfred, each attempt to teach a lover/friend (Julia; Hermann) about the past by reading from the book but meet with resistance or indifference. A curious detail occurs in both novels: Julia and Hermann sleep while the secret book is read, a mark of their lack of interest and of intellectual development.

As in *Swastika Night*, in *Nineteen Eighty-Four* the secret opposition is called a "Brotherhood." Despite the apolitical inclinations of Hermann and Julia, they are each drawn into the protagonist's rebellion and ultimately destroyed by it. But Julia is a far more active rebel than Hermann, even if her rebellion is limited largely to sexual nonconformity. In each novel, too, there are official enemies—Goldstein in *Nineteen Eighty-Four*; the four archfiends, enemies of Hitler, in *Swastika Night*. Finally, in both novels a distortion of sexuality occurs: in *Nineteen Eighty-Four* by the prohibition of sex for pleasure; in *Swastika Night* by the degradation of women, which has turned them into animals and made love and sexual attraction a prerogative of men only. And in both novels sex is encouraged for the sake of procreation, but only with specified people.

Many of the features found in *Swastika Night* appear oddly transformed in *Nineteen Eighty-Four*. The book supposedly written by Goldstein, enemy of the Party, is a fraud, a Party plant, as is the nonexistent Brotherhood. The powerful "rebel," O'Brien, is also a fraud. Even the evidence of the photograph cannot be trusted, for it too may be planted by the Party. In sum, *Nineteen Eighty-Four* evokes a world in which lies predominate. Orwell's preoccupation with the theme of honesty and deceit (which many critics have ingenuously seen as proof of his own personal honesty) is translated into a depiction of a world in which there is nothing but lies. In the process, elements from Burdekin's attack on fascism reappear as part of an attack on socialism and Communism.[30] Even love turns out to be a fraud in *Nineteen Eighty-Four*, since betrayal invariably occurs in the well-named (in Newspeak) Ministry of Love, where love is replaced by hate and only Big Brother can emerge as the beloved.

In her ironically titled 1934 novel *Proud Man*, Burdekin criticizes Aldous Huxley's *Brave New World* for its assumption that human beings would be the same even under totally different conditions.[31] She herself does not make that mistake. Her women, in *Swastika Night*, have indeed become like ignorant and fearful animals. Their misery seems to be their only recognizably human feature. Burdekin is also careful to show each of her male characters as seriously flawed by his environment. There are no simple heroes in her book, but there are men struggling toward understanding, and each is able to overcome his conditioning to some extent. Burdekin allows the reader some hope—that knowledge will somehow survive, that the secret book will be passed on, that a girl child may be raised with a smattering of pride. But Orwell offers only the bleak prospect of perpetual domination.

Swastika Night and *Nineteen Eighty-Four* are both primarily about the interactions of *men*. Burdekin addresses this issue in her exposé of the cult of masculinity; but Orwell, taking the worst male type as the model for the human species, seems to believe that the pursuit of power is an innate characteristic of human beings. Thus Orwell's despair and Burdekin's hope are linked to the degree of awareness that each has of gender roles and patriarchal power as social rather than biological facts.

The main contribution of *Nineteen Eighty-Four* to modern culture probably resides in the catchy names, such as Newspeak and doublethink, that Orwell invented for familiar phenomena. But Orwell cannot and does not provide a name for the key concept that explains the Party's preoccupation with domination, power, and violence: These are all part of what Burdekin calls the cult of masculinity. Because Burdekin is able to see and to name this phenomenon, her depiction of a totalitarian regime has a dimension lacking in Orwell's novel. What Orwell can only, helplessly, attribute to human nature, Burdekin traces to a gender polarization that can degenerate into the world of *Swastika Night*, with its hypertrophied masculinity on the one hand and its Reduction of Women on the other. Male egos and female bodies; male persons and female animals—these are the extremes of which an ideology of male supremacy is capable. As Orwell uses the Stalinist framework to launch his attack on totalitarianism, so Burdekin uses the Nazis as the focal point of her attack on the cult of masculinity. But she makes clear that the Nazi preoccupation with manhood was itself merely an extrapolation of a quite routine gender ideology. Unlike Orwell in his idealized portrayal of female maternal figures, Burdekin recognizes that it is but a small step from the male apotheosis of women as mothers to their degradation to mere breeding animals. In both cases women are reduced to a biological capacity, out of which is constructed an entire social identity.

While Nazi ideology overtly expressed this preoccupation with gender roles, recent studies have noted the centrality of male dominance and the "masculine principle" in all forms of fascism.[32] Burdekin only needed to exaggerate the male supremacy she saw around her to envision Europe after seven centuries of Nazi domination as engulfed in the cult of masculinity. Thus, in *Swastika Night*, phallic pride has become the overt organizing principle of Hitlerian society. Through her dystopian fantasy, Burdekin thus gives dramatic form to something Virginia Woolf had written some years earlier: "Women have served all these centuries as looking-glasses possessing the magic and delicious power of reflecting the figure of man at twice its natural size. Without that power probably the earth would still be swamp and jungle. The glories of all our wars would be unknown."[33]

We cannot yet define the precise contours of the connection between political power and the male gender role, but that there is such a connection is self-evident. The very fact that the exercise of power utilizes a vocabulary associated with male, but not female, gender roles points to this: Control, dominance, strength, aggression, force, authority—all these terms routinely employed in discussing power (both power *over* others, and power to do) also figure prominently in stereotypes of the male personality. Orwell was vaguely aware of some such connection, for he identified the label "Fascist" with "bully" (CEJL, 3:114).

In *Nineteen Eighty-Four*, Orwell treats political power in a social vacuum, without reference to the fact that such power is exercised by males to the exclusion of females and that it is also exercised in the home. The idea of a female revolution is not in and of itself a panacea—Burdekin is right to warn, in *Proud Man*, that unless it challenges the key concept of "importance" it might simply mean a "reversal of privilege"—but to refuse to address the issue of gender roles is to circle fruitlessly around the problem, viewing it as an "essence" rather than as a particular social configuration. Although Orwell seems to believe he is attacking power in itself, in fact he never focuses on male power over females. Thus he fails to note that the abuses of power he describes are simply a further point along the male continuum of a sexually polarized society. But by departing from lofty abstractions about power hunger one arrives at less awesome and less mystifying perceptions: Far from being an innate appetite mysteriously found primarily in males, power emerges as part of a prescribed and self-serving social role.

Despite the popular acclaim of *Nineteen Eighty-Four*, it is not, in the final analysis, an intellectually convincing vision. First of all, Orwell largely disregards 85 percent of the population—the proles—though this is generally forgotten when the novel is characterized as depicting a complete totalitarianism. And by ignoring the material contradictions that still abound in the world of Oceania (for example, someone must produce the luxury items used by Inner Party members; in this already lie the seeds of a class struggle), Orwell is able to conceive of this society as perfectly static, which is essential to his argument since it increases the feeling of entrapment and hopelessness that he sought to convey.[34] In *Nineteen Eighty-Four* reality has *not* been brought into line with Party policy; hence the need for Newspeak, doublethink, crimestop, constant revisions of the newspapers, and so on. Despite its apparent disregard for the written word and history, the Party, in its endless revisions, reveals that it is in fact obsessed with these very things. Burdekin's solution is much simpler: Restrict literacy, promote ignorance, issue no books or papers at all. Thus there is nothing to revise, nothing to censor beyond the initial acts of destruction of the past (which, she says, took about fifty years). Whereas Orwell envisions that cities such as London in some unexplained fashion will have survived an atomic war, Burdekin's postwar society is still, seven hundred years later, organized into small towns, befitting a destroyed civilization. Each scenario involves different mechanisms of control. Orwell appears to be most interested in techniques of intellectual control. He overestimates the value of Newspeak as a static language of repression, for much more likely is the slow distortion of language that complements an entire ideology—a phrase here, a word there. Yet Orwell himself may have been aware that Newspeak was not to be taken too seriously, for in the end his novel relies on old-fashioned physical abuse and terror.[35]

Burdekin, however, envisions a reality that has in fact been brought into line with official policy. No solipsism is necessary here, no doublethink. The habitual disparagement of women has been perfected; the possible positive meanings of female have been eliminated by the well-named Reduction of Women. Once women are reduced to an animal-like existence (but without an animal's unconsciousness), the semantic range associated with the female, which has always differed from that of the male, is reduced as well. The gender ideology that situates the male at the positive pole and the female at the negative has finally found its fulfillment in reality.

This is a more ingenious and horrifying solution. Other dystopias attempt to deal with the potentially disruptive attraction between males and females in a variety of ways. Huxley, for example, licenses sexual promiscuity and, following (though in less Taylorized form) Zamiatin's lead, opts for sexual discharge as a necessary feature of a stable system. Orwell, by contrast, prohibits sex except for the purpose of procreation, on the assumption that sexual tension could be redirected as passionate hatred of an enemy and passionate love of an abstract leader. But Burdekin follows the logic of our own language and experience and sees that these already contain the seeds for the suppression of the feminine. Given the virgin/whore, angel/demon dichotomy, all that was required in *Swastika Night* was to eliminate the idealized positive pole and then elaborate and exaggerate the demonic negative pole. The tendency to see women as animals did not need to be invented. It was already there and merely required extension. To forbid sexual love and the private life, as Orwell does in *Nineteen Eighty-Four*, is to impose rules that can be broken. It is obviously more effective to degrade an ambivalently desired object and thus stimulate horror of it and hatred for it. In this way, Burdekin insists on the fundamental continuity between her own society and her imaginative vision of its implications.

Orwell does not address the problem of how individual men react once they are deprived of their personal control over women. Since masculine power (embodied in Big Brother) is still valorized in Oceania, there is a potentially serious problem as ordinary Party men find their personal enactment of their gender role thwarted. Winston Smith, a recognizably ordinary character, may not have the same right-to-rape as the men in Burdekin's novel, but he has the same impulses. Orwell takes for granted Winston's dislike of women and anger at their sexual inaccessibility. The connection Orwell reveals between frustrated male dominance and political rebellion invites the speculation that if Winston could rape Julia he might never become a rebel.[36] Winston's protest, such as it is, may ultimately be against the Party's usurpation of many male prerogatives. Big Brother has, in effect, deprived men of their manhood by restricting their individual domination of women. In *Nineteen Eighty-Four*, the general fear of betrayal means also that men fear women in a way that was impossible in the old days that Winston longs for. What this implies in family life is indicated by the detail that it is Mr. Parsons's seven-year-old *daughter* who turns him in to the Thought Police. "Real" masculinity officially belongs only to Big Brother and his representatives, such as O'Brien, and can be acquired by other men only through emotional alliance with these representatives. Orwell's novel thus presents us with a kind of Reduction of Men, without, however, improving the status of women. In Oceania it is not only women who must live under masculine domination. Big Brother and Inner Party members such as O'Brien monopolize the masculine gender role; they reduce men like Winston to a feminine role.[37]

In *Nineteen Eighty-Four* Orwell develops many of the features we have already encountered in *Animal Farm*; but from the mere description of how the animals' revolution was corrupted, Orwell has moved to distinct and neatly labeled phenomena: Newspeak, doublethink, the "mutability" of the past. In keeping with his general disregard of the issue of gender roles, however, Orwell also avoids noting that the Party slogan, "Who controls the past controls the future: who controls the present controls the past," has always applied as an expression of male dominance over women. Knowledge of women's past has repeatedly disappeared into "memory holes," which is why we have needed to rediscover women's history; and why in 1983 Joanna Russ needed to publish a book called *How to Suppress Women's Writing*, to teach us again things that Virginia Woolf had taught us more than fifty years earlier in *A Room of One's Own*, and still others before her—always to have their words disappear, barred by "gatekeepers" from becoming known and recognized.[38] Orwell is blind to the fact that the political manipulation of language did not require twentieth-century totalitarianism or modern technology. Language, including his own, was already such a weapon and had been wielded for centuries by patriarchal society. Newspeak and doublethink are not necessary to make certain things unsayable, unknowable, perhaps finally unthinkable. Ideology need only pass itself off as reality and contrary perceptions can be occluded. As long as manipulation and domination were exercised by men as a group against women as a group, Orwell saw no need to protest. When, however, the relations between the governed and the governors so altered that Orwell saw the possibility of men like himself becoming the victims of censorship and domination, these became spectacularly visible to him.[39]

Orwell never seems conscious of the strongly masculine narrative voice evident in so much of his writing (though I believe it is a major factor in his appeal to other men); similarly, he does not seem to have been aware that his indictment of human behavior in *Nineteen Eighty-Four* is in fact an indictment of male behavior. Gamesmanship is its epitome, for here we have domination pursued for its own sake and not for any practical or material objective. Orwell could not name the ideology of which his own views were a part, but his novel has much to contribute as an allegory of hypertrophied masculinity. Given his habitual disparagement of the female and his acceptance of a male model of behavior, Orwell could not analyze the dynamics of the pursuit of power. Although he called into question many social, political, and economic conventions, he accepted learned male behavior as the human norm. While depicting an essentially masculine ideology (of domination, violence, and aggression), Orwell made the common error of confusing culture with nature. We should clearly recognize that *Nineteen Eighty-Four* contains no indictment of how human beings behave but only of how men in a particular tradition have behaved. What we know of power is linked to the male domination of society. We do not, cannot thus far, know what kind of society we would have if it were not dominated by males who are personally dominating females. No novel with female protagonists could ever have been so readily accepted as describing the generally human, but the identification of the male with the human norm is among the conventions of an androcentric society that is only now being seriously challenged.

The totalitarian nightmare, from this perspective, is neither merely a particular political configuration nor an inevitable human construct but rather a possibility inherent in the cultural polarization of superior male/inferior female. *Nineteen Eighty-Four* warns us against the incursions of big government, against the loss of freedom implicit in the pursuit of power, but it does not warn men against themselves. It does not show Winston Smith coming to an understanding of O'Brien's love of power —his expression of dominance—by recognizing the cult of frustrated masculinity at work in himself. On the contrary, the novel, like Orwell's other work, fosters disdain for women, argues for their inferior consciousness in comparison with men's, and encourages the reader to enjoy the superiority of the protagonist's conscious, protesting, male position. We are meant to admire Winston's courage and take his defeat seriously; Julia's fate hardly matters.

Far from demystifying the values implicit in his novel, Orwell takes them as a given and blames "English Socialism" on the one hand and "human nature" on the other. Orwell could have stripped bare the ideology of masculine supremacy and challenged us to confront it in all its consequences. But had he done so, he would have radically undermined his own position in the world. Instead, he chose the easier way of pessimism and despair.

Nine

Conclusion:

Orwell's Despair

"I feel in the work of the men whose poetry I read today a deep pessimism and fatalistic grief; and I wonder if it isn't the masculine side of what women have experienced, the price of masculine dominance."[1] So writes Adrienne Rich, and her observation casts a positive light on Orwell's despair. If it was a sign of his blindness, it was also a mark of his insight. The history of the twentieth century clearly led to bigger and better killing machines, and Orwell saw what men everywhere were doing —capitalist men, fascist men, "socialist" men; he saw that new technologies and centralization made domination ever easier, and he despaired. New concepts, new models, throw light on Orwell's work, so that today we can understand both his inability to see a solution and his responsiveness to the conditions of life implicit in a sexual polarization in which the masculine is defined in terms of destructive patterns that are justified as, or believed to be, facts of nature. Orwell's uncritical embrace of misogyny and his hostility to feminism are among his most serious shortcomings as a moral witness to his times. But they explain his despair. Clinging to an inherently dangerous and presumably inescapable notion of the masculine, while aware of its deadly potentiality, Orwell can see no way out. In his adherence to a conventional notion of manhood, he cannot discern that the characteristics he laments and the ones he promotes are united by the demands of the male gender role. Instead, he is left puzzled and driven to despair by the possible causes of bullying and power worship, which he considers typical of "human beings."

Orwell cannot imagine any possibility for social progress because he views the "other" as lacking in consciousness and hence incapable of action. At the same time, he believes in a drive for power, which thus becomes the only possible agent for social change—but a change that would necessarily duplicate the structure of domination it is attempting to overthrow (this is the message of *Animal Farm*). Hence the paradox of his argument in *Nineteen Eighty-Four*: Hope lies only in the proles, but there is no hope because the proles are unconscious. Since Orwell cannot call into question the mental model (dominant/submissive; subject/object) of human relations that conditions his thinking, he inevitably loses hope.

Ironically, Orwell himself once wrote a line that could have pointed the way to a solution: "To accept an orthodoxy is always to inherit unresolved contradictions" (CEJL, 4:411). Had Orwell applied this observation to himself, he might have been able to come to terms with the contradictions that pervade his own work. But to do so would have entailed questioning a notion of manhood that he was committed to and unwilling to scrutinize. The view of women as inferior, and their confinement as idealized reproductive, nurturing, and sexual specialists, forms an essential part of that notion and thus does not conflict with Orwell's implicit values. But as an ideology it conflicts with his attacks on hierarchy and injustice, which remain woefully incomplete, even hypocritical. It is instructive that critics, while proclaiming Orwell's moral stature, have largely ignored this contradiction. Indeed, it is unlikely that misandry would have gone unrecognized in a woman writer or that she would have been considered a great moral teacher, a promoter of justice and equality, had her works revealed contempt for men as consistently as Orwell's reveal his misogyny. However much Orwell may seem to have challenged his own society, in a fundamental way he not only failed actually to do so but in fact affirmed and disseminated a central ideological tenet of that society.

Orwell's sensitivity to doublethink—holding two contradictory thoughts in one's mind simultaneously and believing both of them without experiencing the contradiction—perhaps stemmed from his own experience with this mental mode, manifest throughout his texts. But the tension produced by such mental gymnastics must have been difficult, and the essentialistic vision of human nature as striving for power perhaps gave him at least the semblance of a resolution, even if a wholly negative one. The embrace of pessimism also has an important side effect: It allows Orwell's ideological presuppositions, to which he was fiercely committed, to continue unacknowledged. To put it differently: It seems to me that Orwell cares more for his continuing privileges as a male than he does for the abstractions of justice, decency, and truth on behalf of which he claims to be writing. But suppressing recognition of women's oppression and ignoring the issue of patriarchy lock Orwell, not surprisingly, in an insoluble bind, and the inability to express this contradiction and then think it through undermines all his work.

Orwell's essays and journalism are full of striking observations that make all the more revealing his inability to examine the particular ideological cluster that pervades his own work. In a discussion of anti-Semitism and nationalism, for example, he affirms that an intellectual's status derives from the "fact that he can feel the emotional tug of such things, and yet see them dispassionately for what they are." He urges intellectuals to begin not with the question of why these irrational beliefs appeal to other people but with the question: Why do they appeal to *me?* What is there about them that I feel is true? In this way, Orwell suggests, intellectuals may discover their own rationalizations and perhaps also what lies beneath them (CEJL, 3:341). In another essay he notes: "One prod to the nerve of nationalism, and the intellectual decencies can vanish, the past can be altered, and the plainest facts can be denied" and adds that "as soon as fear, hatred, jealousy and power worship are involved, the sense of reality becomes unhinged" (3:378–79). The only defense, he concludes, is to recognize your biases "and prevent them from contaminating your mental processes"—but this requires a moral effort that, he says, "few of us are prepared to make" (380).

Orwell holds an essentially simplistic notion of the relationship between politics and language, as is apparent in his statement, in the essay "Politics and the English Language," [2] that one should "let the meaning choose the word, and not the other way about." Even here, his rhetoric (which consists of setting up oppositions) is familiar: "In prose, the worst thing one can do with words is to surrender to them" (CEJL, 4:138). Orwell here assumes a predetermined meaning standing in opposition to preexisting words. Totalitarianism, which to Orwell is a deviation from a normal reality "out there," must therefore try to control language and ultimately thought, to the point where clear "meanings" in the outside world will no longer be available. But this simple notion of the relationship between language and political awareness is activated only by those things Orwell already considers to be legitimate concerns—and his very language is constantly defining and shaping these areas of legitimacy so that other, different, ones cannot emerge into consciousness. He does not see that his thoughts, his language, made public, also help maintain a certain reality in place. Orwell's blindness when it comes to the demands of masculinity and the fact of male dominance reveals the limits of both his language and his conception of what is "out there" in the world. He creates an ideologically weighted discourse that— to the extent that Orwell is uncritically admired—can only contribute to women's continued oppression and men's continued domination. His writings about language do not let him become aware of his own biases.

It is above all in relation to gender roles that Orwell is unable to sustain any distance and he is therefore unable to "see" this feature of his society as a problem. Until now critics have so closely identified with this particular aspect of their social world that, even while disagreeing about Orwell's overt politics, few have been able to note those important ideological elements that Orwell duplicates and reinforces in his writing. This is not to say that Orwell's overt politics are not themselves contradictory; they often are. But at least these contradictions are part of the very issues he wishes to raise and thus invite further discussion. In the case of his androcentrism, however, this is not what happens, for it is never questioned, never allowed to come into focus as an issue. If we follow Orwell's lead in this matter we will simply reproduce this ideology in ourselves; or, rather, we will passively let it work in us to reinforce this particular way of seeing things. Orwell's "seeing," as the preceding chapters have shown, is coherently limited, and by exploring those limits I have tried to make visible those things that his language obscures.

In *Nineteen Eighty-Four*, Winston Smith's breakdown is

finally signaled by his inability to see what is objectively there; he can no longer tell the difference between O'Brien's four or five fingers. What is real ceases to matter, as belief in his tormentor's power to mold reality takes over. In an individual's duplication of a dominant ideology we have the same kind of inability to "see." But it is not only what is *not* seen that matters, for what *is* seen also undergoes the distorting process. Androcentrism is such a distorting lens. In Orwell's work, whether women are absent and ignored or present and denigrated, the contrasting (masculine) self is marked by the distortion, shaped by the exclusion or denigration. How he sees and what he refuses to see finally become the form and the substance of what he is able to speak. It is not only women who are muted in Orwell's work. He himself, trapped by both his manhood and his misogyny, in the end fails to achieve the resonance of a fully human language.

Notes

CHAPTER ONE
INTRODUCTION: THE ORWELL MYTH

1. For a general guide to Orwell criticism, see Jeffrey Meyers and Valerie Meyers, *George Orwell: An Annotated Bibliography of Criticism* (New York: Garland, 1977). Itself a reflection of the Orwell myth, this volume frequently labels serious critiques of Orwell as "unreasonable," "distorted," and "attacks," while never making comparable strictures on the far more numerous laudatory comments about Orwell.

2. V. S. Pritchett, "George Orwell," *New Statesman and Nation*, January 28, 1950, p. 96.

3. V. S. Pritchett, "George Orwell," in Gilbert Phelps, ed., *Living Writers* (London: Sylvan Press, 1947), p. 115.

4. Bernard Crick, who recently published the first authorized biography of Orwell, provides many instances of this strategy. Indeed, Crick's biography, valuable as it is as the first thoroughly researched and documented account of Orwell's life, is marred by constant apologetics shading off into hagiography. See his *George Orwell: A Life* (Boston: Little, Brown, 1980), p. 88, for an example.

5. See, e.g., David Smith, *Socialist Propaganda in the Twentieth-Century British Novel* (London: Macmillan, 1978), pp. 2, 132. Smith explains why he has had to omit *Animal Farm* and *Nineteen Eighty-Four* from his book, despite Orwell's self-definition as a socialist.

6. *National Review*, March 5, 1982, p. 212. This was followed a year later by an article by Robert C. de Camara, "Homage to Orwell," *National Review*, May 13, 1983, pp. 566–74. De Camara discusses Orwell's ambivalence toward socialism, only to argue that antisocialism emerges as Orwell's final truth. Likening the capitalist/communist conflict to a struggle between Good and Evil or God and Satan, de Camara concludes: "The forces of darkness have huge armies, a bigger and better arsenal, liberation movements, and the whores' allegiance. The forces of light have Orwell on their side and draw strength from it" (p. 574).

7. Henry Fairlie, "Political Commentary," *Spectator*, September 2, 1955, p. 296.

8. Rael Jean Isaac and Erich Isaac, "The Counterfeit Peacemakers: Atomic Freeze," *American Spectator* 15, no. 6 (June 1982): 8–17.

9. Norman Podhoretz, "If Orwell Were Alive Today," *Harper's*, January 1983, p. 30.

10. Christopher Hitchens and Norman Podhoretz, "An Exchange on Orwell," *Harper's*, February 1983, pp. 56–58.

11. T. R. Fyvel, in his recent book *Orwell: A Personal Memoir* (London: Weidenfeld and Nicolson, 1982), pp. 177–82, recollects his disagreements with Orwell over "the Jewish issue" and his impression that Orwell was "curiously distant" about the fate of Jews in Europe, but ends on a conciliatory note with a comment of Arthur Koestler's to the effect that each of us can "produce only a limited amount of calories of indignation." Of greater interest is David Walton's "George Orwell and Antisemitism," in *Patterns of Prejudice* 16, no. 1 (1982): 19–34. Walton documents Orwell's anti-Semitism, then praises Orwell for understanding "that while it is not always possible to change subjective feelings, one can ensure they do not 'contaminate' one's mental processes and prevent one acting decently" (p. 34), an unwarrantedly mild conclusion given the evidence Walton has himself cited.

12. John Wain, "George Orwell as a Writer of Polemic," in Raymond Williams, ed., *George Orwell: A Collection of Critical Essays* (Englewood Cliffs, N.J.: Prentice-Hall, 1974), pp. 89–102; quote is on p. 90.

13. E. P. Thompson, "Outside the Whale," *The Poverty of Theory and Other Essays* (New York: Monthly Review Press, 1978), pp. 211–43.

14. Interestingly, Julian Symons is one of the few people who has written about Orwell with genuine affection. In his "Orwell, a Reminiscence," *London Magazine* 3 (September 1963): 35–49 (reprinted in *Critical Occasions* [London: H. Hamilton, 1966], along with some other pieces on Orwell), Symons admires Orwell for this retraction and writes: "To like him you had first not to be too much annoyed by the original outrageous statement, and then to appreciate the generosity of the public retraction." In fact, Orwell's entire "London Letter" of December 1944 is devoted to the mistakes he made in his four years of writing for *Partisan Review*. He acknowledges these mistakes only to comfortably ensconce them in a crowd, writing: "I think the first admission we ought to make is that *we were all wrong*" (CEJL, 3:294; his emphasis). He analyzes his errors and decides that "I was often right as against the bulk of the left-wing intelligentsia" (3:296) and then, after some more confessions, states that "So far as I can see, all political thinking for years past has been vitiated in the same way" (3:297). The net effect of the article—and why should one not assume this was its intent?—is to inoculate the reader against Orwell's real mistakes (see chap. 5, below, on Roland Barthes's description of the inoculation technique) while increasing confidence in his truthfulness and, not incidentally, attacking left-wing intellectuals once again.

15. Jeffrey Meyers, in *The Enemy: A Biography of Wyndham Lewis* (London: Routledge and Kegan Paul, 1980), pp. 296–97, calls Orwell's comment about Lewis "a smear, an irresponsible and highly improbable assertion" based on gossip that Orwell did not bother to investigate.

16. The notebook (currently held at the Orwell Archive, along with Orwell's other papers) contains, pasted into its back cover, a list of Communist-front organizations taken from the *New Leader* (June 14, 1947) and, on the facing page, a list of additional organizations. Bernard Crick, in his *George*

Orwell (pp. 388; 454, n. 49) mentions this notebook but makes far too little of it.

17. This style of writing recalls Mary Ellmann's comment: "The male body lends credence to assertions, while the female takes it away." In *Thinking about Women* (New York: Harcourt Brace Jovanovich, 1968), p. 148, Ellmann comments about the subliminal assumption that "from weight must come weight: men's shoes alone seem a promise of truth." Many writers on Orwell have commented on his size-twelve feet and the difficulty of procuring boots large enough to fit him. I have often wondered why they considered this a significant detail. Ellmann provides an explanation.

18. David Caute refers to this in a discussion of the "varying degrees of unreality" demonstrated by the editors of *Partisan Review* (for which Orwell wrote) as they assessed political opinion. Caute quotes from a letter that Philip Rahv "wrote to Orwell warning that *Animal Farm* might be less well received in the US than in England because 'public opinion here is almost solidly Stalinist, in the bourgeois as well as the liberal press.'" This, in 1946! See Caute, *The Fellow-Travellers* (New York: Macmillan, 1973), p. 327.

19. Mary McCarthy, "The Writing on the Wall," *The Writing on the Wall and Other Literary Essays* (New York: Harcourt, Brace and World, 1970), p. 167. McCarthy wonders whether Orwell's socialism "was not an unexamined idea off the top of his head: sheer rant" (p. 170) and feels it impossible to guess where he would stand on current issues, especially on the war in Vietnam (p. 168). Indeed, a number of writers in the late sixties and early seventies were concerned about establishing Orwell's position on Vietnam and, like Podhoretz and Hitchens more recently, came to opposing conclusions.

20. Anthony Powell, *Infants of the Spring* (New York: Holt, Rinehart and Winston, 1976), p. 92. Powell's comments on Orwell are largely drawn from an earlier piece in the *Atlantic Monthly*, October 1967, pp. 62–68.

21. Powell, *Infants of the Spring*, p. 93.

22. Ibid., pp. 94, 95.

23. Malcolm Muggeridge, "Knight of the Woeful Countenance," in Miriam Gross, ed., *The World of George Orwell* (New York: Simon and Schuster, 1971), pp. 168, 169.

24. Malcolm Muggeridge, *Like It Was: The Diaries of Malcolm Muggeridge*, sel. and ed. John Bright-Holmes (New York: William Morrow, 1982), p. 195.

25. Ibid., p. 376.

26. Muggeridge, "Knight of the Woeful Countenance," p. 169.

27. Thompson, "Outside the Whale"; Raymond Williams, "George Orwell," *Culture and Society, 1780–1950* (New York: Columbia University Press, 1958), pp. 285–94, and also his *Orwell* (Glasgow: Fontana/Collins, 1971); McCarthy, "The Writing on the Wall"; Terry Eagleton, "George Orwell and the Lower Middle-Class Novel," *Exiles and Emigrés: Studies in Modern Literature* (London: Chatto and Windus, 1970), pp. 71–107; Frank Gloversmith, "Changing Things: Orwell and Auden," *Class, Culture, and Social Change* (Sussex: Harvester, 1980), pp. 101–41. Recently, D. S. Savage ("The Fatalism of George Orwell" in Boris Ford, ed., *The New Pelican Guide to English Literature* [Harmondsworth: Penguin Books, 1983], vol. 8, *The Present*) has published a critique of Orwell's contradictions and attacked his inflated reputation.

28. David A. Martin, *Pacifism: A Historical and Sociological Study* (London: Routledge and Kegan Paul, 1965), p. 146, comments: "It is in [Edward] Carpenter's *Civilization: Its Cause and Cure* (1889) that one finds an archetypal source of the ideas which gave the Labour Party a fatal attraction for all those

whom George Orwell labelled as fruit-juice drinkers, nudists, sandal-wearers, sex-maniacs, and nature-cure quacks." Orwell himself referred to Carpenter as a "pious sodomite" in a 1936 letter (CEJL, 1:216). On the subject of Carpenter, *History Workshop* 6 (Autumn 1978): 222, contains a letter by Bernard Henry recalling how his father had brought him up with Edward Carpenter's ideas as a near "religion" and stating that from Carpenter he learned two things: toler-ance and compassion (and this though his father thought Carpenter "was not sound on Sex"). Orwell might have benefited from such an education.

29. In her book *The Troublesome Helpmate: A History of Misogyny in Literature* (Seattle: University of Washington Press, 1966), pp. xii–xiii, Katharine M. Rogers includes as "manifestations of misogyny in literature not only direct expressions of hatred, fear, or contempt of womankind, but such indirect ex-pressions as misogynistic speeches by dramatic characters who are definitely speaking for the author and condemnations of one woman or type of woman which spread, implicitly or explicitly, to the whole sex," as well as "attacks on human follies or vices which focus inappropriately or disproportionately on women." Rogers does not consider the mere expression of a widely held belief, such as that women are inferior to men, to be misogynistic except when an au-thor insists on such a view with a harshness that is exceptional even for his time. As we shall see, this is indeed the case with Orwell.

30. Orwell regularly used ridicule and scorn as a means of discrediting and shutting up his opponents, and it is instructive to see some of his admirers wielding the same weapons against those who dare to criticize Orwell. In the *Times Literary Supplement*, February 3, 1984, Peter Kemp describes a sympo-sium held at London's Barbican at which several women voiced criticisms of Orwell. Kemp heaps ridicule on these dissidents and uses Orwell's terms New-speak and Duckspeak as clubs with which to silence them. He refers to their comments as "diatribes," "speech thick with delusion," expressing "cracked notions"—all adding up to a "dismal morning"—and then cozily congratulates a male speaker who affirmed "Orwell's courage, honesty, and dedication to the English language." Though Kemp is also critical of some male speakers (e.g., Raymond Williams, who "convolutedly groused about *Nineteen Eighty-Four*"), he is not venomous in describing them—again in appropriate imitation of Orwell's own differential treatment of males and females. Not for an instant does Kemp consider the possibility that there may be some legitimacy to the women's critiques of Orwell, which, however, have roused him to supposedly crushing (and predictably misogynist) retaliation.

31. I take the term "disrupting the intended meaning" from Janice Win-ship, "Handling Sex," *Media, Culture, and Society* 3, no. 1 (January 1981): 25–41. She uses it in the context of a discussion of advertising.

32. Jenni Calder, in *Chronicles of Conscience: A Study of George Orwell and Arthur Koestler* (London: Secker and Warburg, 1968), provides an example of a male-identified reader. Especially in discussing Orwell's *Clergyman's Daugh-ter*, which she agrees is his least successful novel, Calder gives a kind of gender-less account that cannot explain the weaknesses of the novel. For an important study of conventional masculine narratives and their effect on female readers, see Judith Fetterley, *The Resisting Reader: A Feminist Approach to American Fiction* (Bloomington: Indiana University Press, 1978). Jacintha Buddicom, in *Eric and Us: A Remembrance of George Orwell* (London: Leslie Frewin, 1974), is one of the few readers to note peculiar attitudes toward sex and women in Orwell's writings; see her chapter "Eric and Sex." The title of Buddicom's book refers, of course, to the fact that Orwell's real name was Eric Arthur Blair.

33. Crick, *George Orwell*, p. 56. Crick's description of the story is actually an interesting illustration of how hard it is for men even to notice the issue of gender roles. As a result, he misses the point (the only point of interest in a rather ordinary piece of writing) and misrepresents the story.

34. The story is reproduced in full in Peter Stansky and William Abrahams, *The Unknown Orwell* (London: Constable, 1972), pp. 93–94.

35. Dale Spender, *There's Always Been a Women's Movement This Century* (London: Routledge and Kegan Paul/Pandora Press, 1983).

36. The review, on file in the Orwell Archive, appeared in the *Manchester Evening News*, August 2, 1945. Orwell describes Woolf's book as "a discussion of the handicaps which have prevented women, as compared with men, from producing literature of the first order. What she believes to be the main reason is alluded to in the title of the book. If a writer is to do his best, she says, he needs £500 a year and a room of his own, and far fewer women than men have enjoyed these advantages.

"But there are other disabilities, and Miss Woolf invents, among other things, a sister for William Shakespeare, not less fitted than her brother, but cut off by the very nature of the society she lives in from any chance of using her rights. At times this book rather overstates the drawbacks from which women suffer, but almost anyone of the male sex could read it with advantage."

CHAPTER TWO
ROLES OF EMPIRE

1. Malcolm Muggeridge, "World Review" (June 1950), in Jeffrey Meyers, ed., *George Orwell: The Critical Heritage* (London: Routledge and Kegan Paul, 1975), p. 55.

2. David Newsome, *Godliness and Good Learning: Four Studies on a Victorian Ideal* (London: John Murray, 1961), explains that to the "muscular Christian" school, associated with Charles Kingsley and Thomas Hughes, manliness no longer meant being adult (as it had, for example, to Coleridge) but rather was used as the opposite of effeminate. The stress now fell on the masculine connotations of "manliness" as it came to be associated with robust energy, spirited courage, and physical vitality (pp. 197–98). These ideals, along with the respect for duty fostered in the public schools by, among other things, the establishment of a Rifle Corps, reflected upper-middle-class British opinion in an age of imperial expansion and were further intensified in the Edwardian period as patriotism increased along with the prospects of war (pp. 200–2). Newsome criticizes the ideal of muscular Christianity for degenerating into a code of living "so robust and patriotic in its demands that it could be represented as reaching its perfection in a code of dying." To die in fighting for one's country became the ultimate expression of this ideal (p. 238).

3. Allen J. Greenberger, *The British Image of India: A Study in the Literature of Imperialism, 1880–1960* (London: Oxford University Press, 1969), p. 51.

4. Ibid., pp. 43–44.

5. In "Shooting an Elephant," Orwell puts it this way: "A white man mustn't be frightened in front of 'natives'; and so, in general, he isn't frightened" (CEJL, 1:240). Conceiving of all the "natives" as women may help in reducing fear, since men do not usually anticipate or fear violence from women, even in groups, in our society.

6. Orwell goes on to say: "With one part of my mind I thought of the British Raj as an unbreakable tyranny, ... with another part I thought that the

greatest joy in the world would be to drive a bayonet into a Buddhist priest's guts" (CEJL, 1:236).

7. Maung Htin Aung, "George Orwell and Burma," in Miriam Gross, ed., *The World of George Orwell* (New York: Simon and Schuster, 1971), p. 24, describes the episode, which he witnessed in 1924, in which some Burmese schoolboys accidentally bumped against Orwell at a railway station in Rangoon. "Blair was furious and raised the heavy cane which he was carrying, to hit the boy on the head, but checked himself, and struck him on the back instead." Htin Aung comments: "Blair was, of course, merely reflecting the general attitude of his English contemporaries towards Burmese students." Christopher Hollis, in *A Study of George Orwell: The Man and his Works* (London: Hollis and Carter, 1956), p. 27, recalls running into Orwell (whom he had known at Eton) in Rangoon in the summer of 1925. Hollis describes one of the evenings they spent together: "We had a long talk and argument. In the side of him which he revealed to me at that time there was no trace of liberal opinions. He was at pains to be the imperial policeman, explaining that these theories of no punishment and no beating were all very well at public schools but that they did not work with the Burmese—in fact that 'Libbaty's a kind 'o thing / Thet don't agree with niggers.' "

8. Terry Eagleton, "George Orwell and the Lower Middle Class Novel," *Exiles and Emigrés* (London: Chatto and Windus, 1970), p. 77.

9. Ibid., p. 85.

10. John Gross, "Imperial Attitudes," in Miriam Gross, *World of George Orwell*, p. 32. Gross's sentence in fact continues: "and when he finally broke free, he recoiled to the opposite extreme. In an unjust world, his place was with the victims, and the four years following his return from Burma saw him repeatedly submerging himself in the lower depths." It is instructive that Gross retreats from his own perception, so much so that his sentence is something of a non sequitur. The "opposite extreme," after the trap of an "unmanly" role, would surely be a "manly" one—and this is indeed one aspect, as we shall see, of Orwell's experiences down and out. Again and again critics of Orwell's work approach the awareness that a particular social role, a masculine one, is at work, informing the texts they analyze and shaping Orwell's life. And again and again these critics beat a hasty retreat from this perception, even when, as in the passage cited above, doing so breaks the logic of their observations.

11. Katharine Burdekin published an antiutopian novel, *Swastika Night*, in 1937, under the pseudonym "Murray Constantine." This novel, which bears some remarkable similarities to *Nineteen Eighty-Four*, as we shall see in chapter 8, links the reduction of women to an animallike state in a future fascist society to this male inability to accept female self-determination, with the possibility of rejection of males that this implies.

12. The phrasing of the middle part of this passage, with its exclamation of "Heavens, what numbers of them!" suggests Flory's possible pride in his Don Juanism, rather than the unalloyed shame with which the paragraph ends.

13. Alick West, as cited by Jack Lindsay in *After the Thirties: The Novel in Britain and Its Future* (London: Lawrence and Wishart, 1956), p. 100, notes that in *Burmese Days* "The theme of how 'all of us,' the class, are corrupted by imperialism gives way to the theme of how the secret revolt against imperialism corrupts the individual." West goes on to make the astute observation that Flory "does not seek to join with the revolt of others; he does not abandon the secrecy of the revolt, but the revolt itself." Lindsay

deduces from this detail that there is an "adolescent masochism in Orwell's attitude," revealed again in *Nineteen Eighty-Four*, as evidenced by the fact that the only possible revolt conceived of is a "secret revolt" (p. 101).

14. Ellis is, in effect, placing Flory at a level even lower than that of the "niggers" with this slur. Greenberger, *British Image*, p. 18, points out that in the model elaborated by Kipling the East appears as a passive negative world and the West as an active positive one; by rejecting Ellis's code of cultural purity, Flory has thus put himself in a position more humiliating even than that of the feminized East, for he has abdicated his masculinity and taken the role (metaphorically) of the passive homosexual male.

15. Barry D. Adam, *The Survival of Domination: Inferiorization and Everyday Life* (New York: Elsevier North-Holland, 1978), p. 8. Adam studies Jews, blacks, and gay people but recognizes that his analysis is valid for other oppressed groups as well.

16. Pat Barr, in *The Memsahibs: The Women of Victorian India* (London: Secker and Warburg, 1976), by focusing on women who wrote about their experiences in India, attempts to correct the omissions of earlier chroniclers who judged the activities of the thousands of British women living in India during the Victorian age as unworthy of recording. Barr discusses the effect on British women of the "male-dominated imperial scenario" and the transmission through fiction, especially by Kipling, of an image of the typical memsahib as frivolous, snobbish, and selfish (p. 1). Barr writes: "The qualities that Kipling most admired—courage, resolution, a dogged devotion to duty—were those born of imperial necessity and were, in his view, essentially masculine; the imperial challenge was to him a proving ground for young men only. His womenfolk, though allowed a certain cleverness and wit, were invariably poor creatures compared to the heroes of Empire, whom they are lamentably prone to distract from life's sterner duties. It is unfortunate that Kipling did not broaden his canvas to include as much diversity of character among them as he developed for his male characters, because it is his stereotyped and superficial version of the nineteenth-century Anglo-Indian woman that has remained current ever since as being truly representative of the whole species" (p. 197). Similarities between Kipling and Orwell have been studied by Richard Cook in his "Rudyard Kipling and George Orwell," *Modern Fiction Studies* 7, no. 2 (Summer 1961): 125–38. Cook is one of the few critics to have noted Orwell's "basic masculine tendency," which, like Kipling's, produces negative portrayals of women. He concludes that "the typical Orwellian heroine has strong similarities to the Kipling women who disrupt men's lives" (p. 132).

17. Orwell held perfectly conventional views about the "taint" of prostitution and the way it marks a woman, as is apparent in some of his passing comments about sirens and prostitutes in movies he reviewed, and in his famous comment—made about male politicians—"Once a whore, always a whore" (CEJL, 3:227).

18. Orwell later commented that the hunting instinct is probably universal in human beings (CEJL, 3:106), though the men's amused and complicitous reaction to Elizabeth's joy in hunting suggests that, even if "universal," this "instinct" is not appropriate in certain groups of women.

19. Maung Maung, *Law and Custom in Burma and the Burmese Family* (The Hague: Martinus Nijhoff, 1963), pp. 55–66.

20. Orwell Archive. These comments recall Orwell's 1946 essay "Politics vs. Literature: An Examination of *Gulliver's Travels*," in which Orwell states that, although politically and morally he is against Swift, yet "curiously enough

he is one of the writers I admire with least reserve" (CEJL, 4:220). Orwell calls the notorious poem "The Lady's Dressing Room" one of Swift's "most characteristic works" and comments upon it and a "kindred poem" entitled "Upon a Beautiful Young Nymph Going to Bed": "Which is truer, the viewpoint expressed in these poems, or the viewpoint implied in Blake's phrase, 'The naked female human form divine'? No doubt Blake is nearer the truth, and yet who can fail to feel a sort of pleasure in seeing that fraud, feminine delicacy, exploded for once?" (4:222). Orwell then goes on to discuss the problem of the linkage between pleasure and disgust in generic terms, referring to "the human body," totally oblivious of the misogyny he has just revealed (expressed in his characteristic coercive rhetoric: "who can fail...").

21. In Charles Allen, ed., *Plain Tales from the Raj: Images of British India in the Twentieth Century* (New York: St. Martin's Press, 1975), p. 42.

22. Edwin Ardener, "The 'Problem' Revisited," in Shirley Ardener, ed., *Perceiving Women* (London: Malaby Press, 1975), p. 22. The term "muted" comes from Charlotte Hardman.

23. Cheris Kramarae, *Women and Men Speaking: Frameworks for Analysis* (Rowley, Mass.: Newbury House, 1981), p. 1.

24. Mary Hiatt, *The Way Women Write* (New York: Teachers College Press, Columbia University, 1977), pp. 90–106, discusses this belief.

25. See Howard S. Levy, *Chinese Footbinding: The History of a Curious Erotic Custom* (New York: Walton Rawls, 1966). Andrea Dworkin, drawing on Levy, in *Woman Hating* (New York: E. P. Dutton, 1974), p. 96, describes footbinding as "a political institution which reflected and perpetuated the sociological and psychological inferiority of women." It was also an index of economic status: The more tightly bound the foot, the higher the woman's status; if her husband was sufficiently well off, she did not "need" her feet. Levy says that westerners generally considered foot-binding to be "unnatural" and were opposed to it. Thus Orwell may be stressing Flory's unusual position as an Englishman who "appreciates" a different culture.

26. Orwell's treatment of the Burmese practice of male bigamy is another indication of the specifically male vision of reality articulated in the novel. Ko S'la, Flory's servant, is depicted as burdened with two screaming, fighting wives, and it is he, not either of them, who is referred to as one of the "obscure martyrs of bigamy" (*Burmese Days*, 48), surely intended to induce a complicitous laugh on the part of the (presumably male) reader while denying any possible female perspective on the practice.

27. In a letter to F. Tennyson Jesse in 1946, Orwell takes her to task for not stressing, in her book on Burma, the "disgusting social behavior of the British." He then mentions his own grandmother who spent forty years in Burma and never learned a word of Burmese, "typical of the ordinary English-woman's attitude," Orwell says (CEJL, 4:114).

CHAPTER THREE
VAGABONDAGE AND LABOR

1. Details of Orwell's experiments with poverty in London and Paris between 1928 and 1931 are provided in Peter Stansky and William Abrahams, *The Unknown Orwell* (London: Constable, 1972), pp. 179–246; and Bernard Crick, *George Orwell: A Life* (Boston: Little, Brown, 1980), pp. 104–36.

2. Cited by Michael Howard, "Empire, Race, and War in Pre-1914 Britain," in Hugh Lloyd-Jones, Valerie Pearl, and Blair Worden, eds., *History and*

Imagination: Essays in Honor of H. R. Trevor-Roper (New York: Holmes and Meier, 1981), p. 344.

3. Peter Keating, ed., *Into Unknown England, 1866–1913: Selections from the Social Explorers* (Manchester: Manchester University Press, 1976), pp. 12–13. George Woodcock, *The Crystal Spirit* (Boston: Little, Brown, 1966), p. 151, notes: "Books of reportage were in vogue during the 1930's; they fitted in with the prevalent atmosphere of Mass Observation and fashionable bolshevism."

4. Keating, *Into Unknown England*, pp. 16, 17.

5. Stansky and Abrahams, *The Unknown Orwell*, p. 192, state that Jack London was "already a world-famous author" in 1902 when he arrived in London and decided to study the East End. Crick repeats this in his book (*George Orwell*, p. 109). In both cases the aim seems to be to establish Orwell's unusual courage and to distinguish him from Jack London. Stansky and Abrahams say Jack London provides a contrast, which "emphasizes the strangeness of what Blair did" (p. 192). But John Perry, in *Jack London: An American Myth* (Chicago: Nelson-Hall, 1981), p. 106, suggests otherwise. After showing that London's work is itself highly dependent on Charles Booth's *Life and Labour of the People of London* (1902–3), Perry notes "striking similarities" between London's book and Jacob A. Riis's *Battle with the Slum*, which had come out a year earlier—Riis's book and London's looked like twins, having the same size, typeface, layouts, even photographic format—and wonders: "Was *The People of the Abyss* planned as a spin-off? London, still an obscure author, didn't gain fame until *The Call of the Wild*—also published by Macmillan Company in 1903." For a further critique of *People of the Abyss* and its sources, see Andrew Sinclair, "A View of the Abyss," in Jacqueline Tavernier-Courbin, ed., *Critical Essays on Jack London* (Boston: G. K. Hall, 1983), pp. 230–41. Sinclair, however, knows less about Orwell than about Jack London and, as a result, subscribes to the Orwell myth and praises *Down and Out*, as so many have done, for its author's "thorough immersion in the debilitation" of his "months of tramping" (p. 239). Since London revealed in his book that he kept available and utilized an escape route from the abyss (while Orwell, as Sinclair is perhaps unaware, intentionally obscured the actual time spent and alternatives available while down and out), Orwell wins the hardship competition—which immediately translates, in Sinclair's mind, into a text of greater "endurance as well as truth."

6. Keating, *Into Unknown England*, p. 18.

7. Ibid., pp. 20–21.

8. Ibid, p. 21.

9. Peter Beresford, "The Public Presentation of Vagrancy," in Tim Cook, ed., *Vagrancy: Some New Perspectives* (London: Academic Press, 1979), pp. 144–45.

10. Ibid., p. 145.

11. Ibid.

12. Solutions similar to Orwell's had already been implemented in various countries by the time he wrote *Down and Out*. See Muriel Kent, "Vagrancy: A National Problem," *Contemporary Review* 142 (July 1932): 76–84.

13. Beresford, "Public Presentation," p. 146. Beresford also argues (p. 145) that "Even if we ignore discordant notes like Orwell's fastidiousness, his disdainful talk of 'brats,' 'dirty old habitual vagabonds,' 'a graceless, motley crew' and his obtrusive upper class ignorance," Orwell presents a version of the problem of vagrancy very similar to the official versions he seems to challenge. Bereford's comment about the social control perspective that sees vagrants as

oddities calls to mind an early (unsigned) notice about *Down and Out* in the *Times Literary Supplement*, January 12, 1933, p. 22. The reviewer states that many of the characters Orwell "met on his adventures are as odd as any in Dickens—which is probably responsible for their uncomfortable lives."

14. Crick, *George Orwell*, p. 132. A letter from Orwell to his agent, Leonard Moore, dated July 6, 1932, suggests that the book be called "The Lady Poverty" or "Lady Poverty," from Alice Meynell's lines: "The Lady Poverty was fair, / But she hath lost her looks of late" (CEJL, 1:85). On August 12, 1932, however, Orwell wrote to Moore suggesting "In Praise of Poverty" as a better title (the letter is in the Berg Collection, New York Public Library). In November 1932, Orwell and Victor Gollancz, his publisher, had still not agreed on a title, and Orwell wrote to a friend that Gollancz wanted to call it "The Confessions of a Down & Out." Orwell adds: "I am protesting against this as I don't answer to the name of down & out, but I will let it go if he thinks seriously that it is a taking title" (1:105). Orwell had earlier expressed his desire to use a pseudonym, saying: "I have no reputation that is lost by doing this and if the book has any kind of success I can always use the same pseudonym again" (1:85), and it was he who provided four possible pseudonyms (including P. S. Burton, "a name I always use when tramping etc"), giving his own preference for "George Orwell" (1:106).

15. There is nothing unusual about contemporary reviews of *Down and Out*. Most of the reviewers (see Jeffrey Meyers, *George Orwell: The Critical Heritage* [London: Routledge and Kegan Paul, 1975], pp. 39–49, for a sampling) are interested in the book as a sociological account and discuss it in those terms rather than as literature. It is only retrospectively that the book seems to many Orwell admirers so important. Several of the reviewers (later ones as well) are impressed because they believe Orwell had no choice but to be down and out, and they read the book as a kind of cautionary tale. Many apparently did not read it with sufficient care to note that the narrator does have available "escape routes" from his poverty but often chooses to postpone utilizing them. This is the "creaking" Stansky and Abrahams hear in the text (*The Unknown Orwell*, pp. 229–30).

16. *Manchester Guardian*, January 9, 1933, p. 5.

17. Basil de Selincourt, *The Listener*, March 8, 1933, p. 368.

18. Granville Hicks, *New Leader*, February 25, 1950.

19. *New English Weekly*, February 16, 1933. Orwell's friend Brenda Salkeld recollected having similar doubts about the authenticity of Orwell's experience: "If you've put on tramp's clothes and walked, well, that didn't make you a tramp. It was the attitude of mind that was much more important; and how could you claim to have the attitude of a tramp, or know it and understand it, if you knew that you could always go back home?" (cited in Stansky and Abrahams, *The Unknown Orwell*, p. 234). Bernard Crick takes issue with this statement saying that Orwell "never claimed to have become a tramp, only to have been among tramps" (*George Orwell*, p. 127). In fact, in *The Road to Wigan Pier* Orwell states: "You can become a tramp simply by putting on the right clothes and going to the nearest casual ward, but you can't become a navvy or a coal-miner" (136). Orwell himself seems to have fallen into the trap of thinking that one simply and immediately "becomes" what one "does"—for however brief a time. Since a tramp, in his view, merely tramps, by dressing like him and walking beside him Orwell has "become" a tramp. To become a worker is, naturally, more difficult, because one would need to get a working-class job. Orwell says, in *Wigan Pier*, "You

couldn't get a job as a navvy or a coal-miner even if you were equal to the work" (136), but he continues to maintain an ingenuous attitude toward the issue of class breaking, consistent with his emphasis on merely sensorial details.

20. Alex Zwerdling, *Orwell and the Left* (New Haven and London: Yale University Press, 1974), discusses the "curious impersonality" of *Down and Out* (p. 164), the narrator's "lack of identity" and absence of "a point of view" (p. 165).

21. Jenni Calder, *Chronicles of Conscience: A Study of George Orwell and Arthur Koestler* (London: Secker and Warburg, 1968), pp. 32–34. Raymond Williams, in *Orwell* (Glasgow: Fontana/Collins, 1971), p. 43, holds a similar view: "The author is present, but only insofar as these things are happening to him along with others. His own character and motivations are sketched as briefly as those of anyone else met in the kitchen or on the road. He is neither 'inside' nor 'outside'; he is simply drifting *with* others—exceptionally close to them but within the fact that they are drifting, that this is *happening* to their bodies and minds." But Williams here disregards the nature of narrative, which necessarily implies a perspective. *Down and Out* is not, after all, a film in which we *see* Orwell as one among several individuals whose adventures we follow; it is a text through which we *hear* Orwell's narrative voice commenting on his and other men's experiences. Precisely because of this the author is "present" in a way quite unlike the other characters in the book, and the reader is exposed not to what is "happening" but to the author's account of perceived reality, which is his semifictional creation.

22. Another example: In Valenti's story about nearly starving and praying to "Sainte Eloise," the last paragraph of the story (though supposedly in Valenti's words) reveals the characteristic Orwellian explanation (*Down and Out*, 79).

23. Richard Mayne, "A Note on Orwell's Paris," in Miriam Gross, ed., *The World of George Orwell* (New York: Simon and Schuster, 1971), states that the area in which Orwell lived was not, in fact, a slum, and cites Hemingway, who had earlier called that area (in the fifth arrondissement) "the best [i.e. most typical] part of the Latin Quarter" (p. 41; Mayne's brackets). In writing of such a neighborhood, with its North Africans, foreign workers, immigrants, and transients, rather than ordinary French workers, Orwell was, in Mayne's view, "characteristically seeking the typical in the extreme. A hostile critic might accuse him of 'romanticism.'" Mayne also argues that too much has been made of Orwell's "guilt" and that at least in Paris Orwell was looking not for squalor and failure but for time and freedom to write, as many other artists and writers had done before him (pp. 40–41).

24. Elizabeth Aries, "Interaction Patterns and Themes of Male, Female, and Mixed Groups," *Small Group Behavior* 7, no. 1 (February 1976): 13–14, has studied themes and patterns of conversation and concludes: "The themes of superiority and aggression were often merged in the male groups. Stories were told of . . . pranks played where participants humiliated, threatened, and terrorized others. The theme of victim or victimizer ran through most stories, often evoking themes of castration and fears of loss of masculinity and potency." Compared to female groups, the "males engaged in dramatizing and story telling, jumping from one anecdote to another, and achieving a camaraderie and closeness through the sharing of stories and laughter. Females discussed one topic for a half hour or more, revealing more feelings, and gaining a closeness through more intimate self-revelation. The findings . . . reflect the themes of intimacy and interpersonal relations for women, and themes of

competition and status for men." Aries associates these distinctive styles also with the developmental stage of the group members: "Adolescence is a period when individuals face strong pressures of socialization into their sex role, and it is through aggressive play and competition, confronting and differentiating oneself from others that a male establishes his own potency, competence, and independence."

25. Frank O'Connor, in a sensitive essay on Guy de Maupassant, discusses the danger of using sex as a source of inspiration, "for it so easily becomes ambivalent, and stories and novels that in their conception were a passionate protest against the exploitation and degradation of sex easily become merely another way of exploiting and degrading it." O'Connor then raises the key issue: "How, if one is not one of the exploited, does one describe them without being one of the exploiters?" (*The Lonely Voice* [Cleveland and New York: World, 1963], pp. 71, 72). O'Connor's question is echoed by Clancy Sigal in a review in *The Nation*, May 21, 1983, p. 646, of a recent book, Robert Hamburger's *All the Lonely People: Life in a Single Room Occupancy Hotel*. Clancy begins his review: "It is hard to write about the poor without exploiting them. No matter how lofty a reporter's motives, his story can easily become just another titillation on the charity circuit.... Unless it leads to action, journalism reinforces the very system it seeks to reform: it contributes to readers' sense of privilege without moving them to involvement."

26. Evelyn Tension, a working-class writer angry at glorification of working people, comments that when middle-class people decide to go poor they still do not really experience the humiliation of being told they're poor because they're inferior, inferior because they're poor. "On the contrary, they gain status. Even when they're poor they're better," she writes ("You Don't Need a Degree to Read the Writing on the Wall," *No Turning Back: Writing from the Women's Liberation Movement, 1975–80* [London: Women's Press, 1981], p. 87). She is obviously right, for even so astute an observer as Mary McCarthy, perhaps unaware both of the rich tradition of social explorers in England and of the brevity of Orwell's excursions into poverty, honors Orwell for his social descent: "what he did with poverty ... is not only quite marvellous but extremely unusual in modern literature, or modern politics for that matter. In this kind of inquiry he himself was the subject and the guinea pig, and he really died of it, in my opinion. The only other example I can think of off-hand is Simone Weil" ("A Discourse on Nature," *The Listener*, June 11, 1970, p. 786). More accurately, Adrian Cunningham, in a review of the Penguin edition of *Down and Out*, in *Granta*, February 15, 1964, pp. 24–25, takes issue with Orwell's creation of a false impression: "The book sets out to give the impression that Orwell spent a considerable time tramping.... 'Down and Out' was accepted as a factual documentary and still is, the blurb of the Penguin edition calls it a humane and factual piece of reporting, 'Orwell faithfully put down what he had seen and above all what he had experienced.' This is simply untrue." Cunningham finds it "hard to escape the conclusion that at the time he [Orwell] deliberately set out to mislead." Citing Jack Common's remark about Orwell ("I was disappointed to find him unmistakeably a public-school man who had not known the desperation that makes the real tramp"), Cunningham notes Orwell's "neurasthenic aversion to dirt and physical contact, and a masochistic fascination about them," and objects to Orwell's "self-regarding disgust," which tends, in his view, to disqualify Orwell from understanding vagrancy and instead reveals his "fundamentally public-school" values; he concludes that *Down and Out* has "dubious honesty" and that Or-

well's masquerade as a vagrant and attempts to "expiate" his guilt by this social descent "were no less a seedy form of romanticism."

27. Of his first experience of Christian charity, Orwell tells the reader how "we" hated the religiosity of it, claiming his identity with this *we* even as he serves up the experience to readers of his own class. For an account of the assumptions vagrants, as opposed to journalists, make about their own lives, see Peter Phillimore, "Dossers and Jake Drinkers: The View from One End of Skid Row," in Cook, *Vagrancy*, pp. 29–48. Woodcock, *Crystal Spirit*, p. 110, in discussing the various motives evident in *Down and Out*, mentions also "a kind of *nostalgie de la boue*, a fastidious man's urge to submerge himself in a hideous and malodorous setting, rather as the decadent poets did in an earlier generation."

28. Mrs. Cecil Chesterton, *In Darkest London* (London: Stanley Paul, 1926), p. 13.

29. Stansky and Abrahams, *The Unknown Orwell*, p. 222, note the "curiously boyish" tone of *Down and Out*, "not a defect, of course: so is the tone of *Huckleberry Finn*—and it is made more noticeable by the exclusion from the narrative of even one female character of any consequence to 'I' who tells the story and is at the centre of the action. Seldom can a book set in the lower depths of Paris have had so little to do with sexuality. Given its autobiographical nature, however, and given Blair's limited experience of women, it could hardly be otherwise." It is instructive to see the leap in Stansky's and Abrahams's thoughts here. Thus, no female characters means, to Stansky and Abrahams, not the exclusion of half the world and its experiences but merely the exclusion of the dimension of sexuality from a heterosexual man's life. It does not suggest to them the narrow range of such a portrait of "life."

30. Beresford, "Public Presentation," p. 27, remarks that to qualify for attention as a social problem, an issue must be instantly recognizable, extraordinary, extreme, dangerous, or dramatic: "Thus it is, for example, that the few people living in lodging houses are singled out for attention, while the many whose lives are constrained by the dreardom and meanness of rooming houses are ignored."

31. R. W. Breach and R. M. Hartwell, *British Economy and Society, 1870–1970: Documents, Descriptions, Statistics* (London: Oxford University Press, 1972), p. 137.

32. Sean Glynn and John Oxborrow, *Interwar Britain: A Social and Economic History* (New York: Harper and Row/Barnes and Noble, 1976), pp. 149–50, note the apparently higher unemployment rate among men than among women during this period but comment: "With female workers the situation is complicated by the fact that there is no way of knowing how many unoccupied women would have been willing to seek paid employment, at prevailing wage levels, if it had been available. There is no doubt that many married women, who were not entitled to unemployment benefits, did not trouble to register themselves as unemployed. In some industries and areas there were social pressures which dictated that married women should be the first to lose their jobs, but this did not always make economic sense from the point of view of employers when women were paid lower wages than men for equivalent work. Many of the industries dominated by female labour, especially in the tertiary sector, suffered rather less from unemployment than some of the basic, male-dominated, manufacturing industries."

33. Chesterton, *Darkest London*, p. 13.

34. Ibid., p. 11.

35. Ibid., p. 118. Mrs. Chesterton's reporting of this situation in a Sunday newspaper led to an improvement.

36. Ibid., p. 121.

37. Ibid., p. 170.

38. Dan Jacobson, "Orwell's Slumming," in Gross, World of George Orwell, p. 50. Peter Thirlby, "Orwell as a Liberal," Marxist Quarterly 3 (1956), notes that Orwell's romantic search for destitution is a characteristically liberal stance rather than a socialist one: "The miscellaneous tramp group strike a very resonant chord in the liberal mind, for they more than anyone else correspond with classical liberal free men" (cited in Zwerdling, Orwell and the Left, p. 72). Thirlby goes on to say that Orwell had little contact with the class-conscious proletariat. Zwerdling cites Wigan Pier as proof that this was no longer the case by 1936 and accepts Orwell's own view of the "typicality" of the miners—about which I comment later in this chapter.

39. In addition to Mrs. Chesterton's book, as a result of the Depression and the increasing numbers of homeless women, a spate of articles on this subject appeared in the late 1920s and early thirties. An especially interesting one is Walter C. Reckless's "Why Women Become Hoboes," American Mercury 31 (February 1934): 175–80, which begins with some general observations about the differences in status between homeless women and homeless men—observations equally valid for England, with its gender ideology similar to that of America. He explains that "men can be transient and homeless with greater ease than women" because of the sociological conditions that prevail for each sex. "Ours is still largely a man's world, the freedom of the road notwithstanding." He points out that in the United States homeless men "have a culture and a society of their own," while women "have not had time to build up their own communal homeless life." Reckless suggests that, as homeless women make the adjustments necessary for life on the road, men will cease to have this advantage over them, and he considers this another instance of women successfully encroaching on an originally male preserve. "The indications are that women are making pretty good hoboes as hoboes go" (p. 175). But a long interview with one woman on the road reveals special problems that women can expect to face unless they appear on the road in numbers equal to men's. This woman "has been attacked and raped on several occasions and has given in on several more" (p. 176). She says: "Another time a man said to me if you don't give in, you have no business on the road. . . . I don't want them to bother me. I am not afraid of them. But there is always a certain fear. Men on the road never have a woman and when there is a woman they always come around every time. It ain't the looks of me but it's just because I'm a woman" (p. 178).

Two related (American) articles from this same period are Cliff Maxwell, "Lady Vagabonds," Scribner's Magazine 85, no. 3 (March 1929): 288–92; and "Ladies of the Road," Literary Digest, August 13, 1932, p. 33. The former is especially interesting because in distinguishing vagabonds from hoboes and arguing that there are no "lady hoboes," only lady vagabonds, Maxwell reinforces the male mystique of the hobo life. In American culture, especially, this mystique has been very powerful, even in its literary manifestations. See, e.g., Frederick Feied, No Pie in the Sky: The Hobo as American Cultural Hero in the Works of Jack London, John Dos Passos, and Jack Kerouac (New York: Citadel Press, 1964). More recently, Barbara Ehrenreich, in The Hearts of Men (New York: Doubleday, 1983), p. 54, has discussed Kerouac and the Beats as men escaping the world of women and responsibility for the "ecstatic possibilities of male adventure," modeled on an image of lower-class males. In England a rather different interpretation of vagrancy has been offered by Philip O'Connor, *Britain in the Sixties: Vagrancy: Ethos and Actuality* (Harmondsworth: Penguin Books, 1963). O'Connor concentrates on the spiritual conditions of vagrancy and sees in the vagrant a variety of Christian virtues including asceticism and poverty. "Tramps are the raw material of a future enlightenment," he writes (p. 20).

40. The 1930 Ministry of Health *Report of the Departmental Committee on the Relief of the Casual Poor*, Cmnd. 3640 (London: HMSO, 1930), is of special interest as an illustration of the gender ideology behind social policy. The report reaffirms the Ministry of Health's established position that women should be provided with relief in an institution rather than by creating special casual wards for them: "Aged women should be urged to settle down in an infirmary or other institution" (p. 42). Apparently, a less visible form of poverty was favored in the case of women, and thus the government is interested in taking women, rather than men, off the streets.

41. "The Art of Fiction" [interview with Henry Miller], *Paris Review* 28 (1962): 146. Miller goes on to say: "Though he was a wonderful chap in his way, Orwell, in the end I thought him stupid. He was like so many English people, an idealist, and, it seemed to me, a foolish idealist. A man of principle, as we say. Men of principle bore me."

An interesting illustration of the connection for Orwell between acting out a masculine role and being down and out is provided by Anthony Powell in *Infants of the Spring* (New York: Holt, Rinehart and Winston, 1976), pp. 96–97, who recollects that Orwell once asked him:

"Have you ever had a woman in the park? . . ."
"No—never."
"I have."
"How did you find it?"
"I was forced to."
"Why?"
"Nowhere else to go."

Bernard Crick, at the University of London on May 27, 1982, in a lecture on the nature of biography and the art of Orwell, mentions this episode as an example of Orwell's pleasure in teasing his upper-class friends by misinformation. However, the story as related by Powell reveals not so much teasing as one-upmanship. Presumably Orwell scored points for this exchange.

42. Ian Hamilton, "Along the Road to Wigan Pier," in Gross, *World of George Orwell*, p. 55, observes: "Orwell's sojourn in the north is often spoken of as if it were a heroic act of self-sacrifice; as if, even, Orwell's suffering were as significant as the suffering he went to study." Hamilton suggests that Orwell's brief investigation needs to be seen in a less heroic mode.

43. Crick, *George Orwell*, p. 181, tells us that Victor Gollancz was responsible, via the commission and advance he offered Orwell in January 1936, for the project. But Orwell may have had some such investigation in mind as early as the winter of 1935, judging by a letter he wrote to Leonard Moore on November 8, 1935 (LL). According to a letter from Eileen Blair to Moore, dated February 11, 1937 (LL), it was only at about that time that the final decision was made to use *Wigan Pier* as the Left Book Club selection for March 1937. Victor Gollancz wanted to offer Left Book Club members the first part of *Wigan Pier* as a separate supplementary book for May 1937, having added his own critical introduction to the whole book expressing his objections to part 2 when

it first appeared. Eileen Blair granted permission for this separate edition while Orwell was in Spain, as revealed by her letter to Moore.

44. Crick, *George Orwell*, p. 183, cites Jim Hammond's account of how Orwell ended up at the Brookers: "He could have gone to any of a thousand respectable working-class houses and lodged with them or stayed right where he was. But he doesn't do that. He goes to a doss-house, just like he's down and out in Paris still. You see, when they've left the upper class, they've got to go right down into muck and start muckraking.... Did he have a taste for that sort of thing?" Orwell's quite open disgust with the Brookers and their household raises the issue, since they were atypical, of why he gave them such pride of place in his account.

45. In his "*Road to Wigan Pier* Diary" (CEJL, 1:170–214), Orwell describes "Mrs F"—the model for Mrs. Brooker—as "ill with a weak heart" (1:178). It is interesting that he changed this to gluttony and sloth in the final book. Bernard Crick points out (*George Orwell*, p. 182) that the "diary" itself was composed after the events it describes and may well be an early effort to organize the material for a book. (For Orwell's special revulsion from gluttonous women, see chap. 8, n. 22, below.)

46. As in *Down and Out*, so in *Wigan Pier* Orwell's upper-class tone emerges in his frequent use of words like "dreadful," "beastly," "frightful," etc., to describe what he encounters. Hamilton, "Along the Road to Wigan Pier" (p. 57), calls these words Orwell's "posh-pejoratives."

47. This episode is discussed in chapter 4, below, in relation to Orwell's difficulty in attributing full consciousness to people unlike himself—women, blacks, natives, proles. Woodcock, *Crystal Spirit*, holds a different view of Orwell's occasional sympathetic portraits of women in *Wigan Pier*. He notes the faces that "tell silently of unspeakable degradation, and always a woman's face, for it is the women who bear the hardest brunt of poverty, and whom chivalry —a code Orwell implicitly obeyed—demands that we first protect" (p. 158). He later comments: "If the women are the perpetual victims in the tragedy of poverty which Orwell writes in these early chapters, the men often appear as the heroes. Orwell admired energy and toughness, and in his case this was no mere adulation of the inactive intellectual for the man of action, since he was always ready, as he showed that same year in Spain, to tax his strength and his powers of endurance to the utmost degree" (p. 159). See chap. 5, n. 1, below, for more on critics' affirmation of Orwell as a warrior.

48. Jane Lewis, "In Search of a Real Equality: Women between the Wars," in Frank Gloversmith, ed., *Class, Culture, and Social Change* (Sussex: Harvester Press, 1980), provides an excellent overview of the real situation of women during this period.

49. By contrast, Margery Spring Rice, in *Working-Class Wives: Their Health and Conditions*, (Harmondsworth: Penguin Books, 1939), p. 26, based on a sample of 1,250 women, notes the evidence that it was impossible for these women to "maintain after marriage the standard (often low enough) of health and well-being which was possible to them as unmarried working girls."

50. Noreen Branson and Margot Heinemann, *Britain in the 1930's* (New York: Praeger, 1971), p. 145.

51. Ibid., pp. 146–47.

52. Elizabeth Wilson, *Women and the Welfare State* (London: Tavistock, 1977), pp. 119–20.

53. Michael Young, "The Distribution of Income within the Family," *British Journal of Sociology* 3 (1952): 305–21, in arguing against the assumption

"that some members of a family cannot be rich while others are poor," notes that "many outstanding social investigators have recorded that the bread-winners are often the meat-eaters" (p. 305). Young traces this theme in various writers' accounts between 1892 and 1948. The Pilgrim Trust's 1938 study, *Men without Work*, noted what was apparently invisible to Orwell: "It was a matter of daily experience to observe the obvious signs of malnutrition in the appearance of wives of unemployed men with families. They obviously did without things for the sake of their husbands and children, and it was by no means certain that they keep for their own use the 'extra nourishment' provided expressly for them in a large number of cases by the Unemployment Assistance Board" (cited by Young, p. 306). Laura Oren, "The Welfare of Women in Laboring Families: England, 1860–1950," in Mary S. Hartman and Lois Banner, eds., *Clio's Consciousness Raised: New Perspectives on the History of Women* (New York: Harper and Row, 1974), pp. 226–44, also pursues this theme and cites Magdalen Stuart Reeves's *Round about a Pound a Week* (1914) and B. S. Rowntree and May Kendall's *How the Labourer Lives: A Study of the Rural Labour Problem* (1913) as two important early studies that "reported family menus in sufficient detail to reveal the allocation of food by sex" (p. 229). The Women's Cooperative Guild volume, *Maternity: Letters from Working Women* (1915), provides ample evidence of the way women stinted themselves, especially "during pregnancy in order to save for the coming confinement" (Oren, p. 230), and Reeves noted that as the number of children increased, the husband often made the wife the same allowance and expected the same amount of food for himself (cited in Oren, p. 231). Oren writes: "As the family grew, the woman once again met the extra expense out of her own standard of living" (p. 230). Peter Stearns, "Working Class Women in Britain, 1890–1914," in Martha Vicinus, ed., *Suffer and Be Still: Women in the Victorian Age* (Bloomington and London: Indiana University Press, 1972), p. 116, also states that as wages rose toward the end of the century "men took the bulk of the gain for themselves," resulting in a "clear deterioration in the position of the proletarian wife." A pamphlet by Maud Brown, "Stop This Starvation of Mother and Child," published by the National Unemployed Workers' Movement in 1935, notes the importance of sound nutrition for pregnant women and cites a doctor who says that when economic circumstances get worse "the mother denies herself the necessities of life to improve the lot of her husband or children" (pp. 4–5). Another highly informative book about the position of women at this time was Winifred Holtby's *Women and a Changing Civilisation* (London: John Lane, 1934). In short, Orwell's blindness to those aspects of poverty and unemployment that especially affect women cannot be attributed to the unavailability of more informed views in his own time. In fact, Orwell was able to imagine—and criticize—unequal distribution of food when it occurred between two women, as is apparent in his 1935 novel, *A Clergyman's Daughter*, in which Mrs. Creevy, a detestable character, routinely deprives Dorothy Hare of her fair share of food (80, 90).

54. Stearns, "Working Class Women," pp. 107–8; 223, n. 33, discusses the practice among miners of turning all or most of their salaries over to their wives, who thus managed the family's finances. He suggests that even before 1914 this had changed to the limited allowance system used by factory workers. Orwell does not enter into any such details of family life and economics. Of course, even if the woman does manage all of her husband's money, this does not insure that she will eat her "fair share" of a generally inadequate diet. The ideology of the lesser "worth" and importance of the woman in com-

parison with her wage-earning husband and growing children (especially boy children, who could in turn become better wage earners than could the girls) is not, however, restricted to the working class or to conditions of immediate financial hardship. A pathetic and disturbing illustration of the same principle at work occurred in Orwell's own life. His first wife, Eileen Blair, died on March 29, 1945, while undergoing what Orwell called routine surgery but was in fact a hysterectomy (which he disapproved of) and removal of a possible cancerous growth. Orwell was on the Continent doing some journalism at the time of the operation. In discussing this matter, Bernard Crick for once is moved toward criticism of Orwell for his willful ignorance of his wife's health problems. Crick cites a letter that Eileen Blair wrote to Orwell a few days before the operation (adding that it is not known if Orwell ever read the letter), in which she writes, among other things, of her fears for her life and her anxiety about the cost of the operation. She comments in some detail about the surgeon's fees and hospital costs and then says, "but what worries me is that I really don't think I'm worth the money. On the other hand of course this thing will take a longish time to kill me if left alone and it will be costing some money the whole time." Orwell's income was then over 500 pounds a year, so that he did not qualify for "really cheap rates," as Eileen Blair says. She goes on to discuss at length possible but less desirable ways of getting the surgery done more cheaply. She had not discussed all this before with Orwell because "I wanted you to go away peacefully anyway" (Crick, George Orwell, pp. 329–30.

55. Richard Hoggart, "Introduction to The Road to Wigan Pier," in Raymond Williams, ed., George Orwell: A Collection of Critical Essays (Englewood Cliffs, N.J.: Prentice-Hall, 1974), p. 42. Hoggart's essay is itself an example of the rhetoric of masculinity, full of references to ordeals and proofs of manhood.

56. Zwerdling, Orwell and the Left, p. 21.

57. Glynn and Oxborrow, Interwar Britain, p. 92.

58. Compare Orwell's discussion of the dangers of coal mining with Allen Hutt's less colorful but far more informative book, The Condition of the Working Class in Britain (London: Martin Lawrence, 1933), pp. 23–29, which explains the economics of safety (or, rather, lack of safety) in the mines. By contrast, Orwell merely says that a miner's safety depends "largely on his own care and skill" (Wigan Pier, 41), by which he means the ability to detect imminent disasters. Characteristically, Orwell does not question the structures of exploitation in themselves, or the economics on which they are based, but examines individual responses within that context, from which he then generalizes. Hutt in every respect is better informed, has a broader vision, a larger scale, and yet similar details. Orwell may well have relied on Hutt's work—certainly he includes many of the same sorts and forms of information: brief descriptions of individual houses, summaries of family members and statuses, sample diets, financial sketches, and so on (though much of this is also found in Jack London's People of the Abyss). Even the sequence of Orwell's book is similar to Hutt's—but of course different in emphasis.

59. Peter N. Stearns, Be a Man! Males in Modern Society (New York: Holmes and Meier, 1979), p. 39. Stearns discusses the ways in which gender distinctions intensified with the advent of industrialization (p. 40), noting that "Early industrialization increased the number of jobs requiring heavy labor, such as metallurgy or construction. Pride in physical prowess was at least as great in nineteenth century labor as before, an important aspect of working-class masculinity" (p. 41). Technical change was frequently resisted by men

who continued to associate strength with production (p. 42). As we shall see, Orwell embraces this besieged working-class concept of manhood that involves all aspects of life, from the adulation of physically demanding work to the belief that potency proves manhood (and the resultant hostility to contraception). Perhaps Orwell's attitude is typical of that emotion known as nostalgia —it is usually not for a past we have actually known but for that idealized past of which we were deprived.

60. Woodcock, *Crystal Spirit*, p. 160.

61. Stearns, *Be a Man*, p. 59.

62. Richard Titmuss, "Industrialization and the Family," *Essays on "The Welfare State,"* 3rd ed. (London: Allen and Unwin, 1976), p. 110.

63. Glynn and Oxborrow, *Interwar Britain*, p. 38, repeatedly touch on this point. For more detailed statistical information, see the chapter on health in A. H. Halsey, ed., *Trends in British Society since 1900: A Guide to the Changing Social Structure of Britain* (London: Macmillan, 1972).

64. Richard Titmuss, "The Position of Women: Some Vital Statistics," in *Essays on "The Welfare State,"* p. 91.

65. Ibid., pp. 96–97.

66. For a good antidote to the romantic view of working-class life in the Edwardian age, see the Women's Cooperative Guild volume, *Maternity: Letters from Working Women*, ed. Margaret Llewelyn Davies (1915); and Magdalen Stuart Reeves, *Round about a Pound a Week* (1914). In addition to works cited earlier, see also O. R. McGregor, "The Social Position of Women in England, 1850–1914: A Bibliography," *British Journal of Sociology* 6, no. 1 (March 1955): 48–60. On the ideology of motherhood and its political and economic ramifications, see Anna Davin, "Imperialism and Motherhood," *History Workshop* 5 (Spring 1978): 8–65. Of course, Orwell was writing at a time when the average birthrate reached a record low (it was 14.8 per 1,000 population in the period between 1931 and 1940, according to Jane Lewis, "In Search of a Real Equality," p. 210), which meant that more women would be looking for work (if it were available). Working-class women, however, were under real pressure from their husbands not to work, as Peter Stearns notes in *Be a Man*: "A working wife was a disgrace to her husband, an admission of basic failure as a man" (p. 68).

67. No wonder, then, that readers as different as Frank Gloversmith and Malcolm Muggeridge have concluded that Orwell believed the working class smells. Gloversmith, in "Changing Things," in Gloversmith, *Class, Culture and Social Change*, p. 113, says that Orwell "offensively reiterates" that the working class smells. Muggeridge, "Knight of the Woeful Countenance," in Gross, *The World of George Orwell*, p. 168, writes that Orwell "seems to have seriously believed that the poor smell, as he thought he did" compared with richer boys at St. Cyprian's and Eton. Muggeridge also disagrees with Orwell's characterization of middle-class beliefs, as is apparent in a diary entry dated April 8, 1951, after Muggeridge had read *Wigan Pier*. He writes: "Odd manias—as that the poor are believed by the middle-classes to smell, and that this is the basic cause of class feelings; that Orientals have pleasanter bodies than Occidentals because they are less hairy. Many of his statements extravagantly false.... The fact is he knew nothing about the ordinary life he specialised in describing—George Orwell, the unproletarian proletarian" (*Like It Was: The Diaries of Malcolm Muggeridge* (New York: William Morrow, 1982), p. 436). Edward M. Thomas, *Orwell* (Edinburgh: Oliver and Boyds, 1965), p. 33, notes Orwell's repetition that the lower classes smell and comments, "it does

seem that he is getting some pleasure from rubbing in to the reader a fact which *he* is willing to face, but which he suspects the reader is not." Thomas thinks the adjective "pathological" comes to mind here and considers the whole passage a mistake because it antagonizes and shocks readers, but in general he praises Orwell's argument.

68. Not a great deal is known about the physiology and psychology of the sense of smell in human beings, but a number of researchers have argued that olfactory responses take on emotional significance by a process of association with life experiences. See Havelock Ellis, *Studies in the Psychology of Sex* (Philadelphia: F. A. David, 1906), vol. 4, *Sexual Selection in Man*, who notes that the sense of smell has an exceptionally strong power of suggestion, and odors "are thus specially apt both to control the emotional life and to become its slave." Personal idiosyncracies of all kinds, says Ellis, "tend to manifest themselves in the sphere of smell" (pp. 54–55). A recent researcher, Trygg Engen, in *The Perception of Odors* (New York: Academic Press, 1982), also argues that "the sense of smell is shaped by experience; that is, odors become meaningful through association with other events" (p. 169). In view of the prominence—and notoriety—of Orwell's "analysis" of class antagonisms as rooted in the sense of smell it is surprising that no serious attention has been devoted to the question of what this tells us about Orwell. Michael Kalogerakis, "The Role of Olfaction in Sexual Development," *Psychosomatic Medicine* 25, no. 5 (September–October 1963): 420–32, offers a hypothesis (concerning the role of olfaction in a young boy's psychosexual development) that may well be applicable to Orwell.

There is an echo of Orwell's ambivalence about working-class bodies in his reaction to urine and urination. In "Such, Such Were the Joys" (CEJL, 4:330–69), he describes his childhood experiences of humiliation and punishment as a result of wetting his bed. In *Down and Out* one of the most frequently mentioned unpleasant odors is that of urine. Yet in one of Orwell's final bits of fiction, written in his last notebook probably in the spring of 1949 (Orwell Archive), there is a distinct fascination with urinating as an emblem of masculine vigor, closely associated with sexual performance. The passage describes an unnamed male character's recollections of his squalid room in a hotel in the Latin Quarter. Through the thin partitioning, he heard the daily routine in the next room of a "lusty" errand boy of about eighteen as he came home each evening, kissed his girl, and then noisily urinated into a tin slop-pail. It is the loudness and strength of the urinating that impress the listener. After this, kisses and a creaking bed are heard, along with groans.

69. Gregory K. Lehne, "Homophobia among Men," in Deborah S. David and Robert Brannon, eds., *The Forty-Nine Percent Majority: The Male Sex Role* (Reading, Mass.: Addison-Wesley, 1976), p. 66.

70. Ibid., pp. 77–80. Homophobic men, says Lehne, do not participate in "sissy, womanly, 'homosexual' activities or interests." For a complementary view of the development (and fragility) of male gender identity in a society in which the child's primary caretaker is typically a female, see chap. 6 below. Orwell spent his childhood in a household of women, until, at the age of eight, he was shipped off to St. Cyprian's—about which he wrote (with the usual misogyny) in "Such, Such Were the Joys."

71. Orwell apparently believed that "female odors" are not only different but uniquely detectable even in a room filled with chemical, vegetal, and animal smells. This, at least, is the implication of one of the final entries

found in his last notebook (in the Orwell Archive). Perhaps there is also a hint here of the idea that women—their smells and all—are a "civilizing" influence on an otherwise dirty and unrestrained "bachelor" existence: "The room stank as only a bachelor's room can stink. It was immediately clear that no female odour, not even a female bad odour, had ever invaded it. ——— inferred in his wordless way that even the cousin-housekeeper was not admitted into this room...." Note Orwell's use of the verb "invade" to describe a female odor in a male bastion.

72. Martin Ceadel, *Pacifism in Britain, 1914–1945: The Defining of a Faith* (Oxford: Clarendon Press, 1980), pp. 83–84, states that "Orwell's cruel caricature of the I.L.P. socialist of the thirties was perhaps more accurate as a satirical portrait of a rank-and-file pacifist of the twenties." Ceadel notes the strong connection between pacifism and vegetarianism in the twenties, explained by the unwillingness to take life.

73. Among early reviewers of *Wigan Pier*, one of the few to notice Orwell's aggressive masculinity is Hugh Massingham who, in "A Bourgeois Joins Up," *Observer*, March 14, 1937, p. 9, writes that the book would have been better if Orwell "had not been so anxious to show that he is a real live He-man. You do not give an edge to your argument by using such phrases as 'outer-suburban creeping Jesus,' nor take anybody in by sentences starting with 'anyone who uses his brains knows—.'" Terry Eagleton, in *Exiles and Emigrés* (London: Chatto and Windus, 1970), p. 79, also comments on the "tough, swaggering sense of self-righteous masculinity" in *Wigan Pier*.

74. Kingsley Amis, "One World and Its Way," *What Became of Jane Austen? And Other Questions* (London: Jonathan Cape, 1970), p. 42, says, "I often feel I will never pick up a book by Orwell again until I have read a frank discussion of the dishonesty and hysteria that mar some of his best work." Not only has this call generally gone unheeded, but commentators such as Bernard Crick contribute to the Orwell myth by dismissals of these traits of Orwell's. Crick does this in an especially interesting way, by a rapid allusion to Orwell's "magnificently comic and violent tirade" against socialism. This is a two-edge ploy: the brief, in-passing reference to an important feature of the book, and the hearty transformation of this revealing tirade into magnificent comic writing. A neat attempt to dispose of the problem—which, however, persists.

75. In one isolated case Orwell departs from his usual androcentric view for a few sentences and specifically includes women in a discussion of human heroism. This occurs in his 1941 essay "The Art of Donald McGill" (CEJL, 2:155–65), which, in other respects, is full of gender stereotypes. In a still later piece, "Pleasure Spots" (CEJL, 4:81), dating from 1946, Orwell asks what "man's" needs are, and, reaffirming both the view and the rhetoric utilized in *Wigan Pier* ten years earlier, answers that man needs to learn that "the highest happiness does *not* lie in relaxing, resting, playing poker, drinking and making love simultaneously. And the instinctive horror which all sensitive people feel at the progressive mechanisation of life would be seen not to be a mere sentimental archaism, but to be fully justified. For man only stays human by preserving large patches of simplicity in his life, while the tendency of many modern inventions—in particular the film, the radio and the aeroplane—is to weaken his consciousness, dull his curiosity, and, in general, drive him nearer to the animals."

76. Gloversmith, "Changing Things," p. 114.

CHAPTER FOUR
MASCULINE/FEMININE IN THE EARLY FICTION

1. There is a problem in dealing with Orwell's two novels of the mid-1930s: He later renounced both *A Clergyman's Daughter* and *Keep the Aspidistra Flying,* specifically objecting to Penguin Books' project to reprint these works, as is evident from his letters to his agent. In 1938, when Allen Lane first suggested to Orwell that Penguin publish some of his work, Orwell wrote to Leonard Moore, his agent, suggesting *Down and Out, Burmese Days,* and *Aspidistra* as possibilities (letter dated November 28, 1938, LL). By 1944, however, Orwell's attitude toward *Aspidistra* had also changed, and he wrote to Moore (May 27, 1944, LL): "I don't think I can allow this book to be reprinted, or 'A Clergyman's Daughter' either. They are both thoroughly bad books and I would much rather see them go out of print." He then suggested that Penguin reprint *Coming Up for Air* instead. Orwell later left instructions in his will that certain of his books, including these two novels, not be reprinted, instructions that were subsequently disregarded. What, then, should be the critic's position in relation to such works? We do not know what particularly Orwell objected to in these novels, which were, of course, a part of his development. Given this situation, I will deal briefly with the two novels, commenting on the ways in which they relate to the ideological cluster characteristic of Orwell's work as a whole.

2. Raymond Williams, *George Orwell* (Glasgow: Fontana/Collins, 1971), p. 44; his emphasis.

3. V. S. Pritchett commented in an early review that Orwell seems uncertain if Dorothy is a "half-wit" (in Jeffrey Meyers, ed., *George Orwell: The Critical Heritage* [London and Boston: Routledge and Kegan Paul, 1975], p. 59). Geoffrey Stone, in the same volume (p. 64), refers to her as "an earnest but not especially bright girl." This is a curious reading of Dorothy, given that early in the novel, for example, we are told that in her arguments with Mr. Warburton (of which, however, we hear only his side, while hers is merely alluded to), "though Dorothy was always *right,* she was not always victorious" (69; Orwell's emphasis). To the extent that Dorothy emerges as a person at all within the novel, she is clearly Orwell's mouthpiece and as bright as he. For example, in the description of her responses to the desperately ignorant schoolgirls she teaches, we see Orwell's own creative response to this problem. What the critics who fault Dorothy's intelligence seem to have missed, then, is that she is not an authentic character at all but rather a blank, a transparent screen for Orwell's own perceptions. Peter Quennell, in a 1935 review (also in *Meyers, Critical Heritage,* p. 61), did get the point and referred to Dorothy as "a cipher . . . a literary abstraction to whom things happen."

4. The *nouveau roman* of the 1950s and beyond, as developed by such novelists as Michel Butor, was to utilize this *you* in an innovative way for fictional purposes. This is not, however, what Orwell does.

5. For example, Lawrence's description of the transformation of the vicar's wife from "a self-assured young woman" to one pitifully wrestling with tradesmen's bills and unable to "be impressive" is not accompanied by any narrative disdain. Instead, he writes:

"Wounded to the quick of her pride, she found herself isolated in an indifferent, callous population. She raged indoors and out. But soon she learned that she must pay too heavily for her outdoor rages, and then she only raged within the walls of the rectory. There her feeling was so strong that she frightened herself. She saw herself hating her husband, and she knew that, unless she were careful, she would smash her form of life and bring catastrophe upon him and upon herself. So in fear she went quiet. She hid, bitter and beaten by fear, behind the only shelter she had in the world, her gloomy, poor parsonage.

"Children were born every year; almost mechanically, she continued to perform her maternal duty, which was forced upon her. Gradually, broken by the suppressing of her violent anger and misery and disgust, she became an invalid and took to her couch" (D. H. Lawrence, "Daughters of the Vicar," *The Prussian Officer* [Harmondsworth: Penguin Books, 1945], pp. 51–52). From all this Orwell seems to have borrowed simply the fact of an unhappy marriage (Dorothy's father's), made more unhappy by being hidden.

Orwell himself associated successful writing with masculinity and potency, as is evident in a comment he makes in a letter written while he was at work on—and dissatisfied with—*A Clergyman's Daughter*. Reading Joyce's *Ulysses*, he says, gives him an inferiority complex: "When I read a book like that and then come back to my own work, I feel like a eunuch who has taken a course in voice production and can pass himself off fairly well as a bass or a baritone, but if you listen closely you can hear the good old squeak just the same as ever" (CEJL, 1:139).

6. Orwell was perfectly aware of his difficulties in putting the novel together (though he seems not to have questioned how much of this difficulty was due to his choice of a female protagonist). In a letter written to his friend Brenda Salkeld in 1934, he states: "As for the novel I am now completing, it makes me spew even worse [than *Burmese Days*], & yet there *are* some decent passages in it. I don't know how it is, I can write decent passages but I can't put them together" (CEJL, 1:138). In another letter shortly thereafter, he writes: "My novel, instead of going forwards, goes backwards with the most alarming speed. There are whole wads of it that are so awful that I really don't know what to do with them" (1:139). And a letter to his agent, at the time he sent the novel in, states: "I am not at all pleased with it. It was a good idea, but I am afraid I have made a muck of it—however, it is as good as I can do for the present. There are bits of it that I don't dislike, but I am afraid it is very disconnected as a whole, and rather unreal" (1:141).

7. Alex Zwerdling, in *Orwell and the Left* (New Haven and London: Yale University Press, 1974), p. 134, notes that, "when Orwell lists the contributors to a BBC program he is arranging during the war, he politely mentions himself last—except for the sole Indian (Mulk Raj Anand), whose name follows his." Zwerdling sees this as an outbreak of "ancient habit." Interestingly, even Zwerdling fails to notice Orwell's androcentrism (as opposed to his ethnocentrism) and writes that Orwell "came to despise the forms of hierarchy the world had invented, whether of birth, wealth, race, or even talent" (p. 17), asserting that Orwell's socialism "is a vision of an end to all forms of privilege" (p. 18).

8. Orwell's letters during his own bookshop days, while he was discouraged about the writing of *A Clergyman's Daughter*, foreshadow the tone and vocabulary he utilizes in *Aspidistra*. The idea for *Aspidistra*, however, goes a good deal further back. In the April 1931 issue of *The Adelphi*, Orwell published a review of *Hunger and Love*, Lionel Britton's novel about poverty. The virtue of the novel, he says, is "that it rubs in the irritating, time-wasting nature of poverty; the nasty, squalid little things which by their cumulative effect make life on less than two pounds a week radically different from life on even three or four pounds." The novel's hero "wants love, but love costs

money; he gets moments with half-witted shop-girls, or prostitutes." Concluding that the book is "almost worthless" as a novel, Orwell then adds: "Obviously the thing to do with such important material—the world of an intelligent poor man—was to make it into a memorable story."

9. In his interesting essay "Boys' Weeklies," Orwell briefly comments on women's papers, noting that they are read "for the most part by girls who are working for a living" and are therefore more realistic than the boys' papers. But, says Orwell, for all their sensible advice columns, women's papers such as the *Oracle* and *Peg's Paper* present "a pure fantasy-world. It is the same fantasy all the time, pretending to be richer than you are" (CEJL, 1:480–81). Orwell does not analyze why this fantasy, so different from the ones he finds in the boys' papers, should take this particular form, or what it has to do with the real positions of males and females in his society.

10. Terry Eagleton, "George Orwell and the Lower Middle Class Novel," in his *Exiles and Emigrés* (London: Chatto and Windus, 1970), p. 94, points out that Gordon's attitude merely reflects the views of the bourgeois world, to which he is bound by a simple inversion. "Gordon rejects middle-class society from what are essentially middle-class premises: his extraordinary sensitivity to such matters as the social significance of kinds of doorbell indicates the depth of his obsession with the insignia of a social structure he is supposed to reject."

11. On the theme of the significance of sterility, Bernard Crick has an odd contribution to make in his *George Orwell: A Life* (Boston: Little, Brown, 1980), p. 174. Noting that Orwell believed he was sterile and mentioned this to several people, Crick comments: "Precisely why he believed this is unclear. Perhaps it was simply that, as he told a woman friend ten years later, [he and Eileen] had tried to have children and failed. But odd that he should shoulder the blame so self-critically; it takes two to make a child." It seems unlikely that, if Eileen were the one who had believed she was sterile, Crick would be making an issue of it.

12. John A. Glusman, "The Style Was the Man," *Literary Review* 25, no. 3 (Spring 1982): 442, notes that for Orwell sex was tied up with power and rarely associated with love: "It is forced on the moment, pursued for its sake, as power hungers after subjection."

13. Gordon here seems to express Orwell's own thoughts, which George Woodcock called "truly reactionary" on the subject of population policy and abortion; see *The Crystal Spirit: A Study of George Orwell* (Boston: Little, Brown, 1966), p. 261. Woodcock notes that "Patriots are usually interested in population" and sees Orwell's authoritarianism in this respect as an indication of his "vitalism," which explains "also the rooted and persistent hostility which he shows towards supporters of birth control, and, indeed, towards any interference with sex as a natural function leading eventually to procreation." Orwell's remarks in "The English People," which occasioned Woodcock's strictures, are discussed in chapter 7, below.

14. E. M. Forster, *Aspects of the Novel* (New York: Harcourt, Brace and World, 1955), p. 38.

15. In a final comic attack on advertising, Orwell describes the agency's new campaign for a deodorant. On the model of the famous "Night-starvation" ads, Gordon's colleague, Mr. Warner, invents "Pedic Perspiration" (*Aspidistra*, 263), a new horror with which to frighten the public and increase sales. Posters all over the country demand with "sinister simplicity": " 'P.P.' WHAT ABOUT

YOU?" Surely Orwell intentionally echoed this slogan in the posters describing Big Brother in *Nineteen Eighty-Four.*

16. Woodcock, *Crystal Spirit,* pp. 149–50, writes that if we accept the novel's conclusion "as a defeat, then Rosemary, like all the women in Orwell's novels about men, is ultimately the enemy." Woodcock later remarks: "As for Rosemary, it is true that she plays the part of the seductive and eventually rapacious siren, but it is difficult, when one reads the juvenile dialogue that goes on between her and Gordon and when one sniffs the smell of hockey-field heartiness that hangs over her, to imagine how she succeeds" (p. 345).

17. The notebook is in the Orwell Archive. Bernard Crick also cites this passage in his *George Orwell* (p. 13) and discusses Orwell's ambivalence toward his mother. Crick sees some "balance" lacking in Orwell's mother between "the over-protectiveness of a conventional mother and the up-and-away over-practicality of the woman on her own who might have quite liked to have been almost a *femme libre"* (p. 14).

18. Bernard Crick (ibid., p. 46) discusses Orwell's version of life at St. Cyprian's and suggests that "no terrible harm seems to have been done."

19. Anthony West, "George Orwell," *Principles and Persuasions: The Literary Essays of Anthony West* (New York: Harcourt, Brace, 1957), p. 165, finds in *Aspidistra* echoes not only of D. H. Lawrence but also of F. Scott Fitzgerald "and his tormenting feeling that whatever a man was, and whatever he did, he could never capture the glow that emanated from the rich and marked them as superior beings." West notes Orwell's attribution to Gordon of the belief that people—especially shopgirls and other dangerous women—could tell at a glance how much money a man had in his pocket.

CHAPTER FIVE
RITES OF MANHOOD, I

1. The war myth would have trouble surviving without the help of widespread mechanisms for its validation. In his eagerness to portray Orwell in the heroic mode, Bernard Crick, in *George Orwell: A Life* (Boston: Little, Brown, 1980), second-guesses the evidence of Orwell's own words at the beginning of *Homage to Catalonia.* Orwell states: "I had come to Spain with some notion of writing newspaper articles, but I had joined the militia almost immediately, because at that time and in that atmosphere it seemed the only conceivable thing to do" (8). Crick, however, considers this a "reversal of cause and effect once again for dramatic effect" (p. 211). Although Crick cites Orwell's "Notes on the Spanish Militias" (CEJL, 1:316–28), which were found among Orwell's papers after his death, he ignores the following statement from the first paragraph of these notes: "I had intended going to Spain to gather materials for newspaper articles etc, but had also some vague idea of fighting if it seemed worth while, but was doubtful about this owing to my poor health and comparatively small military experience." And in one of Orwell's "As I Please" columns, published in *Tribune* on September 15, 1944 (to which Crick also refers, while not mentioning this detail), Orwell describes his train trip to Spain from France: "About halfway down France the ordinary passengers dropped off. There might still be a few nondescript journalists like myself, but the train was practically a troop train, and the countryside knew it" (CEJL, 3:232).

After discussing the uncertainty as to his motivations among people who knew Orwell, Crick comes down firmly on the heroic side: "But what is reasonably clear is that for Orwell at that time writing was, indeed, a quite secondary motive for coming to Spain" (p. 211). Although Orwell did not make an issue of his motives, Crick does, and his interpretation makes Orwell out to be more reckless, adventure-prone, and war-hungry than he probably was.

Crick opens his chapter on Orwell in Spain with a discussion of Orwell's attack on W. H. Auden's poem "Spain." In his essay "Inside the Whale," Orwell had objected to Auden's line, "The conscious acceptance of guilt in the necessary murder," commenting: "Personally I would not speak so lightly of murder" (CEJL, 1:516). Wanting to defend Orwell from the "charge" of hesitancy in killing, Crick rapidly affirms that "Orwell himself was not a squeamish liberal when it came to 'necessary murder' " (p. 208). Crick continues building on Orwell's status as a fighter and, after recounting the episode in which Orwell could not shoot an enemy soldier who was holding up his trousers as he ran, comments: "This was not opting out of the business of killing. In an account of the night raid on the enemy trenches, Orwell made clear that grenades that he threw almost certainly proved deadly. He had also tried to bayonet a man running away down a communication trench as he ran along the top, but could not catch up" (p. 217). Crick's constant emphasis on Orwell's bravery and valor reveals that to him these are touchstones of the man's worth. In addition, Crick's concern with promoting a masculine image of Orwell on occasion leads him into absurdities, as in his description of Orwell's dog, a black poodle: "the manly, hunting-dog sort," Crick reassures us, "not a lap-dog poodle" (p. 234).

Other writers on Orwell, long before Crick, of course helped establish Orwell's connection with the war myth. A few examples will suffice. Richard Rees, *George Orwell: Fugitive from the Camp of Victory* (London: Secker and Warburg, 1961), p. 154, saves for the last page of his book the following recollection: "Orwell did once make a remark to me which seems to give a clue to the obscurer part of his character. Speaking of the first world world war, he said that his generation must be marked for ever by the humiliation of not having taken part in it. He had, of course, been too young to take part. But the fact that several million men, some of them not much older than himself, had been through an ordeal which he had not shared was apparently intolerable to him." Rees comments that "this is an example of his exaggerated sense of honor carried to the point of Promethean arrogance" and then closes his book with a paean to Orwell's heroism, disinterestedness, and courage.

Rees's recollection is borne out by a notebook (Orwell Archive) that Orwell kept containing an outline for what was to become *Nineteen Eighty-Four*. In a passage set in 1918, the character "H." realizes he has been living as if no war was on: "Suddenly H. knows that the war is going on, that people older & more responsible than he are fighting it & think it supremely important to win it. He has a sudden terrible vision of the life of the trenches going on & on while he & his kind are safe in the background" and can forget that the war is happening. The passage concludes: "His death in Spain in 1937 is the direct result of this vision."

Lionel Trilling, in an essay that originally appeared in 1952 in the American edition of *Homage to Catalonia*, "George Orwell and the Politics of Truth" (in Raymond Williams, ed., *George Orwell: A Collection of Critical Essays* [Englewood Cliffs, N.J.: Prentice-Hall, 1974], p. 65), discusses the meaning of calling Orwell "a virtuous man" and says that "by some quirk of the spirit of the language," the form of the sentence "He is a virtuous man" appropriately "brings out the primitive meaning of the word virtuous, which is not merely moral goodness, but also fortitude and strength in goodness." The word "virtue" comes from *vir*, a man, and very quickly acquires the connotation of a man worthy of the name. The two, of course, are not identical except in the concept of male gender identity as requiring heroic deeds. Trilling (p. 74) cites Orwell's quarrel with the intelligentsia which, he says, at times made Orwell sound like a leader writer for the *Times*; and he then validates Orwell's warrior status in the comment: "But he was not a leader-writer for the *Times*. He had fought in Spain and nearly died there, and on Spanish affairs his position had been the truly revolutionary one."

Even Raymond Williams, in his far more critical appraisal in *George Orwell* (Glasgow: Fontana/Collins, 1971, p. 94), subscribes to the warrior myth, and he too considers Orwell's role as a warrior so important that he alludes to it in his closing paragraph, while, in the very same breath, urging us to move beyond Orwell: "The thing to do with his work, his history, is to read it, not imitate it. He is still there, tangibly, with the wound in his throat, the sad strong face, the plain words written in hardship and exposure."

2. Stanley Weintraub, *The Last Great Cause: The Intellectuals and the Spanish Civil War* (New York: Weybright and Talley, 1968).

3. Carl von Clausewitz, *On War*, ed. and trans. Michael Howard and Peter Paret (Princeton: Princeton University Press, 1976), p. 87.

4. Quoted by Stansky and Abrahams, who refer to the poem as "debased Kipling or Newbolt," in *The Unknown Orwell* (London: Constable, 1972), p. 52.

5. Ibid., p. 64.

6. A few years before Orwell, Christopher Isherwood made precisely this point (as did others of this generation) but with more awareness of its implications: "We young writers of the middle twenties were all suffering, more or less subconsciously, from a feeling of shame that we hadn't been old enough to take part in the European war. . . . Like most of my generation, I was obsessed by a complex of terrors and longings connected with the idea 'War.' 'War,' in this purely neurotic sense, meant the Test. The test of your courage, your maturity, of your sexual prowess. 'Are you really a Man?' Subconsciously, I believe, I longed to be subjected to this test; but I also dreaded failure. I dreaded failure so much—indeed, I was so certain that I should fail—that, consciously, I denied my longing to be tested altogether" (*Lions and Shadows: An Education in the Twenties* [London: Hogarth, 1938], pp. 74–76).

7. In an interview conducted in December 1940, Orwell comments that even the poems written about the Spanish Civil War "were simply a deflated version of the stuff that Rupert Brooke and Co were writing in 1914" (CEJL, 2:38).

8. *Evening Standard*, December 1, 1945, on file in the Orwell Archive.

9. On the subject of the taste for noise, Charlotte Perkins Gilman, *The Man-Made World; or, Our Androcentric Culture* (New York: Charlton, 1911), p. 211, says: "In warfare, *per se*, we find maleness in its absurdest extremes. Here is to be studied the whole gamut of basic masculinity, from the initial instinct of combat [which she thought could be countered by developing men's *human* qualities], through every form of glorious ostentation, with the loudest possible accompaniment of noise." In "My Country Right or Left," Orwell comments on his time at the front: "Even on the rare occasions when all the guns

in Huesca and outside it were firing simultaneously, there were only enough of them to make a fitful unimpressive noise like the ending of a thunderstorm" (CEJL, 1:538).

10. In "The Lion and the Unicorn," however, written shortly after "My Country Right or Left," Orwell states that Hitler and Mussolini rose to power largely because they grasped the fact that patriotism (which Orwell here defines as "national loyalty") is a positive force capable of inspiring men (CEJL, 2:56). Orwell's ambivalence is also apparent in this essay in his pride at the English "hatred of war and militarism" (2:60), while at the same time he deplores the military incompetence and general decline in leadership of Britain's ruling class. He then, however, says: "One thing that has always shown that the English ruling class are *morally* fairly sound, is that in time of war they are ready enough to get themselves killed" (2:72; his emphasis). Orwell criticizes intellectuals for regarding "physical courage" as barbarous and says that the war will make it possible for patriotism and intelligence to come together again (2:75). In his essay "Patriots and Revolutionaries," in Victor Gollancz, ed., *The Betrayal of the Left* (London: Victor Gollancz, 1941), Orwell makes many of the same arguments about socialism and the fight against fascism that appear in "The Lion and the Unicorn."

11. Hugh Thomas, *The Spanish Civil War*, rev. ed. (New York: Harper and Row, 1977), p. 347.

12. Franz Borkenau discusses the role of women in the Spanish Civil War to some extent in *The Spanish Cockpit* (1937; rpt., Ann Arbor: University of Michigan Press, 1963). He refers to the basic poise and health of the Spaniards and comments that a striking aspect of the Spanish revolution "is the absence of any deep upheaval in sex life. Something in this line does of course occur, but much less than during the Great War in any country, and nothing at all to compare with the complete dissolution of standards of sexual morality in the Russian Revolution. As for the participation of some women in the fighting, it has always been traditional in Spain. To a surprisingly small degree is the Spanish civil war a psychological crisis." Borkenau was writing after a trip to Spain at the beginning of the war. Elsewhere he comments on one militiawoman who had followed her lover to the front and fought bravely, which made the men proud of her. "The whole position of this isolated girl among a crowd of men was the more remarkable because of the complete isolation of the militia-men from the village girls, who in accordance with the strict Spanish tradition refused even to speak to strangers." Borkenau describes the changed position of women as "one remarkable aspect of the streets" of Madrid in August 1936. Girls could be seen walking in pairs, unchaperoned, collecting money for the International Red Help. "They enjoy it enormously; for most of them it is obviously their first appearance in public, and now they are even allowed to talk to foreigners and sit down at their ease in the cafés for a chat with the militia-men." Orwell, along similar lines, describes village girls he saw in Montflorite in late March 1937 as "splendid vivid creatures with coal-black hair, a swinging walk, and a straightforward man-to-man demeanor which was probably a by-product of revolution" (*Homage to Catalonia*, 78).

A different aspect of the position of women in Republican Spain emerges in Carmen Alcalde, *La mujer en la guerra civil española* (Madrid: Ed. Cambio 16, 1976), pp. 162–65. Discussing the problem of prostitution, of which the anarchist press was more conscious than any other, Alcalde refers to a 1938 article complaining that revolutionary morality was not very different from bourgeois morality. The war had not provoked any heightened awareness among men of the situation of women, she says. The sexual satisfaction of soldiers was considered, as in other war situations, an instinctual necessity, and prostitutes were supplied. Orwell comments on the difficulties of long intervals between leaves and the general problem of keeping "the men in the line for unnecessarily long periods" (in "Notes on the Spanish Militias," CEJL, 1:322) and argues that it would have been possible to grant more frequent leaves "and to provide some kind of amenities for the troops not in the line." Among those "amenities" he lists: "hot baths, delousing, entertainments of some kind, cafés (actually there were some very feeble attempts at these) and also women. The very few women who were in or near the line and were get-atable were simply a source of jealousy. There was a certain amount of sodomy among the younger Spaniards" (1:323).

13. Temma Kaplan's article "Women and Spanish Anarchism," in Renate Bridenthal and Claudia Koonz, eds., *Becoming Visible: Women in European History* (Boston: Houghton Mifflin, 1977), pp. 400–21, describes the difficulties male anarchists had in attracting women to their cause. Orwell mentions the destruction of churches in Catalonia; Kaplan describes the church as "the core of poor women's society just as the local bar or café was the center of poor men's social life" (p. 402), and she explains women's resistance to male anarchist ideology in terms of the lack of alternatives offered to women by this ideology. She also notes that male anarchists did not seriously promote equality for women but rather sought their support for male goals (p. 403). Anarchist attacks on the family similarly ignored poor women's responses. Mujeres Libres (Liberated Women) was an anarchist women's association that by 1938 had 20,000 members in branches throughout the Republican areas of Spain. This group argued that "winning the Civil War and winning their rights as women workers were mutually dependent" (p. 416) and promoted autonomous women's organizations. But Kaplan concludes that "the persistence of traditional norms in anarchists' attitudes leads one to believe that had the anarchists triumphed, female anarchists as well as other women would still have faced a struggle" (p. 417), for in their revolutionary programs for reorganizing society, male anarchists were ambivalent about how such changes would affect them as individuals. Kaplan's analysis casts an ironic light on the conflict between the Communists and the anarchists, which turns out to have been in effect duplicated among anarchists themselves: Male anarchists often felt that women's goals and needs should be subordinated to the general anarchist struggle (p. 418), which men defined in such a way that social and psychological issues were given low priority.

14. Orwell continues: "Sometimes it is a comfort to me to think that the aeroplane is altering the conditions of war. Perhaps when the next great war comes we may see that sight unprecedented in all history, a jingo with a bullet-hole in him" (*Homage to Catalonia*, 65). Is it partly resentment against those who do not fight that accounts for Orwell's later attack on Vera Brittain's concern over the bombing of civilians in World War II? Orwell sets forth a specious argument that, since war is of its nature an atrocity, it is absurd to be upset about one or another form of war. He argues that protection of civilians makes war possible and that indiscriminate killing might end war and also notes that this would be demographically more sound than the killing of young male soldiers only (CEJL, 3:151). He does not seem to be facetious when making this argument, and it is one of the rare occasions on which he speaks up for equal treatment of women. He elsewhere states (CEJL, 2:399): "People don't have scruples when they are fighting for a cause they believe in."

15. Thomas, *Spanish Civil War*, p. 653.

16. This theme of reversal was addressed by Orwell some years later. In an entry in his wartime diary dated June 14, 1940, he writes: "How much rubbish this war will sweep away, if only we can hang on throughout the summer. War is simply a reversal of civilised life; its motto is 'Evil be thou my good,' and so much of the good of modern life is actually evil that it is questionable whether on balance war does harm" (CEJL, 2:348).

17. In an unsigned review of *Homage to Catalonia* in *The Listener*, May 25, 1938, the very charges against the POUM that Orwell's book attempted to combat are asserted, but the reviewer goes on to praise Orwell's "masterly description" and then adds that Orwell "has made almost concrete for the reader the horror and filth, the futility and comedy, and even the beauty of war."

18. Nancy Huston, "Tales of War and Tears of Women," *Women's Studies International Forum* 5, nos. 3/4 (1982): 271–72; her emphasis.

19. Ibid., p. 273.

20. Huston (ibid., p. 274) writes: "during World War II, both the fascist countries and the Allied Forces used triumphal discourse to account for what was happening. Since Hitler lost, the second version is now accepted as historical truth. Overcoming Germany meant, besides compelling the nazi troops to surrender, eliminating the triumphal discourse concerning the extermination of the Jews and allowing only the bombs dropped upon German territory to go down in history as 'beneficial' bombs." Orwell was well aware of this tendency and noted in 1944 that "History is written by the winners" (CEJL, 3:88). Later that year Orwell writes: "Hitler can say that the Jews started the war, and if he survives that will become official history" (3:149). These writings develop many of the themes later found in *Nineteen Eighty-Four*, especially Orwell's fears for the fate of "objective truth." Both Orwell and Huston, however, fail to do justice to the tendency toward revisionist historiography appearing everywhere within a few years of victory.

21. Orwell's letter to Gollancz is quoted in Crick, *George Orwell*, pp. 230–31. Some years later, however, Orwell took quite a different approach to the business of accusations. In the summer 1946 "London Letter" for the *Partisan Review*, Orwell accused Konni Zilliacus of being a "crypto-Communist." Zilliacus objected in a letter published by *Tribune*, January 17, 1947, and Orwell replied in turn. In an extraordinary piece of sophistry, Orwell now cast the following accusation at Zilliacus: "This letter of his, I should say, somewhat supports my thesis. For if what I have suggested is obviously untrue, why does he get so hot and bothered about it? Recently I found myself described by an American paper as a Fascist. I did not write a letter denouncing this as a 'slander,' because no one whose opinion mattered would pay any attention to it. Why does not Mr Zilliacus feel himself equally able to disregard the suggestion that he himself is a 'crypto'?" (CEJL, 4:193). Should the reader with a memory of Orwell's own angry protests of the late 1930s conclude that Orwell was indeed pro-Franco?

22. Arnold van Gennep, *The Rites of Passage*, trans. Monika B. Vizedom and Gabrielle L. Caffee (Chicago: University of Chicago Press, 1960; orig. pub. 1909).

23. Joseph Henderson, "Ancient Myths and Modern Man," in C. G. Jung, ed., *Man and His Symbols* (New York: Dell, 1968), p. 120.

24. Mircea Eliade, *Rites and Symbols of Initiation: The Mysteries of*

Birth and Rebirth, trans. Willard R. Trask (New York: Harper and Row, 1958), p. x.

25. Ibid., p. 103.

26. Eileen Blair to Leonard Moore, April 12, 1937 (LL). This letter verifies that Orwell was keeping a diary in Spain and already had plans for a book.

27. Robert Briffault, *Reasons for Anger* (1936; rpt., Freeport, N.Y.: Books for Libraries Press, 1969), p. 144, writes against the view that men are innately destructive: "A highly organized and complicated technique of propaganda, the resources of oratory, the assistance of the police, the cooperation of academic learning, of the churches, of the press, are required to wheedle the collective combativeness of twentieth-century man into facing a machine gun. Were it not so, no existing institution which excites his exasperation would be safe for a day."

28. Mircea Eliade, *Myth and Reality*, trans. Willard R. Trask (New York: Harper and Row, 1963), p. 8.

29. Gerardus van der Leeuw, *Sacred and Profane Beauty: The Holy in Art*, trans. David E. Green (New York: Holt, Rinehart and Winston, 1963), p. 7.

30. Mircea Eliade, *The Myth of the Eternal Return*, trans. Willard R. Trask (Princeton: Princeton University Press, 1954), p. 4.

31. Ibid., pp. 32, 38.

32. George Woodcock, *The Crystal Spirit: A Study of George Orwell* (Boston: Little, Brown, 1966), p. 175.

33. Gerardus van der Leeuw, *Religion in Essence and Manifestation* (New York: Harper and Row, 1963), 2:414.

34. Eliade, *Myth and Reality*, p. 141.

35. Roland Barthes, *Mythologies*, trans. Annette Lavers (London: Jonathan Cape, 1972), p. 143.

36. Ibid., pp. 142–43.

37. In his 1946 essay "How the Poor Die," Orwell writes: "And it is a great thing to die in your own bed, though it is better still to die in your boots" (CEJL, 4:232). Wyndham Lewis is one of the few critics to have commented on Orwell's attitude toward war. In an uneven essay on Orwell, in *The Writer and the Absolute* (London: Methuen, 1952), p. 181, Lewis refers to Orwell's wartime diary and notes the "martial ebullience" and "martial murk" of his thinking about war. Orwell "always has a good word to say for war," Lewis observes. "He never seemed to learn that these total wars were immense orgies of destruction pulling down and trampling under their bombs our civilization." Lewis also writes: "The patriotism of the ordinary club-man order of his 1940–41 Notebook, the joyous acceptance of war as a good purgative, 'la bonne guerre,' is that of the extreme Right rather than the extreme Left."

38. Michael Walzer, *Just and Unjust Wars: A Moral Argument with Historical Illustrations* (New York: Basic Books, 1977), p. 142.

39. See Emanuel Edrich, "Naïveté and Simplicity in Orwell's Writing: *Homage to Catalonia*," *University of Kansas City Review* 27, no. 4 (1961): 289–97.

40. Barthes, *Mythologies*, p. 150. Cf. also pp. 41–42, where Barthes discusses the inoculation technique specifically in relation to the army.

41. Julian Symons, *The Thirties: A Dream Revolved*, rev. ed. (London: Faber and Faber, 1975), p. 109.

42. Ibid., p. 115.

43. Woodcock, *Crystal Spirit*, p. 165.

44. Ibid., pp. 170–71.

45. Nancy Harstock, "The Barracks Community in Western Political Thought: Prologomena to a Feminist Critique of War and Politics," *Women's Studies International Forum* 5, nos. 3/4 (1982): 283, notes that "the masculine role of warrior-hero" has been "central to the conceptualization of politics for the last 2500 years."

46. Paulann Hosler Sheets, personal communication, October 24, 1983.

47. A fascinating study of the literature and myths produced by the Great War is Paul Fussell, *The Great War and Modern Memory* (London: Oxford University Press, 1975). Fussell writes: "At the same time the war was relying on inherited myth, it was generating new myth, and that myth is part of the fiber of our own lives" (p. ix). In a chapter called "Oh What a Literary War," Fussell discusses the literary models that English participants in the Great War drew on, as well as the impact that the war itself has had on our language. See also Bernard Bergonzi, *Heroes' Twilight: A Study of the Literature of the Great War*, 2nd ed. (London: Macmillan, 1980), who concludes that the writers of the Great War "undermined a whole range of traditional responses: heroism, as a kind of behavior, might still be possible, but not the rhetoric and gestures of heroism" (p. 222). But the rhetoric of heroism is still very much with us, as is apparent in Andrew Rutherford, *The Literature of War: Five Studies in Heroic Virture* (New York: Harper and Row/Barnes and Noble, 1978), which ends in a celebration of the heroic virtue made manifest in the works examined, and as much British reporting of the 1982 Falklands crisis also indicates.

CHAPTER SIX
RITES OF MANHOOD, II

1. Orwell's letters in the Lilly Library also tell us something about the genesis of the novel. As early as December 6, 1937, he wrote to Moore about his projected book: "All I have thought of is this: it will be a novel, it will not be about politics, and it will be about a man who is having a holiday and trying to make a temporary escape from his responsibilities, public and private. The title I thought of is 'Coming Up for Air.'" In a letter dated June 28, 1938, Orwell writes: "I can't do any serious work yet. I have sketched out my novel but don't want to start till I feel completely fit." He now introduces a related subject—another of his manuscripts to have been lost or destroyed: "In the mean time I've been writing a pamphlet more or less on the subject of pacifism." From Marrakech, on October 1, 1938, he again mentions this pamphlet, entitled "Socialism and War," and urges Moore to offer it to Warburg for publication, saying he wants no money for it. But on November 28, 1938, he writes to Moore: "Please don't give yourself any more trouble with that wretched pamphlet. I am sorry you have had so much already. As you say, there is no sale for pamphlets." Orwell's mood at the time can be gauged by a letter to Jack Common, dated September 26, 1938, in which Orwell says that even if war does break out, he will not return to England sooner than planned: "The whole thing seems to me so utterly meaningless that I think I shall just concentrate on remaining alive" (CEJL, 1:351).

2. Bernard Bergonzi, *Reading the Thirties: Texts and Contexts* (Pittsburgh: University of Pittsburgh Press, 1978), p. 104, discusses the prevalence of bombing imagery in British poetry and prose of the late 1930s.

3. A particularly graceless instance of this occurs early in *Nineteen*

Eighty-Four in a description of Winston's reactions: "This, he thought with a sort of vague distaste—this was London" (6).

4. See chapter 3 (and notes) on Orwell's idealization of the Edwardian age. Donald Read, "Introduction: Crisis Age or Golden Age?" in Donald Read, ed., *Edwardian England* (New Brunswick, N.J.: Rutgers University Press, 1982), pp. 14–15, comments: "Golden quality is recognisable only in retrospect, in the minds of later observers who may or may not have personally enjoyed the supposed golden age." Read quotes an article in the *Times* of January 19, 1909, which "emphasised how contemporary Edwardians 'place the golden age behind them, and assume that no generation ever had to deal with evils so great and perplexing as those of the present day.' "

5. Orwell's love of lists (mentioned in my introduction, above) is thoroughly exercised in *Coming Up for Air*, which includes, among other things, long catalogues of varieties of fish and kinds of bait.

6. Orwell makes the same point in *The Road to Wigan Pier*, see chapter 3, above.

7. In "The English People," an essay Orwell wrote early in 1944, he comments on the changes in physical type over the preceding century and asks: "Where are they gone, the hulking draymen and low-browed prize-fighters, the brawny sailors with their buttocks bursting out of their white trousers, and the great overblown beauties with their swelling bosoms, like the figure-heads of Nelson's ships?" (CEJL, 3:5–6).

8. See chapter 3, above. Bowling situates this scene in the summer, but in *Wigan Pier* it is a winter scene. Seven years after writing *Coming Up for Air*, Orwell still envisions such family tableaux. In a column published in the *Evening Standard* on December 8, 1945, p. 6, entitled "The Case for the Open Fire," Orwell argues that a coal fire is necessary in a room that "is to be lived in" because it does *not* heat the whole room and thus forces people into sociable groupings. There then occurs a passage almost identical to the one in *Wigan Pier*, nine years earlier: "To one side of the fireplace sits Dad, reading the evening paper. To the other sits Mum, doing her knitting. On the hearthrug sit the children, playing snakes and ladders. Up against the fender, roasting himself, lies the dog. It is a comely pattern, a good background to one's memories, and the survival of the family as an institution may be more dependent on it than we realise."

9. In 1946 Orwell even wrote a piece for the *Evening Standard* on the subject of the correct preparation of a nice cup of tea—bitter, sugarless, and, of course, strong (CEJL, 3:40–43).

10. This paragraph contains the only point in the novel where the possibility is acknowledged that Bowling's listener or implied reader may be female. Perhaps this can be admitted here because the entire episode depends on differentiating males from females.

11. Nancy Chodorow, *The Reproduction of Mothering: Psychoanalysis and the Sociology of Gender* (Berkeley: University of California Press, 1978), p. 169. Important critiques of Chodorow's work appear in Joyce Trebilcot, ed., *Mothering: Essays in Feminist Theory* (Totowa, N.J.: Rowman and Allanheld, 1984). Another study from about the same time as Chodorow's, developing a related argument, is Dorothy Dinnerstein, *The Mermaid and the Minotaur: Sexual Arrangements and Human Malaise* (New York: Harper and Row/Colophon Books, 1977). Carol Gilligan, *In a Different Voice: Psychological Theory and Women's Development* (Cambridge: Harvard University Press, 1982), utilizes Chodorow's work and extends its implications into the area of the moral de-

velopment of men and women. Gilligan suggests that, unlike men, women construe a moral problem as one "of care and responsibility in relationships rather than as one of rights and rules" (p. 73). Gilligan concludes: "From the different dynamics of separation and attachment in their gender identity formation through the divergence of identity and intimacy that marks their experience in the adolescent years, male and female voices typically speak of the importance of different truths, the former of the role of separation as it defines and empowers the self, the latter of the ongoing process of attachment that creates and sustains the human community" (p. 156).

12. Chodorow, *Reproduction of Mothering*, pp. 166–67.

13. Ibid., p. 167.

14. Ibid., p. 168.

15. Ibid., p. 165.

16. Ibid., p. 9.

17. Orwell devotes several pages to Bowling's boyhood reading (*Coming Up for Air*, 88–90), stressing his identification with "Donovan the Dauntless," which inspired in Bowling a state of "pure bliss" (90). In his 1939 essay "Boys' Weeklies" (CEJL, 1:460–84), Orwell considers this type of mass culture from the point of view of its ideological content. Even in this context, however, he is unable to go beyond considerations of class and nationality and therefore ignores the specific gender ideologies of such papers. In "Boys' Weeklies" Orwell makes the interesting comment: "Personally I believe that most people are influenced far more than they would care to admit by novels, serial stories, films and so forth, and that from this point of view the worst books are often the most important, because they are usually the ones that are read earliest in life" (CEJL, 1:482). J. R. Hammond, *A George Orwell Companion: A Guide to the Novels, Documentaries, and Essays* (New York: St. Martin's Press, 1982), p. 192, points out that in "Boys' Weeklies" Orwell criticizes "the Billy Bunter stories because they are set in an unchanging world of c. 1910 where 'The King is on his throne and the pound is worth a pound' and 'Everything is safe, solid and unquestionable'—yet this is precisely the world looked back upon with such nostalgia in *Coming Up for Air*."

18. These details, as well as major thematic similarities, reveal Orwell's debt to H. G. Wells's *History of Mr. Polly* (1910). For discussions of these two novels, see Hammond, *A George Orwell Companion*, pp. 156–57, and Richard I. Smyer, *Primal Dream and Primal Crime: Orwell's Development as a Psychological Novelist* (Columbia: University of Missouri Press, 1979), pp. 86–93.

19. *Time and Tide*, September 7, 1940, pp. 907–8. This review occurs in the same column as Orwell's review of J. B. Priestley's play *Cornelius*. Orwell makes the point that the quality of tragedy in the play comes from the characters' assumption that the desperate commercial struggle they are involved in is part of the "order of nature." Orwell says: "The tragedy lies simply in the failure of human beings to imagine any other social system than the one they have been bred in," an astute observation that might have led Orwell to further reflection on his own assumptions about the "order of nature" as manifest in male and female character. Once again, in blithely expressing his own sexual stereotypes in the very same column, Orwell reveals his unwillingness to analyze his gender ideology. Orwell's friend Richard Rees, in *George Orwell: Fugitive from the Camp of Victory* (London: Secker and Warburg, 1961), pp. 93–94, tells an interesting story of his visit to Orwell on the island of Jura at a time when Orwell's sister Avril was running the household and taking care of Richard, his adopted son. On this occasion, Rees says, "I remember Orwell re-

turning from the mainland after a very stormy crossing. What had chiefly impressed him was the terrible plight of one of the women passengers. She had been so ill as to seem to be dying. Orwell had been sick too, but he insisted on the impression this poor woman had made on him: 'She had completely collapsed; and it made me think how terrible it must be to be a woman, so weak and easily upset. . . .' His sister, who had never been sea-sick in her life, made no comment."

20. Bowling, it should be noted, is forty-five and "middle-aged"; his wife, Hilda, has a friend, Miss Minns, who is thirty-eight and "old"; Elsie is forty-seven and, as in the passage cited here, is "a fat old woman." Bowling's descriptions of old or older men strike a very different note. They are repeatedly referred to in a semiaffectionate but tough tone as "old devils." The crusty-but-benign characters in the novel include Hodges, the caretaker at Binfield House, "a crabby old devil" (*Coming Up for Air*, 75); Gravitt, the butcher, "a big, rough-faced old devil" (70); and even the down-and-out medium that Hilda's friend Mrs. Wheeler finds for séances, "a seedy-looking old devil" (141).

21. Bernard Crick, *George Orwell: A Life* (Boston: Little, Brown, 1980), p. 209.

22. Ibid., pp. 246–47.

23. See Martin Ceadel, *Pacifism in Britain, 1914–1945: The Defining of a Faith* (Oxford: Clarendon Press, 1980), for a discussion of the struggles experienced by pacifists in the early 1940s as they tried to reconcile conflicting ethical imperatives. Orwell, by contrast, was never a serious pacifist, and the term "anti-militarist," which Crick, *George Orwell*, uses to describe the ILP, is therefore a more accurate designation for Orwell's position at this time.

24. Ceadel, *Pacifism in Britain*, p. 98.

25. A comparison of Orwell's antimilitaristic writing with that of a writer such as Vera Brittain helps us focus on the peculiar quality of Orwell's rhetoric. When Brittain writes against war (see her books *Humiliation with Honor* and *England's Hour*, for examples), she writes *for* people; there is no suggestion that she is too smart to be taken in by warmongering, only a respect and concern for human life. But Orwell's typical antiwar statements—that war is a "racket" or a "swindle"—show him in his usual aggressive stance: He is determined to outsmart the swindlers, which gives even his "pacifist" writings a characteristic tone of attack and smugness. In his essay "Inside the Whale," written in late 1939, Orwell adopts the same tone in explaining why the "passive attitude will come back, and it will be more consciously passive than before. Progress and reaction have both turned out to be swindles" (CEJL, 1:527). As E. P. Thompson comments in the essay "Outside the Whale," in his *The Poverty of Theory and Other Essays* (New York and London: Monthly Review Press, 1978; the essay was originally published in 1960), p. 224: " 'Swindle' is an imprecise tool of analysis, a noise of disgust."

26. "Political Reflections on the Crisis," *The Adelphi*, December 1938, p. 110. See also my introduction, above, for further illustrations of Orwell's rhetoric.

27. In a 1946 essay entitled "George Orwell, Nineteenth Century Liberal," *Politics*, December 1946, p. 387, George Woodcock commented that at times the general superficiality of Orwell's attitudes leads him "to sincere but unjust condemnation of people or groups, because he has not been able to understand their real motives." This, Woodcock believed, explains Orwell's attacks on pacifists. One of Orwell's main faults, according to Woodcock, is that he "does not seem to recognize general principles of social conduct. He has

ideas of fair play and honesty; concentration camps, propaganda lies and so forth are to be condemned. But in a more general sense his attitude is essentially opportunist"—e.g., jail fascists during wartime but leave them alone afterward; conscript men during war but resist this infringement of civil liberties otherwise. Woodcock considered Orwell's promotion of patriotism in "The Lion and the Unicorn" similarly opportunistic, for it disregards the "fundamentally evil nature of patriotism as a producer of war and a bulwark of authority," and he concluded that Orwell resembles an old-style nineteenth-century liberal.

28. Bowling's reaction to Porteous's insouciance calls to mind that Orwell himself was a recent convert to concern with German fascism. His assumption that if he had not thought of something it could not be important and could not have captured anyone else's attention is apparent in a comment he makes in a letter dated December 28, 1938: "I think it's really time someone began looking into Fascism seriously" (CEJL, 1:370). A similar note is struck in a 1947 column in which Orwell comments that he believes anti-Semitism "has never been looked into, or only in a very sketchy way" (CEJL, 4:311). This, not that many years after Orwell himself had evoked anti-Semitic stereotypes. In his wartime diary (which he later tried, unsuccessfully, to have published), for example, he comments (entry dated October 25, 1940): "What is bad about Jews is that they are not only conspicuous, but go out of their way to make themselves so.... What I do feel is that any Jew, i.e. European Jew, would prefer Hitler's kind of social system to ours, if it were not that he happens to persecute them. Ditto with almost any Central European, e.g. the refugees. They make use of England as a sanctuary, but they cannot help feeling the profoundest contempt for it. You can see this in their eyes, even when they don't say it outright" (CEJL, 2:377–78). In 1943, Orwell is attributing this viewpoint about Jews to "many thoughtful people" (2:290) in a discussion of anti-Semitism full of caricatures of pushy "Jewesses."

29. Rose Laub Coser, "On *The Reproduction of Mothering*: A Methodological Debate," *Signs* 6, no. 3 (Spring 1981): 490.

30. Smyer, *Primal Dream*, p. 83.

31. In his 1935 review of *Tropic of Cancer* (which he seems to have largely incorporated into the later essay), Orwell also praised Miller for "brutally insisting on the facts" and attributed Miller's attitudes to ordinary men (CEJL, 1:155–56). In effect, Orwell here praised Miller for the two narrative strategies (voice-of-the-people and voice-in-the-wilderness) he himself was cultivating.

32. Orwell, however, is quite capable of noting sex bias—when, that is, the observation costs him nothing. In another section of "Inside the Whale," Orwell examines fashions in literature and analyzes the popularity of A. E. Housman among young men of Orwell's generation, commenting that he doubts whether Housman "ever had the same appeal for girls" since in his poems "the women's point of view was not considered," she [sic] is merely the nymph, the siren, the treacherous half-human creature who leads you a little distance and then gives you the slip" (CEJL, 1:505).

33. In "The English People," Orwell describes women of the "working classes" as having a tendency "to grow dumpy in early middle life" (CEJL, 3:1).

34. Bowling disapproves of his wife's friendships. In none of Orwell's novels is a genuine attachment between women depicted. Instead, Orwell likes to keep his heroines even more isolated than his heroes. In *Keep the Aspidistra Flying*, when Rosemary and Julia (Gordon's sister) get together out of a com-

mon concern over Gordon's fate, they are described as being "in feminine league against him" and sharing only "their feminine rage against his 'maddening' behaviour" (232).

35. George Woodcock, *The Crystal Spirit: A Study of George Orwell* (Boston: Little, Brown, 1966), p. 346, notes that George and Hilda's marriages suggests Donald McGill postcards. Elsewhere (p. 187) Woodcock admires Bowling's "central toughness."

36. John Wain, "Here Lies Lower Binfield: On George Orwell," *Encounter* 17, no. 4 (October 1961): 78.

37. Robert J. Van Dellen, "George Orwell's *Coming Up for Air:* The Politics of Powerlessness," *Modern Fiction Studies* 21, no. 1 (Spring 1975): 68. Van Dellen sees Bowling as "the archetypal Common Man" (p. 66). The tendency to exalt Bowling—and Orwell's achievement in creating this character—has increased over the years, no doubt fed by the growing mythification of Orwell. It is ironically fitting, as well, that a review of *Coming Up for Air* was the last thing read to Orwell's father before his death. Little is known about Orwell's relationship with his father, but a letter, dated July 14, 1939 (LL), from Orwell to his agent, makes this comment about the elder Blair's death, which occurred on June 28, 1939: "I am very glad that latterly he had not been so disappointed in me as before. Curiously enough his last moment of consciousness was hearing that review I had in the Sunday Times. He heard about it and wanted to see it, and my sister took it in and read it to him, and a little later he lost consciousness for the last time." The review in question, by Ralph Straus (whom Orwell had earlier lambasted for his constant praise of new novels; see CEJL, 1:253–55), *Sunday Times*, June 25, 1939, summarizes Bowling's story as that of a much-put-upon typical fellow and calls the novel "brilliant."

38. David Kubal, *Outside the Whale: George Orwell's Art and Politics* (Notre Dame: University of Notre Dame Press, 1972), p. 119. Kubal also sees George Bowling as "the crystal spirit."

39. Orwell also commented on his difficulties as a novelist in a May 1948 letter to Julian Symons: "*Coming Up for Air* isn't much, but I thought it worth reprinting because it was rather killed by the outbreak of war and then blitzed out of existence.... Of course you are perfectly right about my own character constantly intruding on that of the narrator. I am not a real novelist anyway, and that particular vice is inherent in writing a novel in the first person, which one should never do. One difficulty I have never solved is that one has masses of experience which one passionately wants to write about, e.g. the part about fishing in that book, and no way of using them up except by disguising them as a novel" (CEJL, 4:422).

40. Alex Zwerdling, in *Orwell and the Left* (New Haven: Yale University Press, 1974), p. 124, writes: "It seems probable that Orwell felt unhappy about the narrowness of the appeal of his early fiction and deliberately tried to expand his audience to include people like Bowling when he wrote *Coming Up for Air.*"

41. Kubal, *Outside the Whale*, pp. 119–20, at one point gets so carried away as to fault Orwell's plotting of Bowling's "character development" in these terms: "It seems out of keeping with Bowling's common sense and intellectual development" that he should become an insurance salesman and marry "a dried-up, emotionless shrew, a daughter of an effete Anglo-Indian family."

42. See Jack W. Sattel, "The Inexpressive Male: Tragedy or Sexual Politics?" *Social Problems* 23, no. 4 (April 1976): 469–77, for a discussion of this

ploy. By contrast, as we shall see in chapter 8, Winston Smith's desire for O'Brien's respect leads him to offer every vestige of his inner self for the other's approval.

43. Jeffrey Meyers, *A Reader's Guide to George Orwell* (London: Thames and Hudson, 1975), p. 105. Meyers later compares Bowling to James Joyce's Bloom, saying that, though Bowling is "more brash and hardened, they both are intelligent, curious, perceptive, sympathetic, good-natured, humorous and vulgar, and both are nostalgic about a happier past" (p. 111).

44. For example, Katharine Bail Hoskins, *Today the Struggle: Literature and Politics in England during the Spanish Civil War* (Austin: University of Texas Press, 1969), pp. 122–23, asserts that *Coming Up for Air* ends in almost total despondency but that the character of the hero is what remains with the reader, since his "humor, resilience, decency, and basic good sense brighten even his blackest moods." Jenni Calder, *Chronicles of Conscience: A Study of George Orwell and Arthur Koestler* (London: Secker and Warburg, 1968), pp. 163–64, also comments on Bowling's resilience: "and so we feel that he will survive his stultifying home, his dried-up wife and the bombs being dropped on London." She further states: "Mrs. Bowling's neurotic penny-pinching is shown to be ludicrous as well as intolerable. Through the first-person narrative George Bowling's hatreds and criticisms are solid, a direct confrontation with reality"; and she feels that Bowling "retains the sensitivity and warmth this childhood [in the country] gave him."

45. Judith Fetterley, *The Resisting Reader: A Feminist Approach to American Fiction* (Bloomington: Indiana University Press, 1978), p. xii.

46. Cheris Kramarae, *Women and Men Speaking: Frameworks for Analysis* (Rowley, Mass.: Newbury House Publishers, 1981), pp. 151–53, discusses the common belief that men's speech is direct, blunt, and straightforward, which implies that there "is nothing strategic in men's speech. It is heard as representing logic, reason." Women's speech, however, is perceived as having "frills and quirks; when it is not silly it is often devious. The implicit and explicit connection between men's speech and rationality is made continually." In a comment that could well be a description of George and Hilda Bowling's last argument, Kramarae suggests that "women's speech to men is thought to be more strategic and manipulative than is men's speech to women primarily because women's attempts to control are regarded as socially illegitimate."

CHAPTER SEVEN
POLITICAL FICTION AND PATRIARCHAL FANTASY

1. Gay Clifford, *The Transformation of Allegory* (London: Routledge and Kegan Paul, 1974), pp. 7–8.

2. Ibid., p. 45.

3. Ibid., p. 36.

4. Frye's *Anatomy of Criticism* is cited by Clifford, ibid., p. 47.

5. Ibid.

6. In 1982 and 1983 I conducted an informal survey of young Americans' exposure to Orwell. About five hundred questionnaires were distributed to undergraduates in state universities on the East Coast, the West Coast, and in the Midwest. Although nearly half the students said they had read either *Animal Farm* or *Nineteen Eighty-Four* (occasionally both), usually in junior high school or high school, few could remember anything about the books. Most could not comment on Orwell's politics, but those who did so almost

unanimously identified him as an anti-Communist, or, as one student wrote: "I would say that Orwell is anti-communist (socialist)." Others wrote: "He was concerned with the rise in socialism and the control it was coming to have"; "Believed nothing should take away from strength of private sector, that is, the individual. Despised totalitarianism but was not totally satisfied with complete democracy either"; "Society is heading toward a state of socialism and totalitarian rule"; "He likes animals." Rarely did a student know that Orwell considered himself a socialist. Several students had read *The Road to Wigan Pier* in an English history course at one university. Of these, one said Orwell was "anti-industrialist," and another said "he was a socialist." One student had read *Animal Farm* in a course on satire the year before and commented that in this work Orwell "acknowledged the fact that men are not of equal intelligence and, therefore, will not be able to achieve a pure social and political equality. He saw corruption as an inherent trait of any governing body." A student who remembered *Animal Farm* from junior high school wrote: "There will always be a ruling class—the lower class, upon taking over the upper class, will in turn become the ruling, upper class."

The Berg Collection, New York Public Library, holds several letters from Orwell to Leonard Moore in July 1949 in which Orwell expresses his willingness to subsidize a translation of *Animal Farm* made by some Russian Displaced Persons in Germany who wanted to smuggle the translation through the Iron Curtain.

7. Thomas N. Carter, "Group Psychological Phenomena of a Political System as Satirized in 'Animal Farm': An Application of the Theories of W. R. Bion," *Human Relations* 27, no. 2 (June 1974): 525.

8. Ellen Douglass Leyburn, *Satiric Allegory: The Mirror of Man* (New Haven: Yale University Press, 1956), p. 60.

9. Katharine Burdekin [Murray Constantine], *Proud Man* (London: Boriswood, 1934), p. 17.

10. For an insightful discussion of the role of womb envy in the maintenance of misogyny and patriarchy, see Eva Feder Kittay, "Womb Envy: An Explanatory Concept," in Joyce Trebilcot, ed., *Mothering: Essays in Feminist Theory* (Totowa, N.J.: Rowman and Allanheld, 1984), pp. 94–128. In this, as in other respects, Katharine Burdekin was ahead of her time. For further discussion of the relevance of Burdekin's work to Orwell's, see chapter 8, below.

11. Letter to Leonard Moore, December 17, 1947, Berg Collection, New York Public Library. Quoted in Alex Zwerdling, *Orwell and the Left* (New Haven and London: Yale University Press, 1974), p. 90.

12. For a book almost universally acclaimed, *Animal Farm* has been subjected to very little serious analysis. Writing in 1950, Tom Hopkinson declared it to be one of two contemporary books before which the critic had to abdicate (cited in John Atkins, *George Orwell* [New York: Frederick Ungar, 1954], p. 221). This perspective was adopted by many critics, perhaps as justification for their lack of response (beyond the obvious political one) to the work. Thus, for example, Atkins himself declared, "There is only one thing to do with *Animal Farm* at this stage, apart from reading it" (p. 222), and proceeded to give, yet again, the political parallels between Orwell's text and Soviet history in the period between 1917 and 1943. George Woodcock, *The Crystal Spirit: A Study of George Orwell* (Boston: Little, Brown, 1966), p. 193, repeats this line of commentary, stating that Orwell succeeded admirably in achieving his aim (of fusing political purpose and artistic purpose in one whole, as Orwell himself had explained in "Why I Write"), and then says that in

Animal Farm Orwell "produced a book so clear in intent and writing that the critic is usually rather nonplussed as to what he should say about it; all is so magnificently there, and the only thing that really needs to be done is to place this crystalline little book into its proper setting." If this kind of reasoning were genuinely valid, then all literary criticism would stand as a monument to the failure of the works that inspired it! Another typical example of critical treatment of *Animal Farm* is Frank W. Wadsworth's essay "Orwell's Later Work," *University of Kansas City Review*, June 1956. Wadsworth states (p. 285) that *Animal Farm*'s "technical brilliance cannot, of course, be denied" and affirms that it is "a great deal more than mere political satire," but what precisely it is he does not then specify, preferring to turn his attention to *Nineteen Eighty-Four*. It is hard to avoid the conclusion that were *Animal Farm* a satire of capitalism, of equal "technical brilliance," it would not have achieved such fame. Since Orwell's reputation in the world-at-large (as opposed to the smaller world of literary criticism) rests largely on *Animal Farm* and his other anti-Communist work, *Nineteen Eighty-Four*, this is a relevant consideration. But, as Orwell himself stated repeatedly, it is difficult, if not impossible, to separate political from "aesthetic" responses to a work. Nor can one argue that Orwell is "not responsible" for the conservative political uses made of his work. As Louis Althusser comments, in "Cremonini, Painter of the Abstract," *Lenin and Philosophy and Other Essays* (New York and London: Monthly Review Press, 1971), p. 242, "a great artist cannot fail to take into account in his work itself, in its disposition and internal economy, the ideological *effects* necessarily produced by its existence. Whether this assumption of responsibility is completely lucid or not is a *different* question" (Althusser's emphasis). Orwell in effect acknowledges this. One of his letters (in the Berg Collection, New York Public Library) to Leonard Moore, dated January 9, 1947, comments on the serialization in a "reactionary" Dutch publication of a translation of *Animal Farm*. Orwell writes: "Obviously a book of that type is liable to be made use of by Conservatives, Catholics etc."

13. Robert A. Lee, *Orwell's Fiction* (Notre Dame, Ind.: University of Notre Dame Press, 1969), notes that Boxer's stupidity "suggests interesting qualifications about Orwell's reputed love of the common man, qualifications which become even stronger in light of the description of the proles in *1984*." Lee further comments that "Clover is more intelligent and perceptive than is Boxer, but she has a corresponding lack of strength. Her 'character' is primarily a function of her sex. Her instincts are maternal and pacifistic. She works hard, along with the other animals, but there is no picture of any special strength, as there is with Boxer. And even with a greater intelligence, her insights are partial" (p. 123). "A paradigm appears," Lee concludes: "Boxer is marked by great strength and great stupidity; Clover has less physical power but has a corresponding increase in awareness; the equation is completed with Benjamin [the donkey] who sees and knows most—perhaps all—but is physically ineffectual and socially irresponsible" (p. 124). Lee's commentary on *Animal Farm* is far more interesting and insightful than most.

14. J. R. Osgerby, " 'Animal Farm' and 'Nineteen Eighty Four,' " *The Use of English* 17, no. 3 (Spring 1966): 237–43, discusses the theme of compassion and the "protective gesture" in these two books, noting the permutations of this gesture until it culminates in a grim parody at the end of *Nineteen Eighty-Four* as Winston clings to O'Brien like a baby.

15. Orwell's description of Clover as "the motherly mare approaching middle life" recalls his preference for such maternal figures. In a column de-

scribing an ideal (imaginary) pub, "The Moon under Water," he specifies that the barmaids "are all middle-aged women" who call everyone "dear" rather than "ducky"; the latter, he says, is typical of pubs with "a disagreeable raffish atmosphere" (CEJL, 3:45).

16. As an illustration of how little the terms of such denigration have changed, consider the misogynistic satire of Semonides of Amorgos who, in the seventh century B.C., wrote a poem describing ten types of women, most of them formed by Zeus out of different animals. All except the hardworking bee are depicted in negative terms. Semonides describes the "mare-woman" thus: "Another was the offspring of a proud mare with a long mane. She pushes servile work and trouble on to others; she would never set her hand to a mill, nor pick up a sieve nor throw the dung out of the house, nor sit over the oven dodging the soot; she makes her husband acquainted with Necessity. She washes the dirt off herself twice, sometimes three times, every day; she rubs herself with scents, and always has her thick hair combed and garlanded with flowers. A woman like her is a fine sight for others, but for the man she belongs to she proves a plague, unless he is some tyrant or king [who takes pride in such objects]" (in Hugh Lloyd-Jones, "Females of the Species: On 118 Lines of Semonides," Encounter, May 1975, p. 53; Lloyd-Jones's brackets). I am indebted to Barbara Halporn of Indiana University for this reference.

17. Batya Weinbaum, The Curious Courtship of Women's Liberation and Socialism (Boston: South End Press, 1978), chap. 8. A related critique is Heidi Hartmann, "The Unhappy Marriage of Marxism and Feminism," reprinted in Lydia Sargent, ed., Women and Revolution: A Discussion of the Unhappy Marriage of Marxism and Feminism (Boston: South End Press, 1981).

18. Richard Mayne recently pointed out, in the Times Literary Supplement, November 26, 1982, that Orwell's most famous line is in fact borrowed from another writer, Philip Guedalla. Guedalla's "A Russian Fairy Tale," The Missing Muse (New York: Harper and Brothers, 1930), is a brief anti-Communist satire in which there appears a Good Fairy "who believed that all fairies were equal before the law, but held strongly that some fairies were more equal than others" (p. 206). Guedalla, however, throws the line away, while Orwell creates a context that makes it unforgettable. Nonetheless, it is instructive that the one line in all Orwell's prose that critics repeatedly point to as the pinnacle of Orwell's achievement in clarity and concision in fact was not composed by him. Raymond Williams, for example, in Orwell (Glasgow: Fontana/Collins, 1971), p. 74, cites this line as an example of the "exceptionally strong and pure prose" Orwell was "able to release" in Animal Farm. Orwell himself, incidentally, did not hesitate to use the word "plagiarism" in relation to far less precise borrowings, as when he commented, in a letter to Fred Warburg, that Aldous Huxley had clearly "plagiarized" to some extent from Eugene Zamiatin's We in composing Brave New World (CEJL, 4:485).

19. "As I Please," Tribune, March 21, 1947, p. 13; on file in the Orwell Archive. In Crystal Spirit, p. 284, George Woodcock notes that Orwell saw the family "as a morally regenerating institution; and birth control and abortion as manifestations of moral degeneration," but Woodcock disregards the gender ideology expressed by these attitudes.

20. Weinbaum, Curious Courtship, p. 96.

21. Heidi I. Hartmann, "The Family as the Locus of Gender, Class, and Political Struggle: The Example of Housework," Signs 6, no. 3 (Summer 1981): 372. Hartmann in this essay challenges the idea that the family is an active agent with unified interests and focuses on housework to illustrate the different

material interests among family members caused by their differing relations to patriarchy and capitalism. She shows that men's work in the house does not increase proportionally to women's work outside of the house and concludes that "patriarchy appears to be a more salient feature than class" in understanding women's work in the home (p. 386). She refers to studies indicating this is also true in very different societies, e.g., Bangladesh, which confirm that men's lives are more altered by class distinctions than women's.

CHAPTER EIGHT
GAMESMANSHIP AND ANDROCENTRISM

1. For a schematic discussion of Dostoevski, Zamiatin, Huxley, and Orwell, see D. Richards, "Four Utopias," *Slavonic and East European Review* 40 (1961): 220–28. Of greater interest is Andrew Hacker's critique of contemporary liberal theorists' assumptions about individual autonomy, "Dostoyevsky's Disciples: Man and Sheep in Political Theory," *Journal of Politics* 17, no. 4 (1955): 590–613.

2. This section and the following one owe much to Bernard Suits's thought-provoking book, *The Grasshopper: Games, Life, and Utopia* (Toronto: University of Toronto Press, 1978).

3. Roger Caillois, *Man, Play, and Games*, trans. Meyer Barash (New York: Free Press of Glencoe, 1961); Johan Huizinga, *Homo Ludens: A Study of the Play-Element in Culture* (Boston: Beacon Press, 1955).

4. Jacques Ehrmann, "Homo Ludens Revisited," in Jacques Ehrmann, ed., *Game, Play, Literature* (Boston: Beacon Press, 1968), pp. 31–57.

5. Philip Rahv, "The Unfuture of Utopia," *Literature and the Sixth Sense* (Boston: Houghton Mifflin, 1969), pp. 331–39. This review of *Nineteen Eighty-Four* originally appeared in the *Partisan Review* 16, no. 7 (July 1949).

6. In *Darkness at Noon*, trans. Daphne Hardy (1941; rpt., New York: Bantam Books, 1966), Arthur Koestler comments ironically that soon the Party would even "publish a new and revised edition of the back numbers of all newspapers" (p. 96), in addition to the new histories and even new "memoirs" of dead heroes that were already appearing in Stalinist Russia. But Orwell also drew on his own experience of intentionally dishonest journalism during the Spanish Civil War, as recounted in *Homage to Catalonia*.

7. The literature on game theory is vast. For the purposes of this chapter, the following works were helpful: Morton D. Davis, *Game Theory: A Nontechnical Introduction* (New York: Basic Books, 1970); T. C. Schelling, "What Is Game Theory?" in James C. Charlesworth, ed., *Contemporary Political Analysis* (New York: Free Press, 1967), pp. 212–38, and Martin Shubik, "The Uses of Game Theory," ibid., pp. 239–71. Nigel Howard, in his book *Paradoxes of Rationality* (Cambridge: MIT Press, 1971), uses game theory to analyze Pinter's play *The Caretaker* and comments that this approach makes no sense for symbolic or otherwise nonrealistic actions since "game theory is about real people" (p. 146). An interesting application of game theory to literary texts (which also reveals its limitations) is Steven J. Brams, *Biblical Games: A Strategic Analysis of Stories in the Old Testament* (Cambridge: MIT Press, 1980). I am grateful to Joel Souto-Maior for first introducing me to game theory.

8. Anthony Burgess, in his *1985* (Boston: Little, Brown, 1978), observes: "there is something chesslike [in *Nineteen Eighty-Four*] about the relationship between the State and its members, as there is something chesslike also in the intellectual techniques which sustain the system. To use doublethink is to

play chess ... to use Newspeak is to play a complex game with a limited number of semantic pieces" (p. 88). Burgess correctly notes many of the inconsistencies and problems of Orwell's text, then follows his critique with his own rather unoriginal antisyndicalist dystopia. A more interesting version of the antiunion vein is worked by Diane Boswell in her dystopian novel *Posterity* (London: Jonathan Cape, 1926).

9. Walter Goldschmidt, "Game Theory, Cultural Values, and the Brideprice in Africa," in Ira R. Buchler and Hugo G. Nutini, eds., *Game Theory in the Behavioral Sciences* (Pittsburgh: University of Pittsburgh Press, 1969), pp. 60–74.

10. James Connors, " 'Do It to Julia': Thoughts on Orwell's *1984*," *Modern Fiction Studies*, 16 (Winter 1970/71): 463–73.

11. Caillois, *Man, Play, and Games*, p. 173.

12. Fredric Jameson, "The Great American Hunter; or, Ideological Content in the Novel," *College English* 34, no. 2 (1972): 182.

13. Stuart H. Walker, *Winning: The Psychology of Competition* (New York: W. W. Norton, 1980), p. 3.

14. Earlier in his life Orwell explicitly rejected the idea that the pursuit of power is "natural." In one of his "As I Please" columns in 1946, Orwell wrote: "curiously enough the desire for power seems to be taken for granted as a natural instinct, equally prevalent in all ages, like the desire for food. Actually it is no more natural, in the sense of being biologically necessary, than drunkenness or gambling. And if it has reached new levels of lunacy in our own age, as I think it has, then the question becomes: What is the special quality in modern life that makes a major human motive out of the impulse to bully others?" (CEJL, 4:249). As an afterthought, Orwell suggests that possibly our age is not worse in this respect than preceding ages.

15. Irving Howe, "Enigmas of Power," *New Republic*, year-end issue, 1982, p. 25.

16. Much of the pioneering work on social roles in game situations has been done by Erving Goffman. See especially his essay "Fun in Games," *Encounters: Two Studies in the Sociology of Interaction* (Indianapolis and New York: Bobbs-Merrill, 1971). There is an interesting but so far insuffient literature on sex differences in game playing and decision making. W. Edgar Vinacke, e.g., concludes his study "Sex Roles in a Three-Person Game," *Sociometry* 22 (March 1959): 359, by suggesting that "males are primarily concerned with winning, whereas females are more oriented towards working out an equitable outcome, as satisfactory as possible to all three participants." Harold H. Kelley in studying female pairs involved in negotiations concludes that typically at least one member of each pair is reluctant to maintain the "tough, competitive stance" characteristic of male bargainers. See his "Experimental Studies of Threats in Interpersonal Negotiations," *Journal of Conflict Resolution* 9 (March 1965): 92. Clarice Stasz Stoll and Paul T. McFarlane, in their article "Player Characteristics and Interaction in a Parent-Child Simulation Game," *Sociometry* 32 (September 1969): 270, examine the ways in which external characteristics (one's real-life situation and social role) impinge on game activity. They conclude that the "expression of masculine role behavior [militated] against taking a cooperative stance in the game, *even though the game highly rewarded cooperation*" (their emphasis). A recent article by Otto C. Brenner and W. Edgar Vinacke on sex and managerial stereotypes also concludes that males are exploitative but that females are accommodative—at least as far as reported behavior is concerned. See their "Accommodative and Exploitative Behavior of

Males versus Females and Managers versus Nonmanagers as Measured by the Test of Strategy," *Social Psychology Quarterly* 42, no. 3 (1979): 289. It should not be thought that I am arguing here for the notion of inherent behavioral differences between the sexes. The growing literature on gender roles and on the formation in early childhood of distinctively masculine and feminine modes of behavior supports the view that these behaviors are learned.

17. Stevie Smith, *Me Again* (London: Virago, 1981), p. 315. Julia's anarchism, of course, like her concern for material pleasures, is another female stereotype. Whatever we may say about this stereotype, how it comes into being and how it is used to keep women in their place, it is nevertheless a model of behavior that is far less destructive than the male stereotype of what it means to "be a man." For this reason, to study the behavior of women is to realize that there are alternatives to the traditional male patterns. For a study of male thinkers' views of the female as chaotic and (ironically, in my view) lacking in civic virtues, see Carole Pateman, " 'The Disorder of Women': Women, Love, and the Sense of Justice," *Ethics* 91, no. 1 (1980): 20–34.

18. Jeffrey Meyers, *A Reader's Guide to George Orwell* (London: Thames and Hudson, 1975), pp. 148–49, traces the boot image back to book 4 of *Gulliver's Travels*.

19. In a book review published in the *Manchester Evening News* on December 9, 1943, Orwell, in taking one of his digs at the Left, makes a related comment: "The young Nazi [in Koestler's *Arrival and Departure*] contributes the penetrating remark that one of the strongest arguments against all the Left-wing movements is the ugliness of their women." It is presumably Orwell who finds this remark "penetrating." The review is available at the Orwell Archive. In a 1944 "As I Please" column, Orwell reveals his inability to connect women's use of makeup to the institution of patriarchy: "One of the big failures in human history has been the age-long attempt to stop women painting their faces. The philosophers of the Roman Empire denounced the frivolity of the modern woman in almost the same terms as she is denounced today. In the fifteenth century the Church denounced the damnable habit of plucking the eyebrows. The English Puritans, the Bolsheviks and the Nazis all attempted to discourage cosmetics, without success. In Victorian England rouge was considered so disgraceful that it was usually sold under some other name, but it continued to be used" (CEJL, 3:134).

20. This monstrous but admirable breeder contrasts sharply with the "scrawny but muscular" exercise instructress who exhorts Winston from the telescreen with the words "I'm thirty-nine and I've had four children. Now look!" (*Nineteen Eighty-Four*, 33)—and who is a fanatical Party woman.

The last few pages of Orwell's last notebook (in the Orwell Archive) contain bits of fiction that he probably wrote during the final months of his life. One such passage, calling to mind the "monstrous" prole woman in *Nineteen Eighty-Four*, reveals that Orwell was trying to write more openly about sexual matters, though his stereotypes remain unaltered. The sketch describes the ongoing affair between a man, X., and a thirty-eight-year-old woman named Portia. Their relationship, depicted from the point of view of the man, has continued for thirteen years, right through his marriage, for a simple and "unmentionable" reason: X.'s necessity, about every two months, "to have dealings with a woman who was large, brawny, peasant-like and frankly animal." X. values Portia more as, over the years, she has developed greater bulges in the appropriate places. What he wants is "a large, mature, peasant-like woman, with monstrous thighs, with breasts that menaced you through her dress like the fore-guns of a battleship, & with arms that almost cracked your ribs when she embraced you." Though this passage recalls George Bowling's description of his mother who, with her enormous bosom, resembled the figurehead of a battleship, the sketch quickly takes quite a different turn as X. describes Portia's "impenetrable stupidity," which has perhaps led her to betray the identity of a man, Dr. Levinski, whom X. had entrusted to her care. The last page of Orwell's notebook contains another paragraph on this subject, as X. thinks that what Portia needed "was to be given a beating with a dogwhip—but a really terrible beating, which she would remember till her dying day—& then to be set to work with a pail & scrubbing brush for the rest of her life." But, in a flash of self-knowledge, X. realizes that Dr. Levinski's destruction was really due to X.'s "own unfortunate weakness for women with fat legs."

21. See, for example, Erwin Hester, "Women in 1984," *PMLA* 98, no. 2 (March 1983): 256–57.

22. The review appeared in *Time and Tide*, August 24, 1940, p. 866. It, along with the one mentioned below, is on file in the Orwell Archive. See also the text, *Take Back Your Freedom*, by Winifred Holtby and Norman Ginsbury (London: Jonathan Cape, 1939). Similarly, in an early review in the *New English Weekly*, August 1, 1935, pp. 317–18, Orwell completely misses the point of R. G. Goodyear's novel *I Lie Alone* (London: Boriswood, 1935), about a wretched woman leading the empty, submerged life of a poor spinster with neither real work nor real emotional ties. This character's one pleasure in life is eating. The novel successfully conveys the harrowingly empty and claustrophobic quality of such a life, but all Orwell sees in the book is "an entirely worthless slut whose every thought turns on food or drink, usually food." Orwell concludes that after reading this novel "one sees more clearly than before why gluttony was included among the seven deadly sins." Interestingly, in another review in the same column Orwell refers to "a worthless little prostitute." In such judgments, his antagonism toward women comes through with embarrassing clarity. A further example of the way in which Orwell's misogyny distorts his appraisal of other writers' works occurs in his article on George Gissing, written in 1948. Orwell sees Gissing's portrayal of female characters as far more unsympathetic than it in fact is. Orwell describes Amy Reardon in *New Grub Street* as Gissing's "odious heroine"—which tells us more about Orwell than about Gissing. Misunderstanding *The Odd Women*, Orwell concludes that "in his heart Gissing seems to feel that women are natural inferiors," a view Orwell himself evidently holds (CEJL, 4:428–36).

23. James Hadley Chase, *No Orchids for Miss Blandish* (Berne: Alfred Scherz, 1946), p. 190. Other page references to this novel will appear in my text. Orwell also mentions the hero of another Chase novel, *He Won't Need It Now*, who "is described as stamping on somebody's face, and then, having crushed the man's mouth in, grinding his heel round and round in it" (CEJL, 3:218). Perhaps this reinforced Orwell's attraction to the "iron heel" image he had earlier noted in Jack London. See also n. 18, above.

24. Brian Foster, *The Changing English Language* (London: Macmillan, 1968), p. 14.

25. William Steinhoff, in *The Road to "1984"* (London: Weidenfeld and Nicolson, 1975), examines Orwell's indebtedness to a number of other writers. Especially interesting is Steinhoff's discussion of the similarities between *Nineteen Eighty-Four* and Cyril Connolly's satirical short story "Year Nine" (originally published in the *New Statesman and Nation*, January 26, 1938; reprinted

in Connolly, *The Condemned Playground: Essays, 1927–1944* (New York: Macmillan, 1946). Rejecting Isaac Deutscher's contention that *Nineteen Eighty-Four* owes a great deal to Zamiatin's *We*, Steinhoff writes: "If Orwell had borrowed as much from *We* as Deutscher says he did—in effect plagiarizing it—he would not have been likely to give it so much publicity and to try to get it into print" (p. 24). But, in fact, many well-known plagiarists have somewhat compulsively left clear trails for others to follow. This point is made in Peter Shaw's article "Plagiary," *American Scholar*, Summer 1982, pp. 325–37. Shaw writes: "As it develops, giving the game away proves to be the rule rather than the exception among plagiarists" (p. 330). In any case, the problem with Orwell is rather his debts to a great many sources, some of which I introduce in this section. According to Steinhoff, Orwell projected James Burnham's arguments into the future in order to refute them (*Road to "1984,"* p. 54)—but a reading of the novel, and its emphasis on Winston Smith's defeat and the Party's inevitable successes, does not bear this out. More convincing is Adrian Cunningham's criticism that Orwell incorporated into *Nineteen Eighty-Four* the very words and phrases he most objected to in Burnham's *Managerial Revolution*, without ever having retracted his attacks on Burnham. Cunningham's argument is made in the course of a review (in *Granta*, February 15, 1964, pp. 24–25) of *Down and Out in Paris and London*, an Orwell book that, Cunningham says, aims to mislead. Certainly Orwell's own criticisms of the sadistic and power-worshiping aspects of both Burnham and Jack London apply equally well to his own scenario in *Nineteen Eighty-Four*. But this is not unusual; Orwell often borrowed from other writers the very things he most criticized in them. Another instance of this occurs in relation to Chase's *No Orchids for Miss Blandish*, which Orwell takes to task for its sadistic and fascistic elements and its pornographic violence—only to duplicate all these in *Nineteen Eighty-Four*. An alternative explanation, however, is that Orwell was consciously trying to write a sensationalistic novel that would attract attention; hence the graphic emphasis on torture, which often gives the novel the tone of an adolescent horror story.

26. The review appeared in *Horizon*, June 1940, pp. 458–60, and is on file at the Orwell Archive. In 1936 Orwell had reviewed W. F. R. Macartney's *Walls Have Mouths* (in *The Adelphi*, November 1936, pp. 121–22). Shocked at Macartney's depiction of homosexuality and masturbation in prison, Orwell makes the revealing comment that Macartney "gives a horrible account of the way in which homosexuality gradually overwhelmed himself, first of all through the medium of his dreams" (p. 122). But Macartney's book does not express such horror; he even depicts a few romances and love stories that occur within the prison and makes no mention of homosexual rape or violence other than some fights over a boy. See *Walls Have Mouths: A Record of Ten Years' Penal Servitude* (London: Victor Gollancz, 1936).

27. Jim Phelan, *Jail Journey* (London: Secker and Warburg, 1940), p. 25. Phelan's account stresses that the basic technique one must learn for survival in prison (as in *Nineteen Eighty-Four*) is deception. The convicts' perceptions are scrambled by contradictions such as "talk-but-no-speech," referring to the fact that prisoners officially have the right to speak to one another but cannot disobey the warders' command that they not do so (p. 49). Phelan even uses composite words that suggest the vocabulary of Newspeak: "jail-mind" refers to intervals of mental blankness; "talk-friend" is someone to talk to, usually a person in for similar offenses; "black-thinking" and "black thought" are Dartmoor names for "wakeful worry and depression" (pp. 68, 142). And the convict,

like Winston Smith, must learn to abandon logic. Phelan describes a prisoner who "could never learn that two and two make nine-and-thirteen-sixteenths if a jailer says so, and was always in trouble" (p. 146). For the sake of proceeding with his scheme to escape, Phelan overtly conforms: "If they had said the [one-pint] cup held a gallon of porridge and a ton of sugar I would have concurred and proved it if necessary" (p. 148). But gradually he realizes that the authorities know everything he is "doing, hoping, *thinking*" (p. 151; his emphasis). A convict has no brain and no genitals, he writes (p. 262), and he sees the long-term aim of the prison system as "trying to lop my masculinity from me" (p. 272). Like Winston Smith in his room, Phelan in the Dartmoor prison forge where he worked found "a tiny space, and the only one in the shop, about seven inches wide, where for a second or two one was out of sight. An intelligent well-trained prisoner could snatch a smoke, or a glance at a newspaper, in a second and a few inches. Or he might scribble. For months I lived in a weird four-dimensional pocket universe, measuring seven inches on one side and a few seconds on the other" (p. 96). Like the Party in its pursuit of power, so at Dartmoor, "they wasted no words. The guns and the clubs were openly carried, and no one pretended they were quaint old-world ornaments.... The Moor was a real jail," without "nonsense about 'esprit de corps' or democracy or being 'out for the prisoner's good.' No waste words. No chances. No pseudo trust" (pp. 98–99).

28. Anthony West, "George Orwell," in *Principles and Persuasions: The Literary Essays of Anthony West* (New York: Harcourt, Brace, 1957), pp. 164–76. West sees Orwell's vision of 1984 "in which all children are treacherous and cruel, all women dangerous, and all men helpless unless cruel and conscienceless" to reveal a "hidden wound" that Orwell's actual experiences at school—despite the parallels—cannot explain (p. 176).

29. Katharine Burdekin [Murray Constantine], *Swastika Night* (London: Victor Gollancz, 1937).

30. Andy Croft of the University of Leeds has been studying socialist novels in Britain in the 1930s. He considers *Swastika Night* to be especially important as "one of the first anti-Fascist dystopias produced in Britain in the late 'thirties." Croft has also noted Orwell's apparent debt to *Swastika Night*, "especially the way he adapts some of the anti-Fascist techniques and ideas from the book into anti-Socialist ones." Croft further comments: "If only more were known about novels like *Swastika Night*, like the host of lively, original, moving and funny anti-Fascist dystopias produced in the late 'thirties, then *Nineteen Eighty-Four* wouldn't seem such an isolated and original work" (personal communications, August 31, 1982, and May 6, 1983).

31. Katharine Burdekin [Murray Constantine], *Proud Man* (London: Boriswood, 1934). For a more detailed study of Burdekin's work, see my article, "Orwell's Despair, Burdekin's Hope: Gender and Power in Dystopia," *Women's Studies International Forum* 7, no. 2 (1984).

32. Stanley G. Payne, "The Concept of Fascism," in Stein Ugelvik Larsen et al., eds., *Who Were the Fascists? Social Roots of European Fascism* (Bergen: Universitetsforlaget, 1980), pp. 14–25. See also George Mosse, "Toward a General Theory of Fascism," *Masses and Man: Nationalist and Fascist Perceptions of Reality* (New York: Howard Fertig, 1980), pp. 159–96. Mosse (pp. 184–85) describes the "new fascist man" who provided the stereotype for all fascist movements: "He was, naturally, masculine: fascism represented itself as a society of males, a result of the struggle for national unity that had created fellowships such as 'Young Italy,' or the German fraternities and gymnastic societies.

Moreover, the cult of masculinity of the fin de siècle, which Nietzsche himself so well exemplified, contributed its influence. More immediately, a male society continued into the peace the wartime camaraderie of the trenches, that myth of the war experience so important in all fascism. The masculine ideal did not remain abstract, but was personified in ideals of strength and beauty." Mosse goes on to identify the "inner characteristics of this new man," which were "more clearly defined: athletic, persevering, filled with self-denial and the spirit of sacrifice. At the same time, the new fascist man must be energetic, courageous, and laconic. The ideal fascist was the very opposite of muddle-headed, talkative, intellectualizing liberals and socialists—the exhausted, tired old men of the old order. Indeed, Italian fascism's dream of an age-old masculine ideal has not vanished from our own time." This catalogue of the new fascist man's inner characteristics comes uncomfortably close to qualities Orwell repeatedly extols.

33. Virginia Woolf, *A Room of One's Own* (New York: Harcourt, Brace, 1929), p. 60.

34. Ronald Segal, *The Struggle against History* (London: Weidenfeld and Nicolson, 1971), p. 86, argues that *Nineteen Eighty-Four* is incompatible with "the nature of the very system whose totalitarian premise he [Orwell] saw.... For the world of *1984* works, and can only work, through a retreat from the priorities of property; while the fascist momentum of liberal capitalism, including that of its constituent left, lies not in the relative denial of such priorities, but rather in the blind devotion to them. To see the consummation of the system as the pursuit of corporate power through a state in mass material decay, is socially untenable. Such a development would be interrupted soon enough, whatever the excuses of occasion, by the popular force that supplies the system with its decisive following, in the bulk of labour. If so many people have proved deludable by material bribes, it is by material bribes that they have been deluded. Indeed, the survival of the system, and certainly not least in its final refuge of fascism, lies precisely in its continuing capacity to provide such material bribes."

35. Mary Louise Pratt and Elizabeth Closs Traugott, *Linguistics for Students of Literature* (New York: Harcourt Brace Jovanovich, 1980), pp. 107–9, argue that Newspeak is not a "real human possibility" because it is based on an "incomplete view of what human language is."

36. In an unpublished notebook of Orwell's (in the Orwell Archive) that contains an outline of part of *Nineteen Eighty-Four*, he wrote the comment: "W's longing for a woman of his own (connection in his mind between sexuality & Rebellion?)." And in criticizing Aldous Huxley's *Ape and Essence*, in a 1949 letter to Richard Rees, Orwell wrote: "And do you notice that the more holy he gets, the more his books stink with sex. He cannot get off the subject of flagellating women. Possibly, if he had the courage to come out & say so, that is the solution to the problem of war. If we took it out in a little private sadism, which after all doesn't do much harm, perhaps we wouldn't want to drop bombs etc." (CEJL, 4:479). These comments also appear, in almost identical words, in Orwell's last notebook (Orwell Archive).

37. See Maria-Antonietta Macciocchi, "Female Sexuality in Fascist Ideology," *Feminist Review* 1 (1979): 67–82. In her introduction to this essay, Jane Caplan notes that for Macciocchi the fascist leader is sexually exploitative of men as well as women: "the Leader symbolically castrates all men in the act of expropriating the sexual capacity of women." Caplan summarizes: "Macciocchi is saying that you can't talk about fascism unless you are also

prepared to discuss patriarchy. This may seem to be a rather obvious remark, yet I think it is actually more subtle than its simplicity suggests. It locates the originality of fascism not in any capacity to generate a new ideology, but in its conjunctural transformation and recombination of what already exists" (p. 62).

38. The term "gatekeeping" comes from Dorothy Smith, "A Peculiar Eclipsing: Women's Exclusion from Man's Culture," *Women's Studies International Quarterly* 1, no. 4 (1978): 282–95. On this subject, see also Dale Spender, *Man Made Language* (London: Routledge and Kegan Paul, 1980); Lynne Spender, *Intruders on the Rights of Men: Women's Unpublished Heritage* (London: Routledge and Kegan Paul/Pandora Press, 1983); Joanna Russ, *How to Suppress Women's Writing* (Austin: University of Texas Press, 1983). Elaine Showalter has described the problem as follows: "each generation of women writers has found itself, in a sense, without a history, forced to rediscover the past anew, forging again and again the consciousness of their sex" (*A Literature of Their Own: British Women Novelists from Brontë to Lessing* [Princeton: Princeton University Press, 1977], pp. 11–12). Orwell also acted as a gatekeeper by his general disregard for women writers, who are hardly mentioned in all his work.

39. This is apparent in the introduction that Orwell planned for *Animal Farm* after that manuscript had been rejected by several publishers who were worried that its publication would offend England's then ally, the Soviet Union. This introduction, never published in Orwell's lifetime, contains some rallying calls about the freedom of the press, which reveal that Orwell has himself in mind and not those members of the community whose access to the press has always been restricted. See "The Freedom of the Press," *Times Literary Supplement*, September 15, 1972, pp. 1037–39.

CHAPTER NINE
CONCLUSION: ORWELL'S DESPAIR

1. Adrienne Rich, "When We Dead Awaken: Writing as Re-Vision," *College English* 34, no. 1 (October 1972): 25. I am grateful to Alex Zwerdling of the University of California, Berkeley, for suggesting to me the applicability of Rich's words to my analysis of Orwell. In discussing Orwell's despair, however, it is important to keep in mind that although *Nineteen Eighty-Four* happened to be Orwell's final book, it should not be regarded as the culmination of his work or as his swansong. I believe that Bernard Crick is right in his repeated objections to interpretations of *Nineteen Eighty-Four* as a dying man's final testament. My interpretation of Orwell's despair rests on an analysis of his ideology, not of the state of his health. Orwell's notebooks and correspondence during the last year of his life show that he had other projects in mind and not only hoped but expected to recover his health.

2. Randolph Quirk, "1984 and '1984'," *London Review of Books*, February 16–29, 1984, pp. 10–11, makes a serious critique of Orwell's ideas on language. Quirk not only describes the "intellectual framework displayed in the principles of Newspeak" as "very weak and damagingly inconsistent," but also notes Orwell's unacknowledged debts to the Fowler brothers' 1906 work *The King's English*, whose first page sets out the five maxims that Orwell simply expanded in his "Politics and the English Language."

Index